City of Trees

City of Trees

*The Complete Field Guide
to the Trees of Washington, D.C.*

revised edition

Text by Melanie Choukas-Bradley
Illustrations by Polly Alexander

Photographs by Melanie Choukas-Bradley
and Polly Alexander

The Johns Hopkins University Press
Baltimore and London

For our grandparents: Dr. Michael Choukas and
Gertrude Choukas, Amelia Crane Crosby, Eleanor
Town Andrews, and Madeline Dyer Alexander.

© Copyright 1981, 1987 by Melanie Choukas-Bradley
and Polly Alexander
All rights reserved
Printed in the United States of America

Originally published in 1981 in hardcover by Acropolis
Books Ltd. as *City of Trees: The Complete Botanical and
Historical Guide to the Trees of Washington, D.C.*

Johns Hopkins Paperbacks edition, 1987

The Johns Hopkins University Press, 701 West 40th
Street, Baltimore, Maryland 21211
The Johns Hopkins Press Ltd., London

Library of Congress Cataloging in Publication Data

Choukas-Bradley, Melanie.
  City of Trees.

  Bibliography: p.
  Includes index.
    1. Trees in cities—Washington (D.C.)—Identification.
  2. Trees—Washington (D.C.)—Identification.
  3. Washington (D.C.)—Description—1981-
  —Guidebooks.
  I. Alexander, Polly. II. Title.
  SB435.52.W18C48 1987   917.43'044   86-20912
  ISBN 0-8018-3320-5 (alk. paper)

Photographs by Melanie Choukas-Bradley: The Mag-
nolias; The Dogwoods; The Pea Family; The Japanese
Flowering Cherry Trees; Golden-Rain-Tree; Paulownia;
Linden; Hawthorn; Flowering Crabapple.
Photographs by Polly Alexander: Common Horse-
Chestnut; Crape-Myrtle; Catalpa; Fringe-Tree; Pear.
Cover photo taken by Greg Pease/Baltimore, MD

CONTENTS

FOREWORD

by Dr. John L. Creech
Retired Director, United States National Arboretum

One day in the spring of 1978 two young women sat across from me in my office at the National Arboretum.

"We", announced Melanie Choukas-Bradley, introducing her cohort, Polly Alexander, "intend to publish a book on the trees of Washington."

I wondered if these two young women realized the monumental nature of what they were undertaking and whether or not they had the background to carry out so formidable a task. But after listening to their plans and seeing their enthusiasm, I was won over.

There is a wealth of information on trees at the National Arboretum, plus a vast range of scientific expertise, so I took the aspiring authors to visit several members of the Arboretum staff, who agreed to provide technical assistance.

As a result, I was to see this delightful twosome on numerous occasions during the development of their book as they hurried through our Administration Building with materials for review with one or more of the Arboretum staff. Their steady progress has evolved into a book that portrays the remarkable history and locations of the important tree collections in the nation's capital and also provides technical descriptions of each species along with the line drawings so essential to a thorough review.

Washington is indeed a city of trees, more so than any other world capital because of the diversity of the species involved. In a city with so many transient residents and a complexity of federal agencies, the common interest in trees is surprising.

Trees have been planted to commemorate historic, scientific, and diplomatic events. Other plantings were integral elements of various architectural plans for the capital and still other trees were planted by presidents, congressmen and visiting dignitaries in keeping with a tradition begun in the early days of the city. This enthusiasm for trees is of an enduring nature, making Washington, D.C. a special kind of "window on the world". In the spring of 1981, for example, a tree planting ceremony was held at the Freer Gallery on the occasion of the visit of the Prime Minister of Japan. Secretary of the Smithsonian Institution S. Dillon Ripley selected the small flowering cherry, *Prunus incisa*. It is a pendulous form, probably not planted elsewhere in Washington as a commemorative tree. It grows wild in the vicinity of Mount Fuji, and was therefore a most appropriate choice.

The trees of Washington hold their own histories, some relating to our heritage, others reflecting the views of architects, and still others involving diplomatic exchanges, moments of anxiety, and even amusing side-issues. Some trees have been mislabeled, others displaced by construction—although there are numerous instances where the tree took priority over the building. Because these histories are often relegated to archives or reposited only in the recollections of contemporary scientists and historians scattered about the city, we have lacked a compiled record. Thus many tourists and even longtime residents depart knowing only the most conspicuous specimens. With this book, visitors and others can now acquire a new and exciting understanding of the living monuments of the nation's capital.

Walk under the gracious flowering cherries around the Tidal Basin or stand in the majestic grove of Chinese metasequoias (or dawn redwoods) at the National Arboretum. Pause to reflect on the probability that in their distant homelands, people seemingly of a foreign nature are sharing the same sort of experience under the same trees. Or read the complex story of how these trees were introduced into this country. Then you will understand why Washington can truly be called a "window on the world".

Let us hope that those who are the temporary stewards of this gracious heritage of our nation's capital will gain a new insight into the importance of the trees of Washington. For myself, I am simply grateful for the day Melanie and Polly walked into my office at the National Arboretum.

PREFACE

by *Melanie Choukas-Bradley*

It is a midsummer evening in Washington, D.C. The Japanese pagoda trees are in bloom on Massachusetts Avenue. The dark pink crape-myrtles are out on every block. And the mimosa tree in the courtyard drops blossoms in my hair. It is cool, clear and breezy. The air feels as if it has never held a drop of uncomfortable humidity.

Soon it will be autumn and the air will feel this way every night. The marble monuments will glitter and the Tidal Basin will fill with fallen cherry leaves.

Autumn is my favorite season in the City of Trees. It is the time of year I imagine Thomas Jefferson returning. In my fantasy he strolls around the Tidal Basin, amazed at what they've done to the Potomac flats. He smiles when he sees the marble replica of Monticello and its ripply reflection in the water. Walking under the trees, with their strange, foreign aura, he is overcome with a sudden, inexplicable peace.

The sun goes down over the Potomac. The pines and hollies encircling Jefferson's memorial darken.

Thomas Jefferson feels the magnetism of the memorial—*his* after all—as he slowly circles the basin. A full moon is rising and the air is an unnatural blue. As the sky grows darker, the structure seems to glow from within. Mesmerized, he scales the seemingly endless marble stairs. With a shiver, he beholds the mammoth statue of himself inside. Just then, the most pleasant fragrance seems to materialize out of the night air. Flowers, in November?

He walks over to the holly trees that brush against the pillars and the sweet smell intensifies. But the hollies aren't in flower.

At that moment he sees them. Tiny white flowers all over a large, holly-like bush. Never has he seen this plant in Washington, Charlottesville, or even in France.

Thomas Jefferson turns around and surveys the whole scene for the first time. Nothing is the same but the rising moon. The swamp has become a lake. Horses have metamorphosed into self-propelled machines that are lit up like fireflies. And the capital is filled with trees and shrubs that *he—an accomplished horticulturist—*has never so much as read about! Shrugging his shoulders, overwhelmed, he decides to enter the memorial. And irony upon irony, while every part of the landscape has evolved to an inscrutable degree, there are Jefferson's *words*, mere *words*, carved in stone. His thoughts—abstractions—have survived while all else has vanished.

I am imagining another evening. It is spring. George Washington is riding up on horseback from Mount Vernon where he has just discovered, lo and behold, that the little seedlings he planted on the bowling green two hundred years ago have grown into *huge trees!*

It is a special kind of Potomac evening. A fine mist, teasing rain, brings out the colors in Washington's favorite combination of flowering trees—the purply redbud and the snow white dogwood. Never, he thinks, in all his travels, has any sight rivaled the beauty of a spring evening on the Potomac. And never has he felt more at peace than when riding through this familiar wood, now bursting with soft, spring greens.

He remembers the reason for his journey and nudges his mare. He finds it peculiar, that while so much has changed—the traffic on the river has taken to the air on noisy wings and the old port of Alexandria seems almost land-locked—what strikes him more profoundly than the changes are the things that have stayed the same. He remembers just such a spring evening centuries ago, riding on horseback through these same woods under the flowering dogwood trees.

Suddenly, nearing the capital, one of Washington's worst fears has been confirmed. "They've destroyed the view to the river. And with all those monstrosities sticking up everywhere, including that giant obelisk, the President's house probably won't look a thing like the plan."

Noticing names and signs now for the first time he suddenly sees one that almost makes him fall off his horse. "L'Enfant Plaza? Named for the Frenchman I fired?" Washington comes to his senses when he reasons that it must be another L'Enfant.

Soon George Washington will know whether or not the President's house, begun on his hand-chosen site, was ever completed, and ever survived whatever wars there have been. And if he has time before nightfall he might even trot up to Jenkins Hill to see if they ever completed construction of the Capitol.

His musings are interrupted by the most incredible sight! He won't *have* to ride up to Jenkins Hill to answer his second question. Because there it is, looking larger and more glorious than he ever imagined. "Funny", he thinks, "when Mount Vernon looked so small." But there's no mistaking it—that's the United States Capitol rising out of the spring mist—"and I laid the cornerstone myself!"

George Washington's spirits are soaring. At his feet lies the federal city of his dreams; so much of it, from the President's House down the long green Mall to the Capitol, laid out according to the plan drawn up during his lifetime. And as far as his eye can see, the beautiful groves of trees.

"Every man should be able to live for centuries," he thinks, "if this could be his reward."

When I first moved to Washington, D.C., I remember telling my husband, Jim—who majored in history—that George Washington and Thomas Jefferson seemed no more real to me than the man in the moon. For me, history books had always failed to breathe life into the founding fathers. How strange it is, that I have since come to appreciate George Washington, Thomas Jefferson and many other American leaders—not by studying Revolutionary history or reading the Constitution—but through my research for a book on trees!

When Polly Alexander and I began work on *City of Trees* in 1978, we planned simply to fulfill a need. As I had discovered after moving here from New England, bookstores carried no guide to the magnificent trees of the nation's capital. For weeks I had tried to identify a massive tree with elm-like leaves that grew in a park across from my Capitol Hill apartment. At the end of two months' time, I had made a positive identification: it was not an elm tree.

It would be weeks more before I would find the source to tell me that my mystery tree was a Japanese zelkova. But with one botanical mystery solved, another would inevitably crop up. Polly and I learned to identify southern bald-cypress trees, only to discover that many of them were not bald-cypresses at all, but dawn redwoods from a remote part of China. We didn't believe it possible that we could confuse the Eastern white pine— beautiful conifer of our New England woods—with any other species. But we did. The rare exotic Himalayan pine, sparsely scattered throughout the city, is a near dead ringer.

Washington, we found, is simply filled with exotic trees. And the native American species we came across were just as likely to be indigenous to the Rockies or the Ozarks as they were to the Blue Ridge. Giant sequoias, douglas-firs and several species of magnolias were among the American trees we encountered.

With the help of former Congressman Fred Schwengel, president of the U.S. Capitol Historical Society, we were able to enlist the financial support of the American Forest Institute and the forest products industry. Jane Spivy Keough—then on the staff at the Smithsonian— put her tireless self to the task of historical and botanical research. Botanists at the National Arboretum and the Park Service generously shared their time and expertise.

For months, Polly and I criss-crossed the city, gathering specimens of leaves, flowers and fruit for our own little herbarium, photographing the trees in all seasons, and recording field notes in our journals. Our efforts resulted in the main body of this book, *City of Trees,* Part Two, which is introduced on page 57.

But botanical diversity was only part of the story. George Washington, Thomas Jefferson, John Quincy Adams, and many other American presidents, we learned, were accomplished horticulturists. And the city of Washington had evolved in close accordance with a plan laid out at its founding two centuries ago. That plan— largely the work of Pierre L'Enfant, a French engineer hired by President Washington—had called for tree plantings and parks throughout the capital.

While George Washington, the Revolutionary general, had never really gripped my imagination, I found myself captivated by accounts of his botanical experiments at Mount Vernon. I felt awed standing under living trees he planted two centuries ago. And I grew to respect the man who was just as interested in the homely construction details of the Capitol building and the White House as he was in winning wars and governing a nation.

Thomas Jefferson, whom I'd always admired, also grew in stature for me as I read about his struggles to save the young city of Washington from the haphazard development that threatened to destroy its natural charm. Like George Washington, Jefferson understood that no blueprint for a government could be put to work in a void. Concerned about the sorry state of Pennsylvania Avenue during his presidency, Jefferson drew up plans to line the route from the Capitol to the President's house with Lombardy poplar trees. Eventually, through the early efforts of Washington and Jefferson and like-minded successors, Washington, D.C. came to be known as the "City of Trees."

The story contained in these pages is much more than an accounting of various tree plantings. When George Washington chose the site for the nation's capital, the Tidal Basin where the world-famous cherry trees now bloom each spring was nothing but a tidal marsh.

This book portrays Washington, D.C.'s evolution from tidal swamp to present day world capital. As the Honorable Fred Schwengel always loves to point out, Washington, D.C. is living proof that people working in harmony with nature can even improve on the natural setting.

We hope you spend many hours exploring the City of Trees. Perhaps your explorations will uncover botanical and historical secrets that even we—in our two years of research—have missed.

This book can be enjoyed for its own sake or used as a guide to the trees of Washington, D.C. It is also useful in other cities and towns, particularly in the eastern United States, as a guide to the trees planted in parks and gardens and along streets. Since many city trees are exotic, native field guides are not very useful in settled areas. For instructions on how to use *City of Trees*, Part Two please see page 57.

For my part, I hope to bring my grandchildren to see the cherry blossoms in the twenty-first century. And I hope that throughout my life I continue to feel that if the founding fathers were to return to their capital city, they would be amazed and delighted with its evolution. Their concern for the future, not only of the nation, but of this city, should serve as an inspiration for us all.

ACKNOWLEDGMENTS

The authors gratefully acknowledge the support and assistance of the American Forest Institute, the National Forest Products Association, and the following companies and associations of the forest products industry: International Paper Company, Crown Zellerbach Corporation, American Pulpwood Association, American Paper Institute, Union Camp Corporation, the Bendix Corporation, and Time, Incorporated.

The following people were invaluable to the creation of this book: the Honorable Fred Schwengel, Jane Spivy Keough, James Choukas-Bradley, Roland Jefferson, Peter Mazzeo, Dr. Frederick Meyer, Horace Wester, Ralph Hodges, Joseph McGrath, Don-Lee Davidson, Sharon Connelly, David Kolkebeck, Al Hackl, David Uslan, George Thompson, and the senior staff of the American Forest Institute.

The following people contributed time and energy to *City of Trees*:
Mrs. Lyndon Baines Johnson, Senator Patrick Leahy, Senator Mark Hatfield, Dr. John L. Creech, Dr. Marc Cathey, Joann Klappauf, Robert Hickey, Dick Hammerschlag, Jim Patterson, Dean Norton, R. Bernard and Eleanor Alexander, Michael Choukas, Jr. and Juanita Choukas, Michael A. Choukas, Hubert Bermont, Howell Begle, Nancy Clark Reynolds, Helen Neal, Theodore Dudley, Gene Eisenbeiss, Hans Johannsen, Nash Castro, Rex Scouten, Irvin Williams, Bill Rooney, James Buckler, Jack Mundy, Karen Solit, Don Smith, Elmer Jones, Robert Fisher, Kevin Murphy, Jeffrey Carson, Darwina Neal, Florian Thayn, Tom Beers, Perry Fisher, Paul Pincus, George Berklacey, Dorothy Provine, Peter Atkinson, Richard Howard, John Hall, H. P. Newson, Raphael Sagalyn, Cindy Weaver, Jakie Lewis, David Barrington, and the support staff at the American Forest Institute.

And finally, we wish to thank Carol Ehrlich, Chris Smith, and the rest of the Johns Hopkins University Press staff for devoting so much time and talent to the paperback edition of *City of Trees*.

INTRODUCTION
THE CITY IS BORN
How Washington Came to be Known as the City of Trees

In 1790, President George Washington was granted the authority to oversee the selection of a site for a permanent national capital. The city was to be located on the Maryland-Virginia border, along the Potomac River.

No individual could have been better suited to the task of selecting the capital site than George Washington. The distinguished general and first president of the United States was also a land surveyor and farmer, who possessed a great sensitivity to the land. The site he chose early in 1791 was just a few miles upriver from his estate in Mount Vernon, Virginia.

The eighteenth-century landscape where the city of Washington, D.C. now lies was laid out with picturesque orchards and corn and tobacco fields, set among the lovely woodlands. Native Americans had cleared the land and planted crops along the Potomac centuries earlier. By 1790 Georgetown had become a thriving tobacco port.

George Washington hired Major Pierre Charles L'Enfant, a European-born engineer who has been described as an "artist, adventurer, and spectacularly arrogant visionary"[1] to design the federal city. L'Enfant brought to the task an intimate knowledge of the great capitals of Europe. The Washington city plan benefited from L'Enfant's appreciation of the finest elements of eighteenth century Paris, London and Rome. Broad avenues were laid out in every direction, radiating from the central axis of the Capitol. Spacious grounds were planned for stately federal government buildings and there would be parks aplenty throughout the city.

Both George Washington and Pierre L'Enfant appreciated the need to incorporate trees into the city plan. Every street, avenue, and federal building was to be generously graced by groves of trees.

While his splendid capital is here for the ages, L'Enfant's tenure as the city's designer met an untimely end. Disagreements between the board of commissioners overseeing the city's development and the temperamental engineer put the ever-diplomatic George Washington in an uncomfortable position. For a time, the President managed to placate the commissioners and keep the rebellious L'Enfant in line. But the efforts of the President were doomed to fail. When Daniel Carroll, one of the area's wealthiest men, began erecting a house in the middle of where L'Enfant had envisioned New Jersey Avenue, the Frenchman sent out his assistant to tear it down. When the assistant was arrested, L'Enfant himself attempted to raze the structure. Washington's fatherly scolding, "I must strictly enjoin you to touch no man's property without his consent,"[2] and numerous similar warnings did little to check L'Enfant's impetuous behavior. Eventually he was fired.

L'Enfant later submitted a bill to Congress for $95,000, but he was paid less than $4,000 for designing the capital of the United States. The plan was completed by Andrew Ellicott, who had originally been commissioned to survey the land for the new capital. Ellicott made minor adjustments to the L'Enfant map, then erased L'Enfant's name and signed his own. The map for the new city was known thereafter as the Ellicott map.

One can't help but wonder today how L'Enfant would respond to the huge new plaza in southwest Washington which sits so heavily on his delicate grid of streets, parks, and avenues, and so inappropriately bears his name.

Although the visions of Washington's founders were eventually to become reality, the early years of the capital city were bleak. During his administration, Thomas Jefferson was forced to witness the widespread destruction of the area's trees. Property owners throughout the District cleared the beautiful stands of native timber from their land for profit, and trees were felled by the poor for use as firewood. The staunchly democratic Jefferson even expressed a momentary wish for despotic power, "that, in the possession of absolute power, I might enforce the preservation of these valuable groves." [3]

Despite the despair he felt over the destruction of the city's native trees, Jefferson set to work planting new trees throughout the District. He personally sketched out a plan to plant Lombardy poplars along Pennsylvania Avenue stretching from the Capitol to the White House, and then supervised its execution. This is the first Washington street tree-planting on record. Drawings and paintings that survive the era depict the avenue lined with rows of Jefferson's delicate, columnar trees.

Following the administration of Thomas Jefferson, the capital city experienced its darkest days. Garbage and slops were freely dumped in the streets, the polluted marshland along the Potomac posed a growing health threat, and the death rate was extremely high. Poverty was severe and crime rampant. In her book, *Washington: Village and Capital*, Constance McGlaughlin Green describes the depressing landscape of the 1820s.

> The city L'Enfant had laid out on a scale to represent the genius of the new republic had in fact attained little aesthetic distinction. Partial execution of the plan left large areas untouched, which spoiled the effect.
>
> Most of the Mall was a wasteland of swamps dotted with clusters of sheds along the canal.
>
> Vacant lots occupied much of the city of magnificent distances, and the streets connecting one village with the others that comprised the capital were little more than rutted paths. [4]

As depressing as Washington had become, out-of-doors, it is easy to understand why people flocked indoors during the 1840s to view the botanical wonders housed in the new greenhouse adjacent to the Patent Office Building on F Street. Plants collected in remote parts of the world by government-sponsored expeditions were displayed inside the popular greenhouse, which was a precursor of the Botanic Gardens now located at the foot of Capitol Hill.

Toward the end of the 1840s, interest in beautifying the nation's capital was rekindled. In 1847 the cornerstone for the romantic Smithsonian Castle was laid, and the following year ground was broken for the Washington Monument. Unfortunately, this promising trend was destined to be cut short by the Civil War.

An interesting interlude in the city's landscape design began in the 1850s, when the government hired the eminent landscape gardener Andrew Jackson Downing to take charge of the planting and design of Washington's park system. Downing's ideas differed radically from L'Enfant's. Where L'Enfant called for open spaces and grand vistas, Downing sketched out plans for romantic paths through groves of trees. Downing believed that "the straight lines and broad avenues of the streets of Washington would be relieved and contrasted by the beauty of curved lines and natural groups of trees. . . ."[5]

It was just such a plan that was carried out on the Mall. For many years the open green avenue of today was planted with Andrew Jackson Downing's clumps of trees and curved walkways. Downing was drowned in a steamboat accident in 1852 before he was able to carry out most of the work he'd been commissioned to do. In addition to the landscaping plan for the Mall, his plans for the White House grounds, the Ellipse, and Lafayette Park were more or less executed during and after his lifetime.

During the Civil War (1861–1865), Washington was a grim city, indeed. The Mall was the site of horse and cattle corrals, a fetid and nearly useless canal, and clusters of Union Army tents. The marshlands along the Potomac were growing more unhealthful by the day, and, worst of all, the skyline of the capital was dominated by two disheartening sights: at one end of the Mall, the unfinished Capitol dome, and at the other, the incompleted Washington Monument.

In 1872, a railroad station and tracks were added to the Mall, creating greater distance than ever from the city vision of Washington, Jefferson, and L'Enfant. However, 1872 was a good year for the District of Columbia overall, because something began happening that was to turn Washington into one of the world's most beautiful cities. Alexander R. Shepherd began planting trees.

Alexander Shepherd was the second and last governor of the District of Columbia. A native Washingtonian, his ambitious plans for improving the quality of life in Washington included not only planting 60,000 trees, but also installing crucially needed sewers, and filling in the polluted canal on the Mall. Shepherd also literally tore up the railroad tracks at the foot of Capitol Hill and ran the District of Columbia into debt totalling $10,000,000 over the authorized allowable ceiling. Congress decided in 1874 that the District of Columbia would do better *without* a governor.

However, during his brief reign, the energetic Shepherd turned Washington, D.C. into the world-famous "City of Trees." He appointed three experienced horticulturists to serve as a "parking commission," overseeing the tree plantings throughout the city. During the next decade, under the commission's direction, the streets of Washington were amply lined with maples, poplars, lindens, sycamores, elms, ashes, and many other trees. These early plantings not only beautified the city; for the first time they made Washington truly livable, providing relief from the summer heat as well as a rather mysterious check on the spread of malaria.

An 1889 story in Harper's Magazine described a very different city from the capital the world had grown accustomed to grumbling about:

> The city of Washington, the capital of the nation, exceeds in beauty any city in the world. The grand conception of the plan of its broad streets and avenues paved with asphalt, smooth as marble, and its hundreds of palatial residences erected in the highest style of art, but above all, its magnificent trees, make it without a peer.[6]

For the first time, Washington, D.C. was favorably compared with the great capitals of Europe. Visitors to Berlin claimed that its famous "Unter den Linden," the linden-lined avenue, was a disappointment compared to the miles of lindens planted along Washington's Massachusetts Avenue. There was even talk that the trees of Washington surpassed those of Paris and London in beauty and variety.

Soon Washington was known the world over as the "City of Trees." Although Governor Shepherd was only in office a brief time, his legacy has never wavered. In 1932, Erle Kauffman wrote:

> After (Shepherd) the vision was never lost. The Federal Government, the city fathers, tree loving citizens, even outsiders, labored tirelessly to repair the tragic results of those early depredations. Trees appeared on every street, the parks blossomed in new glory, and tiny seedlings took root on lawns and in backyards. At first the trees were confined to those native to the region, those easily accessible, but soon plants from other sections of the country, from other lands, were flowering in all their exotic beauty. From the Orient came the exquisite cherry trees, the gingko, the umbrella tree, the ailanthus—the Chinese Tree of Heaven—the paulownia and the Scholar tree. From the Holy Land came the cedar and locust, while Asia contributed spruce, thorn, and magnolia. Europe gave the hornbeam, willow elm and holly.
>
> Today in Washington the visitor may find more than two thousand varieties of trees and shrubs, representing nearly two hundred distinct species. It holds, with the exception of a few arboretums, more different kinds of trees and shrubs than any city on earth.[7]

The twentieth century dawned auspiciously for the city of Washington. A commission headed by Senator

James McMillan visited the capitals of Europe, bringing home the conviction that Washington should return to L'Enfant's original conception. Downing's arboretum was to be removed, opening up the vista from the Capitol to the Washington Monument. The railroad station would be torn down and the Mall extended. At the same time, work was already well under way to fill in the polluted tidal flats along the river, creating today's beautiful East and West Potomac Parks.

The McMillan Commission selected the American elm to line the National Mall, choosing it for the "architectural character of its columnar trunk and the delicate traceries formed by its wide-spreading branches." [8] Today these rows of elms, stretching from the Capitol to the "Monument," are a magnificent example of a tastefully designed landscape.

In 1912, the beautiful Japanese flowering cherry trees, a gift to the United States from Japan, were laid out around the newly created Tidal Basin and along the shores of East Potomac Park. And in 1927 Congress authorized the creation of a National Arboretum in the nation's capital.

The early street trees planted by Shepherd's parking commission served as useful experiments in the brand new science of urban silviculture. In time it was learned that the silver maple, planted in the 1870s for the fast shade it provided, was too brittle and prone to storm damage to be a practical city tree. Poplars, also widely planted by Shepherd's commission, turned out to be "surface rooters," tearing up the landscape with their shallow roots. And, ash-leafed maples were found to be particularly prone to insect pests. Norway maples, oaks, plane trees, and ginkgoes proved to be better suited to the urban environment.

As the times changed, so did the problems associated with Washington's street trees. Hungry horses nibbling on the trees they were hitched to—a serious problem in the last century—gave way to the far more destructive automobile. Underground gas leaks became an increasing problem as the city grew; and earlier in the century, ice cream manufacturers wreaked havoc on the city's trees simply by dumping briny water on their roots.

Even the pests changed with the times. During the twentieth century, two devastating diseases were imported on foreign plant material. The chestnut blight virtually destroyed the American chestnut; and Dutch elm disease devastated urban landscapes throughout the country. However, by pooling their expertise, arborists employed by the National Park Service, the National Arboretum, and the District of Columbia, have managed to save many of the historic and beautiful elms of Washington and to make simultaneous strides in the science of urban forestry.

During the 1960s, Lady Bird Johnson's Committee for a More Beautiful Capital inspired the drive to beautify cities across the country with the example it set in the nation's capital. This group of 30 public officials, private citizens, and urban designers revitalized parks throughout the city by planting thousands of trees and flowers and by making extensive physical improvements.

When asked to describe her drive to beautify Washington and the entire national landscape, Mrs. Johnson explained: "To me, in sum, 'beautification' means our total concern for the physical and human quality of the world we pass on to our children."[9]

In recent years, the National Park Service's Center for Urban Ecology, located here in Washington, has zeroed in on the most common problems plaguing natural areas in today's urban environment. The center has studied and implemented soil protection and improvement programs in Washington's parks and it has helped to coordinate citywide efforts to manage tree diseases and pests.

Today, the beautiful "City of Trees" is a living tribute to the human ability to work in harmony with nature. These words from a 1915 volume of *National Geographic* still hold true today:

> Washington rests lightly on its people. In many of the world's larger cities a necessity for 'letting in the country upon the city' is being felt. Such a necessity does not exist in the National Capital, which has been built around the country, leaving many delightful strips within, where a mighty forest is growing in the midst of metropolitan life.[10]

This, then, is the "City of Trees" . . . the magnificent capital of the United States.

PART ONE

Guide to the Highlights of the City of Trees

City of Trees, Part One, is organized in two sections. The first describes tree-viewing sites in the vicinity of the Mall, and the second takes you to outlying areas of the District and beyond. To learn more about the trees you see and to identify unknown species, consult Part Two of this book, where you will find detailed, illustrated descriptions of more than 300 types of native and exotic trees. The index provides a quick and easy way to locate illustrated descriptions of the trees that are mentioned in Part One. And two maps—one of the Mall area, the other of outlying locations—appear on pages 8 and 9. All the areas discussed in Part One are keyed in on the maps.

Tree Viewing around the Mall
THE WHITE HOUSE GROUNDS
Site of Presidential Tree Plantings

President William Howard Taft once wrote: "The view from the White House windows plays an important part in the life of its occupants." The President "can look from the south windows of the White House on a scene of rare beauty."[11]

Occupants of the most demanding, and often the loneliest, office in the land have consistently drawn sustenance from the lovely acres surrounding the White House. During the Cuban missile crisis of 1962, President John F. Kennedy described the White House Rose Garden as the "brightest spot in the somber surroundings of the last few days."[12]

And those who have found solace in the White House surroundings also have a long-standing tradition of leaving the executive mansion grounds an even more beautiful place than that which they've inherited. President Kennedy himself decided to redesign the famous garden just outside the oval office. Nearly every American President, from "the tree-planting Mr. (John Quincy) Adams" on down, has picked up a spade to perform the simple, symbolic ritual of planting a tree at 1600 Pennsylvania Avenue.

Thus, the present occupants of the White House know that spring has arrived when John F. Kennedy's saucer magnolias bloom in the Rose Garden. As the days grow warmer still, John Quincy Adams' American elm leafs out, as it has done every spring for more than a century and a half. The first hot summer days mean there will be warm evenings on the Truman balcony, with the fragrance of Andrew Jackson's southern magnolias in the air.

Individually, the trees of the White House grounds are living memorials to the people who have served in their country's highest office. Together they form a graceful frame for the nation's first home.

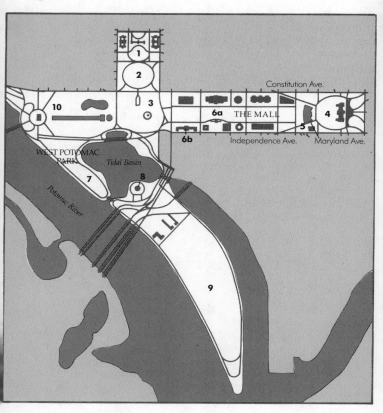

The Mall and Vicinity

  1   The White House Grounds
  2   The National Christmas Tree
  3   The Washington Monument
  4   The Capitol Grounds
  5   The United States Botanic Gardens
 6a   The Smithsonian Museum and Gallery Grounds
 6b   The Department of Agriculture Grounds
  7   The Japanese Flowering Cherry Trees
  8   The Jefferson Memorial
  9   East Potomac Park (Hains Point)
 10   The Lincoln Memorial

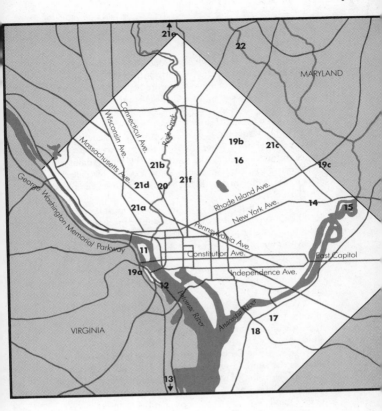

The District of Columbia

HISTORY OF THE GROUNDS

When John and Abigail Adams moved into the newly constructed executive mansion in 1800, the site selected by George Washington bore little resemblance to the White House setting of today. The barren grounds were strewn with tools, rubble, and workmen's shacks. The nation's second first lady described the scene in a letter to her daughter: " 'We have not the least fence, yard or other convenience, without.' "[13] With no private place outdoors to hang the family wash, Mrs. Adams was forced to string up a clothesline in what she called "the great unfinished audience room,"[14] known today as the East Room.

But if the first lady who first set up housekeeping at 1600 Pennsylvania Avenue found some aspects of her situation slightly primitive, she was able to rise above them to make this observation about her new environment: "The President's House is in a beautiful situation in front of which is the Potomac with a view of Alexandr[i]a. The country around is romantic but a wild, a wilderness at present."[15]

When Thomas Jefferson succeeded John Adams to the presidency, he developed a landscaping plan, with the assistance of architect Benjamin Latrobe, that provided privacy for the first family without obstructing the view toward the Potomac. On the eastern and western sides of the south lawn, Jefferson supervised the construction of low, rounded mounds (known appropriately enough as the "Jefferson Mounds" today). These attractive grassy knolls are now shaded by handsome trees. In 1807, an English visitor to the White House, apparently unimpressed by the landscaping innovations in progress, wrote:

> The ground around (the White House), instead of being laid out in a suitable style, is in a condition so that in a dark night instead of finding your way to the house, you may, perchance, fall into a pit, or stumble over a heap of rubbish.[16]

This same British visitor was also unfavorably impressed by Jefferson's rustic wooden fence, the first enclosure ever erected around the executive mansion. According to the guest:

> The fence around the house is of the meanest sort; a common post and rail enclosure. This parsimony destroys every sentiment of pleasure that arises in the mind, in viewing the residence of the President of a nation, and is a disgrace to the country.[17]

While it is hard to imagine the third president concurring with the strong sentiments of his visitor, Jefferson later removed the wooden fence in favor of a low fieldstone wall.

James Madison's lively wife, Dolley, is said to have taken an avid interest in the White House grounds. But in 1814, midway into the Madison administration, the British burned the White House and the president and first lady were forced to live elsewhere. Thanks to a heavy rain, the shell remained intact and the original architect, James Hoban, was able to salvage the

Presidential home. In 1817, James Monroe moved into the reconstructed White House.

Monroe's successor, John Quincy Adams, made the greatest improvements on the White House grounds of any American president. The sixth president spent many hours planting and tending the White House gardens, and trees, an avocation which earned him his nickname, "The tree planting Mr. Adams."[18] Entries in Adams' diaries tell of the joy he derived from his horticultural endeavors, and they give a rough record of what grew on the White House grounds during the late 1820s. The wide range of plants included: " '. . . forest and fruit-trees, shrubs, hedges, esculent vegetables, kitchen and medicinal herbs, hot-house plants, flowers and weeds, to the amount I conjecture, of at least one thousand.' "[19]

In an attempt to boost a national silk industry, President Adams planted white mulberries on the White House grounds, nurturing silkworms on their leaves. His wife, Louisa, performed the delicate task of unreeling the slender silk filaments from the cocoons. Despite their efforts, the industry never really got off the ground.

President Martin Van Buren, the man who occupied the White House from 1837 until 1841, supervised further changes in the grounds. The Van Buren administration installed fountains and stone walls and added more flower gardens around the mansion. When Charles Dickens visited the White House in 1841, his British eye saw the " 'garden walks' " as being " 'pretty and agreeable . . . though they have that uncomfortable air of having been made yesterday.' "[20]

In 1851, with Millard Fillmore in the White House, the prominent landscape architect, Andrew Jackson Downing, was commissioned to formally lay out the grounds. Only sketchy records of the Downing plan and its execution remain, but there is evidence that the architect recommended changing the angular outline of the south lawn to the gracefully curved perimeter we know today. Downing also sketched out a plan for a circular park to be located south of the grounds. The landscape architect met a tragic death just two years after he was commissioned to landscape the White House grounds and other parks throughout Washington. Nevertheless, his plan for a circular park south of the White House was to be carried out after the Civil War during the administration of Ulysses S. Grant.

President James Buchanan's major contribution to the White House grounds was a prominent feature of the landscape for nearly a half century, until it was removed to make way for a new west wing in the early 1900s. Buchanan's niece and White House hostess, Harriet Lane, convinced the fifteenth president to build the first of a series of conservatories (greenhouses) on the west lawn of the mansion. Although the conservatories grew to unsightly proportions over the years, their lush interiors were a panacea for first families needing a break from the interminable round of official duties. A myriad of potted plants, including orchids, camellias, and orange trees, grew in the White House conservatories, providing the mansion with a constant supply of flowers and greenery.

During the Civil War, President Lincoln's view from

the south windows of the White House was indisputably grim. Looking out over Union troops bivouacked on the lawn, the beleaguered president saw a badly polluted canal (where Constitution Avenue runs today) surrounded by fetid marshland. Beyond, cattle and horse corrals stretched up to the unfinished Washington Monument. During the summer months, when the marshland was particularly unhealthy, the president stayed at Soldiers' Home, several miles away.

After the war, the canal and surrounding lowlands were filled in and the present day Ellipse was created, guided by the plan worked out years earlier by Andrew Jackson Downing.

The Teddy Roosevelt era (1901–1909) saw the removal of the White House conservatories. Mrs. Roosevelt also redesigned the outdoor cutting gardens near the mansion, creating an old-fashioned colonial garden instead.

Woodrow Wilson's tenure in the presidency saw two major changes on the White House grounds. The first was decidedly temporary. During World War I, the president installed a flock of sheep on the White House lawns in order to keep the grass trim without wasting money or manpower. The second Wilson innovation has been long-lasting; Mrs. Wilson planted the first White House Rose Garden.

In the 1930s, the Olmsted brothers, sons of the great Frederick Law Olmsted, were commissioned to devise a landscaping plan for the White House. In their 1935 report to the president, the brothers displayed judgment reminiscent of their father's wise treatment of the Capitol grounds more than a half century earlier. The Olmsteds sought to add dignity to the acres surrounding the White House, while simultaneously adapting them to the functional needs of the president.

They advocated the creation of an open swath of land through the center of the south grounds. Modern presidents not only enjoy the unobstructed view of the Washington Monument and Jefferson Memorial, but also appreciate the convenience of being able to land a helicopter on the south lawn.

The Olmsted brothers recommended that trees and shrubs be planted along the perimeter of the grounds. The aesthetics of this arboreal frame for the executive mansion, meticulously maintained by today's White House gardeners, can best be appreciated from the south, where the graceful tree-lined curve of the south lawn meets the opposite curve of the Ellipse.

Today the "President's Park," as it is officially called (including the Ellipse as well as the grounds around the mansion), is cared for by a team of National Park Service horticulturists and gardeners. President John F. Kennedy requested that the Park Service assume responsibility for the grounds during the early sixties.

USE OF THE WHITE HOUSE GROUNDS

Gone are the egalitarian days of the nineteenth century when the public strolled freely under the White House trees. Today the south grounds of the White

House, including the Rose Garden, are generally open to the public twice a year, for the spring and fall garden tours. At Easter time, the children of Washington are invited to participate in an annual egg-rolling celebration on the south lawn, a century-old tradition begun during the administration of Rutherford B. Hayes. Adults are admitted to the festivities only if they are accompanied by children.

Since the turn of the century, the White House grounds have been the scene of a variety of presidential events, from formal receptions for visiting heads of state to picnics and concerts. True to character, it was the great outdoorsman, Theodore Roosevelt, who began the tradition of holding regular White House parties outside the executive mansion walls.

Children living in the White House have also made use of the spacious grounds. Theodore Roosevelt's several rambunctious offspring rode their pony, "Algonquin," around the mansion and walked on stilts through the White House gardens. In recent years, Caroline Kennedy trotted across the south lawn on "Macaroni," while young Amy Carter preferred to survey her surroundings from a tree-house look-out, nestled in the boughs of an Atlas cedar.

Recognizing a child's need for secret space, especially in the White House, Lyndon and Lady Bird Johnson created the "Children's Garden" on the south grounds. Sheltered year round by American holly trees, the garden contains children's chairs and tables, a lily pond, azaleas, and other flowering plants.

THE ROSE GARDEN

Ever since the early 1800s, when the first seed was sown at 1600 Pennsylvania Avenue, the gardens around the White House have been nearly as transitory as the parade of first families who have loved and tended them. One garden, however, has risen in the public imagination to become a lasting and powerful symbol of the presidency.

In 1913, First Lady Ellen Wilson, the first wife of the president, planted roses near her husband's office in the west wing of the White House. Unwittingly, she had chosen the site for America's most historic garden.

In 1928, during the Calvin Coolidge administration, the Washington *Star* reported: "The opinion is that the President's chief interest lies in the White House rose gardens. The larger of these gardens is immediately east of the President's office and contains more than 300 bushes and a dozen or so rose trees. Virtually every known variety and specimen of rose may be found in this garden, and when it is in full bloom, it is a spot of rare beauty." [21]

Each succeeding president has welcomed the opportunity to pause and catch his breath in the shelter of the Rose Garden. It was President John F. Kennedy, however, who made the garden what it is today.

Shortly after his inauguration in 1961, the president and Mrs. Kennedy made a state journey to Europe, where they visited the royal gardens of Austria, France, and

England. This trip sparked the president's desire to create something to equal the beauty of the garden of the French Palais de l'Elysee or the British Buckingham Palace; but he envisioned a garden that would be uniquely American.

The president invited a personal friend and able amateur horticulturist, Mrs. Paul Mellon, to work out a new design for the small piece of land nestled in between the Oval Office and the South Portico. With the help of many gardeners, and under the direct supervision of the president, Mrs. Mellon worked out the plan for a new White House Rose Garden. A pink saucer magnolia would go in each corner of the less than one quarter acre plot; on the north and south sides, lines of lovely white Katherine crabapples; around the trees, neat green osmanthus and boxwood hedges; and, of course, the flowers—tulips and hyacinths for early spring; a rainbow of annuals for summer; chrysanthemums for fall; and the famous staple, roses.

The president took great interest in the way his garde. progressed. According to the architectural critic, Wolf Von Eckardt, "he would always walk through it on his way to his office and back for lunch or dinner. Many times he would stop, and if (Irvin) Williams (the gardener) was in sight ask him one thing or another. As his garden grew, so did his knowledge of its plants and wonders."

When the traditional American garden was all laid out, around a perfect carpet of bluegrass, the president was very proud of it. "It was the only thing he ever bragged about," according to Von Eckardt. "Often late at night he would walk out to clear his mind to seek inspiration. The garden had turned out just as he had hoped it would."[22]

President Kennedy bestowed honorary citizenship upon Sir Winston Churchill in his lovely new garden. There he greeted many guests, and no matter what the occasion, he stole every opportunity to share his new-found knowledge of the trees, shrubs, and flowers with his visitors.

In November of 1963, at the end of the garden's second summer, President Kennedy was tragically killed. Three days after his death, his young widow, Jacqueline, requested that a simple basket of flowers from the Rose Garden be placed beside his grave. The contents of this basket, in the words of the eloquent Von Eckardt, have the cadence and poignancy of a poem: "Roses still blooming, berries from the crabapples and a few flowers that had survived the first frost . . ."[23]

The White House Rose Garden was a great comfort to John Kennedy's successor, Lyndon Baines Johnson, whose presidency saw the country torn apart by the Vietnam war. President Richard M. Nixon's daughter, Tricia, was married in the Rose Garden in the first outdoor White House wedding. So closely has the garden become associated with recent presidents who regularly conduct business there, that more than one incumbent, cloistered in the White House during an election year, has been accused of practicing the so-called "Rose Garden strategy."

Today the garden remains under the constant scrutiny of a National Park Service team of horticulturists and gardeners who weed the grass by hand and carefully tend the flowers, shrubs, and trees.

THE JACQUELINE KENNEDY GARDEN

Before President Kennedy died, he and Mrs. Kennedy had planned another White House garden to be used by the first lady. Located next to the east wing, on the opposite side of the South Portico from the Rose Garden, the first lady's garden was to be as convenient a retreat for her as the Rose Garden was for the president.

When the Johnson family moved into the executive mansion, Mrs. Johnson became determined to finish the garden exactly as the Kennedys had envisioned it. With the help of Mrs. Mellon and the National Park Service White House crew, she set to work.

Beautifying her surroundings comes as naturally to Lady Bird Johnson as breathing, and within months the first lady's garden was completed. In April of 1965 Mrs. Johnson dedicated the garden to Jacqueline Kennedy. In a moving tribute to the former first lady, Mrs. Johnson said:

> The Kennedys brought to the White House many striking qualities, but perhaps above all they brought the lilt of youth, an instinct for the lovely, an infinite quality of grace.[24]

She went on to say that every detail of the garden "reflects the unfailing taste of the gifted and gracious Jacqueline Kennedy."[25]

Gracefully sculpted hollies, a grape arbor, lindens, magnolias, and other trees and shrubs share this lovely plot with tasteful pockets of flowers. A simple plaque attached to a pillar bears a handwritten dedication to Mrs. Kennedy.

The Jacqueline Kennedy Garden is a perfect companion to the Rose Garden. Together they form a moving memorial to the Camelot aura of the Kennedy years.

TREES PLANTED BY PRESIDENTS
Presidential Trees of the Nineteenth Century

There is a special poignancy about the presidential trees at the White House. In the words of former First Lady Rosalynn Carter: "They stand as personal expressions of faith in the future, not only of this place but of our nation."[26] In a sadder sense, the White House trees speak to us of the brevity of human life. They are our only living links with many of the men who achieved their country's highest office and then served so briefly.

The greatest tree enthusiast among our presidents was George Washington, the only chief executive who never resided at the White House. But while the first president probably never got the chance to sow a seed at 1600 Pennsylvania Avenue, Washington planted dozens of trees at his estate in Mount Vernon, Virginia. Several of them are alive today.

Thomas Jefferson shared Washington's reverence for trees, and lined Pennsylvania Avenue, from the White House to the Capitol, with graceful Lombardy poplars.

Although no living trees on the White House grounds can be traced to Jefferson's administration, this quote has survived the great champion of democracy who witnessed the negligent felling of trees in the young capital:

> I wish I was a despot that I might save the noble, the beautiful trees that are daily falling sacrifices to the cupidity of their owners, or the necessity of the poor . . . The unnecessary felling of a tree seems to me a crime little short of murder; it pains me to an unspeakable degree.[27]

The oldest authenticated presidential planting on the White House grounds is the "John Quincy Adams Elm." Planted by our sixth president sometime during the late 1820s, this lovely American elm dominates the eastern "Jefferson Mound" on the White House south lawn. Watchful White House gardeners have helped this historic tree survive the plague of Dutch Elm disease and a lightning bolt which brought down one of the tree's main limbs in the late 1960s.

Andrew Jackson, the Tennessean who was the seventh American president, brought the spirit of the frontier to the White House. He also brought tremendous sadness. His cherished wife, Rachel, had just died following a bitter political campaign in which the circumstances surrounding their marriage (her second) were slandered. "Old Hickory," as he was called, brought a pair of southern magnolias from their Tennessee home, the Hermitage, so that he would have "something green" in Washington to remember her by. These beautiful evergreen magnolias are the pride and joy of today's first family. They stand between the Rose Garden and the South Portico, delighting White House occupants and guests year after year with their lemon-scented blossoms.

On one side of the twenty dollar bill is the bust of Andrew Jackson. On the other, the White House, with the lovely pair of Jackson magnolias plainly visible just to the left of the South Portico!

The *Washington Post Magazine* said of the great frontiersman: "Few people ever knew that 'Old Hickory' was one of the greatest tree lovers ever to occupy the White House. His old plantation home, the Hermitage, near Nashville, Tennessee, is one of the tree show places of the nation."[28]

A tree was featured in a tragedy of a later administration. In 1881, just months after his inauguration, President James A. Garfield was struck down by an assassin's bullet. For more than two months the nation anxiously followed Garfield's unsuccessful struggle to live. Legend has it that periodic bulletins about the President's health were placed on an elm tree outside the White House and that this elm was then known for years hence as the "Bulletin Elm."[29]

Grover Cleveland, the only president to serve two nonconsecutive terms, was also the only chief executive to marry in the White House. Shortly after the 1886 wedding, his 21-year old bride, Frances, planted two delicate "blood-leaf" or "spider-leaf" Japanese maples on the White House south lawn. One of these trees, located to the west of the central fountain on the south lawn, is thriving today. The other was replaced by former First Lady Rosalynn Carter.

While many of the presidential trees that were planted in the last century are no longer alive, President Benjamin Harrison is survived by his handsome scarlet oak, located just inside the fence to the east of the eastern Pennsylvania Avenue gate.

Presidential Plantings of this Century

Charles Henlock, the White House gardener during ten presidential administrations, from 1886 until 1931, told an amusing story after his retirement. During the presidency of William Howard Taft, Mrs. Taft requested that a hedge fence be planted along the west side of the White House for privacy. When Taft's successor, Woodrow Wilson, recruited a flock of sheep to keep the White House lawns clipped during World War I, it seems that the creatures weren't content with an all-grass diet. According to the old gardener, Henlock, "the best thing those sheep ever did was to eat up Mrs. Taft's hedge."[30]

The administration of Warren G. Harding is memorialized by a beautiful southern magnolia which stands between the east wing of the White House and East Executive Avenue. Mrs. Harding spent many hours in the White House gardens, in the company of the family dog, Laddie Boy. On a spring day in the early twenties a Washington paper reported:

> Mrs. Harding and the faithful Laddie Boy have passed some pleasant hours in and out of (the gardens) gathering some blossoms for the sanctum of the second floor and admiring the stately procession of tulips. One of the ancient beliefs is that a dog is destructive to a flower garden, but to see the care with which the Airedale picks his steps following his mistress is to revise this opinion.[31]

President Herbert Hoover gave impetus to a national tree-planting movement in the early thirties by planting an American elm (no longer extant) in memory of George Washington on the White House north lawn. Two stately white oaks on the south lawn survive the thirty-first president's administration.

When Franklin Delano Roosevelt took office in 1933, the *Washington Post Magazine* reported: "The tree-loving nature of Franklin D. Roosevelt has come to rest in a virtual Eden . . . where the personalities of America's most honored citizens are reflected in trees." "For years," read the story, "the planting and management of trees have been his chief hobby on his Hyde Park estate in New York. As governor of New York he set in motion the necessary machinery for one of the greatest tree planting programs a state has ever undertaken."[32]

Several trees planted by FDR are alive and well today: a very full southern magnolia located just to the south of the Harding magnolia on East Executive Avenue; a white oak on the north lawn; and a pair of little-leaf lindens on the south lawn.

However, the best proof of FDR's tree-loving nature is contained in a story in the *Post* which followed one of Washington's violent thunderstorms during Roosevelt's first summer in office: "President Roosevelt, an ardent forest lover, showed himself equally interested in individual trees by his anxiety for the elms on the White House lawn yesterday. Early in the morning, at the request of the President, Mrs. Roosevelt telephoned the White House to learn if the White House trees had suffered in Wednesday's storm. He was pleased to learn that no serious damage had been done to them."[33]

Roosevelt's successor, Harry Truman, planted an American boxwood on the north lawn of the White House directly in front of the North Portico. It can still be seen today, but the most significant tree-related Truman act was the placement of a mature southern magnolia on the eastern side of the South Portico. The story goes that toward the end of his administration Truman declared; "I've been kept so busy I didn't even know I had a backyard. Now I'm going to get it ready for the next tenant!"[34] It was Truman's idea to move the magnolia from another part of the grounds to its present spot close to the portico, in order to balance the Andrew Jackson magnolias on the opposite side.

According to a related tale, after the magnolia had been placed, Truman asked a friend to hand him a twenty dollar bill. (The illustration of the White House on the back of the bill includes the Andrew Jackson magnolias to the west of the South Portico, but not the Truman tree to the east.) Pointing from the south window of the White House the president declared, "It's a counterfeit! See the trees in the engraving of the White House? They don't look like the ones out there, do they?"[35]

Every modern president has felt indebted to Harry Truman for his innovation which is known today as the "Truman balcony." From this second story porch behind the columns of the South Portico, the first family can enjoy the beautiful and historic view of the "President's Park" away from the scrutiny of the public and the press.

President Dwight D. Eisenhower celebrated his seventieth birthday by planting a red oak on the White House lawn. The tree was a gift from the District of Columbia. When asked what he would like for his birthday, and offered the choice of an antique dinner bell or a silver bowl, "Ike" said he would prefer to be given a red oak tree. The tree is alive today, one of three surviving Eisenhower oaks on the White House lawn.

In addition to the four lovely saucer magnolias that President John F. Kennedy planted in the Rose Garden, the thirty-fifth president also added a Pacific pride apple tree to the verdant south lawn of the White House. The apple tree stands just to the southeast of the Jacqueline Kennedy Garden.

It's no surprise that President Lyndon Baines Johnson's plant-wise first lady helped to select the trees that would memorialize his years in the White House. Lady Bird Johnson was disappointed when she learned that the live oak, the poetic mark of the Texas landscape, would be unable to endure many Washington winters. So she and the president decided on a compromise. In October of 1964, the thirty-sixth president planted two oaks just outside the Oval Office: a willow oak and a darlington (also known as laurel) oak, both similar in appearance to the live oak. Like the evergreen live oak, the darlington tends to hold onto its leaves during the winter.

During the simple planting ceremony, President Johnson spoke these words: "I think it is fitting for an occupant of this house to plant trees—not for today, but for the future." "These trees will say 'there lived those who loved this land.' "[36]

On Arbor Day in 1968 Mrs. Johnson added an attractive feature to the White House landscape. With the help of a group of children from the District of Columbia, Mrs. Johnson planted a lovely European fern-leaf beech just to the north of the west wing. During the subsequent administration, First Lady Patricia Nixon added a second fern-leaf beech to the north lawn. The beeches are lovely the year round, but they are especially beautiful in late autumn, with their golden fall foliage.

In the tradition of his predecessors, President Richard M. Nixon took a strong interest in the trees on the White House grounds. For the first time in history a tree from the American west was added to the presidential collection when Nixon planted a giant sequoia, the official tree of his home state of California, on the White House south lawn. Unfortunately, the original Nixon sequoia died. A replacement is alive today, although it will be many years before it approaches the stature of its west coast ancestors.

President Gerald R. Ford created a presidential triangle of trees when he added a white pine to the northeastern portion of the south lawn, just to the north of Eisenhower's seventieth birthday red oak and Kennedy's Pacific pride apple. First Lady Betty Ford planted a scion of the John Quincy Adams American elm on the north lawn of the White House in commemoration of the nation's bicentennial celebration. This descendant of the oldest presidential tree is thriving today.

President Jimmy Carter took an avid interest in the trees at 1600 Pennsylvania Avenue. His request that the White House trees bear name labels was carried out by the National Park service. The Carters brought a young red maple from Plains, Georgia, which the president planted on the north lawn. Former First Lady Rosalynn Carter planted a delicately weeping spiderleaf Japanese maple east of the south fountain, to serve as a companion for the tree to the west of the fountain planted by former First Lady Frances Cleveland. The foliage of this pair of maples is red throughout the season, in dramatic contrast to the brilliant green of the White House south lawn.

During the Reagan years, both fall and spring have seen extra bursts of color at the White House. In 1982, First Lady Nancy Reagan planted a pair of white saucer magnolias in the upper, central portion of the White House north lawn. In early spring, their blossoms are clearly visible to Pennsylvania Avenue passersby. Two years later, President Ronald Reagan brightened up the northern West Wing grounds when he planted a young sugar maple, known for its vibrant autumn leaves.

OTHER TREES ON THE WHITE HOUSE GROUNDS

The White House lawns are graced by many other trees, which do not hold the distinction of having been planted by presidents, but are beautiful nonetheless. Although the White House grounds are usually closed to the public, many trees are clearly visible through the fence. Trees on the south lawn include a camperdown elm, ginkgoes, horse-chestnuts, and buckeyes, Chinese chestnuts, Persian ironwoods, maples, hollies, dogwoods, flowering crabapples, beeches, a yellowwood, and a large golden-rain-tree. The north lawn is shaded by many handsome, venerable trees, with oaks and American elms predominating.

THE NATIONAL CHRISTMAS TREE

The National Christmas tree is a living Colorado blue spruce planted on the park known as the Ellipse, just south of the White House. Traditionally, the president of the United States lights the tree in a ceremony held about two weeks before Christmas.

In 1978, the National Christmas Tree was transplanted from York, Pennsylvania, where it was growing in a private yard. It replaced two previous living Christmas trees which were planted on the Ellipse, the first in 1973 and the second in 1977.

THE WASHINGTON MONUMENT

The summit of the Washington Monument provides the most dramatic view of the "City of Trees." To the east, the elm-lined Mall stretches to the Capitol, flanked by the generously landscaped buildings of the Smithsonian. To the north, the White House is tucked in amongst the trees planted by U.S. presidents. And to the south, the world famous Japanese flowering cherry trees encircle the Tidal Basin. The streets, avenues, and parks of the nation's capital are sumptuously adorned with trees as far as the eye can see.

The Washington Monument itself is wreathed in cherry trees, a fitting though unwitting tribute to the legend associated with George Washington's boyhood.

The memorial to the first president of the United States was forty years in the making—from 1848, when the cornerstone was laid—until 1888, when it was first opened to the public. Scarcity of funds, general controversy, and the Civil War held up construction of the monument. For more than twenty years it stood at a standstill, completed up to less than one-third of its present height. To this day, a subtle change in the color of the marble marks the spot where construction was halted for almost a quarter of a century.

THE TREES

Ever since the late 1960s the springtime beauty of the Tidal Basin has extended up the hill to the Washington Monument, where hundreds of young cherry trees were planted during the Johnson administration. The trees, mostly American grown Akebono cherries, were a gift from the Japanese government. Their masses of pink blossoms against the marble monument and new green grass are extremely beautiful.

Many mature trees grow on the Monument grounds, including two large white mulberries on the hill overlooking Independence Avenue and 17th Street. White pines, several species of maple and oak, lindens, horse-chestnuts, and two species of catalpa are among the trees shading the Independence Avenue and 15th Street sides of the grounds. American (and some Dutch) elms line the perimeter of the grounds and at the corner of 15th and Constitution is a small grove of European hedge maples.

The Washington Monument grounds are striking in late spring and early summer when the horse-chestnuts and catalpas bloom, and in the fall when the winged euonymous planted extensively near Independence Avenue turns flame red.

THE CAPITOL GROUNDS
One of the World's Finest Arboretums

More than three thousand trees from four continents are planted on the U.S. Capitol, Supreme Court, and Library of Congress grounds, making the area known as Capitol Hill one of the finest arboretums in the world. Trees native to most parts of the United States, including 33 official state trees, stand side by side with Asian, European, and nothern African species.

Visitors from the southern states will find five species of native American magnolias thriving here. Westerners may not recognize them yet, but there are three "giant" sequoias growing up under the shadow of the dome. Europeans will see healthy specimens of English, Dutch, and Belgian elms, and visitors from Asia will recognize many familiar trees, including the ginkgo, jujube, Cryptomeria, and several Asian species of magnolia.

No matter what time of year you visit Capitol Hill, you are bound to be struck by the beauty and diversity of its trees and other flowering plants. Beginning with the Japanese flowering cherry trees and Asian magnolias in the early spring, and continuing into December with the fall-blooming cherries, the Hill is adorned by a steady procession of blossoms. If you are able to visit the Capitol grounds in late May or early June, you may be lucky enough to catch the bigleaf magnolias in bloom, with their giant, exotic-looking flowers. In November, just when winter is beginning to take hold, the osmanthus next to the House wing of the Capitol puts forth blossoms that fill the air with a spring-like perfume.

The trees of Capitol Hill are beautiful throughout the

winter months, too. The American beeches, sycamores, and London planes are particularly striking with their ornamental bark, and the Capitol's many evergreen trees and shrubs provide a handsome frame for the building.

Capitol Hill's international tree collection is noteworthy historically as well as botanically. Throughout the years, Congressmen, Senators, and members of state and national organizations have planted trees commemorating important people and events. Dozens of these living memorials grace the Capitol grounds.

THE CAPITOL BUILDING

The long, turbulent history of the Capitol building began in 1793, when George Washington laid the cornerstone on what was then known as Jenkins Hill. By 1800, Congress was in business there.

In 1814, the newly completed House and Senate wings were burned by the British, along with much of the city of Washington. Then, later in the century, midway into construction of the impressive white cast iron dome which is such a familiar landmark today, the Civil War broke out. Throughout the war, while the Capitol was used as a combination barracks, hospital, and bakery for the Union Army, the unfinished dome dominated Washington's horizon, a poignant reminder of the nation's uncertain future. President Lincoln, who recognized the powerful symbolism embodied in the half-finished dome, ordered construction to proceed, despite the division of the country. When the war drew to a close in 1865 and national unity was restored, the beautiful new dome was nearly completed.

THE GROUNDS

While Major Pierre Charles L'Enfant, the man who designed the city of Washington, is said to have called the hill on which the Capitol now stands "a pedestal waiting for a monument," the biological aspects of the pre-Capitol Hill have been described in considerably less lofty terms.

Frederick Law Olmsted, the great landscape architect commissioned by Congress during the 1870s and eighties to design and direct a major overhaul of the Capitol grounds, wrote in 1882: "When government, near the close of the last century, took possession of the site of the Capitol, it was a sterile place, partly overgrown with 'scrub oak.' The soil was described as an *exceedingly stiff* clay, becoming dust in dry and mortar in rainy weather."[37]

Although it is difficult to imagine the now lush and fertile Capitol grounds as a "sterile place," only scanty, short-lived improvements had been made upon the original setting prior to Olmsted's time.

During the first part of the nineteenth century, the western half of Capitol Hill, which is the most magnificent side of the grounds today, was largely ignored. Early Washingtonians believed that the city would grow up to the east, rather than the west, so that today's famous western front of the Capitol was thought of as the "rear" of the building.

A creek, bordered by an alder swamp, flowed along the foot of Capitol Hill, where the Botanic Gardens and Capitol Reflecting Pool now stand. According to Olmsted: "When this stream was in freshet it was not fordable, and members of Congress were often compelled to hitch their riding horses on the further side and cross it, first, on fallen trees, afterwards on a foot-bridge."[38]

While some initial plantings were made, the first notable landscaping efforts were undertaken during the late 1820s under the direction of groundskeeper John Foy. Foy began the execution of a landscaping plan that Olmsted later described as "an enlarged form of the ordinary village-door yards of the time, flat rectangular 'grass plats,' bordered by rows of trees, flower-beds, and gravel walks, with a belt of close planting on the outside of it all." According to Olmsted: "So long as the trees were saplings and the turf and flowers could be kept nicely, it was pretty and becoming. But as the trees grew they robbed and dried out the flower-beds, leaving hardly any thing to flourish in them but violets and periwinkle."[39]

As it became apparent that the city was going to develop to the west as well as the east and interest began to focus on the "rear" of the Capitol, groundskeeper James Maher, a successor to Foy, began planting trees at the foot of the Hill.

Maher also added two circular groups of trees on the eastern side of the grounds which became known as the "Barbecue Groves," "one probably intended for Democratic, the other for Whig jollifications," according to Olmsted.[40]

Although a few of the "barbecue" trees and other plantings made during the Foy and Maher years had survived when Congress commissioned Olmsted to re-landscape the newly extended grounds in 1874, the architect was unimpressed by the arboreal picture he inherited. With few exceptions, he was to order an entire regrading of the grounds.

OLMSTED LANDSCAPING

The man who designed Central Park in New York City as well as countless other parks and campuses throughout the country, exhibited his usual wisdom when he approached the challenge of landscaping the nation's Capitol. Olmsted considered it his first priority to insure "convenience of business of and with Congress and the Supreme Court." He saw his second most important consideration to be "that of supporting and presenting to advantage a great national monument."[41]

"The ground is in design part of the Capitol," he wrote, but is "in all respects subsidiary to the central structure."[42]

With his priorities firmly established, Olmsted tackled his central landscaping problem, which he saw as a conflict between the need to leave enough space to show the Capitol off to its best advantage and accommodate large numbers of people, and the desirability of providing enough shade to combat Washington's summer heat and offset the "glaring whiteness" of the building.

Olmsted solved his problem scientifically, by stationing groves of trees in such a way that unobstructed views of the Capitol could be seen from all sides. In some places he planted only trees with low crowns in order to create views of the dome "rising above banks of foliage from several miles distant."[43] Trees were chosen, not in order to exhibit unusual or exotic specimens, but "with a view of their growing together in groups in which their individual qualities would gradually merge harmoniously."[44]

Olmsted made an exception to this rule around his "summerhouse" on the northwestern part of the grounds. Appropriately, he surrounded this charming brick grotto with trees of a "somewhat quaint or exotic aspect,"[45] including the "cedrella" and "golden catalpa," which are there to this day.

No large conifers, such as spruces, were planted on the grounds, in order that the all-important view remain unobstructed.

Despite his insistence that the particular be subsidiary to the whole, Olmsted was able to account for more than two hundred species and varieties of trees and shrubs, including many exotics, by the time he was through replanting the Capitol grounds. To insure that his thousands of new trees would have something more substantial than "dust" and "mortar" in which to grow, Olmsted went to the following extremes:

> The revised ground having been attained, the ground was thoroughly drained with collared, cylindrical tile, and trench-plowed and subsoiled to a depth of two feet or more from the present surface...It was then ridged up and exposed to a winter's frost, dressed with oyster-shell lime, and with swamp muck previously treated with salt and lime, then plowed, harrowed, and rolled and plowed again. The old surface was laid upon this improved subsoil with a sufficient addition of the same poor soil drawn from without the ground to make the stratum one foot (loose) in depth. With this well pulverized, a compost of stable manure and prepared swamp muck was mixed.[46]

OLMSTED'S LEGACY

Olmsted's painstaking efforts have reached fruition in the twentieth century. Many of the groves that were planted under his meticulous direction "merge harmoniously" today, providing a softly dramatic setting for the nation's most important building. In addition to the extensive plantings and quaint "summerhouse," the Olmsted legacy includes the gently curving walks and drives that lead to the Capitol from every direction, and the spectacular terrace on the western front of the building.

TREE LABELING ON THE HILL

Frederick Law Olmsted also began the tradition of tree labeling on the Capitol grounds, a practice that has survived until the present. In 1882 he wrote: 'There being trees on the ground unknown to many visitors from distant parts of the country, upon a suggestion kindly made by Members of Congress, labels have been placed before a large number. . . ."[47]

While tree labels are a great help in identifying the many unusual woody plants on the grounds, over the years many a tree has stoically borne the indignity of having the wrong name tacked to its trunk. In one case, a mislabeled tree gained national acclaim when it was officially declared the largest of its species in the United States. Proudly bearing a large "Mountain Maple" label for years, this impostor turned out to be a Cappadocian maple, native to the mountains of Asia and Eastern Europe.

TWENTIETH CENTURY IMPROVEMENTS ON THE GROUNDS

This century's most dramatic change in the Capitol grounds occurred in the 1960s. During the Lady Bird Johnson years, when interest in beautification was at a peak, many flowering plants were added to the grounds, including Japanese flowering cherry trees, flowering dogwoods, crabapples, and redbuds. Today the Capitol grounds are managed by a full-time landscape architect and his crew, who work under the direction of the Architect of the Capitol.

HISTORIC TREES OF CAPITOL HILL PAST AND PRESENT

THE CAMERON ELM

This American elm, the loveliest and most venerable tree on Capitol Hill, has managed to survive the twentieth century threats of Dutch elm disease and urban pollution, as well as the even greater nineteenth century threat, Frederick Law Olmsted. Legend has it that Senator Simon D. Cameron of Pennsylvania became so upset when he saw Olmsted's crew about to remove this elm during the relandscaping program of the 1870s that he rushed to the Senate floor and made an impassioned speech on behalf of the tree. Although no record of such a speech has been found, documents housed in the Architect of the Capitol's office confirm that Olmsted's crew was about to remove the tree, and Senator Cameron's influence saved it.

The real proof of this story is evident to any observant visitor to the Capitol grounds. Dominating the rise next to the House of Representatives is the handsome American elm...with a sidewalk winding politely around it.

THE HUMILITY ELM

In 1978, the huge English elm that dominated the northeast grounds between the Capitol and the Russell Senate Office Building fell victim to Dutch elm disease. On the twenty-seventh of June, Senator Edward Kennedy paid this moving tribute to the tree on the Senate floor:

> Few if any trees anywhere were better known or more loved by Members of the Senate. As we walked to the Capitol from the Russell Building, we passed under its giant limb, a cantilevered miracle of nature that stretched out across the sidewalk

and over the roadway. Often we would reach up to touch the limb, or give it a warm slap of recognition and appreciation for its enduring vigil.

President Kennedy, when he was a Senator, liked to call it the Humility Tree, because Senators instinctively ducked or bowed their heads as they approached the limb and passed beneath it. Its loss is a real one, deeply felt.

The records are dim about its origin. But those of us who enjoyed the beauty of this elm can be grateful to the ancestors who planted it long ago. For a century, it graced the grounds of the Capitol of our growing nation. [48]

THE WASHINGTON ELM

Until the late 1940s, a beautiful American elm, known as the "Washington Elm," stood near the eastern entrance to the Senate wing of the Capitol. Two legends widely circulated over the years, neither of which can be substantiated, connect this tree to the first president of the United States. The first, and least likely of the two, is that George Washington planted the tree. The second and more probable story is that Washington stood under the shade of this tree while overseeing the construction of the Capitol.

MEMORIAL TREES

In 1912 formal memorial tree-plantings on the Capitol grounds got their start in earnest when one vice-president (James S. Sherman), five senators, two representatives and the Speaker of the House all spaded up the ground to plant their favorite trees.

Since then, more than 75 commemorative trees have been planted on the Capitol grounds, many of them by, or in honor of, members of Congress. Some of the Capitol's memorial trees commemorate specific events, such as Arbor Day anniversaries. Others are planted in honor of national or state associations.

These are some of the most notable memorial trees:

SAM RAYBURN OAK

On October 11, 1949, the Speaker of the House, Sam Rayburn of Texas, planted a white oak on the southeastern section of the Capitol grounds. Throughout his many years in Washington, Rayburn or an associate frequently visited the tree to measure its growing circumference.

SULLIVAN BROTHERS CRABAPPLES

Five flowering crabapples on the northeastern section of the grounds memorialize one of the most tragic events in Navy history. The trees were planted in honor of the five Sullivan brothers, of Waterloo, Iowa, who were all killed when their ship went down during World War II. The Navy had given the five boys special permission to serve on the same ship.

CHEROKEE INDIAN GIANT SEQUOIA

In 1966, the Cherokee Indian Nation commemorated the bicentennial of the birth of Sequoyah, the famous Cherokee leader and scholar, with a ceremonial giant sequoia planting on the northwest grounds. The original tree died later that year, but was replaced with a tree grown from one of its cuttings in 1969.

SENATOR SAM ERVIN DOGWOOD

In 1974, when Sam Ervin retired from the U.S. Senate, he planted a flowering dogwood, the official flower of his home state of North Carolina, on the northeast Capitol grounds.

THE UNITED STATES BOTANIC GARDENS

The conservatory of the United States Botanic Gardens at the foot of Capitol Hill houses exotic trees and herbaceous plants from around the world, including many tropical species. Among the highlights of this tropical paradise are an ancient "ferocious blue cycad," a tall Mexican thread palm, and banyon, breadfruit, and Litchi nut trees. The orchid collection of the Botanic Gardens is in bloom the year round, lighting up the dark green tropical forest with its brilliant colors and delicate shapes.

Across Independence Avenue from the conservatory is the lovely Bartholdi fountain, designed by Frederic Auguste Bartholdi, the sculptor who created the Statue of Liberty. A beautiful garden surrounds this fountain. During the summer, banana plants are set out around the fountain, and by autumn small bunches of bananas hang from the plants. An ancient jujube and several Japanese flowering cherry trees share this beautiful spot with an interesting collection of conifers.

The Botanic Gardens are administered by the Architect of the Capitol's Office. Many historic trees once graced the grounds of this lovely spot, including, oddly enough, a hornbeam planted by Abraham Lincoln and a bald-cypress planted by his assassin, John Wilkes Booth.

THE SMITHSONIAN, THE NATIONAL GALLERY OF ART, AND THE DEPARTMENT OF AGRICULTURE

The grounds of the Smithsonian Buildings and the National Gallery of Art flanking the Mall are all handsomely landscaped. Many Smithsonian trees are included in Part Two of this book. The United States Department of Agriculture Building, also bordering the Mall, was once an arboretum containing many exotic trees and shrubs. Although little remains of its former glory, it is still surrounded by interesting trees, including the rare pond-cypress, a pair of old ginkgoes, and a Bradford pear planted by Lady Bird Johnson in 1966.

THE JAPANESE FLOWERING CHERRY TREES

For centuries the flowering cherry tree or "Sakura" has stood at the center of Japan's poetic consciousness as a powerful symbol of the beautiful, yet transient nature of life. Ancient legends tell how the cherry blossoms are awakened in spring by "the maiden who causes trees to bloom"[49] or by fairies who visited the emperor at the Palace of Yoshino in the moonlight. Japanese paintings abound with delicate "Sakura" blossoms. Poets throughout the ages have exalted the cherry tree and mourned the brief life of its blossoms, often in the same breath.

The world-famous Japanese cherry trees encircling the Tidal Basin in Washington's West Potomac Park were a gift to the American people from the city of Tokyo. They are probably the world's greatest living symbol of friendship between two nations.

HISTORY OF THE CHERRY TREES

America's loveliest urban acres were the site of dismal swampland just a century ago. By the late 1800s, the area that now comprises West and East Potomac Parks had become an unpleasant and dangerous breeding ground for malarial mosquitoes. In 1882 Congress approved an Act to "reclaim" the tidal marshland along the Potomac.

Today's beautiful Tidal Basin was created for practical rather than aesthetic reasons. Long before the cherry trees and the Jefferson Memorial were even imagined, the Tidal Basin was carved out to catch the tides flowing up from the Potomac through the Washington Channel. The human-made channel (now bordered by East Potomac Park and the Maine Avenue waterfront) was filling up with mud and debris. With the creation of the Tidal Basin and its southern outlet to the Potomac, the incoming tide could freely flow through the channel and eventually back into the Potomac River. This system still cleanses the channel of debris today, making the Tidal Basin a model combination of utility and beauty.

In 1909, the city of Tokyo sent a gift of 2,000 cherry trees to the United States for planting in Potomac Park. Unfortunately, this first gift of trees, which arrived in Seattle on the tenth of December, and was then loaded onto a train bound for the District of Columbia, proved to be infested with insect pests and plant diseases. With great dismay, the United States Department of Agriculture was forced to recommend that the trees be burned.

However, the potentially embarrassing situation did

not weaken the bond between Tokyo and Washington. Tokyo's Mayor Yukio Ozaki simply ordered that special precautions be taken to insure a healthy second shipment of trees. In 1912, 3,000 trees bound for the nation's capital arrived in Seattle, and by the twenty-seventh of March the first cherry trees were planted at the Tidal Basin.

Mrs. William Howard Taft, first lady of the land, planted the first flowering cherry tree; Viscountess Iwa Chinda, wife of the Japanese ambassador, planted the second. The two trees, located on the northwest side of the Tidal Basin, are still alive today.

Twelve selections of flowering cherries were included in the gift of 3,000 trees. Most of the trees planted around the Tidal Basin were specimens of the white or pale pink single-blossomed Somei-Yoshino usually known simply as Yoshino. The Yoshino cherry blooms very early in the spring. The later blooming, double-blossomed varieties were planted extensively in East Potomac Park. Among these trees was the lovely deep pink Kwanzan, which is popular in Washington today. Several specimens of the intriguing Gyoiko, with its pale green blossoms, were planted on the White House grounds.

Of the original twelve, all but the Yoshino and Kwanzan have nearly disappeared from the Washington landscape. However, botanist Roland M. Jefferson of the National Arboretum, during a world-wide survey of cultivated cherry trees, has located specimens of all but one of the original dozen, and he is now in the process of propagating them. Jefferson hopes he will eventually be able to offer the National Park Service, which administers the Potomac Parks, healthy young specimens of each flowering cherry tree that was part of the original Tokyo gift. Roland Jefferson has also made grafted propagations of the old Yoshino cherries planted by Mrs. Taft and Viscountess Chinda. Some day, he hopes to see these historic trees replaced by their progeny.

During the early twenties, Dr. W. B. Clarke selected an unusually pink form of Yoshino from his collection in San José, California for propagation. Clarke christened the tree "Akebono," meaning dawn. The Akebono, which is identical to the Yoshino except for its slightly deeper pink blossoms, is widely planted throughout Washington today; young Akebono trees have replaced some of the dying Tidal Basin Yoshino trees.

The first Cherry Blossom Festival was held in 1935. Since that time, interest in the Washington flowering cherries has spread throughout the world. Today many a Japanese visitor can be seen among the Tidal Basin visitors, proudly beaming his or her approval and trying to capture the elusive beauty of the blossoms on film.

In 1949, the first Cherry Blossom Princesses came to Washington, representing every state and American territory. Each spring since then, the capital has been adorned not only by the cherry blossoms, but by the princesses who represent their home states in the festival.

In 1957, Japan gave the United States the "Miki-moto Pearl Crown," to be worn by the Cherry Blossom Queen who is chosen each year by lot from the group of

Princesses. The crown was valued at $100,000 when it was given to the United States.

Three years earlier, in 1954, Japanese Ambassador Sadao Iguchi had presented the United States with a large, ancient stone lantern in commemoration of the 100th anniversary of the first treaty between Japan and the United States. The Treaty of Peace, Amity, and Commerce was signed by Commodore Matthew Perry in Yokohama on March 31, 1854. Today the ceremonial lighting of this eight and one-half foot lantern marks the official opening of the Cherry Blossom Festival.

In 1958, a second gift commemorating the 1854 treaty was presented to the United States by the Mayor of Yokohama. This simple Japanese stone pagoda, which now stands among the Tidal Basin cherry trees, was dedicated in April of 1958. The year 1965 saw yet another gift from the people of Japan. Thousands of American-grown Akebono cherries were given to the city of Washington. Many were planted on the Washington Monument grounds, providing an attractive frame for the marble monument. And again, the first lady of the United States and the wife of the Japanese ambassador (Mrs. Lyndon Baines Johnson and Mrs. Ryuji Takeuchi) joined in planting two ceremonial cherry trees near the trees planted by Mrs. Taft and Viscountess Chinda in 1912.

In 1981, the Japanese flowering cherries were featured in another gesture of international friendship. Cherry trees along the Arakawa River in Tokyo—the place where the historic Tidal Basin trees originated—had succumbed to the adverse effects of pollution. The National Arboretum's Roland Jefferson, working in conjunction with the National Park Service, selected budwood (propagating material) from healthy trees at the Tidal Basin and the National Arboretum for shipment to Japan. In Japan, the buds of the Washington trees were grafted onto Japanese-grown root stock. In the near future, the young trees arising from this union will replace the cherries that once flourished along the Tokyo waterway.

In February of 1981, First Lady Nancy Reagan took part in a White House ceremony to commemorate the international exchange. Mrs. Reagan presented Japanese Ambassador Yoshi Okawara with a young cherry tree propagated from the original Tidal Basin tree planted by Mrs. Taft.

Today, thousands of people from all over the world converge on the shores of the Potomac for Washington's annual Cherry Blossom Festival. The week-long rite of spring includes a Cherry Blossom Parade and many other events. However, the *main* event does not always come off on schedule. Few envy the National Park Service horticulturist who is given the task of predicting the appearance of the fickle blossoms! Even days before they bloom, the mysterious trees divulge few signs that they are about to flower.

Back in 1934, USDA botanist Paul Russell wrote: "For him who has visited Japan in the spring, as he walks under the flower-laden boughs in the old plantings near the Potomac River in Washington, D.C., there

come memories of the gay kimono-clad crowds in the
Japanese parks, the sound of geta (wooden sandals) on
gravel-covered walks, staccato talk and the vendors'
cries."[50]

Today, springtime in Japan might evoke a similar,
but reverse nostalgia in someone acquainted with the
beauty of the Japanese flowering cherry trees in
Washington. Memory of the beauty of the trees back in
America could be expressed something like this:

> The cherry trees
> Unmindful of this sad world,
> have burst into bloom.
> And in the capital too
> Now must be their glory.[51]

One's thoughts *could* run that way on a spring visit to
Tokyo or Kyoto today. But the poem was not written
by a nostalgic American, nor, indeed by anyone alive
today. It was the work of an anonymous Japanese poet
who wrote it approximately 600 years ago.

THE JEFFERSON MEMORIAL

One of America's most photographed sights is the
white marble Jefferson Memorial framed by a pale pink
cloud of cherry blossoms. While there is no doubt that the
memorial looks its loveliest with the cherry trees in bloom,
Washingtonians know another side of the Jefferson
Memorial that is nearly as pleasing. Day and night
throughout the year, the dark silhouettes of white pine
trees against the lovely white marble structure are a
favorite sight from many of the city's commuter routes.

When the site for the Jefferson Memorial was pro-
posed in the 1930s, friends of the flowering cherry trees
put up a vehement protest. Some women who were particularly outraged by the plans to break ground for the
memorial in the middle of the cherries, actually chained
themselves to the trees! Finally, the furor died down
(although a few trees were sacrificed), and the Jefferson
Memorial was completed in 1942.

President Thomas Jefferson was a serious architect,
as anyone who has visited his lovely Charlottesville
home, "Monticello" or the University of Virginia campus
knows. The Jefferson Memorial was designed in an architectural style reminiscent of that of the third president.
Jefferson was also fond of trees, and the grounds around
the Jefferson Memorial are liberally planted with them.

In addition to the striking white pines that encircle
the memorial, hollies, osmanthus, zelkovas, and American
elms are among the woody plants that provide an attractive setting for one of America's favorite landmarks.

EAST POTOMAC PARK
(HAINS POINT)

It has been said of East Potomac Park: "If Washington has a village green, this is it."[52] Throughout most of

the year, residents of every part of the city can be found on this peaceful point of land spending their leisure hours in the company of family and friends, pursuing their favorite sports, or simply enjoying a few moments of solitude. Joggers and cyclists criss-cross past fishermen and family barbecues while a perennial breeze keeps the willows in motion. Gulls, ducks, and geese share the golf course with golfers and the water with sailors during the warmer months. In the winter the park is a refuge for wildlife, invaded only by the most stoic joggers and fishermen, employees of the National Park Service, and a few straggling sightseers along Ohio Drive.

History of East Potomac Park

East Potomac Park is a promontory of nearly 330 acres stretching out in a southeasterly direction and culminating in Hains Point. The park is surrounded by the Washington Channel to the east and northeast, the Potomac River to the southwest, and the Tidal Basin to the northwest.

As incredible as it may seem, today's popular park was once a major health hazard. A century ago, East Potomac Park was nothing but a tidal marsh, badly polluted by the city's sewers. During the summer months the tidal marshes or "flats" along the Potomac were a breeding ground for malarial mosquitoes and other disease-carrying organisms. Peter C. Hains, the Army engineer who directed much of the work of turning the Potomac marshes into parkland (and for whom Hains Point is named), wrote that sanitary conditions along the river had become so bad during the latter part of the nineteenth century that adjacent "parts of the city had become almost uninhabitable."[53]

An 1882 Act of Congress called for the reclamation of hundreds of acres of marshland along the Potomac. East Potomac Park was the first area to be transformed, under Colonel Hains' guidance, from dismal swamp to pleasant parkland. In 1913, with East and West Potomac Parks successfully reclaimed, the Washington Star reported: "Out of the slimy and reedy marshes of the Potomac River at Washington the government of the United States has created one of the beautiful parks of the world."[54]

East Potomac Park enjoyed early popularity among Washingtonians and visitors to the nation's capital. Where joggers tread today, horseback riders moseyed under the cottonwoods and willows along the Potomac River and newly created Washington Channel.

The Trees

The maritime atmosphere of East Potomac Park is doubly pleasing because of the presence of beautiful trees. Weeping willows trail their delicate, spring-green foliage all along the shoreline. Ohio Drive is lined with Japanese flowering cherry trees which bloom at staggered times. Dozens of other native and exotic trees adorn Washington's "village green." East Potomac Park's weeping willows predate the park itself. Legend says that the park's original willows were propagated from trees brought to the District of Columbia from Napoleon's grave at St. Helena. While this legend may or may not be true, weeping willows are not native and they were on the scene before Colonel Hains.

Ulysses S. Grant III, (grandson of the famous general and U.S. President, and director of the former office of Public Buildings and Public Parks) wrote during the 1920s: "(W)hen . . . East Potomac Park was still a salt water tidal flat, these old willows marked the few high and dry places where one could safely walk and stand."[55]

Nothing could complement weeping willows more perfectly than Japanese flowering cherry trees, and with these the park is well endowed. First to bloom are the delicate weeping cherries, much like small weeping willows in silhouette. While the weeping cherries are still in full flower, more than 1800 Yoshino and Akebono cherry trees (of the same hybrid planted around the Tidal Basin) come into bloom. The Yoshino and Akebono trees were planted along both sides of Ohio Drive by Lady Bird Johnson's Committee for a More Beautiful Capital during the 1960s. The former first lady planted one of the trees personally.

The most famous East Potomac Park cherries are the deep pink, double-blossomed Kwanzans. These trees come into bloom in mid to late April, about two weeks later than the early, single-blossomed cherry trees. When the original Japanese gift of cherry trees was planted in 1912, several double-blossomed forms were planted in East Potomac Park. Of these, only the Kwanzans still survive. While they are not nearly as famous as the Tidal Basin Yoshino and Akebono cherries, the Kwanzans of East Potomac Park are perhaps better loved by Washingtonians, who can enjoy them in relative solitude after most of the tourists have departed.

No observant park visitor will fail to notice the tall, tapered conifers planted on either side of Hains Point. Striking in both summer and winter, with or without their delicate needles which they shed in autumn, the bald-cypresses of East Potomac Park look right at home. And they very nearly are. While these residents of southern swamps are no longer native to the Washington area, botanists theorize that much of Washington was once a cypress swamp. During construction of the Metro subway system, remains of bald-cypress trees dating back thousands of years were unearthed in northwest Washington.

North of the bald-cypress groves, on the eastern side of the promontory, are some very old cottonwoods. The history of planting cottonwoods (or Carolina poplars as they were once called) along the Potomac River dates back to the nineteenth century when it was believed that these trees possessed "wonderful malaria absorbing qualities." While it was not known precisely how the "Carolina poplars" checked the spread of the disease, it was widely believed that stands of trees slowed the spread of malaria. The Carolina poplar seemed especially suited for this purpose, perhaps only because it could survive in wet, mosquito-infested places. There is evidence that by 1890, following massive plantings of cottonwood and other trees along the

Potomac and throughout Washington, the threat of malaria had lessened.

The headquarters of the Park Police and the National Capital Region of the National Park Service on the northwestern side of the park are surrounded by interesting exotic trees. Delicate Japanese red pines and groves of European hornbeams and lindens are among the trees planted as landscaping (or camouflage!) for the collection of austere Park Service buildings.

Among the other noteworthy trees of East Potomac Park are: a grove of Ohio buckeyes close to the point on the Potomac side; Austrian, Japanese black and eastern white pines; London planes and American sycamores; zelkovas; and several oak species and hybrids.

The Lincoln Memorial

The white marble Lincoln Memorial is believed by many people to be the most beautiful monument in Washington. It is especially attractive at night when it seems to glow from within. The cornerstone for the memorial was laid in 1915, but not until 1922 was the completed structure dedicated.

The Lincoln Memorial is surrounded by a brilliantly conceived border of evergreens. Although from a distance the plants around the memorial all appear to be shrubby, up close they comprise a delightful mini-forest that includes southern magnolias, American hollies, and other trees that are green throughout the year. A trip through this little woodland is especially delightful after a snowfall.

The trees lining the Lincoln Memorial Reflecting Pool have baffled botanists for decades. They were imported from Europe as clones of the English elm. However, they are more likely some form of Dutch elm, a hybrid group of trees.

Tree Viewing beyond the Mall

Theodore Roosevelt Island

During the administration of President Theodore Roosevelt five national parks, more than fifty bird and animal refuges, and the U.S. Forest Service were formed.

Today's Theodore Roosevelt Island remains true to the spirit of the great wilderness adventurer and conservationist whom it commemorates. A hiker on one of the island's woodland paths could easily imagine himself somewhere in the wild. Yet the island is just a stone's throw away from the tumult of Washington.

Theodore Roosevelt Island, located midstream in the Potomac between two other presidential memorials—the Kennedy Center, and the George Washington Memorial Parkway—has been known by several names in the past, including Anacostian, Analostan, Barbadoes, and My Lord's Island. For many years it was owned by the family of the Virginia patriot, George Mason, and was generally called Mason's Island. During the latter part of the eighteenth century, George Mason's son, John, built an estate on the island, where he raised sheep, cotton, and other crops. The island changed hands several times before the Roosevelt Memorial Association purchased it in the early 1930s and turned it over to the federal government as a memorial to Teddy Roosevelt.

The Association hired the Olmsted Brothers (sons of Frederick Law Olmsted) to draw up a landscaping plan for the island. The Olmsted plan, which was carried out during the thirties, called for the removal of all human-made structures on the island and the planting of thousands of trees and shrubs.

During the 1960s, federal funds were appropriated to construct a formal memorial to Theodore Roosevelt in the interior of the island. Today this unique memorial is a haven for those who, in Roosevelt's words, "delight in the hardy life of the open." A giant bronze statue of the former president overlooks an expansive terrace which is surrounded by a picturesque moat. The moat is crossed by stone footbridges and is lined with willow oaks. On a still day, when the reflection of oaks and sky in the moat is interrupted only by families of ducks, the effect is truly hypnotic.

Footpaths radiate outward from the terrace to all parts of the island. The trees under which hikers pass include large oaks, maples, elms, ashes, and tulip poplars. Willows grow along the shorelines. Pawpaws and spicebush are also part of the island's varied woody plant community.

LYNDON BAINES JOHNSON MEMORIAL GROVE AND LADY BIRD JOHNSON PARK

Lyndon Baines Johnson, the great legislator who became the thirty-sixth president of the United States, was a tireless promoter of his "Great Society" programs. Yet he once wrote: "I would have been content to be simply a conservation President...My deepest attitudes and beliefs were shaped by a closeness to the land, and it was only natural for me to think of preserving it."[56]

During the Johnson years, more than three and a half million acres were added to America's National Park system, including the famous Redwood National Park. The "Wilderness Act," first of its kind in the world, was signed into law. And important laws were passed to control the growing problems of air and water pollution.

LBJ, as he was so often called, grew up in the hill country of central Texas. In the tradition of many American presidents, he possessed a deep understanding of the close relationship between the land and its people. For Lyndon Baines Johnson and his wife, Lady Bird, social equality and environmental awareness were not separate issues; they were integral elements of a healthy society.

In 1973, soon after his death, family friends began planning a memorial to the former president. It did not take them long to agree that a traditional monument was not in keeping with the spirit of LBJ. A grove of trees was decided upon.

The Lyndon Baines Johnson Memorial Grove would be located within Lady Bird Johnson Park on the Virginia side of the Potomac. A seventy-member committee was formed to work on the plan, which included a nationwide fund-raising drive. Meade Palmer, a Virginia landscape architect, was commissioned to design the grove.

Seventeen acres were laid out with peaceful walkways among plantings of white pine, flowering shrubs, and daffodils. A roughly hewn, 43-ton block of granite was transported from a Texas quarry to serve in place of a traditional statue. In September, 1974 the ground was broken, and less than two years later the grove was ready for formal dedication.

More than a thousand people gathered under the young pine trees on a lovely April day in 1976 for the official opening of the grove. President Gerald Ford spoke for all who knew the former president when he said: "It is entirely fitting that in this city of bronze and marble monuments we choose to remember Lyndon Johnson with a living memorial of pines."[57]

Lady Bird Johnson, who "grew up listening to the wind in the pine trees of east Texas woods,"[58] spoke of the "joy in the outdoors" that she and Lyndon had shared together. "If I were to make one wish for today," she told the crowd, "that wish is that this bower of trees will forever set people dreaming."[59]

THE LBJ GROVE TODAY

In 1977, a footbridge across the boundary channel was completed, creating a new access to the grove. From this western approach one crosses the channel, a favorite haven for water birds, to the heart of the grove without having to contend with parkway traffic.

Today the young white pines are thriving and the spring procession of daffodils, dogwood, cherry laurel, viburnums, azaleas, and rhododendrons is spectacular. In addition, the National Park Service has added wildflowers to the grove flora.

Surrounding the memorial plantings are many lovely old trees, including pears, cottonwoods, maples, and willows.

LADY BIRD JOHNSON PARK

On November 12, 1968, Secretary of the Interior Stewart Udall christened Columbia Island "Lady Bird Johnson Park" in honor of the First Lady who inspired the drive to beautify cities and towns across the United States. Nowhere are her efforts more apparent than in Washington.

Lady Bird Johnson Park lies directly across the Potomac from the city, providing a spectacular view of the Lincoln and Jefferson memorials and the Washington

Monument. The Lyndon Baines Johnson Memorial Grove is located within the park.

The Lady Bird Johnson Park is beautiful year round, but is in its glory in the spring. During the former first lady's beautification drive of the mid-sixties, thousands of flowering plants were added to the island's acreage. Members of area garden clubs helped plant hundreds of thousands of daffodils along the river. A profusion of flowering dogwoods and other trees were also planted, and a biking and walking path was added to the shoreline.

The innovations of the sixties enhanced what was already a pleasing spot. Many mature trees, including pears, willows, American elms, and willow oaks, bend in the wind along the riverside.

George Washington's Mount Vernon

The tall, fierce-tempered general who marched to war at the head of the Continental Army, defeated the British, and then served as the first United States president, had a gentle side. On a Mount Vernon spring day in 1786, General George Washington wrote:

> The warmth of yesterday and this day forwarded vegetation much; the buds of some trees, particularly the weeping willow and maple, had displayed their leaves and blossoms and all others were ready to put forth. The apricot trees were beginning to blossom and the grass to show its verdure![60]

While no man could have served his country better or loved it more, there is no question that George Washington's heart frequently strayed to his Virginia home. In 1775, as newly appointed Commander-in-Chief of the Continental Army, the general wrote to Martha Washington from Philadelphia: " 'I should enjoy more real happiness in one month with you at home than I have the most distant prospect of finding abroad, if my stay were to be seven times seven years.' "[61]

It's easy to see why George Washington loved Mount Vernon. Fewer homes could be, in the president's own words, more "pleasantly situated." Spacious lawns and open fields overlook a graceful bend in the Potomac. Deer feed at the wood's edge at twilight. And everywhere, there are pleasing groves of trees.

According to Erle Kauffman, who wrote about the first president during the 1930s: "Trees were Washington's really great love in nature."[62] While a less worldly avocation could hardly be imagined for the father of one of the earth's most advanced technological societies, the truth is that George Washington loved to plant and care for trees. His diaries abound with detailed descriptions of the trees and shrubs at Mount Vernon. At least thirteen trees planted by Washington himself are alive today after two centuries.

HISTORY OF GEORGE WASHINGTON
AT MOUNT VERNON

The property lying along the Virginia side of the
Potomac River between Little Hunting Creek and Dogue
Creek had been in the family for years before George
Washington officially acquired it in 1754. During his
childhood, Washington's immediate family had resided
at Mount Vernon for three years, and throughout his
early life, young George had visited relatives living at
the estate.

In 1759 Washington married Martha Dandridge
Custis, a widow and mother of two children. Washington himself was never able to have children, but he took
pride in his stepchildren and their offspring. In 1781,
following the death of Martha's son, John Parke Custis,
Washington adopted John's two youngest children.

The years between 1759 and the outbreak of the
Revolution in 1775 were peaceful ones for the Washing-
tons. George lived the life of a prosperous farmer, overseeing his estate and constantly devising ways to increase
its productivity and beauty. He was interested in every
detail of the workings of his farm, from growing wheat
to grinding flour. During these years, Washington supervised the creation of two beautiful gardens which have
been authentically restored by the Mount Vernon Ladies'
Association: the "kitchen garden" and the "flower garden."

Following the Revolution and prior to becoming
president, the general again took up the life of a farmer
and horticulturist. To satisfy his ever-increasing desire
for knowledge about the plant world, Washington built
a greenhouse to house citrus trees and other plants from
warmer climates during the winter. He even created his
own botanical garden, where he experimented with
exotic seed from places as far away as China.

It was during the hiatus between the Revolution and
his presidency that Washington laid out the lovely
Serpentine road and walkways on the "Bowling Green,"
the lawn in front of the main entrance to the mansion.
For the most part he chose native trees and shrubs to
line the graceful curves of the Serpentine road and outer
edges of the Bowling Green. Some of the original plantings in these "wildernesses" and "shrubberies," as he
called them, are alive today.

Washington was no purist about planting native
trees, however. In 1785 he wrote to a cousin, William
Washington of South Carolina: "I would thank you my
Good Sir, for the Acorns, Nutts, or seeds of trees or
plants not common in this Country; but which you
think would grow here, especially of the flowering
kind..."[63] This inquiry and numerous others brought
trees from all over the country and the world to the
home overlooking the Potomac. From the south came
the southern magnolia, and the live oak. From Europe
and Asia, the horse-chestnut, weeping willow, and Lombardy poplar. And from New England, spruce and eastern hemlock (one of which survives today).

The great French botanist, André Michaux, brought
seeds, shrubs and trees to Washington from France. And

New York's Governor Clinton sent linden (or lime) trees to Mount Vernon.

It is no historical secret that George Washington reluctantly assumed the responsibility of becoming the nation's first president. Once again, his country needed him and he tore himself away from Mount Vernon. But although the first president was forced to reside in the temporary capitals of New York and Philadelphia for the eight years of his presidency, his heart was never far away from home. And in 1790, the year after he took office, the president was entrusted with the responsibility of choosing the site for the permanent capital of the United States. The city was to be located along the Potomac.

The business of choosing the location for the new "Federal City" and then supervising its design and construction afforded Washington a reason to visit Mount Vernon, just down the river from Georgetown. On one such visit, during the summer of 1792, he happily wrote: " The day and night we reached home, there fell a most delightful and refreshing rain, and the weather since has been as seasonable as the most sanguine farmer could wish...' "[64] The president went on to discuss the salubrious effect the rain would have on his indian corn crop.

In May of 1797, with his eight years as president over, George Washington described his bucolic plans for retirement: " To make and sell a little flour, to repair houses going fast to ruin, to build one for the security of my papers of a public nature, and to amuse myself with Agricultural and rural pursuits, will constitute employment for the years I have to remain on this terrestrial Globe. If...I could now and then meet friends I esteem, it would fill the measure...but, if ever this happens, it must be under my own vine and fig-tree, as I do not think it probable that I shall go beyond twenty miles from them.' "[65]

Though little time was left George Washington, he lived it in precisely the manner he had wished...in the peaceful pursuit of happiness at Mount Vernon. He died on December 14, 1799 at the age of 67. He was survived by Martha, who lived until 1802. The couple are buried at Mount Vernon.

THE MOUNT VERNON LADIES' ASSOCIATION

In 1858 the Mount Vernon Ladies' Association purchased the estate from one of George Washington's heirs for two hundred thousand dollars. A South Carolina woman, Ann Pamela Cunningham, founded the association after she learned that the property had been offered for sale to the United States and the Commonwealth of Virginia and that both had turned it down. The money to purchase the property was raised by public subscription.

It was a happy day for George Washington's trees, gardens, and grounds when the Mount Vernon Ladies' Association became the proprietors of the estate. In 1926, the Association published a report on the trees at Mt. Vernon, written by the eminent botanist and director of the Arnold Arboretum at Harvard University, Charles Sprague Sargent.

Sargent made a careful study of Mount Vernon's trees, comparing them with plantings described in Washington's diaries. Though he has since been proven wrong in a few cases, Sargent concluded that forty-five trees planted by George Washington, or under his direction, were still living in 1926. Several had been brought down just two years earlier by a tornado.

On page one of his report, Sargent wrote: "(N)o trees planted by man have the human interest of the Mount Vernon trees. They belong to the nation and are one of its precious possessions. No care should be spared to preserve them, and as they pass away they should be replaced with trees of the same kinds, that Mount Vernon may be kept for all time as near as possible in the condition in which Washington left it."[66]

In recent years, the Mount Vernon Ladies' Association has treated Sargent's word as gospel. Every effort is made to preserve the health of the original plantings. When they do succumb to old age or storm damage, the original trees are replaced, whenever possible, with their offspring. And no tree or shrub is planted at Mount Vernon today unless it grew on the estate during Washington's time.

George Washington's Trees

On January 12, 1785, George Washington wrote in his diary: " 'Rode to my Mill Swamp...and to other places in search of the sort of Trees I shall want for my Walks, groves and Wildernesses.'[67] An entry recorded one week later read: "Employed until dinner in laying out my Serpentine Road and shrubberies adjoining."[68]

During the next three years George Washington planted between 120 and 150 trees along the Serpentine drive and outer edges of the Bowling Green. Today, twelve of the original trees survive: two tulip poplars, three white ashes, five hollies, one hemlock and one buckeye. The thirteenth surviving Washington tree is a mulberry, located near the entrance to the Bowling Green and probably planted around the same time.

Botanically, the most interesting of the original plantings is the buckeye. Located on the northern side of the Bowling Green, this tree was one of several buckeyes that Washington grew from seeds he collected in 1784 at the mouth of the Cheat River near the present day Pennsylvania-West Virginia border. It is the only original buckeye left, although Sargent reported that four were extant in 1926.

For years the true identity of this tree has eluded the experts. Sargent, who was very interested in the four trees alive in 1926, declared them a variety of the sweet or yellow buckeye (*Aesculus octandra* var. *virginicus* Sarg.). He described the flowers as ranging from rose to flesh-color.

For several decades Sargent's opinion held, although botanists occasionally puzzled over the blossoms, which were unusually pink and red for a species that was supposed to produce yellow flowers. During the mid-1970s, Dr. Frederick Meyer, supervisory botanist at the National Arboretum, became very suspicious when he saw the tree in full bloom. Although hesitant to question the authority of the great Sargent, Meyer also noticed peculiarities in the leaves and, later, in the fruit. Could this famous buckeye be something other than what it was supposed to be?

Meyer had a theory, which has since been supported by a noted buckeye expert, Professor James W. Hardin, curator of the North Carolina State University Herbarium in Raleigh. The tree appears to be a hybrid buckeye (*Aesculus* x *hybrida* DC.), which is a cross between the yellow buckeye (*Aesculus octandra* Marsh.) and the red buckeye (*Aesculus pavia* L.). But with its botanical identity seemingly found, the mystery surrounding Washington's buckeye has increased!

While the yellow buckeye is native to southwestern Pennsylvania and West Virginia, the red buckeye's range does not reach that far north. Therefore, prior to 1784, either the hybrid buckeye was brought to the area surrounding the Cheat River, or the red buckeye was introduced and a natural hybrid occurred between the two species.

The mystery will probably never be solved; but there is no doubt that Washington would be pleased to know that his buckeye trees have caused such a ruckus in the twentieth century!

OTHER TREES AT MOUNT VERNON

The first trees to greet the visitor's eye inside the main gate at Mount Vernon are not "authentic" plantings, although they could not look lovelier or more at home. Records indicate that no London plane trees grew at Mount Vernon in Washington's day. The planes lining the entry way were planted during the late 1880s, prior to the authenticity campaign begun by Sargent. Authentic or not, they are lovely year round, providing shade in the summer and ornament during the winter. The trees are a cross between our native American sycamore and the Oriental plane tree.

A peculiar story is connected with the two tall pecan trees that crown the hill leading up from the Potomac River to the mansion. These trees were reputed to have been a gift to George Washington from Thomas Jefferson, another horticulturally-minded president. The legend was shattered, however, when a photograph taken in 1856 turned up in recent years. The picture shows a bare hillside where the pecans stand today.

The black locust grove just north of the house has an interesting history behind it. In 1776, General Washington wrote to his grounds manager from New York, instructing him to plant "groves of Trees at each end of the dwelling House...to consist...at the North end, of locusts altogether."[69] The general's orders were carried out and for many years a lovely black locust grove graced the northern grounds of the mansion. In 1934, the grove was restored according to Washington's 1776 specifications. These locusts are especially lovely in May, with their pendulous clusters of fragrant, white blossoms.

The grounds of Mount Vernon are liberally adorned by southern magnolia trees. Washington planted several dozen of these flowering trees from a shipment he received from South Carolina in 1785. Although none has survived to the present day, in 1977 the Mount Vernon Ladies' Association planted southern magnolias in two of the original locations recorded in Washington's diary, just to the west of the mansion.

An absolutely beautiful Atlas cedar stands to the southeast of the house, on the hill overlooking the Potomac. Planted during the latter part of the last century, this cedar is native to the Atlas Mountain region of northern Africa. In 1899, a delegation of Masons planted a closely related tree, the cedar of Lebanon, near Washington's grave in commemoration of the centenary of his death. This tree, too, is magnificent today.

Mid-April is undoubtedly the most spectacular time of year to visit Mount Vernon. The eighteenth-century Flower Garden is in full bloom and trees, everywhere, are just beginning to show their softly electric spring green.

The loveliest sight of all is a magical arboreal combination that was known to George Washington, the simultaneous blooming of the redbud and the flowering dogwood. In 1926 Sargent noted: "That (Washington) appreciated the beauty which can be obtained by contrasting the white flowers of the Dogwood with the rose-colored flowers of the Redbud is shown by his planting, on March 1, 1785, 'a circle of Dogwood with a Redbud in the middle.' "[70]

Today, dogwood and redbud trees grow in profusion at Mount Vernon and along the memorial parkway connecting George Washington's home with the capital city named in his honor. The combination of snow white and purply-pink blossoms is particularly beautiful during a soft spring rain. Very appropriately, the loveliest dogwoods and redbuds of all grow close to George Washington's gravesite, where the elegantly landscaped Mount Vernon estate and peaceful native woodland meet.

One final question about the trees in George Washington's life remains: Did he chop down the cherry tree? Sophisticated adults probably know that story was only a fable made up by Parson Weems. Or was it? On August 18, 1785, the first president of the United States confessed that he "(c)ut down the cherry trees in the Court yard."[71]

THE NATIONAL ARBORETUM

The cherry trees bloom but once a year, their blossoms soon scattered by the brisk spring wind. Even the most hardened urbanite must wish for more than that teasing glimpse of their stirring beauty. Washington has its pockets of beauty year round, but does anything even remotely compare with the cherry trees? The answer is yes...the National Arboretum.

Two of the National Arboretum's attractions are equally as awe-inspiring as the sight of the cherry trees in bloom: Mount Hamilton in April and May and the National Bonsai Collection. The first comes alive with an incredible springtime display of azaleas and flowering dogwoods. The second is an experience to refresh the spirit throughout the year—fifty-three miniature trees from Japan that are up to 350 years old, yet stand no higher than seedlings.

The National Arboretum is located in northeast Washington, on 444 acres of varied terrain. The hills and vales of the Arboretum support an outstanding array of native and exotic trees and shrubs, with peaceful drives and footpaths winding through them. From the first spring wildflower in Fern Valley to the last blanket of snow on the groves of dwarf conifers, every part of the Arboretum is worth exploring, every season of the year.

BRIEF HISTORY AND GENERAL BACKGROUND

In the last part of the nineteenth century, Secretary of Agriculture James Wilson dreamed of a place in the nation's capital that would be "a perennial feast of botanical education."[72] Wilson and some of his contemporaries envisioned an extensive plant research center that would also rate among the great botanical gardens of the world. In 1901, the McMillan Commission (which later became the Commission of Fine Arts) gave impetus to the idea by recommending that a combination arboretum and botanical garden be created in Washington. However, not until 1927 did Congress approve the bill to create the present-day National Arboretum.

Two United States Department of Agriculture (USDA) scientists, F.V. Coville and B.Y. Morrison, chose the northeast Washington site and directed the planning for the new arboretum. In 1951, Morrison became the first director of the United States National Arboretum.

While a more pleasant urban getaway than the National Arboretum can hardly be imagined, providing a place for public recreation is not the Arboretum's primary goal. Plant research and education are what the Arboretum is really all about. A large staff of scientists conduct breeding experiments to develop improved varieties of plants. They also evaluate and classify cultivars developed elsewhere. In the tradition of the great plant hunters of yesterday, the National Arboretum scientific staff introduces new plant varieties into the United States from other parts of the world.

Within the administration building, an attractive glass and concrete structure surrounded by pools filled with colorful lilies, lotuses, and exotic fish, is the National Arboretum's herbarium, where half a million pressed plant specimens are kept on file. The specimens in the herbarium are an important resource, not only for the Arboretum staff, but for scientists from around the world who come here to conduct research or are loaned specimens from the collection. The United States Department of Agriculture, which administers the Arboretum, also uses this vast plant library.

In keeping with the Arboretum's educational objectives, members of the staff regularly publish their research findings in government and professional publications. Lectures, films, and exhibits are open to the public, and courses taught by members of the staff are offered through the USDA Graduate School.

THE AZALEAS

It's as simple as this: If you haven't seen the Arboretum's azaleas, you have no idea what you are missing. The world's widest wide-angle lens could not begin to capture the all-encompassing feeling one gets standing in the midst of the Mount Hamilton azaleas. The colors are out of an Impressionist painting: salmon, lilac, rose, orange, and scarlet. Brilliant white flowering dogwoods, including lovely double-bracted forms, are intermingled with the colorful shrubs. Tall trees and wildflowers complete the scene, which seems to have sprung from a romantic fantasy.

In actuality, the Arboretum azaleas have a far less ethereal origin. The majority of the shrubs (those above the roadway on Mount Hamilton) are the result of breeding experiments conducted by the first director of the Arboretum, B.Y. Morrison. Morrison's colorful array of selections are generally known as the "Glenn Dale Hybrids" after the place where they were developed. In addition to the 65,000 specimens scattered across the hillside, a quaint brick-walled garden called the "Morrison Garden" and its immediate surroundings are also planted with Glenn Dale Hybrids. Below the roadway are lovely Ghent and Mollis hybrid azaleas, a gift to the United States from the Netherlands. Other types of azaleas and rhododendrons also adorn the slopes of Mount Hamilton.

THE NATIONAL BONSAI COLLECTION

Seasons change among the bonsai trees. Leaves unfold in the spring, flowers bloom, and autumn foliage turns red or gold before falling. Only the conifers and camellias are green throughout the winter.

Nothing in the world could sound more natural. But in the case of the National Bonsai Collection, two factors elevate these simple phenomena to the level of the extraordinary. Bonsai exhibit all the characteristics of full-sized trees, but they stand only a few inches to a few feet tall; and some trees in the collection are well into their third and fourth centuries of existence.

Standing among the bonsai trees is something like looking at the stars. One is suddenly struck by the immediate presence of time. The feeling of awe stirred by the knowledge that each star's light was created at a different time in the past, despite the illusion that all starlight exists in the present, is strangely akin to the sensation of viewing the bonsai.

One feels the almost eerie presence of dozens of human generations embodied in the tiny trees; generations that have come and gone but are linked to the present by a miniature forest representing centuries of human care.

Philosophy aside, the bonsai trees are one of the most thrilling sights in the nation's capital. And along

with their ancient history, the bonsai are also noteworthy for making recent history.

The bonsai trees, like the famous cherry trees,
were a gift to the United States from Japan. Presented to
the U.S. in honor of this country's bicentennial celebration, it is difficult to imagine a more generous gift from
one nation to another. Japan's Nippon Bonsai Association assembled the trees from some of the finest private
collections in the country. One tree, a 180-year old red
pine, comes from the imperial household. It is the first
bonsai from the imperial household ever to leave Japan.

Bonsai (which, translated, means "to plant in a shallow pot") is an ancient Japanese art which originated in
China. Through careful, periodic pruning of the roots
and limbs during the lifetime of the plant, a perfect, tiny
tree is "created" which looks exactly as it would in
nature, only in miniature. The exacting maintenance of
the ancient trees is carried on today by bonsai specialists
at the National Arboretum.

The trees in the National Bonsai Collection are
housed in a lovely Japanese-style garden near the
Arboretum administration building. They represent
thirty-four species. Tiny "shade" trees include ginkgoes,
Japanese and trident maples, Japanese beeches, and
hornbeams. The little azaleas, quince, flowering crabapples, and camellias are spectacular in spring with their
oversized blossoms. And the miniature conifers, such as
pines, junipers, spruces and yews, nicely complement the
collection year round.

The art of bonsai is rapidly catching on in this
country. But not until the year 2300 can there be an
American-grown bonsai as old as the Japanese white
pine in the Arboretum collection today. It will take
about three centuries to tell whether bonsai is just
another American fad; and that's longer than this country has been in existence.

THE GOTELLI DWARF CONIFER COLLECTION

The National Arboretum also has another forest of
trees in miniature, the Gotelli Dwarf Conifer Collection.
Unlike the bonsai, which require periodic pruning to
keep in miniature shape, the trees in the dwarf conifer
collection are naturally small for their species. Some are
cultivars or naturally occurring varieties. Others have
been dwarfed by mutations or adverse environmental
conditions. Whatever the reasons, the collective result is
a troll-sized forest in the middle of northeast Washington.

The collection, which is technically an assemblage
of "dwarf and slow-growing conifers," is planted outdoors on a five-acre hillside in the northeastern part of
the Arboretum. Donated by William T. Gotelli in 1962,
the planting comprises 1,500 trees. Species represented in
dwarfed form include fir, cedar, pine, yew, spruce, and
many others.

THE DAWN REDWOOD

The enchanting dawn redwood or metasequoia is
often called a "living fossil." Until 1941, when it was

found growing in a remote part of central China, the genus *Metasequoia* was known to the world's botanical community only in fossilized form and was assumed to be extinct.

The present range of the 50,000,000-year old genus seems to include only several small areas in Hupeh and Szechuan provinces. Nevertheless, the trees are doing well in cultivation in many parts of the world. The dawn redwood favors moist mountain ravines and is most abundant in Hupeh province's picturesque Shui sha Valley.

In 1948, just two years after discovery of the dawn redwood was published, young specimens were brought to the new United States National Arboretum. These trees are thriving today. The dawn redwood is planted in charming groves throughout the National Arboretum. The grove on the lower slope of Mount Hamilton looks most at home, however, with a tiny stream flowing through it. Like the native American bald-cypress of southern swamps, which it closely resembles in appearance, the dawn redwood is a deciduous conifer.

BETULA UBER

The dawn redwood is not the only tree on the National Arboretum grounds to have returned from the dead. Another "extinct" species is planted there, and this tree is a Virginia native and recent rediscovery. The story of *Betula uber's* resurfacing has all the elements of a good detective yarn. Even the Latin name of the tree sounds dark and mysterious.

The story begins in the summer of 1963 when a young botanist named Peter Mazzeo (currently on the staff of the National Arboretum) was working as a ranger naturalist in Virginia's Shenandoah National Park. Mazzeo became intrigued by the legend of *Betula uber*, the mysterious birch that hadn't been seen in the Virginia woods since 1914. Some botanists believed the tree to be extinct, but Mazzeo had a strong feeling it was still growing somewhere in the Blue Ridge mountains of southwestern Virginia, and that some day he would find it.

After joining the staff of the National Arboretum, Mazzeo began to pursue his search for *Betula uber* in earnest. The scanty bit of literature on the rare tree only mentioned one locale where it had ever been sighted: Dickey Creek in Smyth County, Virginia. Mazzeo's investigation of the southwestern Virginia creek, like the searches of many botanists before him, yielded no sign of the elusive *Betula uber*.

Then something happened. Among the *Betula uber* herbarium specimens loaned Mazzeo by Harvard University's Arnold Arboretum, he found an undated specimen collected along a stream near Dickey Creek called Cressy Creek. No mention of this second *Betula uber* sighting had ever appeared in the literature. Mazzeo was excited.

Harvard University, however, did not share the young botanist's enthusiasm, and Mazzeo's paper about the new *uber* finding was turned down by the editors of *Rhodora*, the publication of the prestigious New England Botanical Club. The unpublished paper was returned with the comment, "no new material."

In 1975, the Smithsonian published their report on the endangered and threatened plants of the United States in accord with a congressional mandate. The report listed *Betula uber* as "probably extinct." Before the year was out, that assessment was to be challenged.

Meanwhile, the editors of *Castanea*, the journal of the Southern Appalachian Botanical Club, had accepted the *uber* paper for publication. The article was printed in the fall of 1974.

In the summer of '75, while Peter Mazzeo and the Arboretum's Dr. Frederick Meyer were in the process of planning a trip to Smyth County, another botanical sleuth was on the trail of *Betula uber*. Douglas Ogle, a young biology teacher at Virginia Highlands Community College, had seen the *Castanea* article. He too was excited by the new Cressy Creek evidence.

On August 22, 1975, Douglas Ogle rediscovered *Betula uber* on the banks of Cressy Creek. After spotting the characteristic rounded leaves he had seen before only in photographs, Ogle became so excited that he shinnied up the slender tree trunk to break off a leafing branch. Sure enough. It had to be *uber*.

When news of the discovery reached Peter Mazzeo back in Washington he was thrilled. Together the two men were credited with the *uber* find. Several other specimens were also found in the immediate vicinity along Cressy Creek. The refound tree was christened with the common name "Virginia round-leaf birch."

However, although botanists now know *where Betula uber* is, they still don't know for sure *what* it is. According to Mazzeo, it could be a subspecies or a variety rather than a true species. But however the botanists finally classify it, there is no doubt that *Betula uber* is unique.

Several young specimens of the Virginia round-leaf birch are planted at the National Arboretum. Unfortunately, until the fragile continued existence of this endangered tree can be assured, the trees will remain in an undisclosed location. It would take a detective to find them.

OTHER NATIONAL ARBORETUM COLLECTIONS

We have barely scratched the surface when it comes to the delightful attractions of the National Arboretum. Also not to be missed are the new National Herb Garden, Fern Valley (a lovely woodland abounding with native flowers and trees), the camellias, the dogwoods, the flowering crabapples, the hollies, the magnolias, the lilacs, the crape-myrtle, the hibiscus, the maples, the duck ponds, the bald-cypresses, the Cryptomeria, the pyrocantha, the day lilies, the peonies, et cetera, et cetera, et cetera! Many things grow at the National Arboretum that grow nowhere else in Washington. Information and maps are available in the main lobby of the National Arboretum administration building.

THE PLANT INTRODUCTION STATION AT GLENN DALE, MARYLAND

The National Arboretum administers a plant introduction station in Glenn Dale, Maryland where foreign plants imported into the country are quarantined, examined, and propagated. Important research is carried on at Glenn Dale by the Arboretum staff, frequently yielding results with major impact on the nursery trade.

Botanists of the National Arboretum carry on the tradition of Ernest Wilson, David Fairchild, Frank Meyer, and other great plant hunters of the past by traveling to remote parts of foreign continents in search of new trees, shrubs, and herbaceous plants to introduce into this country. It is because of the great American plant hunters that our backyards and our cities are so richly endowed with beautiful plant life today. Plants from foreign continents also contribute to our food supply and to pharmaceutical research.

Although the Glenn Dale station is only open to the public by appointment, several trees growing there must be mentioned. Many exotic flowering cherry trees, including some Japanese selections that probably grow nowhere else in the country, are at Glenn Dale. Other Glenn Dale trees include an old saw-toothed oak, the beautiful Fuji crabapple, and the Franklin tree, which is believed to be extinct in the wild.

KENILWORTH AQUATIC GARDENS

While the Kenilworth Aquatic Gardens are best known for water lilies and other aquatic plants, their colorful pools are surrounded by some very interesting trees. Appropriately, the bald-cypress of southern swamps stands guard over this aquatic park. Japanese raisin trees, Carolina laurelcherries, and saw-toothed oaks are among the unusual species planted at the gardens. A huge willow oak grows next to the small main office. In addition to specific plantings made along the entrance to the park and around the lily pools, many native trees grow in the gardens and surrounding woodlands. The Kenilworth Aquatic Gardens are located along the eastern shore of the Anacostia River and are administered by the National Park Service.

THE SOLDIERS' AND AIRMEN'S HOME

Some of the oldest and most beautiful trees in the District of Columbia are located on the hundreds of rolling acres of the Soldiers' and Airmen's Home in northwest Washington. Soldiers' Home, as it is most often called, accommodates former members of the military who have either served the requisite number of years in the service or have been disabled in the line of duty. It is the oldest soldiers' home in the country.

During the last century, a gray stucco house known as the Anderson Cottage served as a summer White House for Presidents Lincoln, Hayes and Arthur. It is around this historic structure that many of Soldiers' Home's most beautiful trees can be found. Undoubtedly the most striking tree is an ancient osage orange. Ginkgo trees, southern magnolias, and old American hollies also grace the grounds of the Anderson Cottage and adjacent areas. Nearby are a grove of Siberian elms and a mammoth copper beech.

A large, tree-like osmanthus stands in front of the Sherman Building, putting forth fragrant blossoms in the late fall. To the east and down a gentle hill is a handsome grove of shingle oaks.

One of the most unusual trees at Soldiers' Home is a variegated tulip poplar planted near Grant Hall. In the spring and early summer, the leaves of this tree have whitish or pale yellow margins. Not far from the tulip poplar, just south of a miniature golf course, is a Japanese snowbell tree which is very large for the species.

To the south, the complex which includes the Forwood and Lagarde buildings is ringed with many old exotics. The Japanese flowering cherry trees and Japanese maples there are particularly beautiful.

The residents of the trees at Soldiers' Home are as interesting as the trees themselves. Black and albino squirrels scamper from limb to limb along with their less exotic gray-brown companions. The nimble critters have plenty of time to play since the old soldiers keep them fattened up with generous handouts. Their favorite trees are easily identified by the telltale peanut shells on the ground below.

A pastoral duck pond graces the landscape in the southwestern section of the grounds. Bald-cypresses and other interesting conifers have been planted along the shoreline.

THE FREDERICK DOUGLASS HOME (CEDAR HILL)

Cedar Hill, the colonial-style home of the renowned nineteenth-century abolitionist and women's rights advocate, is situated atop a tree-shaded rise in Anacostia, overlooking the city of Washington. Although the original red cedars for which the Frederick Douglass home is named are no longer alive, the National Park Service has planted young red cedars around the home, in the hope that some day they will equal the stature of the cedars known to Douglass.

Born a slave in Tuckahoe, Maryland in 1817, Frederick Douglass was a forceful lecturer and writer who befriended not only the oppressed, but President Lincoln, Queen Victoria, and other leaders of his day. Douglass moved to Cedar Hill in 1877 and lived there until his death in 1895.

In 1962, concern for the continued preservation of Cedar Hill resulted in an Act of Congress which was signed into law by President Kennedy. The historic house and grounds are now under the care of the National Park Service.

Most of the mature trees on the grounds are native species. Large tulip poplars, several species of oaks, white ashes, black locusts, tupelos, and hickories surround the house. Good-sized southern magnolias, hackberries, and Norway spruces also adorn the crest of the hill.

In addition to the red cedars the National Park Service has planted young oaks, hickories, and other native trees in an attempt to simulate the setting of Douglass' day.

SAINT ELIZABETH'S HOSPITAL

The extensive grounds of Saint Elizabeth's Hospital at 2700 Martin Luther King, Jr. Avenue in Anacostia are replete with beautiful trees, including many exotic species. The federal facility is spread out on a tract of land which overlooks the Anacostia River and provides a magnificent view of the city. The trees at Saint Elizabeth's include Himalayan pines, deodar cedars, fern-leaf European beeches, English elms, umbrella magnolias, live oaks, silverbells, and Kentucky coffee trees. Saint Elizabeth's is noted in the botanical guide section of this book as a location for other species of trees.

TREES OF HISTORIC CEMETERIES

Old gravestones are not the only historic landmarks found in Washington's cemeteries. The area's graveyards are among the finest places for old and historic trees. Washington area cemeteries are also liberally endowed with flowering trees such as magnolias and dogwoods. Here we mention only the cemeteries with trees tied to the nation's history.

ARLINGTON CEMETERY

One of the most pampered trees of all time stands next to the grave of President John F. Kennedy in Arlington Cemetery. This ancient post oak has seen the dawning of at least two centuries.

During 1965, the architect employed to design the permanent gravesite of the former President was concerned that the tree, which has been known for many years as the "Arlington Oak," would be unable to withstand the shock of the construction going on around it. So, at a cost of several thousand dollars, an elaborate aeration, drainage, and soil improvement plan developed by National Park Service plant pathologist Horace Wester was carried out. Today the "Arlington Oak" is healthy and vigorous. Each year thousands of people pass beneath its boughs to pay homage to the former president.

Before the Union Army claimed the land that is now Arlington Cemetery, the property was owned by several generations of prominent Virginians. George Washington's stepson, John Parke Custis (son of Martha Custis Washington), purchased the land in 1778. In turn, his son, George Washington Parke Custis (who had become George Washington's ward following John's death), built the beautiful Greek Revival mansion on the hill. And to increase the confusing entanglement of famous Virginia families, George Washington Parke Custis' daughter, Mary Ann Randolph Custis (his only child to reach maturity) married Robert E. Lee! The Lee family owned the property at the outbreak of the Civil War.

The elegant house that overlooks the cemetery is known today as the Custis-Lee Mansion, or simply "Arlington House." It stands in the shade of one of Washington's most outstanding trees: a huge deodar cedar with massive branches and feathery evergreen foliage. The cedar dominates the grounds in back of the house. In front of the mansion is a ginkgo tree of magnificent proportions. Beneath its branches many small ginkgo seedlings reveal the identity of the parent tree, a female, and producer of the infamously odorous fruit.

A little known landmark of the hill on which the Custis-Lee mansion stands is the permanent gravesite of Major Pierre Charles L'Enfant, designer of the city of Washington. In recent years, L'Enfant's remains were moved from another cemetery to the present site overlooking the city he designed.

Arlington Cemetery is shaded by many beautiful trees. Ancient natives are interspersed with exotic conifers and numerous flowering trees and shrubs.

ROCK CREEK CEMETERY

The man who lined Washington's streets with thousands of trees in the 1870s is buried in Rock Creek Cemetery, near Soldiers' Home in northwest Washington. Largely because of the efforts of District of Columbia Governor Alexander Shepherd, Washington became known as the "City of Trees."

Rock Creek Cemetery is the home of the famous "Glebe Oak." According to legend, this ancient white oak was alive in the early 1700s when the first church was built in what is now the District of Columbia. It is called the "Glebe Oak" because the area that is now Rock Creek Cemetery was once known as a "glebe," a parish-owned tract of land used to raise money for the church. The old oak stands next to Saint Paul's Church, which was built just prior to the Revolution to replace the original chapel built in 1712. The present day church has undergone major restorations since 1775.

There are many other striking trees in Rock Creek Cemetery. A huge Atlas cedar dominates the hillside inside the southeastern gate. Tall incense cedars from the West Coast grow in the vicinity of the church. Also, an absolutely beautiful, fern-leaf Japanese maple is planted on the church grounds.

FORT LINCOLN CEMETERY

Fort Lincoln Cemetery, just across the District line in Maryland, is the site of a sprawling tree known as the "Lincoln Oak." The old white oak is showing its age; several of its limbs have been amputated in recent years. But still the ancient tree holds on. The Lincoln Oak stands next to one of the oldest structures in Maryland, the "Old Spring House," built in 1683. During the Civil War, President Lincoln is said to have drunk from the "Old Spring House" spring and to have conferred with his commanders under the oak that now bears his name.

THE NATIONAL ZOO

Although their competition is formidable, the trees at the National Zoological Park are worth at least a small portion of the attention that is lavished upon the animals. For instance, the exotic cats on lion-tiger hill sleep in the shade of equally exotic Himalayan pines. The big cats also share the hill with rare West Coast incense cedars.

Young dawn redwood trees and sweetbay magnolias add dimension to the swampy ambience of Beaver Valley. And although the bamboo growing in the Giant Pandas' front yard must look mouthwatering to Hsing Hsing and Ling Ling, it's out of reach and strictly there for show along with the weeping willows.

Spectacular native and exotic trees and shrubs grow everywhere at the National Zoo. Even the parking lots are handsomely landscaped. The lot near Connecticut Avenue is surrounded by exotic saw-toothed oaks and golden rain trees, with handsome rows of yellowwoods and Bradford pears nearby. The duck pond parking lot also has its share of golden rain trees.

So take a hint from a couple of animal lovers. The National Zoo is one of the best tree places in town!

STORYBOOK GARDEN SETTINGS

Almost every structure in Washington, from the tiniest townhouse to the most lavish ambassador's residence, has its garden. And the gardens of the District of Columbia are particularly pleasing, benefiting as they do from a potpourri of influences: a touch of the Deep South; a large slice of Europe; and an abundance of Oriental flowering trees. Dumbarton Oaks and other garden settings mentioned here are exceptionally beautiful.

DUMBARTON OAKS

The Dumbarton Oaks Estate in Georgetown is surrounded by one of the world's loveliest landscaped settings. Its quaintly terraced hillside, laid out in the best seventeenth and eighteenth century European style, flows downward into a romantic sea of flowering trees and shrubs. Dumbarton Oaks seems to be part of another world. Yet the gardens are largely the work of two twentieth-century women.

HISTORY OF THE GARDENS

In 1702, the land where Dumbarton Oaks is now situated was granted to Ninian Beall, who was born at Dumbarton on the Clyde in Scotland. Beall named his new home the "Rock of Dumbarton." The estate changed hands and names several times before it was purchased as "The Oaks" by diplomat Robert Woods Bliss and his wife, Mildred, in 1920. Combining the estate's oldest and newest names, the Blisses christened it "Dumbarton Oaks."

While traveling the world with her diplomat husband, Mildred Bliss had developed a vision of a garden of her own, inspired especially by the landscapes of France, Italy, and England. In 1922, she was fortunate enough to find the perfect person to execute that vision, the brilliant landscape architect, Beatrix Farrand. Farrand, too, was well acquainted with the finest gardens of Europe.

Together, the women planned the romantic gardens for which Dumbarton Oaks has become so famous. Both believed that a garden should be a place to *live* in, so they planned a series of small gardens, each with its own special atmosphere. Many have likened these cozy spaces to the rooms of a house. Trees and shrubs were only a part of the plan. Intricate stone carvings, fountains, romantic benches, quaint stone walls, and iron gates were carefully conceived to give the garden its rich, intimate atmosphere.

Farrand and Bliss had a challenging setting to work with. The "back yard" of the Georgian mansion slopes rather steeply into a Rock Creek Park ravine. In order to link the wilderness of the natural woodland below with the imposing appearance of the brick mansion, Farrand planned a series of terraced gardens, progressing gradually from formality to informality. On the crest of the hill close to the mansion, the "Green Garden," the "Beech Terrace" and the "Urn Terrace" are neatly surrounded by brick walls. However, as one progresses down the hill, through the series of terraces, the vista opens up and plantings are no longer confined within rectangular spaces. The landscape finally "ends" in an orgiastic display of springtime abandon, a golden hillside of forsythia bordered by a storybook grove of pink and white Japanese flowering cherry trees.

Beatrix Farrand's clients included Rockefellers, Roosevelts, and Mrs. Woodrow Wilson. Her abilities were even recognized by the western world's gardening elite, the British, who invited her to recreate the grounds of Dartington Hall in Devonshire. However, before she died in 1960, Beatrix Farrand described her work at Dumbarton Oaks as "the most deeply felt and the best of a fifty years' practice."[73] With few exceptions, today's Dumbarton Oaks gardens look precisely the way Beatrix Farrand planned.

In 1940 the Blisses gave Dumbarton Oaks to Harvard University. Four years later this romantic setting was the scene of the international conference that led to the

establishment of the United Nations. Today the Harvard
Center for Byzantine studies is located in the mansion.
Exhibits of Byzantine and Pre-Columbian Art are open
to the public. The gardens and grounds are accessible from
the entrance near the corner of 32nd and R Streets, N.W.,
and at this printing are open only in the afternoon. Phone
Dumbarton Oaks for more information.

THE TREES AT DUMBARTON OAKS

Selecting the trees for special mention at Dumbarton
Oaks is like trying to find the brightest stars in the sky.
Every tree is beautiful in its own right and is an integral
part of the landscape. So much perfection inspires the
eye but boggles the mind of this writer!

The estate is entered from R Street to the south. An
expansive lawn is surrounded by tall trees, many of
them evergreen. Most notable on the south lawn is a
large Yulan magnolia directly in front of the little
"orangery" to the east of the mansion. In early spring
this rare Asian tree dons beautiful cream-white blossoms.
According to chief gardener Don Smith, Mrs. Bliss nick-
named this magnolia "The Bride." Also on the grounds
around the south lawn are two huge katsura trees. The
bigger of the two is probably the largest katsura in the
area. Nearby are a pair of venerable though delicate
Japanese maples.

Directly in back of the orangery, on the crest of the
northern slope, is the Green Garden, home of three of
Dumbarton Oaks' old oaks. The largest is a black oak,
and the other two are red oaks. Unfortunately, few of
the ancient white oaks which were once so common are
alive today. But many old white oaks survive in nearby
Montrose Park.

A handsome American beech dominates the Beech
Terrace east of the Green Garden. In the early spring bright
blue flowers come up between its exposed silvery roots.

Two delicate kobus magnolias, unfortunately rare in
the Washington area, light up the Urn Terrace in spring
with their star-like white blossoms. The Urn Terrace
overlooks the Rose Garden, a major attraction during
the summer months.

A pleasant box-wood walk leads down the hill past
the exotic pebble garden (a post-Farrand innovation),
passing under many pleasant trees. A striking feature of
the mid-level northern slope is the Ellipse (also added
after Farrand's time). This garden space contains a central fountain surrounded by a very European-looking
elliptical planting of closely clipped hornbeams.

The Prunus Walk nearby is lined with rare purple-
leaved plums (*Prunus* x *blireiana*) which produce deep
pink blossoms and reddish-purple leaves. The Prunus
Walk leads downward to Dumbarton Oaks' most romantic grove, on a slope known as "Cherry Hill." In the
spring, several varieties of Japanese flowering cherry
trees produce a delicate pink and white canopy over the
newly green hillside. One could easily imagine a wedding
here, although choosing a date to coincide with the elusive blossoms would be a daring gamble.

While the cherry trees are in bloom, the crowning

glory of Dumbarton Oaks, Forsythia Hill, is a sea of golden blossoms. Looking downward from the higher terraces or across from Cherry Hill, the view of this wild forsythia garden is an experience never to be forgotten. A walk through the weeping golden branches on a winding stone path is pleasantly reminiscent of the fabled Yellow Brick Road in the land of Oz.

Later in the spring the flowering crabapples on Crabapple Hill, just above Forsythia Hill, are beautiful. And the "North Vista" is lined with stately conifers, pink weeping cherries, and other attractive trees.

Finally, a tree that can't go unmentioned is a massive copper beech, located near Lovers' Lane Pool in the easternmost section of the grounds. During the spring, wildflowers come up between the large, sprawling roots of this tree.

While it would be nice to linger at Dumbarton Oaks forever, it's time to bid it adieu. Not, however, without a brief stop at neighboring Montrose Park. The ancient, white oak-studded acres of Montrose Park perfectly complement the elaborately landscaped estate next door. The park radiates the same romantic aura of past centuries. Many of the native and exotic trees of Montrose Park are mentioned in the botanical guide section of this book.

HILLWOOD ESTATE

Another Georgian mansion overlooking Rock Creek Park also has extensive, elaborately landscaped grounds. The home of the late Mrs. Marjorie Merriweather Post (daughter of the founder of the Post cereal company) is surrounded by many lovely gardens, which blend as the gardens of Dumbarton Oaks do, into a single, romantic whole. The late heiress took great interest in the gardens and grounds. She even created a cemetery for her pets, complete with engraved headstones. Among the highlights of Hillwood Estate is a picturesque Japanese garden. Japanese maples, Cryptomeria, and other lovely trees shade the miniature bridges that cross the garden's hillside stream. The trees of Hillwood also include stately old American elms and an abundance of conifers: dawn redwoods, spruces, hemlocks, arborvitae, and many others. The grounds are replete with flowering shrubs such as roses, azaleas, and rhododendrons.

OTHER "STORYBOOK" GARDEN SETTINGS OF THE WASHINGTON, D.C. AREA

- ☐ Franciscan Monastery (1400 Quincy Street, N.E.)
- ☐ Bishop's Garden, Washington Cathedral (Near corner of Wisconsin and Massachusetts Avenues, N.W.)
- ☐ Brookside Gardens (1500 Glenallan Avenue, Wheaton, MD.)
- ☐ Meridian Hill Park (16th and W Streets, N.W.)
- ☐ Japanese ambassador's residence (Not open to the public)

THE PRESIDENTS' TREE

Although the "Hieroglyphics Tree" would be a more descriptive name for this tree in its present condition, the American beech at the corner of Sligo Creek Parkway and Maple Avenue in Takoma Park is officially named the Presidents' Tree. It has even been honored with its own private fence and an impressive plaque.

The story goes that back in the 1860s a farmer named Samuel Fenton carved the names of all the presidents from Washington to Andrew Johnson on the bark of this beech tree. He also included the name of "Lieutenant General" Ulysses S. Grant, who later became president.

In 1948 the Maryland-National Capital Park Commission officially declared the tree a Civil War Memorial and erected an iron fence around it to protect it from modern day beech bark carvers. A plaque explaining its history was added in 1960.

Although it takes a good deal of imagination to decipher the writings engraved on the tree today, this American beech is another one of the great living memorials of the Washington area.

PART TWO

Illustrated Botanical Guide
to the City of Trees

Identifying trees is great detective work, especially
in a city with more than 300 species from all over the
world. Washington, D.C.'s outstanding tree collection
has evolved from a centuries' old tradition of planting
and caring for trees, an avocation that traces back to the
founding fathers. The mild climate of the city—which
lies on the geologic boundary of the Atlantic coastal
plain and the piedmont—has made it possible for a vast
number of trees that could not survive in cooler or
hotter climates to flourish here.

City of Trees, Part Two is an illustrated botanical
guide to Washington's hundreds of native and exotic
trees. With the exception of the National Arboretum,
which harbors many rare woody and herbaceous plants
encountered nowhere else in the area, *City of Trees*, Part
Two describes every mature tree commonly grown in
Washington, D.C. Nurseries are constantly offering new
species, varieties and cultivars, so some young specimens
may not be covered in this edition of *City of Trees*.
And, there is always that chance—which has fueled tree
enthusiasts in the District of Columbia for decades—that
your back yard may cloister an exotic tree so rare that it
is found nowhere else in the area!

City of Trees, Part Two is also useful in cities and
towns throughout temperate eastern and central North
America as well as parts of Europe and Asia. It is a
guide to *cultivated* trees (trees planted for shade and
ornament). Many of the trees planted in Washington,
D.C. can also be found in Boston, New York, London,
Paris, and Tokyo!

HOW TO IDENTIFY TREES
USING *CITY OF TREES*, PART TWO

First, ask yourself, "Is it a tree?" This query is not
as simple-minded as it sounds. Trees and shrubs are
woody plants, (with stems and limbs containing wood).
Although there is no scientific distinction between a tree
and a shrub, trees tend to be *tall* and *single-trunked*,
while shrubs are shorter, fuller and usually *multi-
trunked* (See Fig. 1, p. 58.) *City of Trees*, Part Two is almost
exclusively a guide to trees, although we have included a
few large shrubs that are particularly showy.

Once you have established that your woody plant is
a tree, turn to the Keys to the Genera, pages 64 and 108.
Instructions on how to use the keys follow.

HOW TO USE THE *KEY TO THE CONIFER GENERA*

First, decide whether your tree is a *conifer* or a *broad-leaved tree*.

Conifers are Gymnosperms (*Gymnospermae*), from the Greek, meaning "naked" seeds. Conifer seeds are not enclosed in an ovary. Most conifers produce *cones*, which contain the seeds that are usually scattered by the wind. In our city flora, there are a few conifers that do not produce cones. They are cited in the *Key to the Conifer Genera*. Conifer foliage is *needle-like* or *scale-like* (with the exception of the ginkgo or maidenhair tree). (See Figure 2 for typical conifer foliage and cones.)

If your tree is a conifer, turn to the *Key to the Conifer Genera* page 64.

The illustrations in the *Key to the Conifer Genera* are grouped according to plant *families*. Five families are included: The pine family (*Pinaceae*); the taxodium family (*Taxodiaceae*); the cypress family (*Cupressaceae*); the yew family (*Taxaceae*); and the unique ginkgo family (*Ginkgoaceae*). Because the only species in the ginkgo family (*Ginkgo biloba*) is a *broad-leaved* conifer, we have also included it in the *Key to Broad-Leaved Tree Genera*.

Botanists classify trees in three categories. The *family* [such as the pine family (*Pinaceae*)] is broken down into many *genera* (plural for genus). The *genera* in the pine family include the spruces (*Picea*), the firs (*Abies*), the pines (*Pinus*), etc. Then, each *genus* is divided into individual *species*. Species in the spruce genus include the Norway spruce (*Picea abies*) and the Colorado blue spruce (*Picea pungens*).

The *Key to the Conifer Genera* is only meant to guide you to the *genus* of which your individual *species* is a member. Therefore, you should not be looking for an illustration with characteristics that are identical to your particular specimen. Rather, look for general characteristics. If your tree has long needles that are grouped in bundles of fives, it is a pine (*Pinus*). It may or may not be the species pictured in the *Key to Conifer Genera*.

FIGURE 1.
WOODY PLANTS

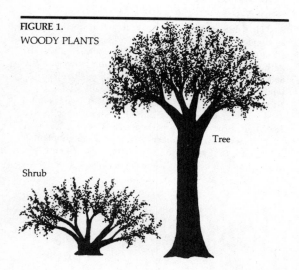

Tree

Shrub

FIGURE 2.
CONIFER CONES AND FOLIAGE

Scale-Like Foliage   Needle-Like Foliage

However, the key tells you to turn to the page where the combination of text and illustrations will help you single out your individual species.

Although the *Key to the Conifer Genera* is meant mostly as a visual aid, see the abbreviated text that accompanies the illustrations. For instance, under "The Spruces (*Picea*)", the text tells you: "Needles more or less four-sided. Cones *pendulous*." These characteristics are important, especially in distinguishing the spruces from the similar firs (*Abies*), which have *flat* needles and *erect* cones.

Once you have found your genus, see "How to Use the Text and Illustrations", later on in this introduction.

HOW TO USE THE *KEY TO THE BROAD-LEAVED TREE GENERA*

If your tree is not a conifer, identification may be a little more difficult at first until you get used to using this book. Most botanical guides contain complicated numerical keys, which are intimidating to anyone without a scientific background. We feel that this illustrated key to the genera makes identifying trees as simple as it can possibly be. If you take the time to read the following instructions, you should be making snap identifications in no time.

Broad-leaved trees belong to the Angiosperms (*Angiospermae*). Unlike the seeds of the Gymnosperms, Angiosperm seeds are contained in ovaries. The fruit produced by the broad-leaved trees may be fleshy (apples, pears) or dry (acorns, chestnuts). See Figure 3 for fruit types produced by broad-leaved trees.

The leaves of broad-leaved trees may be deciduous (falling in autumn) or evergreen. Most broad-leaved trees in our area are deciduous, but some, such as the hollies (*Ilex*) and the southern magnolia (*Magnolia grandiflora*), retain their leaves throughout the year.

FIGURE 3.
BROAD-LEAVED TREE FRUIT

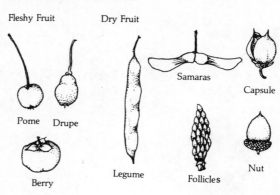

Fleshy Fruit   Dry Fruit

                                                Samaras

                                                            Capsule

Pome   Drupe

                        Legume   Follicles   Nut

Berry

The *Key to the Broad-Leaved Tree Genera* is a key to the *genera* only. Please read "How to Use the *Key to the Conifer Genera*" so that you will understand what a genus is and how the key to the genera is meant to be used.

Once you have established that your tree is a broad-leaved tree or Angiosperm, you must determine which of the following categories it belongs to:

A. Trees with *opposite, simple* leaves
B. Trees with *opposite, compound* leaves
C. Trees with *alternate, compound* leaves
D. Trees with *alternate, simple* leaves

A *simple leaf* is one that is not divided into individual leaflets. Oaks and most maples bear *simple* leaves. (See Figure 4.) A *compound* leaf is divided into leaflets that may be arranged in a *pinnate, palmate* or *trifoliate* pattern. (See Figure 5.)

Leaves are arranged along the branchlet either *opposite* one another or *alternately*. (See Figure 6.) Leaves that are arranged in a *whorled* or *sub-opposite* pattern are also considered to be *opposite*. (See Figure 7.)

In deciding which one of the four categories (A., B., C., or D.) your tree belongs in, make sure you have correctly determined whether your leaves are *simple* or *compound*. From mid-summer through autumn, locate the *axillary bud*, which occurs just above the point where the leaf stalk (petiole) joins the branchlet. At that point the branchlet ends and your leaf begins. Note that there is *no axillary bud* at the base of each individual leaflet (Figure 8).

When you have determined to which of the four categories your tree belongs, turn to the appropriate section of the *Key to the Broad-Leaved Tree Genera*. The pictures and abbreviated text will tell you to what *genus* (oak, maple, beech, etc.) your tree belongs. Then turn to the page number given next to the drawings to find out what *species* your tree is (*Chestnut* oak, *Norway* maple, *European* beech, etc.).

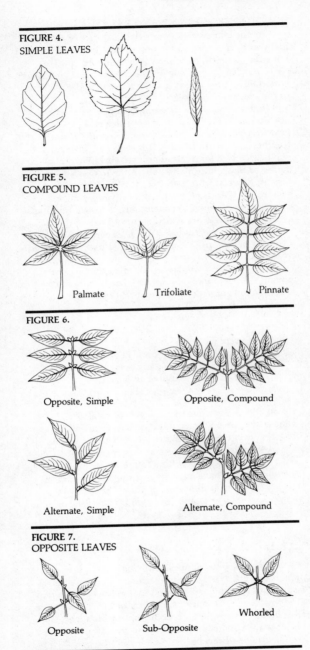

FIGURE 4.
SIMPLE LEAVES

FIGURE 5.
COMPOUND LEAVES

Palmate   Trifoliate   Pinnate

FIGURE 6.

Opposite, Simple   Opposite, Compound

Alternate, Simple   Alternate, Compound

FIGURE 7.
OPPOSITE LEAVES

Opposite   Sub-Opposite   Whorled

FIGURE 8.

Five Simple Leaves

Axillary
Buds

Two Compound
Leaves

HOW TO USE THE TEXT AND ILLUSTRATIONS

You now know that your tree is a spruce or an oak and you have turned to the appropriate pages to determine the species and to learn about the tree.

How can you get the most out of the text, and more importantly, how can you make a positive identification of the species?

In many cases, the illustrations opposite the tree description will tell you what your tree is. In most cases, however, you will need to use the text and illustrations together in order to be sure of the species. Two rules will help you in your tree detective work. First, always gather as much information about the tree as you can (leaves, flowers, fruit, bark, etc.). The more clues you have, the easier your work will be. And, secondly, *never* jump to conclusions. You will find that Washington's trees are crafty. That old oak in the back yard that you thought was a native American tree just may be some Asian or European species that was planted years ago.

In some cases, we have augmented the text with botanical keys to individual species. To use these keys successfully, simply keep in mind that you must make *one* of *two* choices. For instance:

1a) Flowers yellow . . Yellow Catalpa (*Catalpa ovata*)
1b) Flowers white
    2a) Leaf with a foul odor when crushed . . . .
       . . . Southern Catalpa (*Catalpa bignonioides*)
    2b) Leaf with no foul odor when crushed . . . .
       . . . . Western Catalpa (*Catalpa speciosa*)

If you choose 1a, your tree is a yellow catalpa. If you choose 1b, you still have more choices to make. So you proceed to 2, where you must decide between 2a and 2b.

If there had been more than one species that fit the description of 2a, "Leaf with a foul odor when crushed", then you would have been given a third set of choices. Choose between each pair of options, until you are no longer given a choice and your tree is identified for you.

TOOLS YOU WILL NEED TO IDENTIFY TREES

Anyone serious about identifying trees will want to purchase a small hand lens, available at a good hardware store. Sometimes, the only difference between two trees will be the absence or presence of tiny hairs on the leaf blade or stem that are visible only with a lens. Binoculars are also helpful, since many trees bear fruit only on their higher branches.

Some trees are difficult to identify without the presence of flowers and/or fruit. Therefore, you may want to start your own little herbarium or plant library. The only materials required are newspapers, two rectangular pieces of cardboard, and raw-hide, rope or string. Simply place your leaves or flowers inside the pages of a newspaper and record the place and date of collection and any other information you would like to remember on the newspaper. Fold the paper, place it between two pieces of cardboard, and then tie the whole bundle tightly. You may want to place your plant specimen under some books for a few days, while it dries. Plant specimens preserved in this manner will last for years. If you have collected leaves in the late summer, and the tree blossoms in the early spring (before the leaves are out), your herbarium will enable you to examine the leaves and flowers together. Fruit and cones may also be collected, tagged, and kept in egg cartons. Some fruits will last a long time, others will have to be discarded.

You may also want to keep a field notebook to record your arboreal observations throughout the year.

The most essential tool to acquire is a botanical vocabulary. We have kept this guide as simple as we possibly can without sacrificing vital information. You *will* come across words you have never seen before. When you do, consult the illustrated glossary.

Don't be intimidated by words like "glabrous" or "lanceolate". Once you learn a handful of new words, you will notice that they are used over and over again, quickly becoming an integral part of your vocabulary. Before using the book, you may want to scan the glossary.

We hope you enjoy using *City of Trees*, Part Two as much as we have enjoyed creating it. Keep in mind that the locations given for each tree are only examples. With a little perseverance you will undoubtedly uncover your own rare and beautiful specimens.

KEY TO THE CONIFER GENERA
Gymnospermae
(See introduction to Part Two, for description of how to use this

---

GINKGO FAMILY *Ginkgoaceae*
Leaves fan-shaped, deciduous (falling in autumn).

GINKGO, MAIDENHAIR TREE *Ginkgo biloba*   Page 68

Ginkgo, Maidenhair Tree *Ginkgo biloba*

YEW FAMILY *Taxaceae*
Leaves needle-like. Fruit berry-like.

THE YEWS *Taxus*   Page 106

English Yew *Taxus baccata*

PINE FAMILY *Pinaceae*
Leaves needle-like.
1. Leaves evergreen.

THE PINES *Pinus*   Pages 69–79

Japanese Red Pine *Pinus densiflora*

Eastern White Pine *Pinus strobus*

DOUGLAS-FIR *Pseudotsuga menziesii*   Page 92

Douglas-Fir *Pseudotsuga menziesii*

THE HEMLOCKS *Tsuga*   Pages 90–91

Eastern Hemlock *Tsuga canadensis*

THE SPRUCES *Picea*   Pages 86–90
Needles more or less four-sided. Cones *pendulous*.

Colorado Blue Spruce
Picea pungens
Norway Spruce *Picea abies*

THE FIRS *Abies*   Pages 83–86
Needles usually flat. Cones *erect*.

Momi Fir
Abies firma

White or Colorado
Fir *Abies concolor*

Nordmann Fir
Abies nordmanniana

THE CEDARS *Cedrus*   Pages 80–81

Atlas Cedar *Cedrus atlantica*

2. Leaves deciduous (shedding in autumn)

LARCH *Larix*   Pages 92–93

European Larch *Larix decidua*

GOLDEN LARCH *Pseudolarix*   Pages 93–94

Golden Larch *Pseudolarix kaempferi*

TAXODIUM FAMILY   *Taxodiaceae*
Leaves needle-like or scale-like.

1. Leaves evergreen.

UMBRELLA-PINE *Sciadopitys verticillata*   Page 100

Umbrella-Pine *Sciadopitys verticillata*

CRYPTOMERIA, JAPANESE CEDAR *Cryptomeria japonica*
Page 100

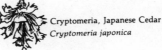

Cryptomeria, Japanese Cedar
Cryptomeria japonica

CHINESE FIR *Cunninghamia lanceolata*   Page 98

Chinese Fir *Cunninghamia lanceolata*

GIANT SEQUOIA *Sequoiadendron giganteum*   Page 99

Giant Sequoia *Sequoiadendron giganteum*

2. Leaves deciduous (shedding in autumn).

DAWN REDWOOD *Metasequoia glyptostroboides*   Pages 96–97

Leaves *opposite*, cone *stalked*.

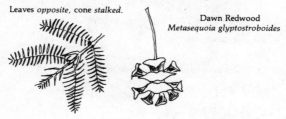

Dawn Redwood
Metasequoia glyptostroboides

BALD-CYPRESS *Taxodium distichum*   Pages 95–96

Leaves *alternate* or *sub-opposite*. Cone *sessile* (no stalk)
or with a very short stalk.

Bald-Cypress *Taxodium distichum*

CYPRESS FAMILY   *Cupressaceae*
Leaves usually scale-like and pressed against the branchlets.

CHAMAECYPARIS *Chamaecyparis*   Pages 102–3

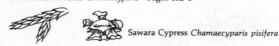

Sawara Cypress *Chamaecyparis pisifera*

EASTERN REDCEDAR, JUNIPER *Juniperus*   Page 104

Eastern Redcedar *Juniperus virginiana*

EASTERN WHITE CEDAR, ARBORVITAE *Thuja occidentalis*
Page 101

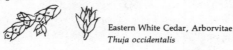

Eastern White Cedar, Arborvitae
Thuja occidentalis

ORIENTAL ARBORVITAE *Platycladus orientalis*   Page 101

Oriental Arborvitae *Platycladus orientalis*

INCENSE-CEDAR *Calocedrus decurrens*   Page 105

Incense-Cedar *Calocedrus decurrens*

LEYLAND CYPRESS x *Cupressocyparis leylandii*   Page 103

Leyland Cypress x *Cupressocyparis leylandii*

Illustrated Descriptions of Conifers

GINKGO
OR MAIDENHAIR TREE
Ginkgo biloba L.
Ginkgo Family *Ginkgoaceae*

The ginkgo tree, one of Washington's most striking Asian ornamentals, may be the oldest living tree species on earth. The enchanting ginkgo has remained almost unchanged since dinosaurs roamed the planet one hundred and twenty-five million years ago. Resistance to disease and immunity to insect pests, attributes that helped the ginkgo outlast the dinosaurs, also make it ideally suited for the rigors of urban life.

NATIVE HABITAT
Eastern China; long cultivated in Japan. (The genus *Ginkgo* was once represented in many parts of the world, including the western hemisphere. *Ginkgo biloba* is the only species in the genus still extant.)

LEAVES
Simple, alternate, deciduous, clustered on short spur shoots. Totally unique; fan-shaped, leathery, with numerous thin parallel veins that give the leaf a "ribbed" look. 1 - 3 in. (2.5 - 7.5 cm.) high, 2 - 4 in. (5 - 10 cm.) wide. May be unlobed or with one or more deep or shallow sinuses. Margin smooth on the sides, wavy across the top. Petiole 1 - 3 in. (2.5 - 7.5 cm.) long. Autumn color: Brilliant yellow in late October or early November. Washington's most spectacular fall tree. (The shape of the ginkgo leaf has suggested many things to many cultures. An old Chinese name for the tree, "ya chio," means "duck's foot." The ginkgo gained the modern common name "maidenhair tree" because the leaf resembles the maidenhair fern.)

FLOWERS
Male and female on separate trees. Males far more common, yellow, in thick hanging clusters, with the new spring leaves. Female looks like a small acorn on a long stalk.

FRUIT
On female trees only. Round or ovoid, pulpy, about an inch (2.5 cm.) long. Smooth and green, becoming yellow and wrinkled; containing an edible center. In the late fall

the fruit rots on the ground, emitting an infamous odor. (Although the edible "nut" is considered a delicacy in China, the idea of ingesting any part of a ginkgo fruit is anathema to most Americans. To avoid the odor emitted by the fruit of female trees, nurseries take great pains to propagate male trees only. However, it is hard to tell the sex of a young ginkgo tree; because only older ginkgoes produce fruit, innocuous "male" trees have been known to surprise their owners even after decades of fruitlessness.)

BARK AND TWIGS
Bark deeply furrowed and prominently ridged on mature trees. Twigs conspicuous in winter with their alternate woody spur shoots, up to an inch (2.5 cm.) long. Winter bud at the end of each shoot.

HABIT
A tall, sparsely branched, truly prehistoric looking tree. On young trees branches are upright or slightly bent inward. Crown spreads out with age.

SIMILAR SPECIES
None!

LOCATIONS
☐ 5th Street, N.W., Chinatown
☐ R Street, N.W. (across from Montrose Park)
☐ Duddington Place and Ivy Street, S.E.
☐ Corcoran Street, N.W.
☐ U.S. Capitol and Library of Congress grounds

FEMALE TREE LOCATIONS
☐ Scott Circle (16th and Massachusetts Avenue, N.W.)
☐ Arlington Cemetery, in front of the Custis-Lee Mansion (Arlington House)
☐ Library of Congress grounds

THE PINES
Pinus L.
Pine Family *Pinaceae*

The pines are the largest and most important genus of conifers in the northern hemisphere. About eighty species are distributed from the Arctic Circle to Central America, northern Africa, and the Malayan Archipelago. Pine trees are widely harvested for timber and frequently planted for shade and beauty.

FOLIAGE
Evergreen. Mature pine needles are borne in fascicled bundles of two - five (rarely one or more than five). The bundles are enclosed at the base in a small sheath that in some species soon falls off.

FLOWERS AND FRUIT
Male and female flowers are produced on the same tree. The small male flowers are usually orange, yellow, or red. The female flowers (which look like tiny cones) develop into the mature cones. Pine cones are made up of many woody scales that open up to release small, sometimes winged, seeds.

The pines in this book are divided into three groups.
The first is the "white" or "soft" pine group, containing
pines with needles in bundles of fives; the second group
contains pines with needles in bundles of twos; the third,
bundles of threes. And finally, in a category of its own,
is the shortleaf pine *(Pinus echinata)*, the state tree of
Arkansas, with needles in bundles of *twos and threes.*

The Soft Pines

The soft or white pine group is characterized by
needles in bundles of fives, pendulous, usually thin-
scaled, thornless cones, and wood that is soft, light and
not very resinous. The eastern white pine *(Pinus strobus*
L.) is by far the most commonly planted white pine in
Washington. However, three other species are in cultivation here.

Needles in Bundles of Fives
Eastern White Pine

Pinus strobus L.
Pine Family *Pinaceae*

STATE TREE OF MAINE & MICHIGAN

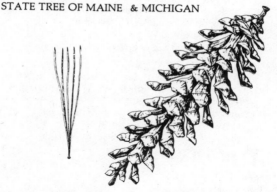

The lovely eastern white pine is one of Washington's most frequently planted conifers. The soft,
subtle beauty of this native tree perfectly complements
Washington's stone monuments: eastern white pines
encircle the Jefferson Memorial; they stand near the
Washington Monument and the Lincoln Memorial; and
the Lyndon Baines Johnson Memorial Grove is a stand
of young white pines. The eastern white pine is one
of America's most important timber trees.

NATIVE HABITAT
Newfoundland to Manitoba; south to Maryland, western
North Carolina, northern Georgia, eastern Tennessee,
and northeastern Iowa.

NEEDLES
Evergreen. Slender, in bundles of five, 2 - 5 in.
(5 - 12.5 cm.) long.

CONES
3 - 10 in. (7.5 - 25.3 cm.) long, slender, slightly tapered.
Scales are thornless.

BARK
Bark is dark purple-gray, deeply fissured, with broad scaly ridges.

HABIT
A tall tree with few horizontal limbs. Older tree trunks are often bare of branches until fairly high up.

SIMILAR SPECIES:
The similar Himalayan pine *(Pinus wallichiana)* is described below. The eastern white pine is far more commonly planted than any other pine with needles in bundles of fives.

LOCATIONS
- Jefferson Memorial
- Lyndon Baines Johnson Memorial Grove
- The White House (tree planted by President Gerald Ford)
- U.S. Capitol grounds (memorial tree)
- Potomac Parkway near Lincoln Memorial
- Washington Monument and the Mall
- National Gallery of Art
- Franciscan Monastery
- The Vice President's House
- National Zoo
- Vietnam Veterans Memorial
- Common throughout the city

HIMALAYAN PINE
OR BHUTAN PINE
Pinus wallichiana A.B. Jacks
(Pinus griffithii McClelland)
Pine Family *Pinaceae*

The Himalayan pine played an important role in the early evolution of *City of Trees*. The tree is so similar to the eastern white pine that it keys out perfectly to *Pinus strobus* in native field guides. The Himalayan was one of our first encounters with a rare exotic that could easily be mistaken for a native tree, a common occurrence in Washington and one of the primary reasons for creating this book!

NATIVE HABITAT: The Himalayas west to Afghanistan. **NEEDLES:** Evergreen, in bundles of fives. Slightly longer than white pine, 4 - 8 in. (10 - 20 cm.), and grayish-green. *Mature needles droop.* **CONES:** Similar to white pine, but usually longer and more resinous. **BARK:** Orange-gray, cracked into small plates. **HABIT:** Pyramidal tree with slightly drooping branches. **SIMILAR SPECIES:** The Himalayan pine's best distinguishing characteristics are its drooping needles and branches and its orangey-gray bark.
LOCATIONS:
- National Zoo (lion and tiger area)
- Maryland Avenue and Second Street, N.E.
- National Arboretum
- British Embassy
- Maryland Avenue, N.E. at 9th and E Streets
- Some private yards throughout the city

OTHER RARE WHITE PINES WITH NEEDLES
IN BUNDLES OF FIVES:

Two other members of the soft or white pine group
are planted in Washington, but they are very rare. The
limber pine (*Pinus flexilis* James), which is native to
mountainous regions of the western states and Alberta,
has 1½ - 3½ in. (3.8 - 9 cm.) needles in crowded, and
often twisted, groups of fives. Limber pine cones have
very *thick scales* for the white pine group; cones are
reddish-yellow in color and 2¾ - 6 in. (7 - 15 cm.) long.

LOCATIONS
☐ U.S. Capitol grounds
☐ Jefferson Memorial (young trees)
☐ Soldiers' Home
☐ National Arboretum

Limber Pine *Pinus flexilis*

The Swiss stone pine (*Pinus cembra* L.) is a rare tree
today, but the nursery trade has recently begun making
it available here. Native to the Alps and Carpathians of
Europe and Asia, this handsome tree has bundles of five
2 - 5 in. (5 - 12.5 cm.) needles, which are green on one
side and blue-white striped on the other. The cones are
egg-shaped or nearly round and 2 - 3¼ in. (5 - 8 cm.)
long.

LOCATIONS:
☐ National Arboretum
   Gotelli Dwarf Conifer Collection

NEEDLES IN GROUPS OF TWOS

AUSTRIAN PINE

Pinus nigra Arnold
Pine Family *Pinaceae*

The Austrian pine is widely cultivated in
Washington.

NATIVE HABITAT
Austria, Italy, Greece, and Yugoslavia.

FOLIAGE
Evergreen. Needles 4 - 6 in. (10 - 15 cm.) long, in
bundles of twos; very stiff, either straight or slightly
curved.

CONES
Yellowish, reddish or grayish-brown. Egg-shaped, 2 - 4
in. (5 - 10 cm.) long.

BARK
Gray or pinkish-gray, deeply cracked, and scaly.

HABIT
Pyramidal or flat-topped crown. Most Washington specimens have short trunks and many level or slightly
ascending branches.

SIMILAR SPECIES
Very difficult to distinguish from the Japanese black pine
(*Pinus thunbergiana*). Habit is the characteristic that
differs most greatly between the two. The Austrian pine
is usually single-trunked and upright, while the Japanese
black pine's trunk tends to lean slightly and to fork into
two or more main limbs.

LOCATIONS
☐ Library of Congress grounds
☐ East Potomac Park
☐ Public buildings and private homes throughout the city

JAPANESE BLACK PINE
Pinus thunbergiana Franco.
(*Pinus thunbergii* Parl.)
Pine Family *Pinaceae*

This tree is quite commonly planted here.

NATIVE HABITAT: Japan. **FOLIAGE AND CONES:**
Very similar to Austrian pine (*Pinus nigra*) but
slightly shorter: needles 2¼ - 4½ in. (5.5 - 11.3 cm)
long; cones 1½ - 2½ in. (3.8 - 6.3 cm.) **BARK:** Dark
gray, fissured. **HABIT:** Mature trees usually slightly
leaning and forked into two or more widely divergent
main limbs; crown often irregular, somewhat jagged in
appearance. **SIMILAR SPECIES:** Even botanists have a
hard time telling the Japanese black pine and the Austrian pine apart. The leaning, forked trunk of the Japanese black pine and its irregular crown are its best
distinguishing characteristics. However, trees do not
assume this in some settings. The best location to see
these two very similar trees growing side by side is East
Potomac Park.
LOCATIONS:
☐ East Potomac Park
☐ Library of Congress courtyard
☐ Hillwood Estate (Japanese garden)
☐ Public buildings and private yards throughout the city
See illustrations for Austrian pine (*Pinus nigra*).

RED PINE OR NORWAY PINE

Pinus resinosa Ait.
Pine Family *Pinaceae*

STATE TREE OF MINNESOTA

Three healthy young specimens of the sturdy red pine were planted on the lawn of the Vice President's House by Minnesotan Walter Mondale in 1979. The Mondale trees came from a nursery in Minnesota.

NATIVE HABITAT
Nova Scotia to Manitoba; south to New Jersey, Pennsylvania, Michigan, and Minnesota.

FOLIAGE
Evergreen. Needles in bundles of twos, 4 - 7 in. (10 - 17.8 cm.) long. Straight, slender, dark yellowish-green.

CONES
Egg-shaped or somewhat elongated, 1½ - 2½ in. (3.8 - 6.3 cm.) long, reddish-brown. When cone falls, it leaves a few scales on the tree.

BARK
Reddish-brown, fissured, and scaly.

HABIT
Broad, rounded, or pyramidal crown. Spreading branches are sometimes slightly pendulous.

SIMILAR SPECIES
The long needles set the red pine apart from other locally planted pines with needles in bundles of twos.

LOCATIONS
☐ The Vice President's House
☐ U.S. Capitol grounds
☐ Some public buildings and private homes throughout the city

JAPANESE RED PINE
Pinus densiflora Sieb. & Zucc.
Pine Family *Pinaceae*

It is hard to understand why the Japanese red pine isn't more widely offered in the nursery trade. Almost any garden could happily accommodate this delicate Asian tree.

NATIVE HABITAT
Japan

FOLIAGE
Evergreen. Needles 2¾ - 4¾ in. (about 7 - 12 cm.) long, in bundles of twos.

CONES
Delicate egg-shaped or oblong cones are ¾ - 2 in. (2 - 5 cm.) long.

BARK
Thin, scaly, orange-brown, or reddish.

HABIT
A small tree with few branches and a broad, flat-topped, or rounded crown.

SIMILAR SPECIES
Size of cones combined with reddish or orange-brown bark separate the Japanese red pine from other species.

LOCATIONS
☐ National Park Service Headquarters,
   East Potomac Park
☐ U.S. Capitol grounds

SCRUB PINE OR VIRGINIA PINE
Pinus virginiana Mill.
Pine Family *Pinaceae*

The most common pine in Rock Creek Park; infrequently cultivated.

NATIVE HABITAT
Southern New York south to South Carolina and Mississippi; west to Tennessee, Kentucky, and southern Indiana.

FOLIAGE
Evergreen. Needles 1½ - 3 in. (3.8 - 7.5 cm.) long in bundles of two. Stout, twisted, grayish-green.

CONES
Egg-shaped, 1½ - 3 in. (3.8 - 7.5 cm.) long; scales thin, with spines.

HABIT
A small tree with a scraggly crown; trunk often crooked.

SIMILAR SPECIES
Jack pine (*Pinus banksiana* Lamb.) (which is rarely cultivated and not included in this guide) has slightly shorter needles and cones; Jack pine cones have no spines or small spines that soon fall off.

LOCATIONS
☐ National Zoo
☐ National Arboretum
☐ Walter Reed Army Medical Center
☐ Rock Creek Park
☐ Hillwood Estate
☐ Some parks and private homes throughout the city

SCOTS PINE

Pinus sylvestris L.
Pine Family *Pinaceae*

An important European timber tree and popular ornamental. Not widely cultivated in Washington.

NATIVE HABITAT: Europe to Siberia. **FOLIAGE:** Evergreen. Short, bluish-green, twisted needles are 1 - 2¾ in. (2.5 - 7 cm.) long, in bundles of twos. **CONES:** Egg-shaped, 1 - 2½ in. (2.5 - 6.3 cm.) long. **BARK:** Reddish-brown, scaly.
LOCATIONS:
☐ National Arboretum
☐ Some public buildings and private yards

Needles in Bundles of Threes

Loblolly Pine

Pinus taeda L.
Pine Family *Pinaceae*

A beautiful southern pine, with a tall, straight trunk and cinnamon-colored bark.

NATIVE HABITAT
Southern New Jersey to Florida; west to eastern Texas.

FOLIAGE
Evergreen. Needles slender, 4½ - 10 in. (11.4 - 25.3 cm.) long, in bundles of threes (rarely twos).

CONES
Conic when closed, egg-shaped when open, 2½ - 6½ in. (6.3 - 16.5 cm.) long. Scales armed with stout, sharp spines.

BARK
Cinnamon-colored and broken into thick scales on mature trees.

HABIT
A tall tree with a long, clear trunk and dense, rounded crown.

SIMILAR SPECIES
Shortleaf pine (*Pinus echinata*) has shorter needles, in bundles of twos and threes, and cones armed with smaller spines.

LOCATIONS
☐ Rock Creek Park
☐ National Arboretum

PITCH PINE

Pinus rigida Mill.
Pine Family *Pinaceae*

A native pine that is not often cultivated.

NATIVE HABITAT: Maine and southern Ontario south to western South Carolina, northern Georgia, and eastern Tennessee. **FOLIAGE:** Evergreen. Stiff, stout, usually twisted needles, 3 - 5 in. (7.5 - 12.6 cm.) long, in bundles of threes. **CONES:** Egg-shaped, 1½ - 3½ in. (3.8 - 9 cm.) long; scales armed with short, stiff spines. **BARK:** Reddish-brown, furrowed. **HABIT:** Nearly horizontal branches and an irregular crown. **SIMILAR SPECIES:** Shortleaf pine (*Pinus echinata*) has straight, not twisted, needles in bunches of twos and threes.

LOCATIONS:
☐ National Arboretum
☐ Rock Creek Park
☐ George Washington Memorial Parkway
☐ Mount Vernon

LACE-BARK PINE

Pinus bungeana Zucc. ex Endl.
Pine Family *Pinaceae*

This rare tree is now carried by some nurseries. It has the most beautiful bark of any pine tree.

NATIVE HABITAT: China. **FOLIAGE:** Evergreen. Dark yellow-green needles, 2 - 3½ in. (5 - 9 cm.) long, in bundles of threes. **CONES:** Egg-shaped, 1½ - 3 in. (3.8 - 7.5 cm.) long; scales are very thick and armed with sharp spines. **BARK:** Absolutely beautiful; more like a plane tree than a pine. Thin gray and olive green outer bark flakes away to leave cream, green, yellow, and pale purple patches. **HABIT:** Somewhat shrubby; usually multi-trunked with a low crown. **SIMILAR SPECIES:** The bark is a give-away. No other pine has anything like it.
LOCATIONS:
☐ National Arboretum

LONGLEAF PINE

Pinus palustris Mill.
Pine Family *Pinaceae*

A lovely southern tree with very long needles. Quite rare in Washington.

NATIVE HABITAT
Southeastern Virginia to Florida; west to eastern Texas.

FOLIAGE
Evergreen. Needles 8 - 18 in. (20 - 45.5 cm.) long, in bundles of threes.

CONES
Conic when closed, egg-shaped when open, 4 - 10 in.
(10 - 25.3 cm.) long. Large scales armed with short, thin,
incurved spines.

BARK
Orange-brown, rough and scaly.

SIMILAR SPECIES
No other pine commonly cultivated in Washington has
such long needles.

LOCATIONS
☐ Arlington Cemetery, in front of the Custis-Lee
   Mansion (Arlington House)
☐ National Arboretum

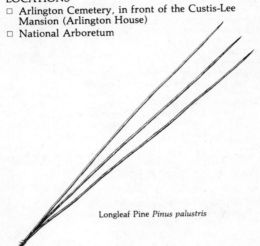

Longleaf Pine *Pinus palustris*

NEEDLES IN TWOS AND THREES
SHORTLEAF PINE
Pinus echinata Mill.
Pine Family *Pinaceae*

STATE TREE OF ARKANSAS

An important timber tree. Sometimes cultivated
for ornament.

NATIVE HABITAT: Southeastern New York to northern
Florida; west to eastern Texas, Oklahoma, and southern
Missouri. **FOLIAGE:** Evergreen. Needles 3 - 5 in. (7.5 -
12.5 cm.) long, *in bundles of twos and sometimes threes.*
CONES: Oblong-conic when closed, egg-shaped when
open, 1½ - 3 in. (3.8 - 7.5 cm.) long; thin scales armed
with small, sharp spines. **BARK:** Reddish-brown and
scaly on mature trees. **SIMILAR SPECIES:** Red pine
(*Pinus resinosa*) has needles in twos and *cones scales
without spines.* Loblolly pine (*Pinus taeda*) has *longer
needles* (usually in threes) and cone scales armed with
stout spines. Pitch pine (*Pinus rigida*) has needles in
threes which are *usually twisted.*
LOCATIONS:
☐ U.S. Capitol grounds
☐ National Arboretum
☐ Some parks and private yards throughout the city

THE TRUE CEDARS

(*Cedrus* Trew.)

Pine Family *Pinaceae*

While the name "cedar" is applied to several trees in our native flora, none of the true cedars is native to this continent. The genus is made up of four closely related species, three of which are in cultivation in Washington. The cedars are the only *evergreen* conifers that bear their foliage on *short spur shoots* on mature branchlets. Like the spruces, the cedars bear *erect cones*.

KEY TO THE CEDARS COMMONLY CULTIVATED
IN WASHINGTON, D.C.

1a) New shoot gently drooping . . . . Deodar Cedar (*Cedrus deodara*)
1b) New shoot stiff; level or ascending.
    2a) Foliage bluish-green to bright blue-white; needles ⅓ - 1 (1 - 2.5 cm.) long. Branches both ascending and level . . . .
    . . . . Atlas Cedar (*Cedrus atlantica*)
    2b) Foliage dark green, grayish-green or bluish-green; needles usually 1 - 1¼ in. (2.5 - 3 cm.) long. Upper branches level and layered . . .
    . . . . Cedar of Lebanon (*Cedrus libani*)

ATLAS CEDAR OR SILVER ATLAS CEDAR, OR ATLANTIC CEDAR

Cedrus atlantica (Endl.) G. Manetti ex Carrière
Cedrus atlantica 'Glauca'
Pine Family *Pinaceae*

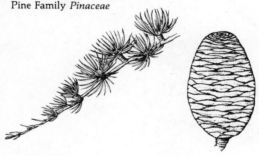

A very impressive tree, with somewhat helter-skelter ascending and level branches. The bright blue-white color of the form most often planted here is breathtaking, especially after a snowfall.

NATIVE HABITAT
Atlas Mountains of Algeria and Morocco.

FOLIAGE
Evergreen. Color varies from blue-gray to blue-white (in the cultivar 'Glauca'). New shoots are *stiff and usually slightly ascending*. Needles on older growth borne in clusters on spur shoots. Each needle stiff, pointed, ⅓ - 1 in. (about 1 - 2.5 cm.) long.

CONES
Erect, egg-shaped or barrel-shaped; greenish, tinged purple when young, becoming purplish-brown at maturity. 2 - 3½ in. (5 - 9 cm.) high, often slightly concave at apex.

BARK AND BRANCHLETS
Bark gray, smooth when young, becoming fissured and
scaly with age. Branchlets with short pubescence and
small, ovoid winter buds.

HABIT
Distinctive combination of ascending and level branches;
crown pyramidal. Easily distinguished from the other
commonly planted cedar (*Cedrus deodara*) by habit alone.

SIMILAR SPECIES
The rare cedar of Lebanon (*Cedrus libani*) has mostly
level branches, greener foliage, and needles that are one
inch long or longer (2.5 - 3 cm.). The deodar cedar has
new shoots that *arch downward.*

LOCATIONS
□ The White House
□ Rock Creek Cemetery
□ Hillwood Estate
□ Franciscan Monastery
□ National Arboretum
□ Washington Cathedral
□ Franklin Park
□ Several specimens between 17th and 18th Streets,
  N.W. near the National Headquarters of the Red Cross

Deodar Cedar

Cedrus deodara (Roxb.) G. Don
Pine Family *Pinaceae*

The true cedars are Washington's most striking conifers. Their tall, dark silhouettes give great depth to the
city's landscape. The deodar cedar is the most commonly
planted of the three species growing here. A magnificent
specimen of this tree stands in back of the Custis-Lee
Mansion (or Arlington House) in Arlington Cemetery.

NATIVE HABITAT: Himalayan Mountains. **FOLIAGE:**
Evergreen. New shoots *arch gently downward.* Needles
on older growth borne in clusters on short spur shoots.
Each needle stiff, sharply pointed, usually triangular in
cross-section; ¾ - 2 in. (2 - 5 cm.) long, gray-green.
CONES: Erect, barrel-shaped or egg-shaped; somewhat
bluish when young, becoming reddish-brown toward
maturity. 2½ - 4 in. (6.3 - 10 cm.) long. Cones take two
to three years to mature. **BARK AND BRANCHLETS:**
Bark grayish-green and smooth on young trees; becoming dark gray or brown, fissured and scaly, with age.
Young branchlets densely pubescent. Winter buds tiny,
ovoid, and pointed. **HABIT:** The most graceful of all the
large conifers planted here. The crown is pyramidal
(except on a few old trees such as the one behind the
Custis-Lee Mansion). The branches are large, dramatically sweeping, and sparsely set, creating an impressive
profile. **SIMILAR SPECIES:** The best way to distinguish
the deodar cedar from the other true cedars in Washington is by the new shoot, which gently arches downward. New growth on the cedar of Lebanon (*Cedrus
libani*) and the Atlas cedar (*Cedrus atlantica*) is level
or ascending.

LOCATIONS:
- ☐ Arlington Cemetery
- ☐ Dumbarton Oaks
- ☐ Hillwood Estate
- ☐ The White House
- ☐ National Zoo
- ☐ Folger Park
- ☐ Common throughout the city

See illustrations for Atlas cedar (*Cedrus atlantica*).

CEDAR OF LEBANON

Cedrus libani A. Rich.
Pine Family *Pinaceae*

The cedar of Lebanon is the famous tree of the Holy Land that provided the wood for King Solomon's temple, according to legend. This tree is rare in Washington, despite the widespread belief that it is commonly cultivated here.

NATIVE HABITAT: Asia Minor, Syria. **DISTINGUISHING CHARACTERISTICS:** The cedar of Lebanon closely resembles the two other true cedars that are commonly planted in the area. It can be distinguished from the deodar cedar (*Cedrus deodara*) by its *stiff, level, or ascending new shoots.* (While the new growth on the cedar of Lebanon may nod toward the very tip of the branchlet, *the entire new shoot on the deodar gently droops.*) It is more difficult to tell the cedar of Lebanon and the Atlas cedar (*Cedrus atlantica*) apart. The blue-white form of the latter species (*C. atlantica* 'Glauca') is readily distinguishable. When the foliage is grayish or bluish-green, the following characteristics should be compared:

CEDAR OF LEBANON

Needles on older growth up to 1¼ in. (3 cm.) long.

Upper branches level and layered; crown often develops a "table top" effect.

ATLANTIC CEDAR

Needles on older growth usually less than 1 in. (2.5 cm. or less long.

Branches *ascending and level*; crown usually pyramidal.

LOCATIONS:
- ☐ The White House (young tree planted by President Jimmy Carter)
- ☐ Fairchild's old estate near the Beltway and Connecticut Avenue, Chevy Chase, MD. (Turkish form of the tree with slightly shorter needles)
- ☐ George Washington's gravesite, Mount Vernon

(See illustrations for Atlas cedar (*Cedrus atlantica*).)

THE FIRS

Abies Mill.
Pine Family *Pinaceae*

Firs are the "Christmas tree genus." Their pleasantly aromatic foliage stays on the tree longer than most other evergreen needles, and their lovely shapes conjure up romantic images of snow-covered forests. The genus is characterized by *erect* cones and usually *flat* needles that are often grooved above and frequently have two pale parallel bands below.

NORDMANN FIR
OR CAUCASIAN FIR

Abies nordmanniana (Steven) Spach.

The lovely Nordmann fir is the true fir most commonly planted in Washington.

NATIVE HABITAT
Caucasus, Asia Minor.

FOLIAGE
Evergreen. Needles stiff, ½ - 1½ in. (1.3 - 3.8 cm.) long. Lustrous above and grooved down the middle; two parallel white bands below. The blunt tip is *notched*. Needles radiate from sides and top of branchlet and most point gently and evenly forward.

CONES
Tall, erect, cylindric; usually on upper branches only. Pale green at first, becoming dark reddish-brown. 4½ - 7½ in. (11.4 - 19 cm.) long.

BARK AND BRANCHLETS
Bark grayish-brown, sometimes becoming fissured with age. Branchlets reddish or grayish-brown, pubescent or nearly glabrous. Winter buds reddish-brown, ovoid, not resinous.

HABIT
Attractive narrow pyramidal form.

SIMILAR SPECIES
No other true fir is commonly planted in Washington. The rare Greek fir (*Abies cephalonica*) has needles that are *not notched* at the tips.

LOCATIONS
- ☐ Along Independence Avenue near the Washington Monument
- ☐ Walter Reed Army Medical Center
- ☐ Lafayette Park
- ☐ Montrose Park
- ☐ Kenilworth Aquatic Gardens
- ☐ Soldiers' Home
- ☐ National Zoo
- ☐ Quite common in parks and private yards throughout the city

MOMI FIR

Abies firma Sieb. & Zucc.
Pine Family *Pinaceae*

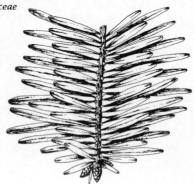

A rare tree, planted in a few parks and private yards.

NATIVE HABITAT
Japan.

FOLIAGE
Evergreen. Needles thick, stiff, ¾ - 1½ in. (about 2 - 4 cm.) long. Usually notched at tip; shallowly grooved above with two gray parallel bands below. Needles arranged on each side of the branchlet like the teeth of a comb (or sometimes with needles radiating from the top of the branchlet, too).

CONES
Erect, cylindric, 3 - 6 in. (7.5 - 15.2 cm.) long. Yellowish-green when young, becoming brown at maturity.

BARK AND BRANCHLETS
Bark dark pinkish-gray, often becoming scaly and fissured with age. Branchlets light grayish or reddish-brown with (usually pubescent) grooves. Winter buds ovoid, reddish-brown, slightly resinous.

HABIT
Pyramidal tree with nearly horizontal branches.

SIMILAR SPECIES
The white or Colorado fir (*Abies concolor*) has slightly longer needles that are irregularly arranged on the branchlet and usually curved.

LOCATIONS
- ☐ Montrose Park
- ☐ National Arboretum

WHITE FIR
OR COLORADO FIR

Abies concolor (Gord. & Glend.) Lindl. ex. Hildebr.
Pine Family *Pinaceae*

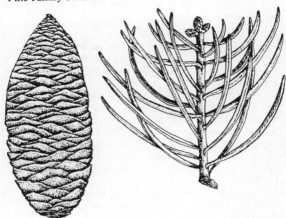

Another handsome fir; not very commonly planted in Washington's public parks but a rather popular backyard tree.

NATIVE HABITAT
Colorado west to California; south to New Mexico and northern Mexico.

FOLIAGE
Evergreen. Needles long, thin, often curved forward or upswept; irregularly arranged on branchlet. 1¼ - 2½ in. (about 3 - 6 cm.) long, dull blue-green or yellow-green above with two slightly paler bands beneath. Needle tip pointed, rounded or rarely with a tiny notch. Foliage emits a strong smell of lemon and balsam when crushed.

CONES
Erect, cylindric, 2¾ - 6 in. (about 7 - 15 cm.) long. Greenish or purplish when young, becoming brown at maturity.

BARK AND BRANCHLETS
Bark gray, smooth on young trees but often growing scaly and fissured with age. Branchlets yellowish or greenish-brown, glabrous or slightly pubescent. Winter buds rounded, resinous.

HABIT
Pyramidal; crown may grow rounded with age.

SIMILAR SPECIES
Momi fir (*Abies firma*) has needles that are *thick, stiff,* and regularly arranged.

LOCATIONS
☐ Washington Monument grounds
☐ Hillwood Estate
☐ Soldiers' Home
☐ Connecticut Avenue and Calvert Street, N.W.

GREEK FIR
Abies cephalonica Loud.
Pine Family *Pinaceae*

A beautiful, but extremely rare tree.

NATIVE HABITAT: Greece and southern Yugoslavia.
FOLIAGE: Evergreen Needles stiff, ½ - 1¼ in. (1.3 - 3.2 cm.) long; upper needles are usually shorter than those on the sides of the twig. Needle tips pointed, sometimes sharply so. Two parallel white bands below. Needles radiate from all parts of branchlet; most point forward.
CONES: Erect, cylindric; greenish-brown when young, brown at maturity. 4½ - 7 in. (11.4 - 17.8 cm.) long.
BARK AND BRANCHLETS: Bark grayish-brown, sometimes becoming fissured with age. Branchlets reddish-brown, glabrous. Needles have bases that look like small suction cups and leave large scars on the twig when they fall. Winter buds ovoid, reddish-brown, resinous.
HABIT: Pyramidal at first, but may become flat-topped with age. Older trees have heavy low-sweeping branches.
SIMILAR SPECIES: Commonly planted Nordmann fir has needles with notched tips.
LOCATIONS:
☐ Across 17th Street from Pan American Union (near corner of Constitution Avenue)

OTHER FIRS (MEMBERS OF THE GENUS *Abies*) IN THE WASHINGTON AREA

A specimen of the handsome Fraser fir (*Abies fraseri*(Pursh) Poir.), native only to the high southern Appalachians, is growing in Fern Valley at the National Arboretum. Several other rare species of fir are also planted at the Arboretum.

THE SPRUCES
Picea A. Dietr.
Pine Family *Pinaceae*

The two spruces most commonly cultivated in Washington are the Norway Spruce (*Picea abies*) and the Colorado Blue (*Picea pungens*). The spruce genus is characterized by usually *four-sided* needles and *pendulous* cones, distinguishing them from the firs which have *flat* needles and bear *erect* cones.

KEY TO SPRUCES COMMONLY CULTIVATED IN WASHINGTON, D.C.

1a) Branchlets drooping, giving the tree a *weeping* look.
    2a) Needles ½ - 1 in. (1.2 - 2.5 cm.) long; cones 4 - 7 in. (10 - 18 cm.) long . . . . Norway Spruce (*Picea abies*).
    2b) Needles less than ½ in. (less than 1.2 cm.) long; cones 3½ in. or less (9 cm. or less) in length . . . .
        . . . . Oriental Spruce (*Picea orientalis*).
1b) Branchlets not drooping or only slightly so.
    3a) Foliage silvery-blue or gray . . . .
        . . . . Colorado Blue Spruce (*Picea pungens*).
    3b) Foliage green or bluish green . . . .
        . . . . see OTHER SPRUCES CULTIVATED IN THE WASHINGTON AREA

NORWAY SPRUCE

Picea abies (L.) Karst.
Pine Family *Pinaceae*

A tall tree with weeping branchlets and long, pendulous cones. Widely planted in temperate North America, including the Washington area.

NATIVE HABITAT
Central and northern Europe

FOLIAGE
Evergreen. Needles *four-sided*, dark green, ½ - 1 in. (1.2 - 2.5 cm.) long.

CONES
4 - 7 in. (10 - 18 cm.) long, pendulous, green when young, ripening to reddish-brown. Cone scales stiff, broadly wedge-shaped.

BRANCHLETS
Drooping, usually glabrous.

HABIT
A tall, conical tree with *weeping* branchlets.

SIMILAR SPECIES
The less commonly cultivated Oriental Spruce (*Picea orientalis*) has shorter needles and smaller cones.

LOCATIONS
☐ National Zoo
☐ Tidal Basin
☐ Arlington Cemetery
☐ Franciscan Monastery
☐ Hillwood Estate
☐ Vice President's House
☐ Washington Cathedral

ORIENTAL SPRUCE
Picea orientalis (L.) Link
Pine Family *Pinaceae*

NATIVE HABITAT
Caucasus and Asia Minor. Similar to preceding species
but far less commonly cultivated. Needles are *shorter*
and cones are *smaller* than those of Norway Spruce
(*Picea abies*). Drooping branchlets are *pubescent*.

LOCATIONS
☐ Franciscan Monastery
☐ Pan American Union
☐ National Zoo
☐ National Arboretum

COLORADO BLUE SPRUCE
Picea pungens Engelm.
Pine Family *Pinaceae*

Many forms of the Colorado Blue Spruce, including
the cultivar 'Glauca', are widely planted throughout the
United States and Europe. Colorado Blue Spruce foliage
is a lovely silvery blue.

NATIVE HABITAT
Rocky Mountains

FOLIAGE
Evergreen. Gray to blue needles are *four-sided*, sharp-
pointed, curved and very stiff, ½ - 1¼ in. (1.2 - 3.2
cm.) long.

CONES
2 - 4½ in. (5 - 11.5 cm.) long, pendulous, green when
young then reddish-brown. Cone scales stiff with irregularly toothed margins.

SIMILAR SPECIES
Foliage color distinguishes the Colorado Blue from other
spruces planted in Washington.

LOCATIONS
- ☐ United States Botanic Gardens
- ☐ Soldiers' Home
- ☐ Rock Creek Cemetery
- ☐ Frederick Douglass Home

OTHER SPRUCES CULTIVATED IN THE
WASHINGTON AREA

WHITE SPRUCE
Picea glauca (Moench) Voss
Pine Family *Pinaceae*

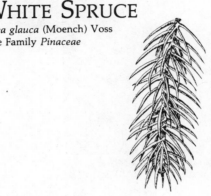

NATIVE HABITAT
Most of Canada, northern U.S. in New England,
Midwest, Plains States and Alaska. Tree with an evenly
conical crown, green or bluish-green four-sided needles
that are bluntly pointed, ⅔ - ¾ in. (2 cm. or less) long.
Pendulous cones are slender, 1½ - 3 in. (3.8 - 7.7 cm.)
long. Cone scales thin, flexible, with rounded margins.

LOCATIONS
- ☐ Hillwood Estate
- ☐ Montrose Park
- ☐ National Zoo

SERBIAN SPRUCE
Picea omorika (Panc.) Purk.
Pine Family *Pinaceae*

NATIVE HABITAT: Yugoslavia. Another rare spruce,
which is now available at some nurseries. The Serbian
spruce has a very narrow, steeple-like crown. The blunt-
tipped or abruptly pointed needles are slightly flattened
and marked with two broad, white bands below. Cones
are small, less than 2½ in. (6 cm. or less) long.
LOCATIONS:
- ☐ National Arboretum
- ☐ Some private yards

TIGERTAIL SPRUCE
Picea polita (Sieb. & Zucc.) Carr.
Pine Family *Pinaceae*

NATIVE HABITAT
Japan. The rare tigertail spruce has stiff, *sharply spined* needles that are actually painful to the touch. They are curved forward and very stout.

LOCATIONS
☐ Montrose Park
☐ National Arboretum

EASTERN HEMLOCK
Tsuga canadensis (L.) Carr.
Pine Family *Pinaceae*

A delicately foliaged evergreen indigenous to the cool, moist woodlands of the northeastern U.S. and southeastern Canada. Its seeds, bark and young shoots provide an important food source for birds, deer and other mammals during the winter months while its sweeping branches serve as an excellent storm shelter. There is nothing quite so peaceful (for human, bird or beast) as a hemlock grove during a quiet snowfall.

NATIVE HABITAT
Southeastern Canada, northeastern U.S.: in the Appalachians south to Georgia; west to the Great Lakes.

FOLIAGE
Evergreen. Needles flat, ⅓ - ¾ in. (1 - 2 cm.) long. Rounded or just barely notched at the tip; usually slightly vertically grooved above, with two pale parallel bands below. Arranged on a horizontal plane.

CONES
Small, delicate, pendulous. ½ - 1 in. (1.2 - 2.5 cm.)
long, with thin, light brown scales. Ovoid, on a
short stalk.

BARK
Reddish brown, separating into large, thin, peeling
scales. Becoming deeply furrowed with age.

HABIT
Medium-sized or large tree with a pyramidal crown,
tapered trunk and long, sweeping branches.

SIMILAR SPECIES
Cones, almost always present, are distinctive of the
genus. See rare Carolina hemlock, described below.

LOCATIONS
□ Dumbarton Oaks
□ Franciscan Monastery
□ National Zoo
□ Hillwood Estate
□ Meridian Hill Park

CAROLINA HEMLOCK

Tsuga caroliniana Engelm.
Pine Family *Pinaceae*

Another beautiful hemlock; rarely planted in
Washington. The Carolina hemlock is native only to the
southern Appalachians, in Virginia, Tennessee, the Caro-
linas and Georgia where it grows next to stream beds
and along the lower slopes of the Blue Ridge. Distinguished from the Eastern hemlock by its needles, which
are arranged *all the way around the branchlet*, rather
than on a horizontal plane and by its cones, which are
slightly longer (1 - 1½ in. (2.5 - 3.8 cm.)), with
longer stalks.
LOCATIONS:
□ Fern Valley, National Arboretum
□ Private yards

Douglas-Fir

Pseudotsuga menziesii (Mirb.) Franco.
(*Pseudotsuga taxifolia* (Poir.) Britt.)
Pine Family *Pinaceae*

In 1974, Washington State's two reigning U.S. Senators, Henry Jackson and Warren Magnuson, presided over
the Capitol Hill planting of a young Douglas-fir. The tree
is an important timber tree in the West.

NATIVE HABITAT
British Columbia to California; south and east to Mexico
and Colorado.

FOLIAGE
Evergreen. ¾ - 2 in. (2 - 5 cm.) long, flat, straight or
slightly curved, vertically grooved above, with pale
vertical bands below. Apex blunt or rounded.

CONES
Very distinctive. Pendulous, 2 - 4 in. (5 - 10 cm.) long,
with *thin, three-pronged bracts hanging below the scales*
(see illustration).

HABIT
Trees in cultivation here rarely attain the stature or form
of those in their native habitat. Trees found in Washington have conical crowns with ascending upper branches.

SIMILAR SPECIES
May be confused with fir, spruce or hemlock. Best distinguished by its cones.

LOCATIONS
□ U.S. Capitol grounds
□ Washington Cathedral
□ Hillwood Estate

European Larch

Larix decidua Mill.
Pine Family *Pinaceae*

Closely related to the tamarack or Eastern larch (*Larix laricina* (Du Roi) K. Koch), not included in this guide, which is indigenous to the northeastern U.S., much of Canada and Alaska. The European larch turns golden before shedding its leaves in autumn.

NATIVE HABITAT
Northern, central and eastern Europe.

FOLIAGE
Clusters of bright green, ¾ - 1¼ in. (2 - 3 cm.) long needles clustered at the ends of *lateral shoots.*

CONES
Cones ¾ - 1¾ in. (2 - 4.5 cm.) long with somewhat wavy scales.

BARK
Gray or pinkish gray, ridged and scaly.

HABIT
Pyramidal crown, growing irregular with age.

SIMILAR SPECIES
See golden larch (*Pseudolarix kaempferi*), below. While it is conceivable that some other members of the genus *Larix* may be planted in some private yards, the European larch is the one most likely to be encountered.

LOCATIONS
□ Saint Elizabeth's Hospital
□ Pan American Union
□ Public buildings and private yards throughout the city

GOLDEN LARCH
Pseudolarix kaempferi Gord.
(*Pseudolarix amabilis* (J. Nels.) Rehd.)
Pine Family *Pinaceae*

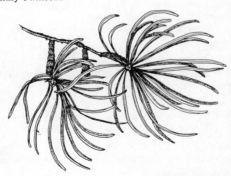

A rarely planted conifer that turns bright orange-bronze before shedding its leaves in autumn and resembles the European larch (*Larix decidua*).

NATIVE HABITAT
Eastern China

FOLIAGE
Needles *coarser* and *larger* than European larch, borne on long, curved spur shoots that are *thickest at the tip* (where needles are joined).

CONES
Resemble a small artichoke, with thick, triangular scales. Cones 1¾ - 3 in. (4.5 - 7.5 cm.) long.

SIMILAR SPECIES
European larch, already described.

LOCATIONS
- ☐ Northeast Capitol grounds
- ☐ Walter Reed Hospital
- ☐ Some private homes, public buildings throughout the city

CRYPTOMERIA OR JAPANESE CEDAR
Cryptomeria japonica (L. f.) D. Don
Taxodium Family *Taxodiaceae*

Cryptomeria is one of Japan's most highly valued trees. It is an important timber tree as well as a favorite ornamental.

NATIVE HABITAT
Japan, China.

FOLIAGE
Evergreen. Needles bright green, ¼ - ¾ in. (6 mm. - 2 cm.) long; widest at the base, tapering to a sharp point, and *curving inward* toward the branchlet. Flattened and ridged on both sides.

CONES
Round, or nearly round, ½ - 1 in. (1.3 - 2.5 cm.) in diameter; remaining on the tree after splitting to release seeds. Wedge-shaped scales bear small, curved spines.

BARK AND TWIGS
Bark reddish-brown, peeling in long thin strips. Branchlets and tiny winter buds concealed under the needles.

HABIT
Trunk straight and tapering; crown narrowly pyramidal.

SIMILAR SPECIES
No tree is apt to be confused with Cryptomeria.

LOCATIONS
- ☐ U.S. Capitol grounds
- ☐ Meridian Hill Park
- ☐ Japanese Ambassador's residence
- ☐ British Embassy
- ☐ Franciscan Monastery
- ☐ Hillwood Estate
- ☐ National Arboretum
- ☐ Quite commonly planted throughout the city

BALD-CYPRESS
OR SWAMP CYPRESS
Taxodium distichum (L.) Rich.
Taxodium Family *Taxodiaceae*
STATE TREE OF LOUISIANA

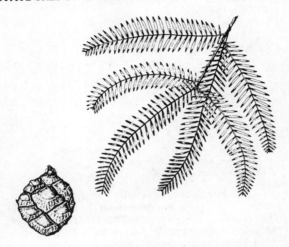

The bald-cypress is the Spanish moss-draped tree of
southern swamps and stream banks that produces "knees",
the peculiar woody root projections that protrude above
the water. Although the bald-cypress is no longer native
to the Washington area, botanists have found evidence
indicating that much of this area was once a cypress
swamp like the ones common in the Deep South.

NATIVE HABITAT
Coastal plain from southern Maryland and Delaware to
Florida; west to Texas and north in the Mississippi River
Valley to southern Illinois and Indiana.

FOLIAGE
Deciduous. Delicate yellow-green needles are *alternately*
arranged on slender, deciduous shoots. Each needle
¼ -¾ in. (6 mm. - 2 cm.) long. Alternately arranged
deciduous shoots vary in length, from 2 - several inches
(5 cm. or more). Foliage turns dull orange-brown in
autumn before falling.

CONES
Round or ovoid, pale green at first, becoming purplish-
brown. ⅔ - 1 in. (1.5 - 2.5 cm.) in diameter; scales
peltately attached (attached at the center, rather than the
base of the cone). Short-stalked or nearly sessile.

BARK AND BRANCHLETS
Bark reddish-brown or grayish-brown, separating into
thin shreds and shallow vertical fissures. Branchlets
reddish-brown with small rounded winter buds.

HABIT
Tall tree with tapered trunk, and nearly horizontal
branches. Base of trunk is *usually fluted*.
Crown pyramidal.

SIMILAR SPECIES
See pond cypress (*Taxodium distichum* var. *nutans*).
Very similar to the dawn redwood (*Metasequoia glyptostroboides*) which has *oppositely arranged* foliage and cones on long stalks.

LOCATIONS
- ☐ Hains Point, East Potomac Park
- ☐ Lafayette Park
- ☐ Kenilworth Aquatic Gardens
- ☐ The Mall
- ☐ Rock Creek Park, near Pierce Mill
- ☐ 15th Street, N.W., between the Federal Triangle and the Ellipse
- ☐ U.S. Capitol grounds
- ☐ National Arboretum

POND CYPRESS

Taxodium distichum var. *nutans* (Ait.) Sweet
(*Taxodium ascendens* Brongn.)
Taxodium Family *Taxodiaceae*

The rare pond-cypress, which some botanists consider a separate species, differs from the bald-cypress in the following minor ways. **NATIVE HABITAT:** Southern Virginia south to Florida, west to Alabama. **FOLIAGE:** Needles are usually *pressed flat against the branchlets* or *strongly incurved*, often appearing scale-like. **BARK:** *Thick, furrowed*, grayish-brown.
LOCATIONS:
- ☐ U.S. Department of Agriculture, the Mall
- ☐ Dupont Circle
- ☐ National Arboretum

DAWN REDWOOD
OR METASEQUOIA
Metasequoia glyptostroboides H.H. Hu & Cheng
Taxodium Family *Taxodiaceae*

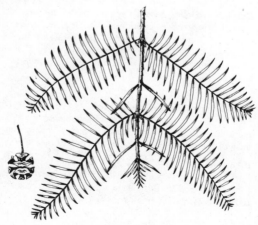

The dawn redwood is often called a "living fossil" because it was believed to be extinct for many years. For information about the recent discovery of living specimens of this ancient tree, see page 45 of this book. The dawn redwood, like the bald-cypress and the larches, is a deciduous conifer.

NATIVE HABITAT
Szechuan and Hupeh provinces, China.

FOLIAGE
Deciduous. Thin, flat, delicate needles are arranged *oppositely.* Each needle ½ - 1½ in. (about 1 - 4 cm.) long; soft spring green. Needles on thin, *oppositely arranged,* deciduous shoots which are 3 - 6 in. (7.5 - 15 cm.) long. Foliage colors bright orange-brown in autumn.

CONES
Round or cylindric, green at first, becoming brown; ½ - 1 in. (1.3 - 2.5 cm.) long. Scales peltately attached (attached at the center rather than the base of the cone). Hanging on a stalk 1 - 2½ in. (2.5 - 6.3 cm.) long.

BARK AND BRANCHLETS
Bark reddish-brown or grayish-brown, cracked and peeling in thin strips. Branchlets also have peeling bark; winter buds small, pale ovoid.

HABIT
Tapered trunk, ascending branches, and pyramidal crown. (Crown may grow somewhat rounded with age.)

SIMILAR SPECIES
Very similar to the bald-cypress (*Taxodium distichum*). The needles and shoots of the bald-cypress are *alternately* arranged (although they can appear to be nearly opposite). Bald-cypress cones are sessile or very short-stalked.

LOCATIONS
☐ National Arboretum
☐ Smithsonian National Museum of Natural History
☐ Hillwood Estate
☐ Redwood Terrace, N.W.
☐ U.S. Capitol grounds

CHINESE FIR OR CHINA-FIR
Cunninghamia lanceolata (Lamb.) Hook
Taxodium Family (*Taxodiaceae*)

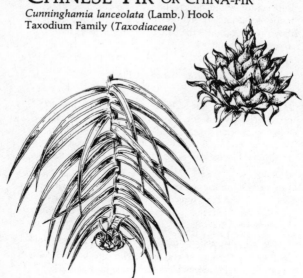

The lovely Chinese fir is an important timber tree
in China.

NATIVE HABITAT
China.

FOLIAGE
Evergreen. Needles thick, widest toward the base, gradually tapering to a sharp point. Thickly set and usually
slightly curved downward. 1¼ - 2¾ in. (about 3 - 7
cm.) long. Flat, bright green, two pale parallel bands
below. Dead foliage often remains on the tree.

CONES
Round or ovoid, 1 - 2 in. (2.5 - 5 cm.) long; wedge-
shaped scales end in sharp, often curved, spines.

BARK AND BRANCHLETS
Bark reddish-brown and peeling. Branchlets greenish,
mostly covered by the clasping bases of the needles.
Buds squatly rounded, covered with leaf-like scales.

HABIT
Pyramidal tree with few, more or less pendulous branches.

SIMILAR SPECIES
Not apt to be confused with any other species, but in the
absence of cones, bears a slight resemblance to the true
firs (*Abies*). Chinese fir needles are longer and more
sharply pointed than the needles of the true firs commonly planted here. Also, the presence of dead foliage is
a common characteristic of the Chinese fir.

LOCATIONS
☐ U.S. Capitol grounds
☐ Franciscan Monastery
☐ Hillwood Estate
☐ National Arboretum
☐ Quite rare in Washington, D.C.

GIANT SEQUOIA
OR BIG TREE OR WELLINGTONIA
Sequoiadendron giganteum (Lindl.) Buchholz
Taxodium Family *Taxodiaceae*
STATE TREE OF CALIFORNIA

Although they've got a little growing to do before they tower over the skyline, bona fide giant sequoias are thriving in Washington! Native to a small mountain area in California, the giant sequoias are the most massive and possibly the oldest living things on earth. The closely related redwood (*Sequoia sempervirens* (D. Don) Endl.) of the California and Oregon coast has not been able to live for long in Washington. While the giant sequoia is considered the most massive overall, the redwood is probably the *tallest* tree in the world. The state of California, apparently unable to decide between the two arboreal giants, adopted both the redwood and the giant sequoia as its official trees.

NATIVE HABITAT
Western slopes of the Sierra Nevada, California.

FOLIAGE
Evergreen. Scale-like, sharply pointed leaves are thickly and spirally arranged on branchlet. Each leaf ¼ - ½ in. (5 - 12 mm.) long, either closely pressed against branchlet or spreading outward. Bluish or grayish green.

CONES
Ovoid; pendulous; green at first, becoming dark brown. 2 - 3½ in. (5 - 9 cm.) long, with peltately attached scales (attached at middle rather than base).

BARK AND BRANCHLETS
Cinnamon-colored bark is very thick, deeply furrowed, and spongy. Slender branchlets are leaf-clad; winter buds small, naked.

HABIT
Some of the tallest trees on record are giant sequoias. The tree has large, spreading branches; lower ones droop, then sweep up. Usually forms a pyramidal crown, although some of the specimens in Washington are rather round-topped.

SIMILAR SPECIES
Combination of bark and foliage separates the giant sequoia from other conifers planted in the area.

LOCATIONS
☐ U.S. Capitol grounds
☐ White House grounds (replacement for giant sequoia planted by President Richard M. Nixon)
☐ Dumbarton Oaks
☐ National Arboretum

Umbrella-pine

Sciadopitys verticillata (Thunb.) Sieb. & Zucc.
Taxodium Family *Taxodiaceae*

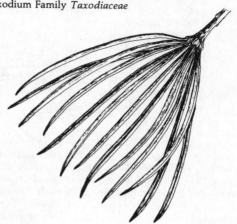

A beautiful and unfortunately rare tree. Named for
its whorled umbrella-shaped clusters of needles, which
slightly resemble the foliage of the true pines.

NATIVE HABITAT
Japan.

FOLIAGE
Evergreen. Deep shiny green clusters of 8 - 30 flat
needles arranged in whorls. Needles 3 - 5½ in. (7.5 -12.5
cm.) long, grooved on both sides, with a bright yellow-
green band below. Small scale-like foliage is scattered on
the branchlet; the tips of these scales form the pronounced
knobs from which the whorls of needles arise.

CONES
Ovoid, 2 - 4 in. (5 - 10 cm.) long; green, then ripening
brown. Loosely attached scales often break off
when handled.

BARK
Reddish or grayish-brown, peeling away in coarse strips.

SIMILAR SPECIES
Not apt to be confused with any other species. The
whorled clusters of grooved, shiny green needles are
unique. (See illustration.)

LOCATIONS
☐ National Zoo, near the old Monkey House
☐ National Arboretum
☐ Rare in Washington, D.C.

EASTERN WHITE CEDAR
OR ARBORVITAE
Thuja occidentalis L.
Cypress Family *Cupressaceae*

NATIVE HABITAT
Northeastern U.S., southeastern Canada.

FOLIAGE
Small, yellowish green, scale-like leaves in flattened
sprays. Each scale lance-shaped, less than ¼ in. (less
than 5 mm.) long, closely pressed against the branchlet.
Scales hugging the middle of the branchlet *glandular*.

CONES
Tulip-shaped, about ½ in. (1.2 cm.) long, with *scales
attached at the base*. 8 - 12 cone scales are thin, light
brown (green when young), somewhat leathery. Seeds
(attached to scales) with 2 narrow wings.

BARK
Thin, reddish brown, shallowly ridged and fissured, with
long peeling scales.

HABIT
Narrowly pyramidal crown, with short branches and a
tapered trunk.

SIMILAR SPECIES
See Oriental Arborvitae (*Platycladus orientalis*), following.

LOCATIONS
☐ Hillwood Estate
☐ National Arboretum
☐ Private yards

ORIENTAL ARBORVITAE
Platycladus orientalis (L.) Franco.
(*Thuja orientalis* L.)
(*Biota orientalis* (L.) Endl.)
Cypress Family *Cupressaceae*

NATIVE HABITAT
China, Korea. Distinguished from the Eastern White
Cedar or Arborvitae (*Thuja occidentalis*) by its *bluish
cones* with their *thick scales* and *wingless seeds*.

LOCATIONS
☐ National Arboretum
☐ Private yards

SAWARA CYPRESS
Chamaecyparis pisifera (Sieb. & Zucc.) Endl.
Cypress Family *Cupressaceae*

The Sawara cypress is the member of the genus *Chamaecyparis* most frequently planted in our area. The most popular form of this tree is the cultivar 'Squarrosa', with its pale bluish foliage.

NATIVE HABITAT
Japan.

FOLIAGE
Scale-like foliage, each tiny scale finely pointed and slightly curved at the tip. Inside bases of scales are white.

CONES
Small, round, brown cone ¼ in (6 - 8 mm.) in diameter. 10 - 12 scales attached at the center (peltate), with a fine point protruding from each scale's slightly depressed center.

BARK
Fairly smooth, thin, reddish brown, peeling in strips.

HABIT
A small tree with a narrow pyramidal shape.

OTHER FORMS
Many forms of the Sawara cypress are in cultivation, the most common in Washington being 'Squarrosa', with its *soft blue foliage* which is mostly *needle-like* rather than scale-like. 'Filifera', another popular form, has drooping, thread-like branchlets.

SIMILAR SPECIES
Compare features with other *Chamaecyparis* species.

LOCATIONS
☐ Franciscan Monastery
☐ Hillwood Estate
☐ Soldiers' Home
☐ Washington Monument grounds
☐ National Zoo
☐ Rock Creek Cemetery
☐ National Arboretum

OTHER MEMBERS OF THE GENUS *Chamaecyparis*
PLANTED IN WASHINGTON:

HINOKI CYPRESS
Chamaecyparis obtusa (Sieb. & Zucc.) Endl.
Cypress Family *Cupressaceae*

Best distinguished from the Sawara Cypress, already
described, by its foliage. Scales are *blunt* or *rounded* at
the tip, rather than pointed. Cones are bright green when
young, then orange-brown. **NATIVE HABITAT:** Japan.
LOCATIONS:
□ Franciscan Monastery
□ National Arboretum

LAWSON CYPRESS
OR PORT ORFORD CEDAR
Chamaecyparis lawsoniana (A. Murr.) Parl.
Cypress Family *Cupressaceae*

The Lawson Cypress is similar in appearance to the
two preceding species, but it has *thick*, furrowed bark
and conspicuous *glands* on the backs of the scale-like
leaves. In the spring this species bears bright red stami-
nate flowers. Lawson Cypress branchlets droop in fan-like
patterns. **NATIVE HABITAT:** Northwestern California,
Southwestern Oregon.
LOCATIONS:
□ Franciscan Monastery
□ National Arboretum

LEYLAND CYPRESS
X *Cupressocyparis leylandii* (A.B. Jacks. & Dallim.)
Dallim. & A.B. Jacks
Cypress Family *Cupressaceae*

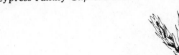

The Leyland cypress arose as a naturally occurring
cross between two different genera, a highly unusual
phenomenon. The tree is a hybrid of the Nootka Cypress
(*Chamaecyparis nootkatensis* (D. Don) Spach) and the
Monterey Cypress (*Cupressus macrocarpa* Hartw.), both
indigenous to the West Coast. Similar in appearance to
the *Chamaecyparis* species already described, the scale-
like leaves are *not so flattened*, are triangular in cross-
section. The cultivar 'Haggerston Grey', with gray-green
foliage, is frequently planted.

LOCATIONS
□ National Arboretum
□ Franciscan Monastery

EASTERN REDCEDAR

Juniperus virginiana L.
Cypress Family *Cupressaceae*

The Eastern redcedar yields the fragrant wood used to construct the old, familiar cedar chest. An abundant tree of the eastern United States; not a true cedar, but a members of the juniper genus.

NATIVE HABITAT
Eastern U.S. from Maine to northern Florida; west to South Dakota and Texas.

FOLIAGE
Evergreen. Of two types (dimorphic): Tiny, bluish-green, *scale-like* leaves are oppositely arranged, closely pressed against the four-sided branchlet and overlapping; needle-like leaves often presnt *on the same tree*, sharply pointed, arranged oppositely or in threes, about ¼ in. (less than 1 cm.) long.

CONES
Small, round, berry-like, about ¼ in. (less than 1 cm.) in diameter. Light green, bluish, then dark blue, with a whitish bloom.

BARK
Reddish brown, shredding into long, thin strips.

HABIT
Small to medium-sized tree, usually with a narrow pyramidal or columnar shape. Some specimens quite spreading.

SIMILAR SPECIES
Rare Chinese juniper (*Juniperus chinensis*), described below.

LOCATIONS
- ☐ Franciscan Monastery
- ☐ Hillwood Estate
- ☐ Very common in area cemeteries, along private drives and in abandoned fields

CHINESE JUNIPER

Juniperus chinensis L.
Cypress Family *Cupressaceae*

The Chinese juniper, native to China, Mongolia and Japan, is rarely planted in the Washington area. The best way to distinguish it from the Eastern redcedar (*Juniperus virginiana*), already described, is by the cone, which is slightly *larger* and *brownish when ripe*, with a thick bloom.
LOCATIONS:
- ☐ National Arboretum

INCENSE-CEDAR

Calocedrus decurrens (Torr.) Florin
(*Libocedrus decurrens* Torr.)
Cypress Family *Cupressaceae*

A gorgeous western conifer which is rare in the Washington area.

NATIVE HABITAT
California, Oregon.

FOLIAGE
Evergreen. Tiny flattened scale-like leaves are whorled in fours and closely pressed against the branchlet. The side leaves overlap the middle two. Each tiny leaf comes to a fine, sharp point. (See illustration.)

CONES
Small, oblong, yellowish-brown leathery cones ripen in late summer and autumn, splitting open to release seeds. Each cone ¾ - 1½ in. (about 2 - 4 cm.) long.

BARK AND BRANCHLETS
Bark reddish-brown, furrowed and very scaly. Flattened branchlets are covered by scale-like foliage. Tiny naked winter buds are inconspicuous.

HABIT
Although the branches of the incense-cedar may be quite spreading in its native western habitat, the trees planted in Washington have narrow, columnar habits. The local specimens are strikingly tall for columnar trees.

SIMILAR SPECIES
Could be confused with other members of the Cypress family from a distance.

LOCATIONS
☐ Rock Creek Cemetery
☐ National Zoo (near the lions and tigers)
☐ Washington Cathedral

The Yews
Taxus L.

Yews are planted throughout Washington. The most commonly grown is the English yew (*Taxus baccata* L.). The Irish yew (*Taxus baccata* 'Fastigiata'), an upright form of the English yew with a broadly columnar crown, is planted in cemeteries and churchyards here and in the British Isles. Asian species are also grown in some private collections here, but yews rarely attain tree stature in Washington, and therefore we treat only the commonly grown species.

English Yew
or Common Yew
Taxus baccata L.
Yew Family *Taxaceae*

NATIVE HABITAT
Europe, northern Africa, Asia Minor.

FOLIAGE
Evergreen. Needles arranged in a comb-like pattern, each ½ - 1½ in. (1 - 4 cm.) long, dark green above, with two pale parallel bands below.

SEEDS
A hard seed surrounded by a *bright red, berry-like* aril which is about ½ in. (1 - 1.5 cm.) across and open at one end. Seed is visible through opening.

BARK
Reddish brown, very thin and flaky, peeling into long strips.

HABIT
A large shrub or small tree with a broad, rambling crown. (The Irish yew has many upright branches that form a jagged, table-topped crown.)

ENGLISH YEW LOCATIONS
☐ U.S. Capitol grounds
☐ Dumbarton Oaks
☐ Public buildings and private homes throughout the city

IRISH YEW LOCATIONS
☐ Rock Creek Cemetery and other area cemeteries

JAPANESE NUTMEG
Torreya nucifera (L.) Sieb. & Zucc.
Yew Family *Taxaceae*

Extremely rare. **NATIVE HABITAT:** Japan.
FOLIAGE: Evergreen. Needles dark, shiny green above
with two pale parallel bands below, ¾ - 1½ in. (2 - 4
cm.) long, tapered to a sharp point. Arranged in a regular, comb-shaped pattern. **FRUIT:** Green, with purplish
streaks, plum-shaped, about an inch (2 - 2.5 cm.) long.
HABIT: Small tree with widely spreading branches.
LOCATIONS:
□ Dumbarton Oaks

KEY TO THE BROAD-LEAVED GENERA
Angiospermae

A .Trees with *opposite, simple* leaves

PAULOWNIA *Paulownia*   Pages 302–3

Paulownia, Royal Paulownia or
Princess Tree *Paulownia tomentosa*

THE CATALPAS *Catalpa*   Pages 303–7
Leaves often *whorled.*

Western, Northern or Hardy Catalpa
Catalpa speciosa

Yellow or Golden Catalpa
Catalpa ovata

THE MAPLES *Acer* (Mostly full-sized trees.
A few species are shrubby.)   Pages 260–76

Japanese Maple *Acer palmatum*

Sugar Maple *Acer saccharum*

Amur Maple *Acer ginnala*

Fern-Leafed Japanese Maple
Acer palmatum 'Dissectum'

Trident Maple *Acer buergerianum*

KATSURA *Cercidiphyllum*   Pages 143–44

Katsura-Tree
Cercidiphyllum japonicum

CRAPE-MYRTLE *Lagerstroemia*   Pages 252–53

Crape-Myrtle *Lagerstroemia indica*

FRINGE-TREE
Chionanthus   Pages 298–99

OSMANTHUS
Osmanthus   Page 297

Fringe-Tree
Chionanthus virginicus

Leaf evergreen

Osmanthus
Osmanthus heterophyllus

VIBURNUM *Viburnum*   Pages 300–301

(A large group of shrubs and small trees.
Leaves may also resemble the Maples'.)

EUONYMOUS *Euonymous*   Page 292
Winged Euonymous *Euonymous alata*

Portion of typically "winged" branchlet.

THE DOGWOODS (INCLUDING THE CORNELIAN CHERRY)
Cornus   Pages 284–88

Flowering Dogwood *Cornus florida*

Cornelian Cherry *Cornus mas*

LILAC
Syringa   Page 299

BOX *Buxus*   Pages 226–27

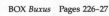

Common Box *Buxus sempervirens*

Common Lilac *Syringa vulgaris*

B. Trees with *opposite, compound* leaves

BOX-ELDER OR ASH-LEAFED MAPLE   *Acer negundo*   Page 270

Box-Elder or Ash-Leafed Maple *Acer negundo*

CORK-TREE *Phellodendron*   Page 256

Amur Cork-Tree *Phellodendron amurense*

THE ASHES *Fraxinus*   Pages 294–97

European Ash *Fraxinus excelsior*

White Ash *Fraxinus americana*

THE HORSE-CHESTNUTS AND BUCKEYES *Aesculus*
Pages 278–83

Common Horse-Chestnut
Aesculus hippocastanum

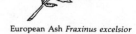

Fruit
Sweet or Yellow Buckeye
Aesculus octandra

CHASTE-TREE *Vitex agnus-castus*   Pages 307–8

Chaste-Tree *Vitex agnus-castus*

C. Trees with *alternate, compound* leaves

JAPANESE PAGODA-TREE, CHINESE SCHOLAR TREE
Sophora japonica   Pages 250–51

Yellow-green blossoms.
Mid-summer.

Japanese Pagoda-Tree *Sophora japonica*

BLACK LOCUST *Robinia pseudoacacia*   Pages 248–49

White blossoms.
Spring.

Black Locust *Robinia pseudoacacia*

YELLOWWOOD   *Cladrastis kentukea (Cladrastis lutea)*   Pages 244–45

White blossoms. Spring.

Yellowwood *Cladrastis kentukea*
(Cladrastis lutea)

LABURNUM, GOLDEN CHAIN TREE *Laburnum*   Page 251

Yellow blossoms. Spring.

Voss's Laburnum *Laburnum* x *watererei*

MIMOSA, SILK-TREE *Albizia julibrissin*   Page 241

Pink (rarely white) blossoms.
Summer.

Mimosa, Silk-Tree
Albizia julibrissin

112   C. Trees with *alternate, compound* leaves

HONEY LOCUST *Gleditsia triacanthos*   Pages 245–46

Yellow blossoms. Spring.

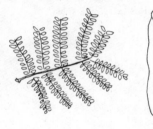

Honey Locust
Gleditsia triacanthos

KENTUCKY COFFEE-TREE *Gymnocladus dioicus*   Pages 246–47

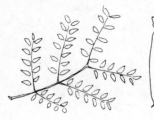

Green and white blossoms
(not particularly showy.)
Spring.

Kentucky Coffee-Tree
Gymnocladus dioicus

MOUNTAIN-ASH *Sorbus*   Page 240

European Mountain-Ash
Sorbus aucuparia

GOLDEN-RAIN-TREE *Koelreuteria paniculata*   Pages 276–77

Golden-Rain-Tree *Koelreuteria paniculata*

TRIFOLIATE ORANGE *Poncirus trifoliata*   Page 257

Winged petiole.

Trifoliate Orange *Poncirus trifoliata*

COMMON HOPTREE *Ptelea trifoliata*   Page 258

Common Hoptree *Ptelea trifoliata*

TREE OF HEAVEN, AILANTHUS *Ailanthus altissima*   Pages 254–55

Tree of Heaven or Ailanthus
Ailanthus altissima

Common.

CHINESE CEDAR, CEDRELA *Cedrela sinensis (Toona sinensis)*
Page 259

Chinese Cedar or Cedrela
Cedrela sinensis (Toona sinensis)

Rare.

THE WALNUTS *Juglans*
Pages 207–8

(One species has leaflets
with smooth margins.)

Black Walnut *Juglans nigra*

THE HICKORIES AND THE PECAN *Carya* Pages 204–6

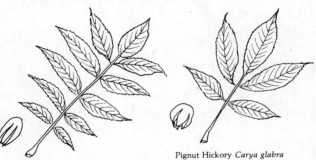

Pecan *Carya illinoensis*

Pignut Hickory *Carya glabra*

DEVIL'S WALKINGSTICK *Aralia spinosa* Page 290
Leaf (not illustrated) is large, pinnately compound. A small tree or
large shrub, best identified by its coarsely spined branches.

Branchlet of Devil's Walkingstick *Aralia spinosa*

D. Trees with *alternate, simple* leaves

Trees with *alternate, simple* leaves are divided into
the following categories:
  I. Common flowering trees of Washington, D.C.
 II. Common shade and street trees of
     Washington, D.C.
III. Rare trees
 IV. Common trees of native woodlands that are
     infrequently cultivated in formally landscaped
     areas of Washington, D.C.
  V. Large shrubs

I. Common flowering trees of Washington, D.C.

THE MAGNOLIAS *Magnolia* Pages 127–38
Blossoms before the leaves or with the young leaves in early spring
(Asian species).

Star Magnolia *Magnolia stellata*

Saucer Magnolia *Magnolia* x *soulangeana*

Blossoms appear after the leaves are out in spring
and summer (native North American species).

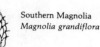

Southern Magnolia
Magnolia grandiflora

Leaf evergreen.

Leaf deciduous. (All other Magnolia species in the Washington area.)

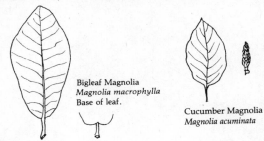

Bigleaf Magnolia
Magnolia macrophylla
Base of leaf.

Cucumber Magnolia
Magnolia acuminata

Umbrella Magnolia *Magnolia tripetala*

THE FLOWERING CHERRIES, PEACHES AND PLUMS *Prunus*
Pages 227–31

A very difficult genus. Common species and hybrids best identified
with the aid of color close-ups.

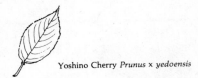

Yoshino Cherry *Prunus* x *yedoensis*

THE FLOWERING CRABAPPLES *Malus*   Pages 232–33

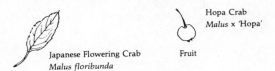

Japanese Flowering Crab
Malus floribunda

Fruit

Hopa Crab
Malus x 'Hopa'

THE PEARS *Pyrus*   Pages 234–35

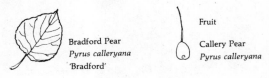

Bradford Pear
Pyrus calleryana
'Bradford'

Fruit

Callery Pear
Pyrus calleryana

THE HAWTHORNS *Crataegus*   Page 239

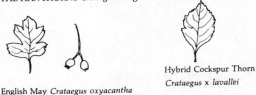

English May *Crataegus oxyacantha*

Hybrid Cockspur Thorn
Crataegus x *lavallei*

THE REDBUDS *Cercis*   Pages 242–43

Redbud *Cercis canadensis*

SMOKE-TREES *Cotinus*   Pages 253–54

European Smoke-Tree
Cotinus coggygria

II. Common shade and street trees of Washington, D.C.

THE PLANES AND THE SYCAMORE *Platanus*   Pages 147–51

London Plane
Platanus x *hispanica*
(*Platanus* x *acerifolia*)

TULIP POPLAR, YELLOW POPLAR OR TULIP-TREE
Liriodendron tulipifera   Pages 138–39

Tulip Poplar *Liriodendron tulipifera*

SWEETGUM *Liquidambar styraciflua*   Pages 144–45

Sweetgum *Liquidambar styraciflua*

GINKGO, MAIDENHAIR TREE *Ginkgo biloba* Pages 68–69
(Not an Angiosperm. Also included in the Key to Conifer genera.)

Ginkgo, Maidenhair Tree *Ginkgo biloba*

COTTONWOOD *Populus* Page 213
(Common in parks along the Potomac.)

Eastern Cottonwood *Populus deltoides*

THE WILLOWS *Salix* Pages 212–13

Weeping Willow *Salix babylonica*

THE BEECHES *Fagus*
Leaves green, purplish, reddish or coppery. Pages 169–72

American Beech
Fagus grandifolia

European Beech
Fagus sylvatica
(including Copper Beech)

Cut-Leaf or
Fern-Leaf Beech
Fagus sylvatica
'Asplenifolia'

THE OAKS *Quercus*   Pages 175–96

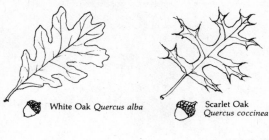

White Oak *Quercus alba*

Scarlet Oak
Quercus coccinea

Chestnut Oak *Quercus prinus*   Blackjack Oak *Quercus marilandica*

Willow Oak *Quercus phellos*

Saw-Toothed Oak *Quercus acutissima*

THE CHESTNUTS *Castanea*   Pages 172–74

Chinese Chestnut *Castanea mollissima*

THE HACKBERRIES *Celtis*   Pages 164–65
Leaf base usually *unequal*. Bark smooth, gray, with "warts".
Ripe fruit red.

Hackberry *Celtis occidentalis*

OSAGE-ORANGE *Maclura pomifera*   Pages 167–68
Bark orange, scaly. Fruit yellow-green.

Osage-Orange *Maclura pomifera*

THE MULBERRIES *Morus*   Pages 165–66
Mulberry fruit white, pink, red, purple, or almost black.
Mulberry leaves often *lobed*.

White Mulberry *Morus alba*

PAPER MULBERRY *Broussonetia papyrifera*   Page 166
Leaves often *lobed* and may be arranged *oppositely*.
Fruit round, orange-red.

Paper Mulberry *Broussonetia papyrifera*

THE HOLLIES *Ilex*   Page 291
(Osmanthus has similar leaves, but arranged *oppositely* along
the branch.)

American Holly *Ilex opaca*

THE LINDENS (LIMES) *Tilia*   Pages 220–25
Fragrant yellow or white flowers in late spring, early summer.
Margin usually unequal at the base.

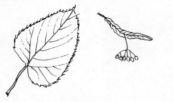

European Linden
Tilia x europaea

American Linden *Tilia americana*

THE ELMS _Ulmus_   Pages 151–61
Leaf margin usually sharply, _doubly_ toothed.
Margin usually _unequal_ at the base.
Fruit is a small, papery samara.

American Elm _Ulmus americana_

Chinese Elm _Ulmus parvifolia_

Scotch Elm _Ulmus glabra_

JAPANESE ZELKOVA _Zelkova serrata_   Pages 161–62
(This tree is commonly planted in Washington. Other Zelkovas,
rarely grown, are included in III. Rare Trees.)
Margin _singly_ toothed. Equal or nearly equal base.

Japanese Zelkova _Zelkova serrata_

THE HORNBEAMS (ALSO KNOWN AS IRONWOOD,
BLUE-BEECH, MUSCLEWOOD) _Carpinus_   Pages 201–2
Bark smooth, "muscular" looking.

European Hornbeam _Carpinus betulus_

THE BIRCHES _Betula_   Pages 198–201
Bark white. In some species gray or brown.

European Birch _Betula pendula_

THE ALDERS _Alnus_   Page 197
Fruit woody, cone-like.

European Alder _Alnus glutinosa_

III. Rare trees

JUJUBE *Ziziphus jujuba*   Page 293
Three main veins radiate up from base.   Base usually unequal.

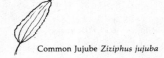

Common Jujube *Ziziphus jujuba*

JAPANESE RAISIN TREE *Hovenia dulcis*   Pages 292–93
Sweet, edible, raisin-flavored fruit.

Japanese Raisin Tree *Hovenia dulcis*

FRANKLIN TREE *Franklinia alatamaha*   Pages 208–9
Blooms in late summer and autumn.

Franklin Tree *Franklinia alatamaha*

DOVE OR HANDKERCHIEF TREE *Davidia involucrata*
Page 289

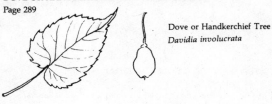

Dove or Handkerchief Tree
Davidia involucrata

Idesia polycarpa   Page 210
Fruits (not illustrated) are reddish brown berries in long,
pendulous clusters.

Idesia polycarpa

PERSIAN IRONWOOD *Parrotia persica*   Pages 146–47
Bark smooth, pinkish or grayish brown, flaky. Short, wide trunk
divides into many limbs.

Persian Ironwood *Parrotia persica*

SILVERBELL *Halesia*   Page 218
Small, bell-shaped flowers in spring.

Carolina Silverbell *Halesia carolina*

SNOWBELL (STORAX) *Styrax*   Pages 216–18
Hanging clusters of fragrant flowers (sometimes hidden by the
leaves) appear in spring.

Japanese Snowbell
Styrax japonica

Fragrant Snowbell or
Big Leaf Storax *Styrax obassia*

CHINESE KAKI PERSIMMON *Diospyros kaki*   Page 220

Chinese Kaki Persimmon
Diospyros kaki

Fruit of the wild
form of the tree.

STEWARTIA (DECIDUOUS CAMELLIA)   *Stewartia
pseudocamellia*   Page 209

A small tree with pretty, orange-brown bark and white flowers
in summer.

Stewartia *Stewartia pseudocamellia*

ZELKOVAS *Zelkova* (Rare species)   Pages 161–63
Leaves singly toothed.

Cut-Leaf Zelkova
Zelkova x verschaffeltii

Caucasian Elm *Zelkova carpinifolia*

THE POPLARS *Populus*   Pages 214–15

Lombardy Poplar
Populus nigra 'Italica'

White Poplar *Populus alba*

CHINESE PARASOL TREE (PHOENIX-TREE) *Firmiana simplex*
Page 226

Chinese Parasol Tree (Phoenix-Tree) *Firmiana simplex*

CHINESE QUINCE *Chaenomeles sinensis*   Page 237
A small tree, with a fluted trunk, mottled bark and
fragrant yellow fruit. Leaves (not illustrated) elliptic-ovate, 2 - 4 in.
(5 - 10 cm.) long, finely toothed.

Chinese Quince *Chaenomeles sinensis* Fruit

MEDLAR *Mespilus germanica*   Page 235

Medlar *Mespilus germanica*

IV. Common trees of native woodlands that are infrequently cultivated in Washington, D.C. (These trees *are*
planted in Washington, but are *more apt to be found
growing in private yards and in the wild than along
streets or in formally landscaped areas.*)

COMMON PERSIMMON *Diospyros virginiana*   Page 219

Common Persimmon *Diospyros virginiana*

TUPELO, SOUR GUM OR BLACK GUM   *Nyssa sylvatica*
Leaves turn scarlet in early autumn. Pages 288–89

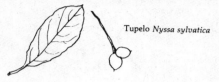

Tupelo *Nyssa sylvatica*

SASSAFRAS *Sassafras albidum*   Pages 142–43

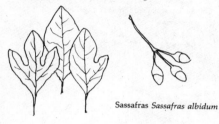

Sassafras *Sassafras albidum*

RIVER BIRCH *Betula nigra*   Pages 200–201
Bark brown, coarsely scaly. Common along Rock Creek.

River Birch *Betula nigra*

SOURWOOD, SORREL TREE   *Oxydendrum arboreum*
A small tree. Leaves turn scarlet and wine in the fall.   Pages 215–16

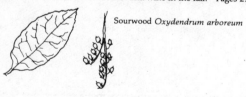

Sourwood *Oxydendrum arboreum*

SHADBUSH, SHADBLOW OR SERVICEBERRY   *Amelanchier arborea*   Page 238
The first tree to bloom in native woodlands. Blossoms are white.
Very common in the wild.

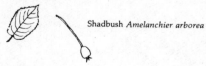

Shadbush *Amelanchier arborea*

V. Large shrubs or small trees (included because of showy blossoms, fruit or foliage).

EASTERN HOP-HORNBEAM *Ostrya virginiana*   Page 204
Bark in narrow peeling strips.

Eastern Hop-Hornbeam *Ostrya virginiana*

SPICE-BUSH *Lindera benzoin*   Page 141
Blossoms pale yellow in spring. A common woodland shrub
or small tree.

Spice-Bush *Lindera benzoin*

PAWPAW *Asimina tribola*   Page 140
A small tree. Common along the Potomac.

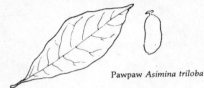

Pawpaw *Asimina triloba*

ROSE-OF-SHARON   *Hibiscus syriacus*
Blossoms pink, red, purple, white or
a combination of colors. Very showy.
Summer—autumn. Common.   Page 225

Rose-of-Sharon *Hibiscus syriacus*

THE TAMARISKS
Tamarix   Page 211
Delicate, feathery
foliage. Wispy pink
blossoms.

Tamarisk *Tamarix*

CHINESE PHOTINIA   *Photinia serrulata* A large shrub or small tree.
Leaves shiny, evergreen. Flowers white, in upright clusters.
Fruit bright red. Page 236

Chinese Photinia
Photinia serrulata

THE FILBERTS OR HAZELNUTS *Corylus*   Pages 202–3
Tall shrubs or small trees with purple, reddish or green leaves.
Fruit (not illustrated) an edible nut.

European Filbert or Hazelnut
Corylus avellana

THE WITCH-HAZELS *Hamamelis*   Page 145–46
Large shrubs or small trees with pale yellow blossoms in late autumn
or early spring.

Common Witch-Hazel
Hamamelis virginiana

COMMON FIG *Ficus carica*   Page 168

Common Fig
Ficus carica

THE DOGWOODS
Cornus Pages 284–88
(This species has
opposite leaves.)

Flowering Dogwood
Cornus florida

Illustrated Descriptions
of Broad-Leaved Trees

THE MAGNOLIAS

KEY TO MAGNOLIAS COMMONLY CULTIVATED
IN WASHINGTON, D.C.

1a) Flowers before the leaves. (Leaves may emerge toward end of blooming time.)

2a) Petals thick, rather stiff; blossoms upright, cup or tulip-shaped.

3a) Usually nine petals and petal-like sepals.

4a) Petals pale pink or purplish (rarely white), usually with
a darker blush toward the base. Six petals; three petal-
like sepals, half as long or nearly as long as petals. Blossom cup-like, but may open quite wide when mature.
(Widely planted large shrub or small tree) . . . .
. . . . Saucer Magnolia (*M. x soulangeana*).

4b) Petals thick, usually white, with a faint yellow blush
toward the base inside. Six petals and three sepals alike.
(Rarely planted tree) . . . .
. . . . Yulan Magnolia (*M. denudata*).

3b) Usually six petals.

5a) Petals wine-red or deep purple. (Shrubby) . . . .
. . . . Lily Magnolia (*M. liliflora*).

2b) Blossoms *not* cup or tulip-shaped. Petals thin, delicately reflexed.

6a) Petals and sepals alike, 12 or more . . . .
. . . . Star Magnolia (*M. stellata*).

6b) Petals 6 - 9, with faint purple line toward base
outside. (Sepals short, green, soon falling) . . . . .
. . . . Kobus Magnolia (*M. kobus*).

1b) Flowers after the leaves.

7a) Leaves evergreen: thick, leathery, glossy
green. Flowers large, white, fragrant, early
summer . . . .
. . . . . Southern Magnolia (*M. grandiflora*).

7b) Leaves deciduous.

8a) Flowers greenish-yellow, erect, 2 - 3½
in. (5 - 9 cm.) high . . . .
Cucumber Magnolia (*M. acuminata*).

8b) Flowers white, creamy, or very pale
yellow.

9a) Leaf base heart-shaped or "ear"-
like, 12 - 36 in. (approx. 30 - 90
cm.) long. Petals huge, white, with
purple splotches at inner bases . . . .
. . . . Bigleaf Magnolia
(*M. macrophylla*).

9b) Leaves wedge-shaped (or rarely
rounded) at base.

10a) Leaf 8 - 24 in. (20.2 - 60.6
cm.) long, widest above the
middle. Flowers in late April
and early May . . . .
. . . . Umbrella Magnolia
(*M. tripetala*).

10b) Leaf 3½ - 6½ in. (9 - 16.5
cm.) long, glossy, somewhat
leathery: flowers late May
through early summer . . . . . .
. . . . Sweetbay Magnolia
(*M. virginiana*).

Southern Magnolia
or Evergreen Magnolia
or Bull-Bay Magnolia

Magnolia grandiflora L.
Magnolia Family *Magnoliaceae*
STATE TREE OF MISSISSIPPI

Although this magnolia is as southern as a mint
julep, it has been planted in places as far from home as
Europe, Asia, Africa, and South America, making it
one of North America's most important native ornamentals. The rest of the world is finding out what residents
of the Deep South have always known—there is nothing
like the smell of southern magnolia blossoms on an early
summer evening.

NATIVE HABITAT
South coastal states from southeastern Virginia to
Florida; west to Texas

LEAVES
Alternate, simple, evergreen. Thick, leathery, shiny green
above, paler and rusty-pubescent below. 5 - 8 in. (12.5 -
20.2 cm.) long, with sharply or bluntly pointed apex and
wedge-shaped base. Margin smooth or slightly wavy.
Petiole stout, pubescent, about an inch (2.5 cm.) long.

FLOWERS
Large, white, cup-shaped blossoms, early to mid-
summer, with a few as late as September. 6 - 8 in. (15.1
- 20.2 cm.) across. Six or more petals and three petal-
like sepals are thick, stiff, and obovate. Strong, sweet,
lemony fragrance. (See color close-up.)

FRUIT
An upright egg-shaped aggregate of follicles, 2¾ - 4 in.
(7 - 10 cm.) high. Bright red in late summer and early
fall, becoming brown by mid-autumn. Densely pubescent. Fruit follicles open to release individual red seeds
hanging on long white threads.

BARK AND TWIGS
Bark gray or light brown, broken into small scales on older trees. Twig stout, pubescent with densely woolly winter terminal bud, 1 - 1½ in. (2.5 - 3.8 cm.) long. Stipular scars encircle twig.

HABIT
Long, straight trunk, with many branches forming a tall, pyramidal crown.

SIMILAR SPECIES
Not likely to be confused with any other species, but see sweetbay magnolia (*Magnolia virginiana*).

LOCATIONS
- ☐ White House grounds
- ☐ Old Executive Office Building grounds, along Pennsylvania Avenue and 17th Street, N.W.
- ☐ Lincoln Memorial
- ☐ Federal Triangle, Constitution Avenue, N.W.
- ☐ U.S. Capitol grounds
- ☐ Franciscan Monastery
- ☐ Mount Vernon
- ☐ Widely planted throughout D.C. in private yards, public parks, and on the grounds of government office buildings and museums

SWEETBAY MAGNOLIA
Magnolia virginiana L.
Magnolia Family *Magnoliaceae*

A small tree with sweet-smelling blossoms. Deciduous in the northern part of its range; evergreen in the south.

NATIVE HABITAT
Swamps and moist woodlands from coastal Massachusetts to New Jersey and Pennsylvania; south to Florida and west through Gulf Coast states (further north in some river valleys) to Texas.

LEAVES
Alternate, simple, deciduous or nearly evergreen. Elliptic-lanceolate. 3½ - 6½ in. (9 - 16.5 cm.) long. Apex bluntly pointed or rounded; base broadly wedge-shaped or (rarely) rounded. Somewhat leathery; glossy green above, *whitish* (glaucous) below; may be silky when young. Margin smooth. Petiole becoming glabrous; ½ - 1 in. (1.2 - 2.5 cm.) long.

FLOWERS
White or yellow-white, fragrant, in late spring and early summer. Cup-shaped, with 9 - 12 obovate petals and shorter, thinner petal-like sepals. Blossom 2 - 3 in. (5 - 7.5 cm.) across.

FRUIT
An erect oblong cone-like aggregate of follicles; dark red, 1½ - 3 in. (about 3.8 - 7.5 cm.) high.

BARK AND TWIGS
Bark gray, fairly smooth. Twigs glabrous, brown or greenish, with encircling stipular scars. Pith chambered. Winter buds greenish, pubescent; terminal bud conspicuous.

HABIT
A large shrub or small tree.

SIMILAR SPECIES
See southern magnolia (*Magnolia grandiflora*).

LOCATIONS
☐ U.S. Capitol grounds
☐ National Arboretum
☐ Beaver Valley, National Zoo
☐ Grounds, gardens, and homes
☐ In the wild, mostly along
   streams and in swampy areas

CUCUMBER MAGNOLIA
OR CUCUMBER TREE
Magnolia acuminata L.
Magnolia Family *Magnoliaceae*

Named for its fruit, which resembles a tiny cucumber.

NATIVE HABITAT
Western New York to southern Illinois; south to Georgia, Louisiana, and southeast Oklahoma.

LEAVES
Simple, alternate, deciduous. Thin-textured, broadly elliptic or ovate. 4 - 10 in. (10 p 25.2 cm.) long. Gradually or abruptly pointed apex; wedge-shaped or rounded base. Yellowy-green above; paler below and usually finely pubescent. Margin smooth or slightly wavy. Petiole 1 - 1½ in. (2.5 - 3.8 cm.) long.

FLOWERS
Yellow-green, erect, bell-shaped, after the leaves in early
May. 2 - 3½ in. (5 - 9 cm.) high. Not as showy as most
magnolias.

FRUIT
Small, erect "cucumber;" brilliant pink to deep red in
late summer and early fall. 1 - 3 in. (2.5 - 7.5 cm.) high.
Fruit follicles split to release scarlet seeds on thin
white threads.

BARK AND TWIGS
Bark brown, furrowed, and scaly. Twig brown,
glabrous, with whitish pubescent winter terminal bud.

HABIT
Medium-sized tree with long, straight trunk and
pyramidal crown.

SIMILAR SPECIES
Bigleaf magnolia (*Magnolia macrophylla*) has much
longer leaves. Umbrella magnolia (*Magnolia tripetala*)
also has longer leaves which are *narrowly wedge-shaped*
at the base. See text and photographs for differences in
flowers and fruits.

LOCATIONS
☐ U.S. Capitol grounds
☐ National Arboretum
☐ Some private homes in D.C.

Umbrella Magnolia

Magnolia tripetala L.
Magnolia Family *Magnoliaceae*

The umbrella-like clusters of leaves at the ends of its
branches give this tree its common name.

NATIVE HABITAT
Mostly in the mountains, from southern Pennsylvania,
Ohio, and Kentucky; west to Arkansas and southeast
Oklahoma; south to Georgia, Alabama, and Mississippi.
The only magnolia native to Shenandoah National Park
in Virginia.

LEAVES
Simple, alternate deciduous. Large, 8 - 24 in. (20.2 - 60.6
cm.) long. *Wedge-shaped base.* Gradually or abruptly
pointed apex. Widest part of leaf above the middle. Usually some pubescence below. Margin smooth or slightly
wavy. Petiole ¾ - 1½ in. (2 - 3.8 cm.) long.

FLOWERS
White or yellow-white, late April - early May. Six to
nine narrow petals, each 3 - 5 in. (7.5 - 12.6 cm.) long.
Three outer petals hang down. (Not as showy as bigleaf,
southern and sweetbay magnolias.)

FRUIT
Erect red cone-like aggregate of follicles. 2¾ - 4 in.
(7 -10 cm.) high, cylindrical. Follicles split to release
scarlet seeds.

BARK AND TWIGS
Bark smooth, brown. Twigs stout, *glabrous*. Terminal winter bud glabrous, purplish. Stipular scars encircle twig.

HABIT
A small tree; tropical looking with its umbrella-like clusters of large leaves.

SIMILAR SPECIES
Bigleaf magnolia (*Magnolia macrophylla*) has larger leaves, with "ear"-like bases. (See other differences in flowers, bark, etc.) The Pawpaw (*Asimina triloba*) has *pubescent* twigs with no encircling stipular scars and dissimilar flowers and fruit.

LOCATIONS
☐ U.S. Capitol grounds
☐ St. Elizabeth's Hospital
☐ National Zoo

Base of leaf.
Bigleaf Magnolia
Magnolia macrophylla

Umbrella Magnolia *Magnolia tripetala*

BIGLEAF MAGNOLIA
Magnolia macrophylla Michx.
Magnolia Family *Magnoliaceae*

The largest-leafed tree in the temperate eastern United States. Bears giant, exotic-looking white flowers.

NATIVE HABITAT
Southern Ohio, southwest Virginia, Kentucky, and Arkansas; south to Louisiana, Alabama, and Georgia.

LEAVES
Alternate, simple, deciduous. Huge! 12 - 36 in. (approx. 30 - 90 cm.) long. Thin textured. Pointed or rounded apex. *"Ear"-shaped*, or heart-shaped base. Silvery-soft pubescent below. Petiole 1½ - 4 in. (3.8 - 10 cm.) long, soft-pubescent.

FLOWERS
Giant, open cup-shaped blossoms in late May and early June. Up to 12 in. (30.4 cm.) across, fragrant. Six creamy white petals, each with purple inside near the base. Sepals slightly shorter than petals.

FRUIT
An upright, round or egg-shaped aggregate of follicles. Rose-colored, pubescent, 2½ - 4½ in. (6.3 - 11.4 cm.) high. Follicles split to release orange-scarlet seeds on white threads.

BARK AND TWIGS
Bark smooth, yellowish (gray on young trees). Twigs greenish, velvety, with white pubescent terminal buds in winter. Stipular scars encircle twig.

HABIT
Never attains great height. Tropical-looking, with giant leaves and yellowish bark.

SIMILAR SPECIES
Only umbrella magnolia (*Magnolia tripetala*) has leaves approaching bigleaf size. Umbrella magnolia leaves are wedge-shaped at base.

LOCATIONS
☐ U.S. Capitol grounds
☐ National Arboretum
☐ Soldiers' Home
☐ Rock Creek Cemetery
☐ Kalorama Road and Tracy Place, N.W.

(Leaf base illustrated)

STAR MAGNOLIA
Magnolia stellata (Sieb. & Zucc.) Maxim.
(*M. kobus* var. *stellata* (Sieb. & Zucc.) Blackburn)
Magnolia Family *Magnoliaceae*

The authors' favorite harbinger of spring. Its delicate, perfumed flowers open before the cherry blossoms.

NATIVE HABITAT
Japan.

LEAVES
Simple, alternate deciduous. 1½ - 4½ in. (3.8 - 11.4 cm.) long. Bluntly pointed or rounded apex; gradually tapering to wedge-shaped base. Glabrous above; may have some pubescence below. Margin smooth. Petioles short, ½ in. (1.2 cm.) or less.

FLOWERS
Fragrant, profuse, white or pale pink; before the leaves in March or early April. Twelve or more narrow white petals and petal-like sepals open wide, suggesting a star. Petals are not as thick as on most magnolias. (See color close-up.)

FRUIT
Reddish, twisted, somewhat carrot-shaped aggregate of follicles, 2 - 4 in. (5 - 10 cm.) long.

BARK AND TWIGS
Bark smooth or slightly roughened, pale gray, with lenticels. Twigs pubescent, with very fuzzy conspicuous terminal buds in winter. Stipular scars encircle twig.

HABIT
A wide-spreading shrub or small tree.

OTHER FORMS
The cultivar 'Rosea' has petals suffused with pink. A rare purple form of the star magnolia (*Magnolia stellata* 'Rubra') is at the National Arboretum.

SIMILAR SPECIES
The kobus magnolia (*Magnolia kobus*) is very similar, but its blossoms have fewer petals (6 - 9), which are faintly lined with purple outside. All other white-flowering magnolias commonly planted here have more or less *cup-shaped blossoms with stiff, thick petals.*

LOCATIONS
- □ U.S. Capitol grounds
- □ Library of Congress grounds
- □ Park near Jefferson Memorial
- □ National Arboretum
- □ District of Columbia cemeteries
- □ Quite common throughout the city

SAUCER MAGNOLIA
Magnolia x *soulangeana* Soul.-Bod.
(*Magnolia denudata* x *Magnolia liliflora*)
Magnolia Family *Magnoliaceae*

A cross between the Yulan (*Magnolia denudata*) and lily (*Magnolia liliflora*) magnolias. The saucer magnolia is more widely planted in the city than either of its parents or any other Asian magnolia. Its blossoms, which are usually pink, open very early, before the leaves. One of Washington's most popular ornamentals.

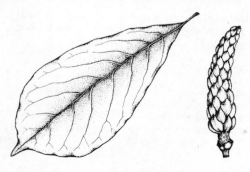

LEAVES
Simple, alternate, deciduous. 3½ - 9 in. (9 - 22.8 cm.)
long. Wedge-shaped base, gradually widening toward
apex, then ending in an abrupt (blunt or sharp) point.
Usually some pubescence below, especially on the veins.
Margin smooth. Petiole ¼ - 1 in. (0.6 - 2.5 cm.) long,
usually pubescent.

FLOWERS
Late March and April.* Color varies from white to deep
purple, but the most common forms are pale pink outside, with a darker rose blush toward the base; white
inside. Six thick petals and three petal-like sepals which
are half as long or nearly as long as petals. Petals and
sepals more or less rounded at the top. Blossom cup-like,
but may open quite wide when mature. Degree of fragrance
varies. (See "OTHER FORMS" for more blossom
descriptions.) (See color close-up.)

*May put forth a few blossoms again during the
summer months.

FRUIT
Bright red, often twisted, somewhat carrot-like aggregate
of follicles, 2 - 4 in. (5 - 10 cm.) long.

BARK AND TWIGS
Bark smooth or slightly roughened, gray or brown, with
lenticels. Twigs reddish-brown, with lenticels; large,
fuzzy white or pale green terminal buds in winter.
Stipular scars encircle twig.

HABIT
A large, full shrub or small tree.

OTHER FORMS
Many forms of the saucer magnolia are planted in Washington. The cultivar 'Lennei' blooms slightly later and
has petals that are purple outside, white inside, and very
broad at the apex. Several forms of saucer magnolia
have creamy white blossoms, barely suffused with pink.

SIMILAR SPECIES
The typical pink-flowering forms are distinct. White-
flowering trees may be confused with Yulan magnolia
(*Magnolia denudata*). The darker-blossomed 'Lennei' and
other purplish forms could be confused with the lily
magnolia (*Magnolia liliflora*). See lily magnolia
for comparison.

LOCATIONS
☐ White House
☐ Old Executive Office Building, along 17th Street, N.W.
☐ British Embassy
☐ Rawlins Park
☐ National Gallery of Art
☐ U.S. Capitol and Library of Congress grounds
☐ Pennsylvania Avenue, S.E. (median)
☐ Pan American Union
☐ Very popular throughout the city

Yulan Magnolia

Magnolia denudata Desrouss.
(*M. heptapeta* (Buc'hoz) Dandy)
Magnolia Family *Magnoliaceae*

A popular Chinese garden tree for centuries, but rare today in the U.S. Scarcity is partially due to propagation problems encountered by nurseries here. Perhaps more to the point, most Americans are unwilling to wait the fifteen years it takes this tree to put forth its first blossoms.

NATIVE HABITAT
Woodlands of central China.

LEAVES
Simple, opposite, deciduous. Deep, even green. 3½ - 6 in. (9 - 15 cm.) long. Wedge-shaped or rounded base; very wide toward apex, then ending in an abrupt point. Margin smooth. Pubescent below, especially on the veins. Petiole pubescent, about ½ - 1 in. (1.2 - 2.5 cm.) long.

FLOWERS
Absolutely gorgeous, large, white, cup-shaped blossoms before the leaves in late March and early April. Nine thick "petals" (actually six petals and three sepals), white outside, very pale yellow inside toward the base. Blossom fragrant, 4½ - 6½ in. (11.4 - 16.5 cm.) across.

FRUIT
Brownish, cylindric aggregate of follicles, 3 - 5 in. (7.5 -
12.5 cm.) long.

BARK AND TWIGS
Young bark smooth, gray, with lenticels. Older bark
dark gray-brown, scaly. Twigs reddish-brown, pubescent,
with large, pale, fuzzy terminal buds in winter. Stipular
scars encircle twig.

HABIT
Small to medium sized tree with long, spreading branches.

SIMILAR SPECIES
May be confused with white-flowering forms of saucer
magnolia (M. x *soulangeana*), but they are barely suffused with pink. Other white-flowering magnolias which
bloom before the leaves (Star and Kobus) have thinner,
narrower petals and less cup-shaped blossoms.

LOCATIONS
☐ Dumbarton Oaks
☐ National Arboretum magnolia collection
☐ Rare in Washington, D.C.

LILY MAGNOLIA

Magnolia liliflora Desrouss.
(*M. quinquepeta* (Buc'hoz) Dandy)
Magnolia Family *Magnoliaceae*

NATIVE HABITAT: China; widely cultivated in Japan.
FLOWERS: A shrub with deep purple or wine-red blos-
soms in mid-April. Blossoms large, tulip-shaped, with six
petals and three small, green lance-shaped sepals which
soon fall. Blossom color paler inside.
SIMILAR SPECIES: Saucer magnolia cultivar 'Lennei'
(*Magnolia* x *soulangeana* 'Lennei'). 'Lennei' has nine
"petals" (six petals and three petal-like sepals), which are
white inside and very broad and rounded at the apex.
LOCATIONS:
☐ Smithsonian National Museum of Natural History
☐ U.S. Capitol grounds
☐ National Arboretum magnolia collection

HYBRID MAGNOLIA

Magnolia x *loebneri* Kache.
Magnolia Family *Magnoliaceae*

A cultivated cross between the star and kobus
magnolias. Several selections are becoming popular,
including 'Leonard Messel,' 'Merrill,' 'Spring Snow,' and
'Star Bright.' These hybrids all have the delicately
reflexed blossoms characteristic of both parents. Color
ranges from white, through shades of pink, to purple.
LOCATIONS:
☐ National Arboretum (Administrative Building terrace)

Kobus Magnolia
or Northern Japanese Magnolia
Magnolia kobus DC.
Magnolia Family *Magnoliaceae*

Similar to the star magnolia (*Magnolia stellata*), but attaining greater height. Quite rare in Washington, D.C. **NATIVE HABITAT:** Japan. **LEAVES:** Simple, alternate, deciduous. Dark green, 2¼ - 6½ in. (5.8 - 16.5 cm.) long. Base wedge-shaped; blade widens toward apex, then ends in an abrupt point. Margin smooth. Some pubescence on veins below. Petiole about ½ in. (1 - 1.5 cm.) long. **FLOWERS:** Late March and early April, before the leaves. Six to nine petals; white, with faint purple line toward the base outside. Petals thin, narrow and delicately reflexed. (Short sepals soon fall off.) Blossom about 4 in. (10 cm.) across.
FRUIT: Pink, cylindric aggregate of follicles, 2 - 4 in. (5 - 10 cm.) long. Follicles split to release red seeds hanging on thin threads. **BARK AND TWIGS:** Bark smooth gray, with lenticels. Becoming somewhat roughened with age. Twigs glabrous. Terminal buds gray, fuzzy, conspicuous in winter. Stipular scars encircle twig. **HABIT:** Shrubby, or a good-sized tree with broadly pyramidal crown. **SIMILAR SPECIES:** Star magnolia (*Magnolia stellata*) has similar blossoms, but with twelve or more petals and petal-like sepals. All other white-flowering magnolias here have more or less cup-shaped blossoms with thick, stiff petals.
LOCATIONS:
☐ Dumbarton Oaks
☐ National Arboretum magnolia collection

Tulip Poplar or Tulip-Tree,
or Yellow Poplar
Liriodendron tulipifera L.
Magnolia Family *Magnoliaceae*

An important timber tree, and the tallest broad-leafed tree in the east. Our native tulip poplar and the Chinese tulip-tree (*Liriodendron chinense* Sarg.) are the only living trees in the world in the genus *Liriodendron*.

LEAVES
Simple, alternate, deciduous. Four-lobed, or sometimes with an extra pair of lobes at the base. 3½ - 6 in. (9 - 15 cm.) high and 4 - 6½ in. (10 - 16.5 cm.) wide. Margin smooth. Leaf nearly flat across the bottom. Top two lobes separated by a widely and shallowly "v"-shaped sinus. Usually glabrous. Petiole slender, 3 - 6 in. (7.5 - 15 cm.) long. Large stipules. The first native tree to leaf out in the spring. Early color bright yellow-green. Autumn color: yellow, early in the season.

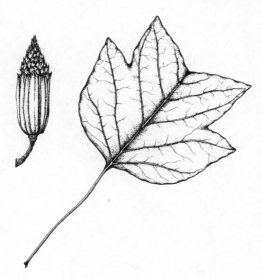

FLOWERS
In May. 1½ - 2 in (4 - 5 cm.) high, tulip-shaped, with six petals, and three down-curved sepals. Petals are greenish at the top with a broad orange band near the base. Many yellow stamens arranged around a yellowish cone in the center of the blossom.

FRUIT
A brown, erect, cone-like aggregate of samaras, 2½ - 3 in. (6.5 - 7.5 cm.) high. In the fall the winged samaras break free and fall to the ground. The central cone-like axis often remains on the tree through the winter.

BARK AND TWIGS
Bark becoming evenly and shallowly furrowed with age. Light brown or gray. Twigs reddish-brown with rounded leaf scars. Stipular scars encircling the twig. Winter buds flattened, shaped like ducks' bills.

HABIT
A tall, handsome tree with a long straight trunk and oblong crown. Visible from far away in winter because of its stature and the many candle-like remains of the fall fruit.

CULTIVAR
Liriodendron tulipifera 'Aureomarginatum.' A rare form with pale yellow leaf margins early in the season.

SIMILAR SPECIES
None. Unmistakable year round: in spring with its brilliant early foliage; in summer with its unique leaves; and in fall and winter with its candle-like fruit.

LOCATIONS
☐ U.S. Capitol grounds
☐ Mount Vernon (tree planted by George Washington).
☐ Montrose Park
☐ National Arboretum
☐ National Zoo
☐ Rock Creek Park
☐ Soldiers' Home

PAWPAW
Asimina triloba (L.) Dun.
Custard-Apple Family *Annonaceae*

The pawpaw is the only member of the largely tropical custard-apple family that is hardy in our area.

NATIVE HABITAT
Scattered distribution from New York south to Florida and west to Nebraska and Texas.

LEAVES
Simple, alternate, deciduous, 6 - 12 in. (about 15 - 30 cm.) long, with a smooth margin, abruptly pointed apex and wedge-shaped base.

FLOWERS
Purple, bell-shaped, just before the leaves in spring.

FRUIT
Greenish-yellow banana-like berry, 2 - 5 in. (5 - 12.7 cm.) long.

TWIGS
Slender, brown, pubescent when young, with dark brown *woolly* winter buds.

HABIT
Small tree.

SIMILAR SPECIES
Easily confused with the umbrella magnolia (*Magnolia tripetala*). In the absence of flowers or fruit, distinguish the two by the twigs. Umbrella magnolia twigs are stout and glabrous *with encircling stipular scars and glabrous winter buds.*

LOCATIONS
☐ Theodore Roosevelt Island
☐ U.S. Capitol grounds
☐ Along the Potomac and C&O Canal
☐ Cultivated in some private yards

SPICE-BUSH
Lindera benzoin (L.) Bl.
Laurel Family *Lauraceae*

Although the spice-bush is a shrub, it can reach a height of more than 16 feet (5 meters). Its twigs, leaves and fruit exude a pleasant spicy fragrance when crushed and have been used to make tea and spice. Deer, rabbits and birds favor the twigs and fruit of the aromatic spice-bush.

NATIVE HABITAT
Southwestern Maine to southern Ontario, Iowa and southeastern Kansas; south to Florida and Texas.

LEAVES
Simple, alternate, deciduous. Obovate or oblong-obovate, 2 - 6 in. (5 - 15.2 cm.) long. Base wedge-shaped; apex abruptly or gradually pointed. Margin smooth. Pale and glabrous or barely pubescent below.

FLOWERS
Before the leaves in early spring; yellow, in dense, rather showy clusters.

FRUIT
Small, red, berry-like drupe in autumn.

TWIGS
Slender, glabrous, brown, with spicy odor when crushed.

SIMILAR SPECIES
Sassafras *(Sassafras albidum)* also has spicy leaves and twigs, but its leaves are often two or three lobed, its fruit is dark blue and its twigs are greenish and glaucous. Dogwood *(Cornus* species) twigs and leaves have no spicy odor when crushed.

LOCATIONS
☐ Theodore Roosevelt Island
☐ Some parks, private homes and public buildings throughout the city

SASSAFRAS

Sassafras albidum (Nutt.) Nees.
Laurel Family *Lauraceae*

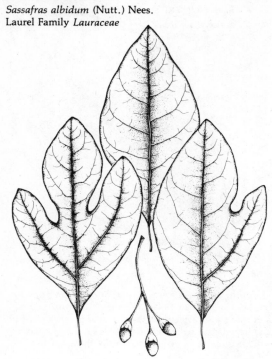

A tree with variable leaves, often unlobed, two-lobed, and three-lobed all on the same tree. Sassafras leaves, twigs, and bark have a pleasant spicy fragrance when crushed. Bark and roots are the source of "oil of sassafras," which is used in soaps. Sassafras tea is made from the roots of the tree.

In 1882 the great landscape architect, Frederick Law Olmsted, who was in Washington landscaping the Capitol grounds, wrote: "The Sassafras which, rarely seen except as a shrub in the far north, is here a stout and lofty tree, richly furnished, very sportive in its form of foliage, and often exceeding all other deciduous trees in picturesqueness."

NATIVE HABITAT
Southern Maine, New Hampshire, and Vermont to northern Florida; west to southeastern Iowa, eastern Kansas, Oklahoma, and Texas.

LEAVES
Simple, alternate, deciduous, 3 - 7½ in. (7.5 - 19 cm.) long. Three major leaf-shapes, often all on the same tree: 1) ovate; 2) mitten-like, with one large lobe and one smaller "thumb"; and 3) three-lobed. Margin smooth. Base wedge-shaped. Glabrous or velvety-pubescent beneath; glaucous. Petiole ⅔ - 1⅔ in. (1.5 - 4.2 cm.) long. Autumn color: orange and red.

FLOWERS
Male and female usually on separate trees. Yellowish green, with the young leaves in spring.

FRUIT
Small, dark blue berry-like drupe, about ⅓ in. (1 cm.) long, on a red or orange 1½ - 2 in. (3.8 - 5 cm.) stalk. Late summer and fall.

BARK AND TWIGS
Bark brown or reddish-brown and furrowed. Twigs greenish, glaucous, with spicy odor when broken. Leaf scar with only one bundle scar. Terminal bud present.

HABIT
Small to medium-sized tree with flat or pyramidal crown.

SIMILAR SPECIES
Spice-bush *(Lindera benzoin)* also has spicy-smelling twigs and leaves, but its leaves are never lobed, its fruit is red, and its twigs are brown.

LOCATIONS
☐ Fern Valley, National Arboretum
☐ Kenilworth Aquatic Gardens
☐ Rock Creek Park
☐ C&O Canal, between Georgetown and
  Great Falls, Md.
☐ Arlington Cemetery
☐ Private yards in the District

KATSURA-TREE
Cercidiphyllum japonicum Sieb. & Zucc.
Katsura-Tree Family *Cercidiphyllaceae*

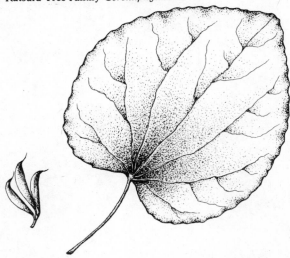

"Monotypic": One of the few trees in the world that is the sole species in its family and genus.

NATIVE HABITAT
Japan, China.

LEAVES
Simple, deciduous, heart-shaped, opposite or sub-opposite. Palmately veined. Green or bluish-green above; pale and slightly glaucous beneath; glabrous. 2 - 4 in. (5 - 10 cm.) high, 1½ - 3½ in. (3.8 - 9 cm.) wide. Wavy-toothed margin. Rounded or bluntly pointed apex; cordate base. Petiole thin, 1 - 1¾ in. (2.5 - 4.5 cm.) long. Autumn color: brilliant yellow.

FLOWERS
Before the leaves in spring; male and female on separate trees. Small reddish clusters of stamens (male tree), and red or purple styles (female tree); no petals.

FRUIT
Small, erect green pods on female tree in summer.

BARK AND TWIGS
Bark gray, shallowly fissured, may become shaggy with age. Twigs glabrous with opposite, pointed, brown winter buds on short spur shoots; conspicuous in winter.

HABIT
Upright when young. May become multi-trunked with age.

SIMILAR SPECIES
Redbuds (*Cercis canadensis* and *Cercis chinensis*) have larger, alternate leaves with smooth margins.

LOCATIONS
☐ Dumbarton Oaks , Georgetown
☐ U.S. Capitol grounds
☐ Smithsonian Museum of
　Natural History
☐ Stanton Park

SWEETGUM
OR REDGUM
Liquidambar styraciflua L.
Witch-Hazel Family *Hamamelidaceae*

Alexander Hamilton was so fond of the sweetgum that he wanted to see it adopted as "America's emblematic tree." Although the sweetgum never did become a national emblem, it has long been a popular ornamental and an important timber tree.

NATIVE HABITAT
Southern Connecticut and New York to Florida; west to Illinois, eastern Oklahoma, and Texas.

LEAVES
Simple, alternate, deciduous. Star-shaped, usually with five pointed lobes. About as long as wide: 3½ - 8½ in. (9 - 21.5 cm.). Sharply toothed. Palmately veined. Glabrous, but for tufts of hair in vein axils below. Petiole slender, anywhere from 2 - 7 in. (5 - 17.7 cm.) long. Autumn color: variable; often with several colors on the same tree.

FLOWERS
Male and female on the same tree. Inconspicuous yellow-green round heads, with the young leaves in spring.

FRUIT
A striking prickly sphere on a long, slender stalk, containing many beaked two-seeded capsules. Sphere 1 - 1½ in. (2.5 - 3.8 cm.) in diameter. Often remains on tree through the winter.

BARK AND TWIGS
Bark thick, furrowed, gray-brown. Twigs often with corky "wings."

HABIT
A large tree with a tall, full crown.

SIMILAR SPECIES
Maples (*Acer* species) have *opposite* leaves and dissimilar fruit. (Although sweetgum leaves are alternate, they may be very closely crowded together.) Plane trees (*Platanus* species) have light-colored peeling bark.

LOCATIONS
☐ U.S. Capitol grounds
☐ Constitution Gardens
☐ National Zoo (near polar bears)
☐ Polo Field, West Potomac Park
☐ Vietnam Veterans Memorial
☐ A common native tree

THE WITCH-HAZELS
Hamamelis sp.
Witch—Hazel Family *Hamamelidaceae*

Witch-Hazels are native to Asia and eastern North America. They bloom either in late autumn or early spring. The blossoms of these small trees or shrubs are usually pale yellow, with delicate, ribbon-like petals. While some Asian witch-hazels are cultivated in our area, they rarely attain tree stature.

COMMON WITCH-HAZEL

Hamamelis virginiana L.
Witch-Hazel Family *Hamamelidaceae*

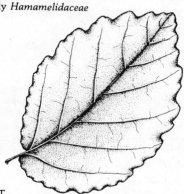

NATIVE HABITAT
Eastern United States, extreme southeastern Canada.

LEAVES
Simple, alternate, deciduous, 2 - 6 in (5 - 15 cm.) long.
Usually unequal at the base, with a scallop-toothed margin.

FLOWERS
Pale to bright yellow. Four ribbon-like petals per
blossom. Small but showy, October-December.

HABIT
Large, multi-trunked shrub or small tree with a broad,
rounded crown.

LOCATIONS
☐ National Arboretum
☐ Capitol Hill and Georgetown gardens
☐ Moderately common

PERSIAN IRONWOOD

Parrotia persica (DC.) C.A. Mey
Witch Hazel Family *Hamamelidaceae*

Two beautiful specimens of this rare tree stand on
the east and west sides of the White House south lawn.

NATIVE HABITAT
Northern Iran to Caucasus Mountains.

LEAVES
Simple, alternate, deciduous. Oblong-obovate or ovate with about six to nine pairs of deeply impressed veins. 2 - 5 in. (5 - 12.5 cm.) long, on a short petiole. Margin wavy or with a few coarse teeth above the middle.

BARK
Smooth, pinkish or grayish brown, breaking off in thin flakes to expose paler patches.

HABIT
Short, wide trunk dividing into many limbs. Although very large, White House specimens look shrubby.

LOCATIONS
☐ White House south lawn
☐ National Arboretum

LONDON PLANE TREE
Platanus x hispanica Muenchh.
(*Platanus x acerifolia* (Ait.) Willd.)
Plane Tree Family *Platanaceae*

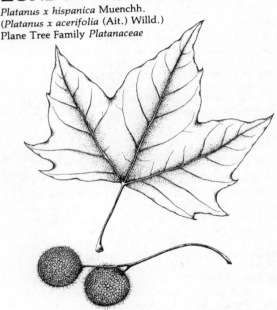

Widely planted in Washington, New York, Philadelphia, London, Paris, and other cities of the eastern U.S. and Europe. Commonly mistaken for its parents, the oriental plane (*Platanus orientalis*) and the American sycamore (*Platanus occidentalis*). The London Plane is the most frequently planted of the three, due to its remarkable resistance to disease, drought, and air pollution. The London plane varies a great deal, because it is actually a large *group* of hybrids. Trees planted in the U.S. often closely resemble the American sycamore, while those in Europe tend to display more characteristics of the oriental plane.

NATIVE HABITAT
Nonexistent in the wild. Arose as a hybrid between the North American and Eurasian species in Europe, probably in the seventeenth century.

LEAVES
Simple, alternate, deciduous. Three- to five-lobed, with pointed *lobes about as long as wide.* Sinuses usually narrow. Blade 4 - 10 in. (10 - 25.2 cm.) across and about as high, with individual leaves varying in size and shape. Glabrous or slightly pubescent, especially on the veins below. Margin with large, sparse, pointed teeth. Petiole short, ¾ in. - 4 in. (2 - 10 cm.) long, thickened at the base. Stipules often fall early.

FLOWERS
Males and females in separate round heads on the same tree in late spring.

FRUIT
Fruit heads round, brown, bristly, about an inch (2.5 cm.) in diameter; hanging on long stalks in *pairs or singly* (rarely in threes in the U.S.). Remaining on the tree until early spring, when individual seeds are scattered by the wind.

BARK AND TWIGS
Bark distinctive. Creamy white and tan on mature trees, often with patches of reddish-brown or gray older bark flaking off in a jigsaw puzzle-like pattern. Twig with winter buds hidden by thickened petiole bases in autumn. In winter, leaf scars nearly encircle buds, stipular scars encircle twig. Bud ovoid, covered by a single scale. Terminal bud lacking.

HABIT
A large tree with a long trunk and tall crown. Very striking in winter with its creamy bark and hanging fruit.

SIMILAR SPECIES
Very similar to the American sycamore or plane tree (*Platanus occidentalis*). Leaves of the American sycamore are usually more shallowly lobed, with shorter, broader lobes. The older bark on the sycamore tends not to peel off as extensively as on the London plane, especially toward the base of the tree, so that the London plane is often *whiter* looking. However, the best way to distinguish the two trees is to examine the fruit balls. American sycamore fruits hang *singly.* London plane fruits hang singly and in pairs. Therefore, if a tree *has any hanging pairs of fruits* (see illustration), it is a London plane. The oriental plane (*Platanus orientalis*), frequently mistaken for the London plane, is extremely rare in Washington. It has fruits hanging *in pairs and in groups of three or more.*

LOCATIONS
- ☐ U.S. Capitol grounds
- ☐ Dupont Circle
- ☐ Hains Point
- ☐ Potomac Parkway
- ☐ Mount Vernon
- ☐ Streets and parks throughout the city

ORIENTAL PLANE TREE

Platanus orientalis L.
Plane Tree Family *Platanaceae*

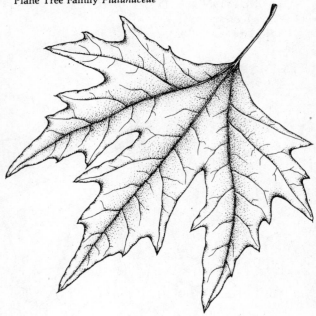

Native to southeastern Europe and western Asia, the Oriental plane tree was one of the world's first trees to be cultivated for shade and ornament. The literature of ancient Greece is replete with references to "the shady plane." The Oriental plane has frequently been confused with the London plane, and the extent of its cultivation in the eastern U.S. has consequently been overestimated. The tree is actually rare in Washington and other East Coast cities.

NATIVE HABITAT
Southern Europe and western Asia, where it has long been cultivated as a shade tree.

LEAVES
Similar to London plane *(Platanus x hispanica)*, but *sinuses are more deeply cut.* (See illustrations.)

FRUIT
Also similar to London plane, but often with *three or more fruitballs per stalk.*

LOCATIONS
□ Stanton Park
□ National Arboretum
□ University of Maryland campus

American Sycamore
or American Plane Tree
or Buttonwood

Platanus occidentalis L.
Plane Tree Family *Platanaceae*

One of the largest trees of the eastern U.S. Common in the wild, but not planted in cities as frequently as the London plane, which has greater resistance to disease, drought, and pollution. American sycamore wood is often used to make butchers' blocks.

NATIVE HABITAT
Southern Maine to southern Ontario and Minnesota; south to Texas and northern Florida. Prefers moist sites such as river basins.

LEAVES
Simple, alternate, deciduous. Three- to five-lobed, with shallow sinuses and *lobes broader than long*. Blade 4 - 10 in. (10 - 25.2 cm.) wide and about as long or slightly shorter. Pubescent along the veins below. Margin covered with large, coarse, pointed teeth. Petiole 1 - 4 in. (2.5 - 10 cm.) long. Stipules leaflike and conspicuous.

FLOWERS
After the leaves in spring. Males and females on the same tree in separate, round heads.

FRUIT
A round, brown fruiting head, about an inch (2.5 cm.) in diameter. Each fruiting head hangs *singly*, on a long stalk, through the winter. The heads break up in early spring, when individual seeds are dispersed by the wind.

BARK AND TWIGS
Outer reddish-brown and gray bark peels off in a jigsaw puzzle-like pattern, revealing yellow-white bark underneath. Outer bark near the base of tree thicker and breaking into smaller scales. Twigs reddish-brown, with conical buds covered by single yellow-brown scale. Stipular scars encircle twig. End buds "false."

HABIT
A large tree, with a long trunk and open crown.

SIMILAR SPECIES
See London Plane (*Platanus x hispanica*) "Similar Species" section.

LOCATIONS
- ☐ U.S. Capitol grounds
- ☐ Rock Creek Park
- ☐ Parks and private yards citywide
- ☐ Some city streets

AMERICAN ELM OR WHITE ELM
Ulmus americana L.
Elm Family *Ulmaceae*
STATE TREE OF MASSACHUSETTS AND
NORTH DAKOTA

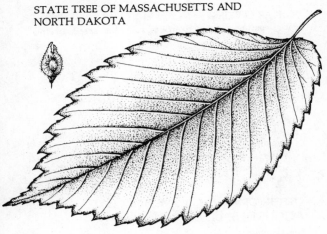

The loveliest of all elms, and one of America's favorite shade trees. Until very recently, the American elm lined the main streets of cities, towns, and villages throughout much of the United States. Unfortunately, Dutch elm disease (a fungus of European origin carried by the elm bark beetle) has all but destroyed the elm-lined avenue. However, arborists working for the National Park Service, the National Arboretum, and the District of Columbia government have helped the American elm stand its ground in Washington. While scientists hold little hope of finding a cure for Dutch elm disease, they have managed to save many of this city's historic trees. Meanwhile, new disease-resistant forms of the American elm are being propagated and tested here and elsewhere.

NATIVE HABITAT
Eastern U.S. and southeastern Canada from Newfoundland to Florida and west to the Rocky Mountains.

LEAVES
Simple, alternate, deciduous. Sharply and doubly toothed margin, long-pointed apex, and unequal base. 2 - 6 in. (5 - 15 cm.) long; oblong-ovate or obovate. More or less rough above, dark green. Paler below and pubescent or glabrous. Petiole ¼ - ½ in. (0.6 - 1.2 cm.) long.

FLOWERS
Early spring, before the leaves. Tiny, reddish, on pendulous stalks.

FRUIT
Flattened, papery samara, deeply notched at apex, containing a central seed. Margin hairy. About ½ in. (1.2 cm.) long. An important food source for migrating birds in the spring.

BARK AND TWIGS
Bark thick, gray, with vertical ridges and fissures. Twigs reddish-brown; winter buds scaly, ¼ in. (0.6 cm.) or more, red or mahogany.

HABIT
Very distinctive vase-shaped habit with long, graceful, more or less pendulous limbs.

SIMILAR SPECIES
Habit separates the American elm from other species of elm.

LOCATIONS
☐ The Mall
☐ U.S. Capitol grounds
☐ White House grounds
☐ West Potomac Park and Jefferson Memorial
☐ National Museum of American Art and National Portrait Gallery Courtyard
☐ 18th Street, N.E. between South Dakota and Montana Avenues
☐ New Hampshire Avenue, N.W.
☐ Streets, parks, grounds, and private yards throughout the city

OTHER FORMS OF THE AMERICAN ELM:
AUGUSTINE ELM
Ulmus americana 'Augustine'

Attractive form with a uniform, rectangular habit. Unfortunately, not as resistant to Dutch elm disease as it was once thought to be.

LOCATIONS
☐ Bladensburg Road, N.E. between Florida and New York Avenues
☐ M Street, N.W. between Connecticut Avenue and 28th Street
☐ L Street, N.W. between New York and Massachusetts Avenues
☐ 17th Street, N.W. between Florida and Massachusetts Avenues
☐ 18th Street, N.E. between South Dakota and Montana Avenues (young trees)

HORACE WESTER ELM

Ulmus americana 'Horace Wester'

Named for the Park Service plant pathologist
who selected and tested this vigorous clone for Dutch
elm disease. Repeated inoculations of the Horace
Wester elm have proven it to be unusually resistant to
the disease. Success appears to lie in the tree's ability to
seal off infected vessels with healthy, immune woody
tissue. Once the disease has been compartmentalized, the
tree is able to ougrow it. This promising new elm comes
into leaf two weeks earlier than is normal for the species
and retains its leaves two weeks later in the fall.

LOCATIONS
☐ White House northwest grounds (2 trees)
☐ Jefferson Memorial (2 trees)
☐ Washington Monument
☐ Custis-Lee Mansion (Arlington House), Arlington
  Cemetery

SLIPPERY OR RED ELM

Ulmus rubra Muhl.
(*U. fulva* Michx.)
Elm Family *Ulmaceae*

A native species, unimportant in cultivation. Similar
to the American elm (*Ulmus americana*), but with
flowers, usually stalkless; fruit pubescent on the *seed*,
but not along the margin; and densely *pubescent* reddish
winter buds. The inner bark is covered with a "slippery"
mucilaginous coating.

LOCATIONS
☐ Rock Creek Park

CEDAR ELM

Ulmus crassifolia Nutt.
Elm Family *Ulmaceae*

NATIVE HABITAT
Arkansas and Mississippi; west to Louisiana, Oklahoma,
and Texas. Very similar to the Chinese elm (*Ulmus parvifolia*) and a good example of the close relationship
between the flora of the southeastern U.S. and that of
parts of China and Japan. The cedar elm differs from the
Chinese species in having "sandpapery" leaves, pubescent
and less abundant fruit, and light gray, vertically furrowed, and scaly bark.

LOCATIONS
☐ The Mall, near the corner of 3rd Street and Maryland
  Avenue, S.W.
☐ Extremely rare in Washington

ENGLISH ELM

Ulmus procera Salisb.
Elm Family *Ulmaceae*

A large elm that looks much like an oak from a distance. A huge English elm dominates the southeast corner of the U.S. Capitol grounds. Until 1978, another English elm of the same age and stature stood on the northeast corner of the Capitol grounds. This tree was dubbed the "Humility Elm" by John F. Kennedy, because it forced tall pedestrians who passed under a low-hanging limb (including U.S. senators) to stoop.

NATIVE HABITAT
Great Britain.

LEAVES
Simple, alternate, deciduous. Shape variable; ovate or rounded. Dark green and rough above, softly pubescent along the veins below. 1⅔-4 in. (4-10 cm.) long. Sharply and doubly toothed, with unequal base and abruptly pointed apex. Petiole pubescent, about ¼ in. (4-6 mm.) long.

FLOWERS
Dark red, short-stalked, before the leaves in early spring.

FRUIT
Rounded, notched samara, about ½ in. (1.2 cm.) across. Single seed located close to the notch; notch closed at apex.

BARK AND TWIGS
Bark dark brown, fissured, often cracked into squarish plates. Twig slender, reddish-brown, pubescent. Winter buds darker red-brown, slightly pubescent.

HABIT
Straight, massive trunk reaching well into the crown. Healthy trees resemble oaks with their long, full crowns.

SIMILAR SPECIES
Similar to smooth-leaved elm (*Ulmus carpinifolia*) and some forms of the Dutch elm (*Ulmus × hollandica*). Smooth-leaved elm has leaves that are smooth above. Dutch elm leaves are smooth above or just barely roughened.

LOCATIONS
☐ U.S. Capitol grounds
☐ Lafayette Park
☐ Independence Avenue, in front of Hirshhorn Museum
☐ St. Elizabeth's Hospital grounds, including a variegated form

DUTCH ELM GROUP
(DUTCH, BELGIAN, HUNTINGDON, COMMELIN, AND BUISMAN ELMS)

Ulmus x hollandica Mill.
(*U. glabra x U. carpinifolia*)
Elm Family *Ulmaceae*

A large, confusing group of hybrids which are a cross between the Scotch elm (*Ulmus glabra*) and the smooth-leaved elm (*Ulmus carpinifolia*). The common name, Dutch elm, is ironic, as this tree and most other forms of the hybrid have shown excellent resistance to Dutch elm disease.

LEAVES
Simple, alternate, deciduous. Broadly elliptic or elliptic-ovate. Very unequal at base, often with one side slightly curled forward. Apex abruptly pointed or long-pointed. Coarsely doubly or triply toothed. 3-6 in. (7.5-15 cm.) long. Smooth or barely roughened above. Pubescent below along veins, which stand out prominently. Petiole pubescent, may be slightly pinkish, less than ½ in. (about 1 cm. or less) long.

FLOWERS
Red, short-stalked, in dense clusters. Early spring.

FRUIT
Single-seeded, notched samara, with seed touching the notch. Elliptic-obovate, ¾-1 in. (2-2.5 cm.) long.

BARK AND TWIGS
Bark vertically furrowed, light and dark gray. Young limbs smooth, light gray, with brown and darker gray cracks and ridges. Twigs stout, medium brown, soon glabrous. Winter buds red-brown, shiny, egg-shaped.

HABIT
Crown usually rounded, (not vase-like). Branches and trunk usually meet at V-shaped angle. Habit varies with different forms of hybrid.

SIMILAR SPECIES
Leaves larger and wider than smooth-leaved elm's (*Ulmus carpinifolia*). American elm (*Ulmus americana*), English elm (*Ulmus procera*), and Scotch elm (*Ulmus glabra*) have leaves that are *rough* to the touch. Zelkovas (*Zelkova* sps.) have *singly toothed* leaves.

LOCATIONS
- ☐ U.S. Capitol grounds
- ☐ The Mall (in front of the Freer Gallery)
- ☐ Tidal Basin
- ☐ Large trees lining the Lincoln Memorial Reflecting Pool are probably some form of this hybrid
- ☐ Experimental forms of the Dutch elm planted throughout the city

OTHER TREES IN THE DUTCH ELM GROUP:

BELGIAN ELM

Ulmus x hollandica 'Belgica.' This form originated in Belgium and is widely planted in Europe. **LEAF** more narrowly elliptic than the Dutch elm's, with a shorter petiole.

LOCATIONS:
- ☐ U.S. Capitol grounds
- ☐ National Academy of Sciences, Constitution Ave.
- ☐ Rarely planted in Washington

HUNTINGDON OR CHICHESTER ELM

Ulmus × hollandica 'Vegeta'

LOCATIONS:
- ☐ Washington Monument grounds

COMMELIN ELM

Ulmus × hollandica 'Commelin.' Form with a very upright, narrow crown and smaller leaves.

LOCATIONS:
- ☐ Tidal Basin

BUISMAN ELM

Ulmus × hollandica 'Buisman'. Resistant to Dutch elm disease, but of poor, unattractive habit.

LOCATIONS:
- ☐ Hains Point Golf Course

JAPANESE ELM

Ulmus davidiana var. *japonica* (Rehd.) Nakai
(*Ulmus japonica* (Rehd.) Sarg.)
Elm Family (*Ulmaceae*)

An elm native to Japan and N.E. Asia which has so far shown good resistance to Dutch elm disease and the elm-leaf beetle.

LEAVES: Simple, alternate, deciduous. Doubly-toothed, long-pointed, 3-4¾ in. (7.5-12 cm.) long. "Sand-papery" and pubescent above, pubescent below. **FRUIT:** Open-notched samara with the seed touching the notch.

LOCATIONS:
- ☐ NW corner of 21st and C Streets, N.W. (State Department Building grounds)
- ☐ Constitution Avenue, between 10th and 12th Streets, N.W.

SCOTCH ELM OR WYCH ELM
Ulmus glabra Huds.
Elm Family *Ulmaceae*

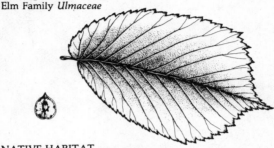

NATIVE HABITAT
Northern and Central Europe, western Asia.

LEAVES
Simple, alternate, deciduous. Large, up to 7 in. (about 18 cm.) long, sharply and doubly toothed. Very unequal base, widening slightly toward apex, then ending in an abrupt point. Many leaves have the suggestion of lobing toward the apex. Sand-papery rough above, pubescent below; on a very short, pubescent petiole.

FLOWERS
Densely clustered, purply red, before the leaves in early spring.

FRUIT
Large for an elm; up to an inch (2.5 cm.) across. Slightly notched, obovate or elliptic samara with a single seed in the middle.

BARK AND TWIGS
Bark smooth for many years; eventually becoming cracked and ridged. Twig reddish-brown with pubescent, red-brown buds.

HABIT
Crown broad with arching, nearly horizontal branches.

SIMILAR SPECIES
Leaf size and shape separate the Scotch elm from other elms planted here.

OTHER FORMS
Camperdown Elm (*Ulmus glabra* 'Camperdown'). Very dramatically weeping form, with branches reaching almost to the ground.

LOCATIONS
- ☐ U.S. Capitol grounds
- ☐ Fort McNair
- ☐ Some parks and private yards

CAMPERDOWN LOCATIONS
- ☐ White House grounds
- ☐ Thomas Circle

Smooth-Leaved Elm

Ulmus carpinifolia Gleditsch.
Elm Family *Ulmaceae*

NATIVE HABITAT
Europe, northern Africa, western Asia.

LEAVES
Simple, alternate, deciduous. Bright, shiny green and *smooth* above. Pubescent below in the vein axils and along the midrib. Doubly toothed margin. Base very unequal; apex long-pointed. Shape varies: elliptic, ovate or obovate. 2-3½ in. (5-9 cm.) long. Petiole pubescent, ¼-½ in. (6-12 mm.) long.

FLOWERS
Early spring in dense red clusters. Stigmas white.

FRUIT
Single-seeded samara with a wedge-shaped base and rounded apex. Seed located near the closed notch at apex.

BARK AND TWIGS
Bark gray or gray-brown with deep, vertical fissures and ridges. Twig slender, soon glabrous, light brown. Winter buds dark red with light brown tips; pubescent.

HABIT
Main limbs upright, with arching branches forming a rounded, usually fairly narrow crown.

SIMILAR SPECIES
English elm (*Ulmus procera*) and American elm (*Ulmus americana*) have leaves that are *rough* to the touch above. See Dutch and Belgian elms (*Ulmus* × *hollandica*).

OTHER FORMS
Ulmus carpinifolia 'Wredei.' Rare form with golden leaves.

LOCATIONS
☐ U.S. Capitol grounds
☐ Quite rare in Washington
☐ Montrose Park

Chinese Elm OR Lace-Bark Elm
Ulmus parvifolia Jacq.
Elm Family *Ulmaceae*

An attractive, fall-blooming elm that is resistant to Dutch elm disease and another common pest, the elm-leaf beetle. Experimental street plantings of the Chinese elm have been made in the District of Columbia.

NATIVE HABITAT
China, Korea, Japan.

LEAVES
Simple, alternate, deciduous. Small, ¾-2 in. (2-5 cm.) long, ½-¾ in. (1.2-2 cm.) wide. Singly (or just barely doubly) toothed. Shiny green and smooth above, paler below and pubescent when young. Ovate-lanceolate, obovate or elliptic. Base unequal or nearly equal; apex sharply or bluntly pointed. Petiole thin, pubescent, about ¼ in. (0.5 cm.) long. Nearly evergreen in the southern part of its range and in warmer parts of the U.S.

FLOWERS: Late summer or early fall. Small, greenish clusters.

FRUIT
Elliptic-ovate single-seeded samara less than ½ in. (about 1 cm.) long. Apex notched. Fruit develops in the fall and remains on the tree into late November or December.

BARK
Bark consists of "lacy" brown and orange scales. Twigs slender, reddish-brown, pubescent, with small reddish-brown buds.

HABIT
Graceful, somewhat vase-shaped, with long, pendulous branches.

SIMILAR SPECIES
The rare, fall-blooming cedar elm (*Ulmus crassifolia*) has leaves that are somewhat "sand-papery" above, very pubescent fruit, and gray, furrowed bark. Siberian elm (*Ulmus pumila*) blooms in the spring and has larger, usually long-pointed leaves.

LOCATIONS
- Library of Congress, southwest grounds
- National Arboretum (next to administration building)
- Fessenden Street, N.W. between Wisconsin Avenue and Reno Road
- Brandywine and 45th Street, N.W.

SIBERIAN ELM
Ulmus pumila L.
Elm Family *Ulmaceae*

NATIVE HABITAT
Eastern Siberia, Northern China, Turkmen

LEAVES
Simple, alternate, deciduous. 1-3¼ in. (2.5-8.2 cm.)
long, singly or slightly doubly-toothed. Usually long-
pointed; equal or nearly equal at the base. Smooth
above; glabrous or nearly so below; except when young.
Elliptic to elliptic-lanceolate. Petiole glabrous, ¼-½ in.
(0.5-1.3 cm.) long.

FLOWERS
Greenish, short-stalked, clustered, in spring.

FRUIT
Small, nearly round samara, ⅓-⅔ in. (about 1-1.5 cm.)
long. Single seed just above the middle. Notch closed at
apex.

BARK AND TWIGS
Bark gray or grayish brown, rough and furrowed. Twigs
light brown or gray, soon glabrous, with rounded, red-
brown, pubescent winter buds.

SIMILAR SPECIES
Chinese elm (*Ulmus parvifolia*) has smaller leaves with
more abruptly pointed apices and orange-brown, scaly
bark. The Chinese elm blooms and fruits in the fall.

LOCATIONS
□ Soldiers' Home
□ Walter Reed Army Medical Center
□ Nevada Avenue and Morrison Street, N.W.
□ Some Georgetown Streets

WINGED ELM
OR WAHOO ELM OR CORK ELM
Ulmus alata Michx.
Elm Family *Ulmaceae*

The common names, "winged" and "cork" elm, refer to the opposite corky "wings" which usually develop on the twigs of this tree.

NATIVE HABITAT: Virginia south to Florida; west to Texas, Oklahoma, and Missouri. **LEAVES:** Simple, alternate, deciduous. 1-2½ in. (2.5-6.3 cm.) long, coarsely doubly-toothed, on a very short petiole. Smooth or slightly roughened above, pubescent below. **FRUIT:** Spring. Single-seeded samara, ⅓ in. or (less than 1 cm. in length, narrowly ovate-elliptic, with 2 incurved beaks at apex. Always fringed at the margin and usually pubescent overall.
LOCATIONS:
□ U.S. Park Service Headquarters, Hains Point

ZELKOVA
OR JAPANESE ZELKOVA, OR KEAKI
Zelkova serrata (Thunb.) Mak.
Elm Family *Ulmaceae*

This elm family member is gaining great popularity in Washington as a street and shade tree.

NATIVE HABITAT
Japan

LEAVES
Simple, alternate, deciduous. Elm-like, but with sharply pointed *single* teeth and an equal or nearly equal base. 2¼-4¾ in. (5.5-12 cm.) long, with up to sixteen pairs of veins. Lanceolate-ovate, with *long-pointed* (acuminate) apex and variable base (rounded, wedge-shaped, straight across, or heart-shaped). *Glabrous* or nearly so. Petiole about ¼-⅔ in. (0.5-1.5 cm.) long. Leaves stay on tree until late fall or early winter.

FLOWERS AND FRUIT
Flowers small, inconspicuous, with the leaves in spring; greenish females in the leaf axils toward the tips of new branchlets, and males clustered in leaf axils toward new branchlet bases. Fruit is a tiny greenish drupe, ⅛ in. or slightly more (3-4 cm.) across.

BARK AND TWIGS
Bark on young trees smooth, gray, with pinkish horizontal stripes and orange-brown lenticels. Mature trees have very attractive scaly orange, brown, and gray bark. Twigs are slender, glabrous, reddish-brown, and somewhat "zigzagged," with small, ovoid, red-brown winter buds.

HABIT
Broad, rounded crown with widely spreading branches. Young tree trunks straight, slightly enlarged at base. Older trees with very large trunks and limbs radiating outward not far from the ground.

SIMILAR SPECIES
See Caucasian elm "Similar Species" section. This zelkova differs from the true elms in having leaves that are *always singly toothed* and nearly equal at the base; distinctive bark and habit; and fruit that is not a samara.

LOCATIONS
- ☐ Sixth and G Streets, S.W.
- ☐ U.S. Capitol grounds
- ☐ Garfield Park
- ☐ Orren Street, N.E.
- ☐ 45th, Van Ness, and Weston Streets, N.W.
- ☐ Jefferson Memorial
- ☐ Hains Point
- ☐ Freer Gallery, Independence Avenue

CAUCASIAN ELM
Zelkova carpinifolia (Pall.) K. Koch.
Elm Family *Ulmaceae*

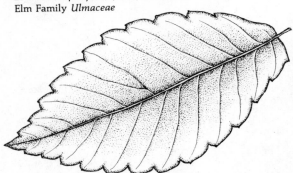

The Caucasian elm should be named "Caucasian zelkova" as it is not a true elm, but a zelkova closely related to the preceding species. Native to the Caucasus Mountains, this tree is very rare in Washington.

LEAVES
Simple, alternate, deciduous. Similar to Japanese zelkova, but *without long-pointed apex* (see drawings) and with fatter, less sharply pointed teeth. 1¾-4 in. (4.5-10 cm.) long, usually with *no more than twelve* pairs of veins. Whitish hairs along the veins below; petiole pubescent.

BARK
Smooth greenish or pinkish gray; scaly, revealing orange underneath.

HABIT
Very striking and unique; trunk fluted, with many limbs arising from the same level, not far from the ground, to form a large, egg-shaped crown.

LOCATIONS
☐ The Mall, near the U.S. Capitol reflecting pool
☐ U.S. Capitol grounds

Cut-Leaf Zelkova
Zelkova x *verschaffeltii* (Dipp.) Nichols.
Elm Family *Ulmaceae*

An extremely rare hybrid. Small leaves, 1¼-2½ in. (about 3-6 cm.) long, have five to nine pairs of large, pointed, slightly outcurved teeth. Rough above, pubescent below. Bark is similar to Caucasian elm's (*Zelkova carpinifolia*). Twigs and tiny winter buds are reddish-brown and pubescent. Large shrub or small tree.

SIMILAR SPECIES
Far more common cut-leaf or fern-leaf beech (*Fagus sylvatica* 'Heterophylla') reaches greater height and has even, gray bark and long, pointed winter buds.

LOCATIONS
☐ Tidal Basin, near the Jefferson Memorial

Schneider's Zelkova
Zelkova schneideriana Hand.-Mazz.
Elm Family *Ulmaceae*

Native to eastern China. Very rare here. Leaves are 1½-3½ in. (4-9 cm.) long with fat, incurved teeth and long-pointed apices; softly pubescent below, on a pubescent petiole. Twigs and small winter buds are reddish-brown and pubescent.

SIMILAR SPECIES: The common Japanese zelkova has *glabrous* leaves. The rare Caucasian elm has leaves *without* long-pointed apices.
LOCATIONS:
☐ U.S. Capitol grounds (south side)

HACKBERRY
Celtis occidentalis L.
Elm Family *Ulmaceae*

Like the beeches, the hackberries have pale gray bark. Hackberry bark is usually marked with conspicuous wart-like protuberances.

NATIVE HABITAT
Québec to Idaho; south to Florida, Arkansas, Oklahoma, and Utah.

LEAVES
Simple, alternate, deciduous. Ovate, 2-5 in. (5-12.5 cm.) long. Usually unequal at base, sharply toothed, (except near the base) and long-pointed. Usually glabrous, but may be pubescent along the veins below.

FRUIT
Small orange-red to purple berry-like drupe.

HABIT
Straight trunk; spreading, sometimes pendulous branches, and a full, rounded crown.

SIMILAR SPECIES
Two other species of hackberry are planted in Washington: the exotic Chinese hackberry *(Celtis sinensis)* and the Mississippi hackberry *(Celtis laevigata)*. Brief descriptions of their differing characteristics follow.

LOCATIONS
☐ Frederick Douglass Home
☐ Parks, private homes, and public buildings citywide

CHINESE HACKBERRY
Celtis sinensis Pers.
Elm Family *Ulmaceae*

The Chinese hackberry has dark green leaves that are thick, almost leathery in texture. The leaf margin of this species is toothed only toward the apex. The dark orange fruit contains a ribbed, pitted stone.

NATIVE HABITAT: China, Korea, Japan.
LOCATIONS:
☐ Garfield Park
☐ A few city parks

Mississippi Hackberry
OR SUGARBERRY
Celtis laevigata Willd.
Elm Family *Ulmaceae*

NATIVE HABITAT: Southern Indiana and Illinois to
Texas and Florida. **LEAVES:** Narrower and thinner than
the two preceding species; oblong-lanceolate. Margins
entire or with a few teeth.
LOCATIONS:
☐ The Mall
☐ Rare in Washington

White Mulberry
Morus alba L.
Mulberry Family *Moraceae*

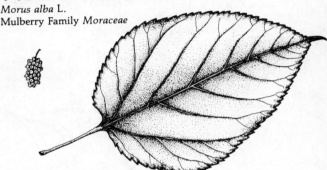

This is the mulberry that nourishes the silkworm.

NATIVE HABITAT
China. (Widely naturalized in Asia, Europe and
America.)

LEAVES
Simple, alternate, deciduous. Ovate, 2-4 in. (5-10 cm.)
long; variously lobed or unlobed. Coarsely toothed,
often with bluntly pointed teeth. Base rounded or
cordate. *Usually smooth above, glabrous below* or
pubescent only along the veins.

FRUIT
The familiar mulberry shape, ⅓-1 in. (1-2.5 cm.) long;
white, pinkish, or purple.

OTHER FORMS
Many forms of the white mulberry are in cultivation in
Washington. Particularly striking is the weeping form
(*Morus alba pendula*), with long, slender, vertically
hanging branches.

SIMILAR SPECIES
The other mulberries in cultivation in Washington, and
the paper mulberry (*Broussonetia papyrifera*) have leaves
that are pubescent below.

LOCATIONS
☐ Washington Monument grounds (two magnificent
trees)
☐ National Zoo (including weeping form)
☐ Soldiers' Home (including weeping form)
☐ Quite common throughout D.C.

Red Mulberry

Morus rubra L.
Mulberry Family *Moraceae*

The red mulberry has leaves that are similar to the white mulberry (*Morus alba*), already described. However, red mulberry leaves are usually at least *slightly rough* above and *pubescent* below. The red mulberry leaf is not nearly as rough above as that of the paper mulberry (*Broussonetia papyrifera*); the paper mulberry can also be distinguished by its *roughly pubescent twigs.* Red mulberry fruit is purple and sweet.

NATIVE HABITAT: Massachusetts to Florida; west to Michigan, Kansas, and Texas.

LOCATIONS:
☐ National Arboretum
☐ Kenilworth Aquatic Gardens
☐ Common in the city

Paper Mulberry

Broussonetia papyrifera (L.) Vent.
Mulberry Family *Moraceae*

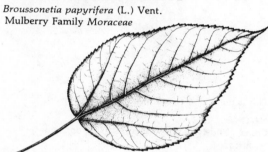

The bark of this tree is used to make paper in Japan.

NATIVE HABITAT
China, Japan.

LEAVES
Alternate, simple, deciduous. (Occasionally leaves are arranged oppositely.) Heart-shaped, or with a rounded base, 3-8 in. (7.5-20 cm.) long, with coarse, outwardly pointed teeth. (Leaves usually lobed.) Rough above, *grayish-green, soft and velvety pubescent below.* Petiole pubescent.

FLOWERS AND FRUIT
Male catkins and round female flowers on separate trees. Fruit ripens round and orange-red on female trees.

BARK AND TWIGS
Bark gray, smooth. Twigs stout, *roughly* pubescent.

SIMILAR SPECIES
True mulberries.

LOCATIONS
☐ National Zoo
☐ C&O Canal, Georgetown
☐ Quite common throughout the city

Osage-Orange ("Bodarc")

Maclura pomifera (Raf.) Schneid.
Mulberry Family *Moraceae*

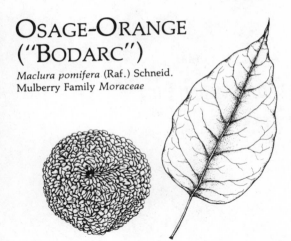

Native to the home of the Osage Indians, who used the wood to make archery bows. The French name which consequently arose, "bois d'arc" (bow wood), became "Bodarc" or "Bodock" in parts of the south-central U.S. This name is still used today. The tree yields a yellow dye.

NATIVE HABITAT
Northern Texas, southwest Arkansas, southeast Oklahoma. Now naturalized in parts of the east.

LEAVES
Simple, alternate, deciduous. Ovate, 2-6 in. (5-15 cm.) long. Shiny green above, paler below, and glabrous at maturity. Margin smooth. May be wedge-shaped, rounded, or slightly cordate at base. Long-pointed apex. Petiole 1-2½ in. (2.5-5.5 cm.) long. Autumn color: clear light yellow.

FLOWERS
Late spring. Males and females on separate trees. Not showy.

FRUIT
Female trees only. Large, round, yellow-green. Surface finely convoluted, like the surface of a brain. Vaguely resembles an orange; hence the name of the tree. May reach grapefruit size. Contains a bitter milky juice.

BARK AND TWIGS
Bark a distinctive dark orange-brown; irregularly ridged and furrowed. Sap milky. Twigs with stout thorns, ½-¾ in. (about 1-2 cm.) long. Winter buds small, rounded, depressed; terminal bud absent.

HABIT
Few branches forming an irregular crown.

SIMILAR SPECIES
From a distance it may be mistaken for a mulberry (*Morus* species). However, the combination of smooth-margined leaves, orange-brown bark, and unusual fruit set the osage-orange apart.

LOCATIONS
☐ Soldiers' Home (huge, ancient tree next to the Anderson Cottage)
☐ Montrose Park
☐ U.S. Capitol grounds

COMMON FIG

Ficus carica L.
Mulberry Family *Moraceae*

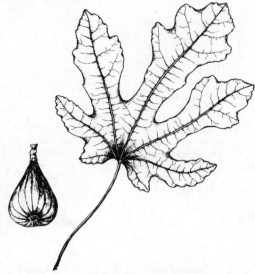

This is the fig that has long been cultivated in Europe and North America for its fruit. Usually a shrub, but may grow to become a small tree. Most other members of the genus *Ficus* are hardy only in or near the tropics.

NATIVE HABITAT
Western Asia, eastern Mediterranean.

LEAF
Simple, alternate, and unlike most members of the genus, deciduous. 4-8 in. (10-20 cm.) long, 3½-7½ in. (9-19 cm.) wide; rough to the touch above and below. Three to five narrow lobes separated by deep sinuses. Margin with large rounded or bluntly pointed teeth. Yellow-white veins prominent, palmately arranged. Petiole 2-4 in. (5-10 cm.) long.

FLOWERS
Borne inside a fleshy receptacle that later develops into the fruit.

FRUIT
The familiar fig; pear-shaped and greenish or brownish-purple when ripe in the fall.

HABIT
A spreading shrub or small tree.

LOCATIONS
☐ Backyards and gardens throughout the District

American Beech

Fagus grandifolia Ehrh.
Beech Family *Fagaceae*

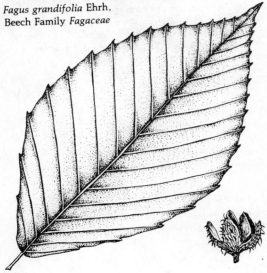

A lovely shade tree with smooth, gray bark and a large, rounded crown.

NATIVE HABITAT
New Brunswick to southern Ontario; south to northern Florida, eastern Texas, and Mexico.

LEAVES
Simple, alternate, deciduous. Ovate-elliptic, 2-4½ in. (5-11.5 cm.) long, with *nine or more pairs of veins*. One sharp tooth at each point where vein meets leaf margin. Veins very straight, pinnately arranged. Apex pointed. Base rounded or wedge-shaped; may be unequal. Sometimes slightly pubescent below, especially when young. Petiole less than ½ in. (0.5 to 1 cm.) long, glabrous or barely pubescent.

FLOWERS
Male and female flowers on the same tree: Males yellowish, numerous, in hanging round clusters; two to four females in a spike at the end of branchlet. In spring, with the leaves.

FRUIT
Two or three edible, triangular nuts, each ¾ in. (2 cm.) or less in length, enclosed in a prickly husk. In the fall, the husk opens and releases the nuts, which are a favorite food of squirrels.

BARK AND TWIGS
Bark an irresistibly smooth gray (the favorite tree of lovers and other initial carvers). Twigs slender with long, pointed, reddish winter buds.

HABIT
Rather short, straight trunk, with many limbs forming a full, rounded crown. A striking winter tree with its silvery limbs and handsome form.

SIMILAR SPECIES
Very similar to the European beech (*Fagus sylvatica*).
The best way to distinguish the two is to count the veins
(see "LEAVES" section for each species). The only other
mature trees with similar bark are the hackberries (*Celtis
sps.*) and yellow-wood (*Cladrastis kentukea*) Hackberry
bark is *warty* in places. Yellow-wood has pinnately compound leaves and naked winter buds.

LOCATIONS
☐ U.S. Capitol grounds
☐ Dumbarton Oaks
☐ Montrose Park
☐ Rock Creek Park (growing wild)
☐ Meridian Hill Park
☐ Sligo Creek Parkway, Takoma Park, MD
☐ Quite common throughout D.C.

EUROPEAN BEECH

Fagus sylvatica L.
Beech Family *Fagaceae*

The European beech is widely planted in Washington. Three different forms of this tree are also popular
here: the copper (or purple) beech; cut-leaf (or fern-leaf)
beech; and the weeping beech. (See "OTHER FORMS".)

NATIVE HABITAT
Central and southern Europe.

LEAVES
Simple, alternate, deciduous. Ovate-elliptic, 2-4½ in.
(5-11.5 cm.) long, with *eight or fewer pairs of veins*.
Leaf margin wavy, or with one blunt tooth at each point
where vein meets margin. Buff pubescence below, especially in vein axils. Petiole ½ in. or more (about 1.5
cm.) long, pubescent. Base usually wedge-shaped and
often slightly unequal; apex bluntly or sharply pointed.
Autumn color: Yellow, orange, late in the season (after
the American beech (*Fagus grandifolia*) has lost its
leaves).

FLOWERS
Male and female flowers on the same tree. In spring,
with the leaves; males in hanging, pale yellow, rounded
clusters; females fewer, on short stalks.

FRUIT
Edible, triangular nut, enclosed in a prickly husk about 1
in. (2.5 cm.) long. Husks open, releasing the nuts, which
are popular with squirrels.

BARK AND TWIGS
Gray, smooth or slightly roughened. Twigs with striking
winter buds: long and narrow, scaly, reddish-brown at
base, light yellow-brown toward the sharply pointed tip.

HABIT
A large tree with a very rounded crown and short trunk.

SIMILAR SPECIES
The American Beech (*F. grandifolia*) has leaves with *nine
or more pairs of veins*, paler bark and slightly smaller
fruit husks.

LOCATIONS
☐ Along Potomac Parkway between the Lincoln
   Memorial and the Kennedy Center
☐ Ellipse

OTHER FORMS

COPPER BEECH OR PURPLE BEECH
Fagus sylvatica f. *purpurea* (Ait.) Schneid.

   Leaves coppery green or deep purple.

LOCATIONS
☐ Folger Park
☐ Dumbarton Oaks (huge tree near amphitheater)
☐ Rock Creek Cemetery
☐ Soldiers' Home
☐ Smithsonian National Museum of Natural History

FERN-LEAF BEECH
OR CUT-LEAF BEECH
F. sylvatica 'Heterophylla,' or 'Asplenifolia'

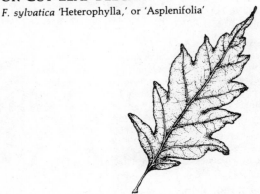

   Leaves narrow, deeply cut, like small oak leaves.

LOCATIONS
☐ White House (trees on the Pennsylvania Avenue side
   planted by Mrs. Johnson and Mrs. Nixon)
☐ Folger Park

Weeping Beech
Fagus sylvatica f. *pendula* (Loud.) Schelle

Branches pendulous. Tree may be tall and narrow, or full and rounded.

LOCATIONS
☐ Private yards throughout D.C.

Chinese Chestnut
Castanea mollissima Bl.
Beech Family *Fagaceae*

The Chinese chestnut holds the ignominious distinction of being the probable source of the Asian fungus responsible for the tragic chestnut blight. In this century, the blight has totally destroyed the magnificent stands of American chestnuts (*Castanea dentata*) that once dominated forests throughout the eastern United States. Ironically, the Chinese chestnut itself is immune to the blight and is therefore planted extensively in Washington and elsewhere. However, it is a poor substitute, in stature and in sweetness of fruit, for the good old American chestnut.

NATIVE HABITAT
China, Korea.

LEAVES
Simple, alternate, deciduous. 3-7 in. (7.5-17.8 cm.) long. Oblong-lanceolate or oblong-elliptic with a rounded, squared, or wedge-shaped base and a gradually or abruptly pointed apex. Margin has coarse, sharply pointed teeth. Dark, glossy green above; whitish or pale green below and softly pubescent.

FLOWERS
Late spring and early summer. Male flowers in showy, bright yellow catkins 4-9 in. (10-22.8 cm.) long.

FRUIT
Painfully prickly bur, 1-2½ in. (2.5-6.3 cm.) across; splits in early autumn to release one to three edible chestnuts. Each nut less than an inch (less than 2.5 cm.) across, "chestnut" brown, with a pale scar across the base.

BARK AND TWIGS
Bark furrowed; twigs pubescent, sometimes with long,
spreading hairs.

HABIT
A small tree with widely spreading branches.

SIMILAR SPECIES
The American chestnut (*Castanea dentata*) almost never
reaches tree proportions any more, due to the blight.
The only common ornamental in Washington that the
Chinese chestnut is apt to be confused with is the saw-
toothed oak (*Quercus acutissima*). The oak has a similar
leaf, but *each of its teeth ends in a long bristle-tip*. In the
fall the trees can be readily distinguished by their fruit.

LOCATIONS
□ Lincoln Park
□ Kenilworth Aquatic Gardens
□ Hains Point
□ National Zoo
□ Parks, streets, public buildings and private homes

AMERICAN CHESTNUT
Castanea dentata Borkh.
Beech Family *Fagaceae*

While foreign trees and other flowering plants have
enhanced the beauty of towns and cities throughout the
country, exotic plants can harbor pests and diseases for
which our domestic flora have no immunity. Earlier in
this century, the European elm bark beetle arrived unin-
vited from Europe (probably on a shipment of elm logs),
bringing the disease that was to denude American elm-
lined avenues throughout the country. But even before
Dutch elm disease began its relentless journey up and
down America's streets, an even more insidious foreign
blight had nearly destroyed the American chestnut, one
of the most beautiful and important deciduous trees of
the eastern United States. Victim of an Asian fungus
probably imported on seedlings of Chinese and Japanese
chestnuts, the American chestnut was the dominant tree
in eastern forests for centuries. It is now unable to survive for more than a few years.

The chestnut blight began killing trees in the northeastern states soon after the turn of the century. The
fungus (*Endothia parasitica*) attacks the bark of the
American chestnut, creating a spreading canker, which
eventually encircles the tree, cutting off the flow of
nutrients. The blight spreads rapidly, and has killed virtually every mature chestnut in the east.

Although science has found no cure for the disease,
the story of the American chestnut is not over. The
roots of the tree are not destroyed by the fungus and
they persist in sending up new sprouts, year after year,
although these eventually succumb to the blight. In
Europe, a new weaker strain of the fungus has developed
which European chestnuts are able to outgrow. Experiments are now being conducted in this country aimed at
duplicating European successes. Therefore, we can hope
for the return of this magnificent tree. Hybrids of the

American chestnut and blight-resistant Asian species have also been developed, but these trees lack the stature of the American chestnut.

Before the blight struck, the American chestnut was used to build furniture and for split-rail fences, musical instruments, home interiors, and shingles in addition to producing its famous nuts which were popular with people and wildlife.

In the Great Smokies of North Carolina, chestnut trees stood 120 feet with trunks 13 feet in diameter.

NATIVE HABITAT: Maine, New York, southern Ontario, and southeastern Michigan to Georgia and northeastern Mississippi. **LEAVES:** Simple, alternate, deciduous. 5-9 in. (12.6-22.8 cm.) long. Oblong-lanceolate to oblong-elliptic. Margin sharply toothed. Base wedge-shaped; apex abruptly or gradually pointed. Yellow-green above and below; glabrous. (May have tiny glands below when young.) **FLOWERS:** Late spring and early summer. Males in yellowish-green catkins 4-10 in. (10-25.3 cm.) long. **FRUIT:** Two to three ½-1 in. (1.3-2.5 cm.) long, edible nuts contained in a sharply spiny bur. **HABIT:** Once a tall tree with a broad, open crown; since the chestnut blight, rarely more than a shrub or small tree in its native habitat. **SIMILAR SPECIES:** The Chinese chestnut (*Castanea mollissima*) is the chestnut most commonly planted in Washington since the advent of the blight. Its leaves are *whitish or very pale green and pubescent below.* The eastern or Allegheny chinkapin (*Castanea pumila* (L.) Mill.), which is not included in this guide, is a *native shrub* with leaves that are *whitish and pubescent below,* with *short,* coarse teeth. The rare Japanese chestnut (*Castanea crenata* Sieb. & Zucc.), also not included, has leaves that are usually pubescent below, at least along the veins.
LOCATIONS:
☐ Mount Vernon (young tree)
☐ Young shoots which soon succumb to the blight in parks throughout the area

SOUTHERN RED OAK
OR SPANISH OAK
Quercus falcata Michx.
Beech Family *Fagaceae*

A very attractive oak, with intriguing, narrow, ir-regularly lobed leaves. Not as frequently planted as the following species.

NATIVE HABITAT
Southeastern New York west to southern Illinois; south-ern Missouri and eastern Texas; south to Louisiana and northern Florida.

LEAVES
Simple, alternate, deciduous. 3½-10 in. (9-25.3 cm.) long, with three to seven narrow, often sickle-shaped, bristle-tipped lobes. Dark green above, paler and more or less woolly below. Petiole 1-2 in. (2.5-5 cm.) long.

FRUIT
Acorn, maturing in two years. Short-stalked, about ½ in. (1-1.5 cm.) long. Enclosed for one-third of its length *or less* by cup covered with pubescent, appressed scales.

BARK AND TWIGS
Bark thick, dark and furrowed. Twigs stout, reddish-brown, usually pubescent. Winter buds ovoid, pubes-cent, dark red.

HABIT
Medium-sized tree with a full, rounded crown.

SIMILAR SPECIES
No other oak in our area has leaves like the leaves of this tree. (See illustration)

LOCATIONS
☐ Smithsonian Arts and Industries Building
☐ Hains Point Golf Course
☐ National Arboretum
☐ Embassy of the Netherlands
☐ Soldiers' Home
☐ Some public buildings and private homes

RED OAK
OR NORTHERN RED OAK
Quercus rubra L.
(*Quercus borealis* Michx.)
Beech Family *Fagaceae*

STATE TREE OF NEW JERSEY

Widely planted throughout the city, along streets, in parks, and around public buildings and private homes.

NATIVE HABITAT
Nova Scotia, Québec, Michigan, and Minnesota; south to southeastern Oklahoma and Georgia.

LEAVES
Simple, alternate, deciduous. 4-10 in. (10-25.3 cm) long. Seven to eleven toothed, bristle-tipped lobes are cut about halfway to the midrib. Lobes point forward. Dull, medium green above, paler below and glabrous, except for small tufts of brownish hairs in the vein axils. Petiole up to 2 in. (5 cm.) long.

FRUIT
Acorn, maturing in two years. Oblong-ovoid, ⅔-1 in. (about 1.5-2.5 cm.) long, sessile or nearly so. Enclosed for one-third of its length *or less* in reddish-brown, saucer-shaped cup with many small, closely appressed scales.

BARK AND TWIGS
Bark thick, dark brown or nearly black, with shallow furrows, and flat, sometimes lighter colored, ridges. Twigs shiny reddish-brown, becoming glabrous, with scaly, ovoid, reddish-brown winter buds. Buds have scales that are *pubescent only at tips.*

HABIT
Medium-sized to large tree with stout, spreading branches forming a broad, rounded crown.

SIMILAR SPECIES
The black oak (*Quercus velutina*) is less commonly planted in Washington. Its leaves are similar in shape, but they are *dark, glossy green above* and usually *pubescent below*. Its acorn is enclosed for up to half of its length in a *bowl-shaped* cup. The scarlet oak (*Quercus coccinea*) and the pin oak (*Quercus palustris) have leaves that are cut more than halfway to the midrib.*

LOCATIONS
- □ White House grounds
- □ U.S. Capitol grounds
- □ Union Station (trees planted by the Daughters of the American Revolution in honor of U.S. Presidents)
- □ Streets throughout D.C., including South Dakota Avenue, N.E., and 34th Place, N.W.
- □ The Vice President's House

SCARLET OAK
Quercus coccinea Muenchh.
Beech Family *Fagaceae*
OFFICIAL TREE OF
THE DISTRICT OF COLUMBIA

The official tree of the District of Columbia is one of the world's *most beautiful* oaks. Its scarlet autumn foliage has earned it the distinction of being one of the city's most popular street trees.

NATIVE HABITAT
Southwestern Maine and southern Ontario west to southeastern Missouri; south to Georgia, Alabama, and Mississippi.

LEAVES
Simple, alternate, deciduous. 3 - 7 in. (7.5 - 17.8 cm.) long. Five to nine (usually seven) toothed, bristle-tipped lobes have *deep, rounded* sinuses between them. Side lobes point straight outward or slightly forward. Bright shiny green above, paler below. Glabrous except for tufts of hairs in the vein axils below. Petiole 1¼ - 3 in. (about 3 - 7.5 cm.) long.

FRUIT
Acorn, maturing in two years. Short-stalked or sessile. ½ - 1 in. (1.3 - 2.5 cm.) long, usually with *several concentric rings near the apex.* Reddish-brown, enclosed for one-half of its length or less by scaly bowl-shaped cup.

BARK AND TWIGS
Bark thick, dark, furrowed, and scaly. Twigs slender, soon glabrous, reddish-brown; red-brown winter buds have silky pubescence on the upper half of their scales.

HABIT
Medium-sized to tall tree with ascending and spreading branches forming an open, rounded crown.

SIMILAR SPECIES
In the absence of fruit, very difficult to distinguish from the pin oak *(Quercus palustris)*. Pin oak acorns are smaller, with shallow, saucer-shaped cups. During the spring and summer, the best way to tell the two trees apart is by their habits. The pin oak has an *egg-shaped crown* and *drooping lower branches*. However, beware of pin oaks that have had their lower branches pruned!

LOCATIONS
☐ New Hampshire Avenue, N.W.
☐ Eastern Avenue, N.E.
☐ White House grounds
☐ Hillwood Estate
☐ Constitution Gardens
☐ U.S. Supreme Court and Capitol grounds

Pin Oak

Quercus palustris Muenchh.
Beech Family *Fagaceae*

Very similar to the scarlet oak *(Quercus coccinea* Muenchh.), but with a distinctive egg-shaped habit, drooping lower branches, and smaller acorns.

NATIVE HABITAT
Southern New England and New York south to North Carolina; west to southeastern Iowa; eastern Kansas and Oklahoma.

LEAVES
Simple, alternate, deciduous. 3 - 7 in. (7.5 - 17.8 cm.) long. Five to seven toothed, bristle-tipped lobes have *deep sinuses* between them. Side lobes point slightly forward or straight outward. Bright green above, paler below and glabrous but for tufts of hair in the vein axils. Petiole ¾ - 2 in. (2 - 5 cm.) long.

FRUIT
Small acorn, about ½ in. (1.3 cm.) long, maturing in two years. Short-stalked or sessile. Light brown, often with thin, vague, vertical stripes. Shallow, saucer-shaped cup is covered with small, reddish-brown scales.

BARK AND TWIGS
Bark grayish-brown; smooth on young trees, becoming furrowed and scaly with age. Twigs reddish-brown, becoming glabrous. Winter buds reddish-brown, scaly, sharply pointed.

HABIT
Egg-shaped or pyramidal crown. Many small branches usually radiate outward from a tall, central trunk; lower branches droop (but are often pruned in the city).

SIMILAR SPECIES
Very similar to the scarlet oak (*Quercus coccinea*). The scarlet oak has a larger acorn which may be enclosed for up to half of its length by a *bowl-shaped cup*. (See illustrations.) In the absence of fruit, the best way to distinguish the two trees is according to habit. The pin oak's central trunk often continues almost to the top of its egg-shaped crown, with *many small branches radiating outward and downward* from it. The scarlet oak splits into *several large, ascending and spreading limbs* that form an open, rounded crown.

LOCATIONS
- ☐ White House grounds
- ☐ U.S. Capitol grounds
- ☐ Hains Point
- ☐ Massachusetts Avenue, N.W. beyond the Naval Observatory
- ☐ Smithsonian National Museum of American History

WILLOW OAK
Quercus phellos L.
Beech Family *Fagaceae*

An absolutely beautiful tree with strong, clean lines and delicate, willow-like foliage. The willow oak was Thomas Jefferson's favorite tree.

NATIVE HABITAT
Southeastern New York to parts of northern Florida; west to eastern Oklahoma and Texas.

LEAVES
Simple, alternate, deciduous. Linear-oblong to lanceolate; 2 - 5 in. (5 - 12.6 cm.) long and about ½ in. (1 - 1.5 cm.) wide. Margin smooth or slightly wavy. Apex bristle-tipped; base wedge-shaped or rounded. Lustrous green and glabrous above; paler below and pubescent or glabrous. Petiole very short.

FRUIT
Small, greenish or yellowish-brown acorn, maturing in two years. Sessile or short-stalked. ½ in. or less (about 1 cm.) in length, and enclosed only at the base by a scaly, reddish-brown, saucer-shaped cup.

BARK AND TWIGS
Bark thick, dark, shallowly furrowed. Twigs slender,
glabrous, reddish-brown. Winter buds small, narrow,
sharply pointed, reddish-brown.

HABIT
Tall tree with a large, straight trunk and handsome,
rounded crown.

SIMILAR SPECIES
The rarely planted laurel (or darlington) oak (*Quercus
laurifolia*) of the southeastern U.S. has similar leaves but
they are *thickly textured*, leathery, and nearly evergreen.

LOCATIONS
☐ Rhode Island Avenue
☐ U.S. Capitol grounds
☐ Kenilworth Aquatic Gardens

CHESTNUT OAK

Quercus prinus L.
(*Quercus montana* Willd.)
Beech Family *Fagaceae*

A large oak, common in Washington both in
cultivation and in the wild.

NATIVE HABITAT
Southwestern Maine to southern Illinois; south to South
Carolina, northern Georgia, Alabama, and Mississippi.

LEAVES
Simple, alternate, deciduous. 4 - 9 in. (10 - 22.8 cm.)
long. Somewhat leathery, usually widest above the middle, with large, rounded or bluntly pointed teeth. Base
wedge-shaped or rounded, apex bluntly pointed. Bright
or yellowish-green above, paler and either pubescent or
glabrous below. Petiole ½ - 1½ in. (1.3 - 3.8 cm.) long.

FRUIT
Acorn, maturing in one year. Short-stalked; ¾ - 1½ in.
(2 - 3.8 cm.) long. Enclosed for one half its length or less
in thin, bowl-shaped cup, with scales pressed quite close
to cup except at their tips.

BARK AND TWIGS
Bark thick, *dark*, deeply furrowed and scaly. Twigs
orange-brown, with softly pubescent, orangish winter
buds.

HABIT
Medium-sized to large tree with a broad, open crown.

SIMILAR SPECIES
Very similar to the rare basket oak (*Quercus michauxii*),
described below.

LOCATIONS
☐ The Vice President's House
☐ The Federick Douglass Home
☐ Soldiers' Home
☐ Fern Valley, National Arboretum
☐ Theodore Roosevelt Island
☐ Common throughout the city

Chestnut Oak *Quercus prinus*

Basket Oak *Quercus michauxii*
Leaf margin

BASKET OAK
OR SWAMP CHESTNUT OAK
Quercus michauxii Nutt.
(*Quernus prinus* L.)
Beech Family *Fagaceae*

This tree is rare in the District of Columbia. Apart from the following characteristics, it is very similar to the chestnut oak, already described.

NATIVE HABITAT
New Jersey to Florida; west to eastern Texas and north in the Mississippi River Valley to southern Illinois and Indiana.

LEAVES
Very much like the leaf of the chestnut oak, but usually with *larger, more deeply cut teeth* that are often slightly mucronate. Autumn color is a rich crimson, while the chestnut oak is dull orange or yellow in color.

FRUIT
Acorn is enclosed in a *thick* cup with wedge-shaped *scales attached only at their bases.*

BARK
Light gray, scaly, sometimes irregularly furrowed.

LOCATIONS
□ Tidal Basin (eastern side, near highway)
□ Some large parks (especially in moist areas)

SAW-TOOTHED OAK
OR JAPANESE CHESTNUT OAK
Quercus acutissima Carruthers
Beech Family *Fagaceae*

Named for its sharply bristle-tipped teeth resembling
the teeth of a saw, this unique Asian tree is one of
Washington's most interesting oaks.

NATIVE HABITAT
China, Korea, Japan.

LEAVES
Simple, alternate, deciduous. 3 - 9 in. (7.5 - 22.8 cm.)
long, 1 - 2½ in. (2.5 - 6.3 cm.) wide. Oblong to
lanceolate with wedge-shaped or rounded base and
sharply pointed apex. Pointed teeth end in long, thin,
bristle-tips. Dark, glossy green above; paler below and
glabrous, except for occasional tufts of hair in the vein
axils. Petiole ½ - 1¾ in. (1.3 - 4.5 cm.) long.

FRUIT
Chestnut brown, round acorn, ½ - 1 in. (about
1 - 2.5 cm.) long; maturing in two years. Sessile. *Almost
entirely enclosed* by a thick cup covered with long,
light brown scales. The cup looks like a shaggy wig (see
illustration).

BARK AND TWIGS
Bark dark gray with rough ridges and fissures. Twig pale
orangish-brown, with small, pointed winter buds of
about the same color.

HABIT
Handsome tree with a rounded, open crown.

SIMILAR SPECIES
Not likely to be confused with any other oak commonly
planted in the District of Columbia. Somewhat similar to
the rare Chinese cork oak (*Quercus variablilis* Bl.) which
is planted only at the Fairchild Estate in Chevy Chase,
Maryland. However, the saw-toothed oak bears a close
resemblance to the Chinese chestnut (*Castanea mollissima*),
which is widely planted around the Washington area.
The Chinese chestnut has leaves that are *whitish* (or very
pale green) and *woolly below*. The Chinese chestnut
produces showy, bright yellow catkins in late spring or
early summer. Its fruit is an edible chestnut, enclosed in
a sharply spiny, greenish husk.

LOCATIONS
☐ National Zoo
☐ Kenilworth Aquatic Gardens
☐ 7th Street, N.W. between Geranium and Juniper
   Streets
☐ Lafayette Park and some other parks in D.C.
☐ Some public buildings and private homes

White Oak

Quercus alba L.
Beech Family *Fagaceae*

STATE TREE OF CONNECTICUT, MARYLAND AND
ILLINOIS

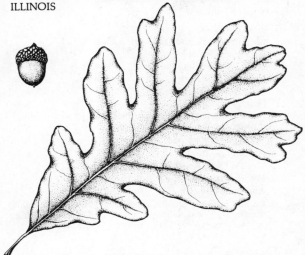

The white oak has long been a friend to human-
kind, both as a shade tree and an important source of
hardwood. White oak wood is used in the construction
of ships, furniture, flooring, and barrels. Some of
Washington's ancient white oaks are older than the city
itself, dating back to the eighteenth century.

NATIVE HABITAT
Eastern U.S. and southeastern Canada from Maine and
southern Québec to Minnesota; south to eastern Texas
and northern Florida.

LEAVES
Simple, alternate, deciduous, 3½ - 9 in. (9 - 22.8 cm.)
long, with five to nine *rounded* lobes. Leaf shape varies;
some leaves have narrow lobes separated by sinuses cut
almost to the midrib, while others have wider lobes and
sinuses cut only about halfway to the midrib. Lobes
point forward and sometimes have one or more *large,
rounded* teeth. Pubescent when they first appear, soon
becoming glabrous; very pale and sometimes slightly
glaucous below. Base wedge-shaped. Petiole ¼ - 1 in.
(0.5 - 2.5 cm.) long. Autumn color deep wine red some
years. Dead leaves often remain on the tree through the
winter.

FRUIT
Acorn, maturing during the first year. Sessile or short-
stalked. ½ - 1 in. (1.3 - 2.5 cm.) long, light brown,
enclosed for about one-quarter of its length by a bowl-
shaped cup covered with thickened scales.

BARK AND TWIGS
Bark pale gray, very scaly and sometimes slightly furrowed. Twigs reddish-brown, soon glabrous, with scaly,
reddish-brown, ovoid or nearly round winter buds.

HABIT
Medium-sized to large tree developing a wide trunk,
large limbs and a full, rounded crown.

SIMILAR SPECIES
May be confused with other trees in the white oak
group. See illustrations for comparisons of
leaves and fruit.

LOCATIONS
☐ Montrose Park and Dumbarton Oaks
☐ Arlington Cemetery
☐ Frederick Douglass Home
☐ Meridian Hill Park
☐ Franciscan Monastery
☐ Hains Point
☐ Parks, cemeteries, private homes, and public buildings
  throughout the Washington area

HISTORIC WHITE OAK LOCATIONS
☐ Glebe Oak, Rock Creek Cemetery
☐ Lincoln Oak, Fort Lincoln Cemetery
☐ Presidential trees, the White House
☐ Ancient white oak, The Vice President's House
☐ Capitol grounds memorial trees, including white oak
  planted by Speaker Sam Rayburn and young seedling
  of the famous Wye Oak in Wye Mills, Maryland

BUR OAK OR MOSSYCUP OAK

Quercus macrocarpa Michx.
Beech Family *Fagaceae*

A tall, handsome tree with large, "mossycupped"
acorns.

NATIVE HABITAT
Scattered distribution throughout the east coast states,
from Maine to Virginia; southeastern Canada, Pennsylvania, Kentucky, Tennessee, and parts of Alabama; west
to Texas, Nebraska, the Dakotas, and eastern
Saskatchewan.

LEAVES
Simple, alternate, deciduous. 4-10 in. (10-25.3 cm.) long.
Leaf usually divided at the middle or just below by one
or two pairs of very *deep sinuses*. The lower portion of
the leaf usually has several rounded or bluntly pointed

lobes that are separated by deep sinuses. The upper half of the leaf is usually one large lobe with several large, rounded or bluntly pointed teeth. Shape varies considerably. Dark green above, paler below and usually slightly woolly. Base wedge-shaped. Petiole ½-1½ in. (1.3-3.8 cm.) long.

FRUIT
Large acorn, maturing in one year. Sessile or short-stalked. Broadly ovoid, ¾-2 in. (2-5 cm.) long, enclosed for ⅓-⅔ of its length by a thick, bowl-shaped cup with the lower scales forming a distinctive fringed margin.

BARK AND TWIGS
Bark thick, grayish brown, deeply furrrowed and scaly. Twigs stout, gray or yellowish-brown, often developing corky wings. Winter buds pubescent.

HABIT
Tall tree with large limbs forming a broad, rounded crown.

SIMILAR SPECIES
The fruit is distinctive; in its absence, however, the tree may be confused with other members of the white oak group. See illustrations.

LOCATIONS
- ☐ The Mall (in front of the Hirshhorn Museum)
- ☐ Hains Point
- ☐ Montrose Park
- ☐ U.S. Capitol grounds
- ☐ Soldiers' Home
- ☐ Fairly common throughout the city

Shingle Oak

Quercus imbricaria Michx.
Beech Family *Fagaceae*

NATIVE HABITAT: New Jersey and Pennsylvania; south to South Carolina; west to Iowa, Missouri, and Arkansas. **LEAVES:** Simple, alternate, deciduous. 3-7 in. (7.5-17.8 cm.) long, 1-2 in. (2.5-5 cm.) wide. Oblong or oblong-lanceolate, with a smooth or barely wavy margin. Rounded or pointed apex is usually bristle-tipped; base rounded or wedge-shaped. Dark green and glabrous above, paler and pubescent below. Petiole ¼-¾ in. (0.5-2 cm.) long. **FRUIT:** Short-stalked acorn, maturing in two years. Ovoid, chestnut brown, ½-¾ in. (1.3-2 cm.) long, enclosed for one-third to one-half its length in a pubescent, reddish-brown cup. **BARK:** Thick, grayish brown, shallowly furrowed. **SIMILAR SPECIES:** The far more common willow oak (*Quercus phellos*) has narrower leaves.
LOCATIONS:
- ☐ Soldiers' Home
- ☐ The Mall, near the Capitol Reflecting Pool
- ☐ Constitution Avenue and 21st Street, N.W.
- ☐ Some parks, public buildings, and private homes citywide

ENGLISH OAK

Quercus robur L.
Beech Family *Fagaceae*

   This lovely exotic oak is similar to our native white oak (*Quercus alba*) but can be distinguished from the American tree by its less deeply lobed leaves and long-stalked acorns. A columnar form of the English oak (*Quercus robur* 'Fastigiata') lines 16th Street, N.W. from Meridian Hill to Lafayette Park. The tree was chosen for this location because its attractive, compact form allows for a long, unobstructed view of the White House.

NATIVE HABITAT
Europe, western Asia, northern Africa.

LEAVES
Simple, alternate, deciduous. 2-6 in. (5-15 cm.) long, with 6-14 *rounded* lobes which are very shallow or cut about halfway to the midrib. *Lobe* margins smooth, wavy or sometimes with a few rounded, shallow teeth. Dull, dark green above, paler below and glabrous. Narrow base often slightly cordate. Petiole short, less than ½ in. (1 cm. or less).

FRUIT
Chestnut brown acorn, maturing during the first year. Oblong-ovoid or ovoid. ⅔-1½ in. (about 1.5-4 cm.) long. Often in pairs on a long stalk, 1¼-3½ in. (about 3-8 cm.) long. Enclosed for one-third of its length or less by a light-colored, bowl-shaped cup.

BARK AND TWIGS
Bark gray, narrowly furrowed. Twigs gray-brown with scaly, brown, pointed ovoid winter buds.

HABIT
Thick, rather short trunk; broad, open crown with stout, wide-spreading limbs.

OTHER FORMS
Fastigiate English oak or Cypress oak (*Quercus robur* 'Fastigiata'). Form with upright branches forming a narrow, columnar crown.

SIMILAR SPECIES
May be confused with other members of the white oak group. See illustrations of leaves and fruit.

LOCATIONS
- ☐ U.S. Capitol grounds
- ☐ Washington Cathedral
- ☐ C Street, S.E. near House office buildings
- ☐ 16th Street, N.W. (Fastigiate form)
- ☐ Some public buildings and private homes in D.C.

POST OAK
Quercus stellata Wangh.
Beech Family *Fagaceae*

A small to medium-sized native tree common in the wild, but infrequently cultivated.

NATIVE HABITAT
Extreme southern New England and New York; south to central Florida; west to Texas, Oklahoma, and southern Iowa.

LEAVES
Simple, alternate, deciduous. 3-7 in. (7.5-17.8 cm.) long. Shape varies, but leaf usually has *five rounded, major lobes* and a few large, rounded teeth. The pair of lobes on either side of the end lobe is the longest, giving the leaf a vaguely cross-like look. Dark green above, paler below and usually pubescent. Base wedge-shaped.

FRUIT
Reddish-brown acorn, maturing in one year. Sessile or short-stalked. ½-¾ in. (1.3-2 cm.) long, enclosed for one-third to one-half its length by a bowl-shaped cup.

BARK
Grayish-brown, furrowed.

LOCATIONS
- ☐ Arlington Cemetery (historic tree next to President John F. Kennedy's grave.)
- ☐ National Arboretum
- ☐ Parks, cemeteries, private homes, and some public buildings throughout the area

Swamp White Oak

Quercus bicolor Willd.
Beech Family *Fagaceae*

NATIVE HABITAT
Quebec to Minnesota; south to North Carolina and
Arkansas.

LEAVES
Simple, alternate, deciduous. 4-9 in. (about 10-23 cm.)
long, 2-4 in. (5-10 cm.) wide. Shape variable. Either
unlobed, with large, rounded or bluntly pointed teeth,
or with a few shallow, irregular, bluntly pointed, or
rounded lobes. Leaf gradually narrows to wedge-shaped
or rounded base. Dark green above, paler below with
felt-like pubescence.

FRUIT
Acorn, maturing in one year. ¾-1¼ in. (2-3.2 cm.)
long, on a *long stalk*, from 1-4 in. (2.5-10 cm.) in length.
Enclosed for about one-third of its length in a thick,
scaly, slightly fringed cup.

BARK
Furrowed, with scaly ridges. Scales sometimes curl back.

SIMILAR SPECIES
May be confused with other oaks. However, English oak
(*Quercus robur*) is the only other oak commonly
planted locally with such long acorn stalks. See leaf
illustrations to compare similar species.

LOCATIONS
☐ U.S. Capitol grounds
☐ Meridian Hill Park
☐ Garfield Park
☐ Some other parks, public buildings, and private
homes citywide

Water Oak

Quercus nigra L.
Beech Family *Fagaceae*

NATIVE HABITAT
Southern New Jersey to central Florida; west to eastern
Texas, Oklahoma, and southeastern Missouri.

LEAVES
Simple, alternate, deciduous. Size and shape variable.
2-6 in. (5-15 cm.) long. Widest at the apex, which may
be *shallowly three-lobed, rounded,* or with as many as
seven lobes. Lobes are usually rounded but sometimes
come to a sharp, abrupt point. Leaf narrows to a wedge-
shaped base. Bluish green and glabrous, except for small
tufts of brownish hairs in the vein axils below. Petiole
short, less than ½ in. (1 cm. or less) long.

FRUIT
Short-stalked or sessile acorn, maturing in two years;
dark, nearly round, ⅓-¾ in. (about 1-2 cm.) long.
Enclosed at base only or for up to one-third of its length
by a shallow cup covered with thin scales.

BARK
Dark gray-black. Smooth or shallowly furrowed and
scaly.

SIMILAR SPECIES
Leaf shape quite unique. Blackjack oak (*Quercus
marilandica*) has leaves with wider apices, and usually
rounded or subcordate bases. Bartram's oak (*Quercus x
heterophylla*) has leaves with narrow, pointed, bristle-
tipped lobes or teeth. See illustration.

LOCATIONS
□ Hains Point golf course
□ Pan American Union
□ Some parks, private homes, and public buildings

Blackjack Oak
Quercus marilandica Muenchh.
Beech Family *Fagaceae*

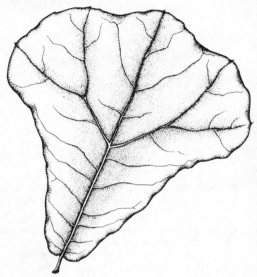

NATIVE HABITAT
Southern New York to northern Florida; west to Kansas and Texas.

LEAVES
Simple, alternate, deciduous. 3-7 in. (7.5-17.8 cm.) long, thick and somewhat leathery. Shape variable, but always very wide at apex and usually rounded or sub-cordate at base. Apex may be *rounded, shallowly three lobed*, or with a few shallow, *rounded*, just barely *pointed*, or *bristle-tipped teeth*. Dark green and glabrous above, pubescent below. Petioles pubescent, ⅓-1 in. (about 1-2.5 cm.) long.

FRUIT
Sessile or short-stalked acorn, maturing in two years. Yellowish-brown, about ¾ in. (2 cm.) long, enclosed for one- to two-thirds of its length in a reddish-brown, pubescent cup.

BARK
Thick, dark gray or black, sometimes separated into squarish segments.

SIMILAR SPECIES
Water oak *(Quercus nigra)* has leaves with narrower apices and wedge-shaped bases.

LOCATIONS
☐ Soldiers' Home
☐ Washington Cathedral
☐ National Arboretum
☐ Some parks, private homes, and public buildings

BLACK OAK
Quercus velutina Lam.
Beech Family *Fagaceae*

NATIVE HABITAT
Maine to Florida; west to Minnesota and Texas.

LEAVES
Simple, alternate, deciduous. 4-10 in. (10-25.4 cm.) long.
Five to nine lobes; with sinuses extending more than
halfway to the midrib. Margin with pointed, bristle-
tipped teeth. *Dark, glossy green above,* paler and usually pubescent below, with prominent tufts of hair in the
vein axils. Petioles stout, 1¼-2½ in. (3.6.3 cm.) long.

FRUIT
Sessile or short-stalked acorn, maturing in two years.
Ovoid, ½-¾ in. (1.3-2 cm.) long, enclosed for one-third
to one-half its length in a pubescent, bowl-shaped cup.
Tips of scales on the edge of cup form a fringe-like edge.

BARK AND TWIGS
Bark thick, furrowed, nearly black. Twigs with *woolly
winter buds.*

SIMILAR SPECIES
The red oak *(Quercus rubra)* is far more commonly
cultivated in Washington. Its leaves are *dull, medium
green above* and glabrous below, except for small tufts
of hair in the vein axils. Its acorn is enclosed for one-
third its length or less in a *saucer-shaped* cup and its
winter buds are *reddish-brown* with *scales that are
pubescent only at tips.* The uncommon shumard oak
(Quercus shumardii Buckl.) has leaves more deeply
lobed and acorns similar to those of the red oak.

LOCATIONS
□ Dumbarton Oaks
□ Frederick Douglass Home
□ National Arboretum
□ Some parks, streets, homes, and public buildings
   citywide

BARTRAM'S OAK

Quercus x *heterophylla* Michx. f.
(Quercus phellos x *Quercus rubra)*
Beech Family *Fagaceae*

An attractive hybrid which is a cross between two native species, the willow oak *(Quercus phellos)* and the red oak *(Quercus rubra)*

LEAVES
Simple, alternate, deciduous. 3-7 in. (7.5-17.8 cm.) long, 1-3 in. (2.5-7.5 cm.) wide. Oblong-lanceolate with a *variable number of pointed, bristle-tipped lobes or large teeth* (rarely with a smooth margin). Medium green and glabrous above; paler below and glabrous except for small tufts of light brown hair in the vein axils. Base rounded or wedge-shaped.

FRUIT
Acorn, similar to red oak, but slightly smaller and rounder.

SIMILAR SPECIES
See water oak *(Quercus nigra)* leaf illustrations.

LOCATIONS
- National Zoo (between the lion and tiger area and the restaurant)
- U.S. Capitol grounds
- Some parks, public buildings, and private homes

Chinkapin Oak

Quercus muehlenbergii Engelm.
Beech Family *Fagaceae*

NATIVE HABITAT
Northwestern Vermont to northwestern Florida (excluding most of the eastern portions of the southeastern states); west to Texas and eastern Nebraska.

LEAVES
Simple, alternate, deciduous. 3-7 in. (7.5-17.8 cm.) long. Margin with *large, pointed, gland-tipped* teeth which are often slightly incurved. Lustrous dark or yellow-green above, paler and pubescent below. Petiole ¾-1½ in. (2-3.8 cm.) long.

FRUIT
Sessile or short-stalked acorn, maturing in one year. Ovoid or nearly round, ½-¾ in. (1.3-2 cm.) long, enclosed for about half its length in a pubescent cup.

BARK
Pale gray, thin, shallowly and irregularly furrowed or scaly.

SIMILAR SPECIES
The far more common chestnut oak (*Quercus prinus* L.) has slightly larger leaves with *rounded or bluntly pointed teeth* and thick, dark, deeply furrowed bark. The rare basket oak (*Quercus michauxii* Nutt.) also has larger leaves. See illustrations.

LOCATIONS
☐ The Mall, near the Capitol Reflecting Pool
☐ National Zoo
☐ Theodore Roosevelt Island
☐ Quite rare in the District

OVERCUP OAK

Quercus lyrata Walt.
Beech Family *Fagaceae*

NATIVE HABITAT
Coastal plain swamps and moist forests from New Jersey to northern Florida; eastern Texas; north in the Mississippi River drainage area to southern Illinois and Indiana.

LEAVES
Simple, alternate, deciduous. 3-8 in. (7.5-20.2 cm.) long. Variably and irregularly lobed with rounded or pointed lobes and teeth. The lowest pair(s) of lobes are usually small and triangular and are separated from the upper lobes by deep, often squarish sinuses. The pair of lobes on either side of the terminal one are usually widest, giving the leaf a top-heavy appearance. The terminal lobe itself is frequently three-lobed. Glabrous and dark green above, felty-pubescent or glabrous below.

FRUIT
The tree's common name refers to the acorn cup, which almost entirely encloses the sessile or short-stalked, ½-1 in. (1.3 - 2.5 cm.) long acorn.

SIMILAR SPECIES
May be confused with post (*Quercus stellata*) and bur (*Quercus macrocarpa*) oaks. See illustrations and text .

LOCATIONS
☐ National Gallery of Art
☐ Soldiers' Home
☐ U.S. Capitol grounds
☐ Some parks, private homes, and public buildings

Downy Oak
Quercus pubescens Willd.
Beech Family *Fagaceae*

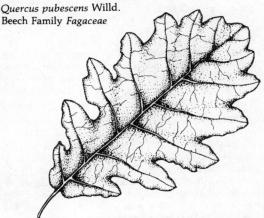

This is the famous Library of Congress "Hungarian Oak", which may have come from Hungary but is not the species (*Quercus frainetto* Ten.) botanists once believed it to be. A very rare tree.

NATIVE HABITAT
Southern Europe, western Asia.

LEAVES
Simple, alternate, deciduous. Lobes rounded or bluntly pointed, sinuses shallow. Pubescent along the veins below and on the petiole.

FRUIT
Acorn ½-1 in. (1.3-2.5 cm.) long with a pubescent cup. Short-stalked or sessile.

HABIT
A small tree.

LOCATIONS
☐ Library of Congress grounds

Compton's Oak
Quercus x *comptonae* Sarg.
(*Quercus lyrata* x *Quercus virginiana*)
Beech Family *Fagaceae*

Compton's oak is a hybrid of two southeastern species; the live oak and the overcup oak, both of which are described. This rare tree has the attractive form of the live oak combined with the greater winter hardiness of the overcup oak.

LEAVES: Simple, alternate, deciduous, persisting until early winter. Oblanceolate, with wavy margin or rounded lobes. FRUIT: Similar to live oak acorn.

LOCATIONS:
☐ Hains Point Golf Course

LIVE OAK

Quercus virginiana Mill.
Beech Family *Fagaceae*

Although not really hardy this far north, some sheltered specimens of the live oak do manage to survive Washington's winters. This lovely evergreen tree is often draped with Spanish moss in the Deep South, where it is beloved as a shade and street tree. The live oak is Lady Bird Johnson's favorite tree.

NATIVE HABITAT: Coastal plain, from southeastern Virginia to Florida and Texas; inland in Texas, Oklahoma and Mexico. **LEAVES:** Simple, alternate, evergreen. 1½-5 in. (3.8-12.6 cm.) long, elliptic to oblong-obovate. Margin smooth, wavy or rarely toothed; slightly rolled back. Apex rounded or bluntly pointed, base rounded or wedge-shaped. Leathery, lustrous dark green above; paler, with grayish or whitish pubescence below. **FRUIT:** Dark brown acorn, maturing in one year. ¾-1 in. (2-2.5 cm.) long, enclosed for one-third to one-half its length in a reddish-brown, pubescent, bowl-shaped cup. **HABIT:** Broad trunk usually divides near the base into several large, widely spreading limbs.

SIMILAR SPECIES: Compton's oak (*Quercus × comptonae*) is a hybrid of the live oak and the overcup oak (*Quercus lyrata*).

LOCATIONS:
☐ St. Elizabeth's Hospital
☐ National Arboretum

OTHER RARE OAKS PLANTED IN WASHINGTON
Turkey Oak *Quercus cerris* L.
Laurel Oak *Quercus laurifolia* Michx.
Carruther's Oak *Quercus variabilis* Bl.
Bamboo-Leaved Oak *Quercus myrsinifolia* Blume

Black Alder
or European Alder
Alnus glutinosa (L.) Gaertn.
Birch Family *Betulaceae*

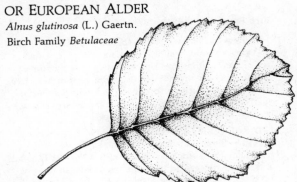

The ripe woody fruit of this tree looks like it belongs on a conifer.

NATIVE HABITAT
Europe to Siberia; northern Africa.

LEAVES
Simple, alternate, deciduous. Obovate, ovate or nearly round. 1½-4 in. (3.8-10 cm.) long, with irregularly toothed margins.

FLOWERS AND FRUIT
Male catkins shed pollen in early spring. Tiny female flowers are reddish when young; they ripen into green ½-¾ in. (1-2 cm.) long fruits, which become woody and brown and remain on the tree through the winter.

BARK
Dark grayish or purplish brown, cracked and fissured.

SIMILAR SPECIES
The rare Italian alder (*Alnus cordata*), below, has heart-shaped leaves. The native hazel alder (*Alnus serrulata* (Ait.) Willd.) is a shrub rarely seen in cultivation.

LOCATIONS
☐ Rayburn House Office Building (Canal Street side)
☐ Some private yards and public buildings

Italian Alder
Alnus cordata Desf.
Birch Family *Betulaceae*

Rare in Washington.

NATIVE HABITAT: Southern Italy, Corsica. **LEAVES:** Simple, alternate, deciduous. Ovate, with a *cordate* base; 2 - 3½ in. (5 - 9 cm.) long. Margin toothed, but smooth near the petiole. **FRUIT:** Similar to black alder (*Alnus glutinosa*) but larger (about an inch (2.5 cm.) long). **SIMILAR SPECIES:** Heart-shaped leaves separate this alder from the more commonly planted black alder.
LOCATIONS
☐ U.S. Capitol grounds

THE BIRCHES

Betula L.
Birch Family *Betulaceae*

The white or paper birch (*Betula papyrifera*) is one of America's most beautiful trees and the official state tree of New Hampshire. Unfortunately, Washington's climate is a little on the warm side for this northern tree. However, the lovely European white birch (*Betula pendula*), which is better suited to the climate, serves as a worthy stand-in for the American species.

CHARACTERISTICS OF THE GENUS
LEAVES: Simple, alternate, deciduous. Ovate or triangular-ovate; toothed. **FLOWERS AND FRUIT:** Male and female flowers on the same tree. Males in hanging catkins. Smaller females develop into catkin-like fruiting cones which release many seeds with butterfly-shaped wings. **BARK:** Typically thin and papery with horizontal lenticels. Often peels off in layers. **DISTRIBUTION:** About forty species of trees and shrubs distributed throughout the Northern Hemisphere.

EUROPEAN WHITE BIRCH

Betula pendula Roth
Birch Family *Betulaceae*

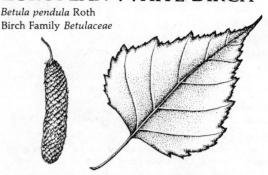

The lovely European white birch is the most commonly cultivated birch in Washington. The native American white or paper birch (*Betula papyrifera*) of the northern U.S. and Canada is not as widely planted here, because Washington's summers don't seem to agree with it.

NATIVE HABITAT
Europe, Asia Minor.

LEAVES
Simple, alternate, deciduous. Triangular-ovate, 1¼ - 3 in. (3 - 7.5 cm.) long. Margin sharply and irregularly toothed. Base straight across or wedge-shaped; apex long-pointed. Glabrous above and below, on a slender petiole.

FLOWERS AND FRUIT
Male catkins, ¾ - 1¼ in. (2 - 3 cm.) long, are on the tree through the winter; in the spring they shed yellow pollen. Smaller female flower stalks ripen into 1 - 1¼ in. (2.5 - 3 cm.) catkin-like fruiting cones; green at first, then turning brown in autumn and breaking up.

BARK AND TWIGS
Bark shiny reddish-brown on very young trees, becoming white, or pinkish white with large, black, horizontal diamonds. The bark peels, but not as readily as the bark of the native white birch. Twigs are *glabrous* and resinous-glandular. Winter buds ovoid, purplish-brown or greenish.

HABIT
A small, graceful tree which is upright when young, but usually assumes an attractive pendulous form with age.

OTHER FORMS
The cultivar 'Darlecarlica' has deeply cut, very sharply toothed leaves.

SIMILAR SPECIES
The gray birch (*Betula populifolia* Marsh), (not included in this guide), is native to the northeastern states and southeastern Canada (extending in the mountains to North Carolina). Its leaves are similar to those of the European white birch, but it is very rare in cultivation. Gray birch bark is a chalky, rather than creamy, white. The white or paper birch (*Betula papyrifera*) has ovate or oblong-ovate (rather than triangular-ovate) leaves and twigs that are pubescent, at least when young.

LOCATIONS
☐ U.S. Capitol grounds
☐ National Arboretum

WHITE BIRCH
OR PAPER BIRCH, OR CANOE BIRCH
Betula papyrifera Marsh.
Birch Family *Betulaceae*

STATE TREE OF NEW HAMPSHIRE

People are not the only living things that find Washington's summer heat unbearable. Despite repeated attempts to coax the white birch into cultivation here, it just doesn't seem to like Washington's climate. However, a few specimens do manage to survive.

NATIVE HABITAT
Newfoundland to Labrador to Alaska; south to Pennsylvania, West Virginia, northern Ohio, northern Iowa, South Dakota, and parts of Nebraska (slightly further south in isolated areas).

LEAVES
Simple, alternate, deciduous. Ovate or oblong-ovate, 2 - 5 in. (5 - 12.5 cm.) long. Coarsely and irregularly toothed.

BARK AND TWIGS
Bark creamy white, marked with horizontal lenticels, peeling off in thin, papery layers to reveal pale orange inner bark. Twigs pubescent, at least when young.

SIMILAR SPECIES
The European white birch (*Betula pendula*), already described, is far more commonly cultivated here. Several other Eurasian and Asian species of white birch, which are very similar to the native American species, are in cultivation at the National Arboretum. A beautiful Japanese white birch stands in front of the Arboretum administration building.

LOCATIONS
☐ Franciscan Monastery
☐ A few private yards and public buildings
☐ National Arboretum

RIVER BIRCH

Betula nigra L.
Birch Family *Betulaceae*

    The river birch grows along streams and rivers throughout the Washington area, though it is rarely cultivated.

NATIVE HABITAT
Southern New England to northern Florida; west to eastern Texas and Oklahoma, much of Missouri, eastern Iowa, and southeastern Minnesota.

LEAVES
(Simple, alternate, deciduous.) Triangular-ovate, 1 - 5 in. (2.5 - 12.5 cm.) long; irregularly toothed and sometimes slightly lobed. Usually pubescent below.

BARK
This tree is easily recognized by its bark, which is a pinkish, reddish or golden brown and separated into large, curly strips.

LOCATIONS
- Rock Creek
- Potomac and Anacostia Rivers
- Some parks, public buildings, and private homes

OTHER NATIVE BIRCHES

The yellow birch (*Betula alleghaniensis* Britton) and the black, sweet, or cherry birch (*Betula lenta* L.) are native to the mountains of western Virginia; both species are planted at the National Arboretum. For the story of another native Virginian birch, one that was believed to be extinct for many years, see page 46 of this book.

EUROPEAN HORNBEAM

Carpinus betulus L.
Birch Family *Betulaceae*

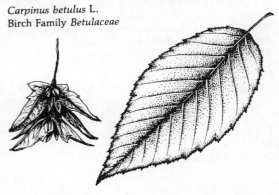

The European hornbeam is very similar to the native American hornbeam, ironwood, musclewood, or blue beech (*Carpinus caroliniana*). It is slightly more frequently cultivated than the native species.

NATIVE HABITAT
Europe, Asia Minor.

LEAVES
Simple, alternate, deciduous. Oblong-ovate, 2 - 5 in. (5 - 12.5 cm.) long with a rounded or cordate base, pointed apex and sharply, finely, double-toothed margin. Glabrous except for some pubescence along the veins below and in the vein axils.

FRUIT
Small nut attached to leafy bract; borne in clustered pairs. Bract with an ovate-lanceolate central lobe and ovate side lobes; margin smooth or with remote teeth.

BARK
Gray, with vertical brown stripes; trunk often fluted. "Muscular" looking.

HABIT
Small tree, frequently with a fluted trunk.

SIMILAR SPECIES
Very similar to the American hornbeam, below.

LOCATIONS
- U.S. Capitol grounds
- National Park Service Headquarters, East Potomac Park

AMERICAN HORNBEAM
OR IRONWOOD OR MUSCLEWOOD, OR BLUE BEECH
Carpinus caroliniana Walt.
Birch Family *Betulaceae*

Very difficult to distinguish from the European species, described above. The American hornbeam is a native tree which grows along the banks of Rock Creek and in woodlands throughout the area.

NATIVE HABITAT: Southeastern Canada to northern Florida; west to eastern Texas and eastern Minnesota.
LEAVES: Very similar to the preceding species; slightly thinner textured, with less deeply impressed veins.
FRUIT: Similar to European tree, but leafy bracts usually with one to several pointed teeth.
BARK: Very "muscular" looking; trunk usually fluted.
LOCATIONS:
☐ Rock Creek Park
☐ National Arboretum
☐ Parks, private yards, public buildings

EUROPEAN FILBERT
OR HAZELNUT OR HAZEL OR COBNUT
Corylus avellana L.
Corylus avellana 'Purpurea'
Birch Family *Betulaceae*

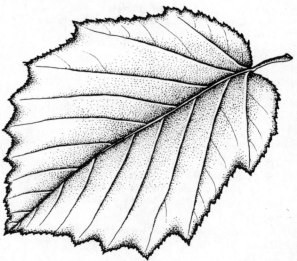

Although the European filbert is usually a shrub, we include it here because it can attain a height of twenty feet (six meters). With its large leaves and interesting fruit, it is very conspicuous, particularly on the Capitol grounds. The European filbert is widely cultivated in this country and abroad for its edible nuts. The form most often planted in Washington is a purple-leaved variety (*Corylus avellana* 'Purpurea').

NATIVE HABITAT
Europe, Asia Minor.

LEAVES
Simple, alternate, deciduous, 2 - 6 in. (5 - 15.2 cm.) long, 1¼ - 5 in. (3 - 12.6 cm.) wide. Margin doubly toothed, often with small, jagged lobules. Broadly obovate, ovate or elliptic. Apex abruptly pointed or rounded; base usually cordate. Green, purplish or reddish. Downy below and sometimes above.

FLOWERS
Spring, before the leaves. Male in catkins 1¼ - 2½ in. (3 - 6.3 cm.) long.

FRUIT
Edible nut, ⅔ - ¾ in. (1.5 - 2 cm.) long; enclosed by two lobed, often toothed, leafy bracts that are a little shorter or (rarely) a little longer than the nut.

HABIT
Usually a tall, broad shrub with many ascending branches.

SIMILAR SPECIES
The rare Turkish hazel (*Corylus colurna*).

LOCATIONS
□ U.S. Capitol grounds
□ Library of Congress grounds
□ Dumbarton Oaks
□ Tidal Basin
□ St. Elizabeth's Hospital

TURKISH HAZEL
OR HAZELNUT OR FILBERT
Corylus colurna L.
Birch Family *Betulaceae*

The following characteristics separate the rare Turkish hazel from the common European filbert, which is described above.

NATIVE HABITAT: Southeastern Europe, Asia Minor, western Asia. **LEAVES:** *Slightly larger than those of the European filbert;* often with distinct, small lobes.
FRUITS: The leafy bracts surrounding the nut are deeply divided into lobes that are somewhat *curled back.*
HABIT: Single trunked *tree* with a *pyramidal crown.*
LOCATIONS:
□ Walter Reed Army Medical Center
□ Glenn Dale Plant Introduction Station, Glenn Dale, Maryland
□ Rare in Washington

Eastern Hop-Hornbeam
Ostrya virginiana (Mill.) K. Koch
Birch Family *Betulaceae*

Very similar to the hornbeams (*Carpinus* sp.), already described. The distinctive characteristics of the hop-hornbeam are its *bark*, which often peels into long, thin strips, and its hop-like autumn fruit. (See illustration.)

NATIVE HABITAT
Eastern U.S., southeastern Canada, Mexico.

LOCATIONS
□ Northeast Capitol grounds
□ National Arboretum
□ Private yards

Mockernut Hickory
Carya tomentosa (Poir.) Nutt.
Walnut Family *Juglandaceae*

A beautiful native tree.

NATIVE HABITAT: Southern New Hampshire, southern New York, southern Ontario, southeastern Iowa to eastern Texas, and northern Florida. **LEAVES:** Alternate, compound, deciduous. 8 - 12 in. (20 - 30.5 cm.) long, with seven to nine leaflets. Terminal leaflet slightly longer than side leaflets. Margins finely or coarsely toothed. Glabrous above; pubescent below. **FRUIT:** Nut enclosed in a rounded or obovoid husk, 1½ - 2 in. (3.8 - 5 cm.) long. Husk ⅛ - ¼ in. (3 - 6 mm.) thick, splitting nearly to base. **BARK AND TWIGS:** Bark thick, dark gray. Shallowly furrowed. Twigs stout, pubescent, grayish to reddish-brown. **HABIT:** A medium-sized to tall tree with a large, open crown. **SIMILAR SPECIES:** Pignut hickory (*Carya glabra*).

LOCATIONS:
□ U.S. Capitol grounds
□ Rock Creek Park
□ Some public buildings, private yards, and parks

Pignut Hickory
Carya glabra (Mill.) Sweet
Walnut Family *Juglandaceae*

The pignut hickory, like the mockernut, is native to Rock Creek Park and surrounding woodlands. Its distribution corresponds closely to that of the above species. The pignut differs from the mockernut in having leaves with *usually 5* (rarely 7) leaflets, which are mostly *glabrous*. The fruit of the pignut is slightly smaller, with a thinner husk that usually splits only part way to the base.

LOCATIONS
☐ Rock Creek Park
☐ Parks, private yards and some public buildings

OTHER HICKORIES
Other hickories that are indigenous to the Washington area or nearby Maryland and Virginia are the bitternut hickory (*Carya cordiformis* (Wangh.) K. Koch), the shellbark hickory (*Carya laciniosa* (Michx, f.) Loud.) and the shagbark hickory (*Carya ovata* (Mill.) K. Koch). None of the three is commonly cultivated in Washington.

PECAN
Carya illinoensis (Wangh.) K. Koch
Walnut Family *Juglandaceae*

Famed for its fruit, the pecan is cultivated throughout the southern states. Several magnificent specimens are growing on the Capitol grounds and in front of George Washington's home at Mount Vernon.

NATIVE HABITAT
Mississippi River Valley from southern Wisconsin to Nebraska, Texas, and Alabama.

LEAVES
Alternate, compound, deciduous. 12 - 20 in. (30.5 - 50.5 cm.) long. Eleven to seventeen toothed, lanceolate leaflets are usually slightly sickle-shaped.

FRUIT
An oblong husk, 1 - 2 in. (2.5 - 5 cm.) long, contains the nut.

BARK
Deeply furrowed.

LOCATIONS
☐ Mount Vernon
☐ U.S. Capitol grounds
☐ National Zoo

BLACK WALNUT

Juglans nigra L.
Walnut Family *Juglandaceae*

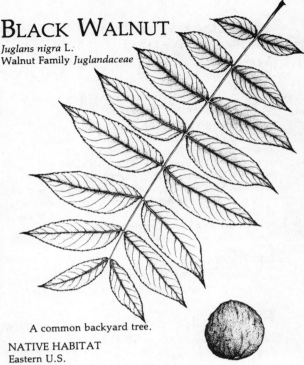

A common backyard tree.

NATIVE HABITAT
Eastern U.S.

LEAVES
Alternate, pinnately compound, deciduous. 8 in. - 2 feet
(20 - 60 cm.) long, with 15 to 23 leaflets. The end leaflet
is smaller than the side ones or absent. Leaflets lance-
shaped, often unequal at the base, sharply toothed.
Yellow-green (turning a clear yellow in the fall),
pubescent below.

FRUIT
A round nut 1 - 2 in. (2.5 - 5 cm.) in diameter, with a
furrowed shell; borne singly or in pairs. Contained within
a green, lime-like husk.

BARK AND TWIGS
Mature trees have dark, deeply furrowed bark. Twigs
have pubescent winter buds.

HABIT
A tall tree with a long, straight trunk and rounded
crown.

SIMILAR SPECIES
The butternut or white walnut (*Juglans cinerea* L.) (not
included in this guide) is native to the eastern U.S., but
is rarely grown in this area. It can be distinguished from
the black walnut by its *four-ribbed* nuts which are borne
singly or in clusters of up to five. The English or Persian
walnut (*Juglans regia*) has smooth-margined, glabrous
leaves with fewer leaflets.

LOCATIONS
☐ Rock Creek Park
☐ National Arboretum
☐ Private homes and public buildings

ENGLISH WALNUT
OR PERSIAN WALNUT
Juglans regia L.
Walnut Family *Juglandaceae*

This tree has been in cultivation in Europe and the U.S. for many years for its fruit and timber.

NATIVE HABITAT: Southeastern Europe, Asia.
LEAVES: Alternate, pinnately compound, deciduous. Leaflets five - nine (rarely more), glabrous, with *smooth* margins. **FRUIT:** Smooth or slightly wrinkled, 1½ - 2 in. (4 - 5 cm.) in diameter, thick-shelled, roundish.
SIMILAR SPECIES: The black walnut (*Juglans nigra*) has *toothed* leaflets. Another extremely rare exotic species is the Japanese walnut (*Juglans ailanthifolia* Carr.). It has *toothed* leaflets and nuts borne in *long, pendulous* clusters. The Japanese walnut is planted at the National Arboretum.
LOCATIONS:
☐ U.S. Capitol grounds
☐ Private homes and public buildings (but quite rare)

FRANKLIN TREE OR FRANKLINIA
Franklinia alatamaha Marsh.
Tea Family *Theaceae*

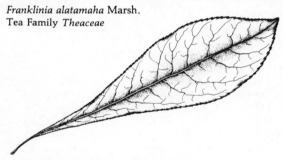

Native to Georgia, the mysterious Franklin tree has not been found growing in its natural habitat since 1790 and is believed, by many, to be extinct in the wild. In 1973, Congress authorized the Smithsonian Institution to prepare a list of the country's extinct and endangered plants. The Smithsonian listed two trees as extinct: The Franklin tree and the Virginia round-leaf birch (*Betula uber*). Since the list was compiled, the latter of the two "extinct" species has been rediscovered in the wild. The Franklin tree is named for the statesman, Benjamin Franklin.

LEAVES
Simple, alternate; deciduous. Bright, lustrous green above, pubescent below. Obovate-oblong, 4¾ - 9 in. (12 - 23 cm.) long, on a short petiole. Remotely toothed.

FLOWERS
Mid to late summer and early fall. Cup-shaped, creamy, with bright yellow centers.

HABIT
Small multi-trunked tree or shrub.

LOCATIONS
- ☐ Glenn Dale Plant Introduction Station, Glenn Dale, MD
- ☐ Fern Valley, National Arboretum

STEWARTIA
OR DECIDUOUS CAMELLIA
Stewartia pseudocamellia Maxim.
Tea Family *Theaceae*

This small Japanese tree has very ornamental bark and attractive blossoms appearing in mid-summer.

NATIVE HABITAT
Japan.

LEAVES
Simple, alternate, deciduous. Ovate-lanceolate to obovate-elliptic, 1¼ - 3¼ in. (3 - 8 cm.) long. Margin wavy or with a few remote shallow teeth. Long-pointed apex; wedge-shaped base.

FLOWERS
White, cup-shaped blossoms, 1¾ - 2½ in. (4.5 - 6.3 cm.) across, with showy orange anthers in the center.

BARK
Orange-brown; peeling away in plane tree fashion to reveal paler orange-brown inner bark.

LOCATIONS
- ☐ U.S. Capitol grounds

IDESIA

Idesia polycarpa Maxim.
Flacourtia Family *Flacourtiaceae*

Extremely rare.

NATIVE HABITAT
Japan, China.

LEAVES
Simple, alternate, deciduous. Heart-shaped, 4 - 10 in.
(10 - 25.5 cm.) long, with large, coarse teeth. Petiole
very long.

FLOWERS
Greenish yellow, fragrant, in long, pendulous clusters.

FRUIT
Very showy hanging clusters of round, reddish brown
berries.

SIMILAR SPECIES
Two other rare trees, the Japanese raisin tree (*Hovenia
dulcis*) and the dove or handkerchief tree (*Davidia
involucrata*) have similar foliage, but the fruit of each is
distinctive.

LOCATIONS
☐ National Arboretum
☐ A few private yards

THE TAMARISKS

Tamarix sp.
Tamarisk Family *Tamaricaceae*

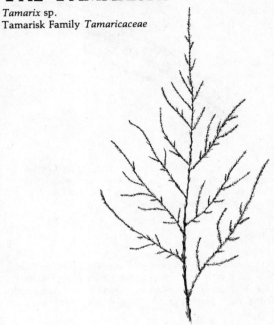

As long as botanists are still puzzling over this confusing genus, we will not attempt to describe species characteristics in detail. Probably most of the tamarisks planted in Washington are the species *ramosissima* Ledeb. which is also known as *chinensis* Lour. or *pentandra* Pall. If you're like us, you'll be happy to enjoy these gorgeous shrubs or small trees on an aesthetic level while the taxonimists worry about how to classify them!

NATIVE HABITAT
The Mediterranean (75 species of tamarisks are found in the Mediterranean area and Asia).

LEAVES
Delicate, fern-like leaves are grayish green. Upon close examination they are scale-like.

FLOWERS
As delicate as the foliage; pink, wispy.

HABIT
Extremely delicate branches, often spreading or weeping.

LOCATIONS
- National Arboretum
- Private yards, especially on Capitol Hill and in Georgetown

Weeping Willow

Salix babylonica L.
Willow Family *Salicaceae*

The weeping willow is such a familiar part of the landscape that most people probably don't realize that it's an exotic tree. Graceful weeping willows line Washington's Potomac shoreline.

NATIVE HABITAT
China.

LEAVES
Simple, alternate, deciduous. Linear-lanceolate, 3 - 7 in. (7.5 - 17.8 cm.) long. Long pointed apex, wedge-shaped base. Margin with rounded or pointed teeth. Dark green above, paler grayish-green below; usually glabrous.

HABIT
One of the world's most beautiful trees, with gracefully pendulous branches and foliage that streams in the wind.

OTHER FORMS
Salix babylonica 'Crispa' has leaves that are spirally curled.

SIMILAR SPECIES
The golden weeping willow (*Salix* x *chrysocoma*), described below.

LOCATIONS
☐ East and West Potomac Parks
☐ National Arboretum
☐ Quite common throughout the city, especially along the water

Golden Weeping Willow

Salix x *chrysocoma* Dode
Willow Family *Salicaceae*

The golden weeping willow is very similar to the weeping willow (*Salix babylonica*), above, but it has golden twigs and branches. The leaves of the golden weeping willow are usually pubescent.

LOCATIONS:
☐ National Arboretum
☐ Quite common in Washington

OTHER WILLOWS OF THE WASHINGTON AREA

The pussy willow (*Salix discolor* Muhl.), the goat willow (*Salix caprea* L.), and the black willow (*Salix nigra* Marsh.) are among the other species of willows grown in Washington. The willows are an extremely difficult genus, even for botanists, so we have described and illustrated only the ones that are important ornamentals in Washington.

Eastern Cottonwood

Populus deltoides Marsh.
Willow Family *Salicaceae*

Several magnificent old cottonwood trees are growing on both sides of the Potomac in the Washington area.

NATIVE HABITAT
Eastern U.S., excluding much of Virginia, Pennsylvania, and northern New England.

LEAVES
Simple, alternate, deciduous. 3 - 7 in. (7.5 - 17.8 cm.) long, deltoid, with large, coarse, rounded or pointed teeth. Glabrous. Petiole thick, flattened, with two conspicuous glands at the point where it attaches to the base of the leaf.

FRUIT
8 - 12 in. (20 - 30.5 cm.) fruiting catkins bear small ovoid capsules that release cottony-haired seeds.

BARK
Greenish and smooth on young trees. Becoming thick, gray, and deeply furrowed with age.

LOCATIONS
☐ East Potomac Park near Hains Point
☐ Lady Bird Johnson Park

THE POPLARS
Populus L.
Willow Family *Salicaceae*

   Once popular (no pun intended) throughout the city, the *Populus* genus is now significantly represented in Washington only by the Eastern cottonwood (*Populus deltoides*), already described. During the last century, poplars were widely planted for their fast growth and attractive foliage. But they proved to be bad city trees: Their shallow roots tore into roads and sidewalks so over the years these "surface rooters", as they came to be called, were replaced by more suitable species. Brief descriptions of three poplars that are still found in the area follow.

LOMBARDY POPLAR
Populus nigra L. 'Italica'

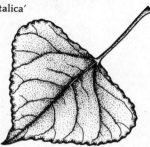

   Thomas Jefferson personally selected this Italian clone for planting along Pennsylvania Avenue during his administration. The tree has triangular leaves and a very distinctive narrow, columnar habit with many small, steeply ascending branches.

WHITE POPLAR
Populus alba L.

   Native to Europe and Asia, the white poplar has become naturalized in many parts of North America. Easily distinguished by its distinctive leaves which are *white and densely pubescent below.*

BIGTOOTH ASPEN

Populus grandidentata Michx.

The bigtooth aspen is native to the northeastern U.S. (including the Washington area) and southeastern Canada. Its leaves are similar to the Eastern cottonwood's, but they are smaller (2 - 3 in. (5 - 7.5 cm.) long,) and *ovate* rather than deltoid.

SOURWOOD
OR SORREL-TREE

Oxydendrum arboreum (L.) DC.

Heath Family *Ericaceae*

This small tree is rather inconspicuous most of the year, but in the fall it steals the show. Decorative hanging clusters of ivory blossoms appear in midsummer, and are followed by showy fruit that is set off by gorgeous, long-lasting autumn color, varying from scarlet to dark wine.

NATIVE HABITAT
Southern New Jersey and Pennsylvania; west to southern Illinois; south to Florida and Louisiana.

LEAVES
Alternate, simple, deciduous, 4 - 7 in. (10 - 17.7 cm.) long. Oblong-elliptic to oblong-lanceolate. Finely and irregularly toothed, broadly wedge-shaped at base, and somewhat abruptly pointed at apex. Glossy and glabrous above; paler below and slightly pubescent along the veins.

FLOWERS
Thin, pendulous, delicately curved clusters of bell-shaped ivory blossoms. Clusters are 4 - 10 in. (10 - 25.3 cm.) long and hang from near the ends of the branches. Midsummer.

FRUIT
Small, pubescent, grayish brown capsules in long clusters. Late summer, autumn.

BARK AND TWIGS
Bark thick, gray, ridged and scaly; often tinged with
red. Twigs reddish to yellow-green, glabrous, with small
winter buds and false end bud.

HABIT
Small tree. Ascending branches form a narrow, rather
top-heavy, rounded crown.

SIMILAR SPECIES
Quite distinctive. The tupelo or sour gum (*Nyssa
sylvatica*) has somewhat similar leaves, but they are
smaller, with *smooth* (or slightly wavy) margins. See,
also, common persimmon (*Diospyros virginiana*),
"Similar Species."

LOCATIONS
☐ Glenwood Cemetery
☐ Arlington Cemetery
☐ Walter Reed Army Medical Center
☐ George Washington Memorial Parkway
☐ Near Washington Cathedral

JAPANESE SNOWBELL TREE
Styrax japonica Sieb. & Zucc.
Storax Family *Styracaceae*

A small tree with slender, widely spreading
branches and attractive white blossoms in early summer.

NATIVE HABITAT
China, Japan.

LEAVES
Simple, alternate, deciduous, 1½ - 3½ in. (3.8 - 9 cm.)
long. Ovate or elliptic with abruptly or gradually
pointed apex and *wedge-shaped base*. Margin wavy,
often with a few irregular, shallow teeth. Soon glabrous
except for tufts of hair in the vein axils below. Petiole
¼ - ⅓ in. (less than 1 cm. long).

FLOWERS
Late spring or early summer. Petals white, usually five;
stamens orange or yellow. Many clusters, each containing three to four blossoms, hang close to the undersides
of the branches. Each blossom an inch or less (1.5 - 2.5
cm.) across.

FRUIT
Smooth, greenish-gray ovoid or rounded drupe, ½ - ⅔
in. (1.2 - 1.6 cm.) long on a long stalk.

SIMILAR SPECIES
The fragrant snowbell (*Styrax obassia*) has fragrant
flowers and larger, rounder leaves.

LOCATIONS
☐ Soldiers' Home
☐ National Arboretum
☐ Private yards and gardens throughout the city
☐ Some parks and public buildings

Fragrant Snowbell
or Big Leaf Storax
Styrax obassia Sieb. & Zucc.
Storax Family *Styracaceae*

        An attractive tree with large, nearly round leaves
and fragrant flowers that open in May.

NATIVE HABITAT
Japan.

LEAVES
Simple, alternate, deciduous. 3 - 8 in. (7.5 - 20.3 cm.)
long and usually *about as wide or slightly wider*. (Some
leaves are narrower.) Very rounded with an abruptly
pointed apex and a wedge-shaped or rounded base.
Margin slightly wavy, often with a few small teeth
toward the apex. Densely and softly pubescent below.

FLOWERS
Similar to the Japanese snowbell but earlier, much
more fragrant, and with more blossoms per cluster.
Hanging clusters are 4 - 8 in. (about 10 - 20 cm.)
long and are often partly hidden behind the leaves.

FRUIT
Gray-green, ovoid or nearly round drupe, about ¾ in.
(2 cm.) long. Pubescent, at least on the persistent calyx.
This and the fruit of the Japanese snowbell are shaped
like tiny eggplants.

SIMILAR SPECIES
Although the flowers and fruit are similar to the
Japanese snowbell, the large, rounded leaves of this
species easily identify it.

LOCATIONS
- ☐ Dumbarton Oaks
- ☐ National Arboretum (near Magnolia Collection and near Mount Hamilton azaleas)
- ☐ Sparsely planted in Washington, mostly in private and public gardens and private yards

CAROLINA SILVERBELL
Halesia carolina L.
Storax Family *Styracaceae*

A small tree or large shrub with bell-shaped spring blossoms.

NATIVE HABITAT
Southeastern U.S., west to Oklahoma. In Virginia only in the mountains.

LEAVES
Simple, alternate, deciduous, 3 - 7 in. (8 - 18 cm.) long. Finely toothed.

FLOWERS
White, in drooping clusters of two - five. Each blossom bell-shaped; petals fused.

FRUIT
Dry, *four-winged* drupe, up to 1½ in. (up to 4 cm.) long.

SIMILAR SPECIES
Compare leaves of the two preceding species, which both have smooth (not winged) fruit.

LOCATIONS
- ☐ National Arboretum
- ☐ Saint Elizabeth's Hospital

COMMON PERSIMMON

Diospyros virginiana L.
Ebony Family *Ebenaceae*

The common persimmon is a very attractive native tree; it is not widely cultivated in Washington.

NATIVE HABITAT
Southeastern New York through all of Florida; west to eastern Texas, eastern Kansas, and southeastern Iowa.

LEAVES
Simple, alternate, deciduous. 3 - 6 in. (7.5 - 15 cm.) long, oblong-ovate to ovate-elliptic; margin smooth. Lustrous green and glabrous above; sometimes slightly pubescent below.

FRUIT
A large, orangy purple berry, 1 - 1½ in. (2.5 - 3.8 cm.) long.

BARK
Very distinctive; dark gray, separated into small, thick squares.

SIMILAR SPECIES
The tupelo (*Nyssa sylvatica*) has fruit that is a small blue-black drupe, and has reddish-brown bark.

LOCATIONS
☐ U.S. Capitol grounds
☐ National Zoo
☐ Some parks and private homes in the District

Chinese Kaki Persimmon

Diospyros kaki L. f.
Ebony Family *Ebenaceae*

Chinese Kaki Persimmon *Diospyros kaki* Fruit

This tree is cultivated in Asia, Europe and North America for its edible fruit.

NATIVE HABITAT
Asia.

LEAVES
Similar in shape to the native species, above, but longer and broader.

FRUIT
1½ - 3½ in. (3.8 - 7.5 cm.) across, rounded to ovoid (often squat like a tomato), bright yellow to orange. (The fruit of the wild form of the tree, *D. kaki* var. *sylvestris* Mak. is considerably smaller.)

LOCATIONS
☐ Lutheran Home, N.E. Washington
☐ Alton Street, N.W.
☐ Hillwood Estate (wild form)

The Lindens (Limes)

Tilia L.
Linden Family *Tiliaceae*

Bees are fonder of lindens than botanists are. Linden nectar makes great honey, but the trees themselves are a nightmare to identify and classify. The European species pose particular problems because they have been so heavily hybridized.

Washington's streets, avenues, and parks are well-endowed with linden trees; their fragrant flowers perfume the air throughout much of the month of June.

CHARACTERISTICS OF THE GENUS

LEAVES: Simple, alternate, deciduous. Usually heart-shaped, with unequal bases and toothed margins.
FLOWERS AND FRUIT: Flowers yellow or whitish, fragrant, in clusters attached to a leafy bract (see illustration). Fruit small, round or ovoid, sometimes conspicuously ribbed; attached to the leafy bract. **TWIGS:** Winter buds quite large, obtuse; terminal bud absent.
DISTRIBUTION: About thirty species distributed throughout most of the northern hemisphere.

AMERICAN LINDEN
OR BASSWOOD (LIME)
Tilia americana L.
Linden Family *Tiliaceae*

During the last century Massachusetts Avenue was lined with lovely American linden trees. Some of the original lindens remain from the 1870 plantings. The city's Department of Transportation tree division still maintains the tradition of planting lindens on Massachusetts Avenue. Today European species are planted along with the American trees. In June, the linden blossoms on this avenue and throughout the city fill the air with a summery perfume.

A 1923 visitor to the capital had this to say about the lindens: "Its praises have been less sung than the praises of the oak, the elm, the maple or the chestnut, but let one drive under the lindens of Massachusetts Avenue on a damp night in June, when the trees are in full bloom, and the haunting fragrance of that drive will long remain. Some day American poets may sing its praises."

NATIVE HABITAT
New Brunswick and Maine; south to western North Carolina; west to southeastern Manitoba, the eastern Dakotas, eastern Kansas, and eastern Oklahoma.

LEAVES
Simple, alternate, deciduous. 4 - 10 in. (10 - 25.3 cm.) long, heart-shaped, with an unequal base. Coarsely toothed, dull dark green above, paler below and usually glabrous except for a few small tufts of hair in the vein axils. Petioles slender, 1 - 2 in. (2.5 - 5 cm.) long.

FLOWERS
Fragrant, yellow, in pendulous clusters of 6 - 15; clusters on a long, slender stalk, attached to a leafy bract, 3 - 5½ in. (7.5 - 14 cm.) long.

FRUIT
Round or ellipsoid, nutlike, without ribs, ¼ - ½ in. (5 - 12 mm.) long; attached in small clusters to leafy bract.

BARK AND TWIGS
Bark gray, becoming narrowly, vertically ridged and furrowed. Twigs glabrous with rather large reddish winter
buds; terminal bud absent.

HABIT
Tall trunk and a dense, rounded crown.

SIMILAR SPECIES
The white basswood (*Tilia heterophylla* Vent.) is considered a separate species by some botanists, and a
variety of the American linden (*Tilia americana* var.
heterophylla (Vent.) Loud.) by others. It ranges further
south and is characterized by leaves that are woolly-
white below. This tree is planted in Washington, though
not nearly as commonly as the American linden. The
European lindens have smaller leaves than the American
species. The leaves of the European big-leafed linden
(*Tilia platyphyllos*), which are almost as large as those
of the American species, are pubescent below with *conspicuous tufts of hair in the vein axils.*

LOCATIONS
□ Massachusetts Avenue
□ U.S. Capitol grounds
□ Streets, parks, and buildings throughout the city

BIG-LEAFED LINDEN
(LARGE-LEAFED LIME)
Tilia platyphyllos Scop.
Linden Family *Tiliaceae*

NATIVE HABITAT: Europe, the Caucasus, Asia Minor.
LEAVES: Alternate, simple, deciduous. Variable in size,
2½ - 6½ in. (6.3 - 16.5 cm.) long. More or less heart-
shaped, with an unequal base, and sharply toothed
margin. Pubescent below, especially along the veins,
with conspicuous tufts of hairs in the vein axils. Petiole
pubescent. **FLOWERS AND FRUIT:** The first linden to
bloom in Washington (late May or early June). Flowers
yellow-white, fragrant, attached to a leafy bract. Fruit
small, round, and nutlike; conspicuously five-ribbed,
pubescent, attached to the leafy bract. **OTHER FORMS:**
An absolutely beautiful specimen of the cultivar
'Vitifolia' stands behind the Smithsonian castle
(Independence Avenue side). Many of its leaves are
slightly three-lobed. They tend to be less pubescent than
the common form. **SIMILAR SPECIES:** The common
American linden (*Tilia americana*) has larger leaves that
are glabrous except for small tufts in the vein axils. The
white basswood (mentioned in the American linden
"Similar Species" section) has leaves that are whitened
below.
LOCATIONS
□ U.S. Capitol grounds
□ East Potomac Park
□ Smithsonian Castle
□ Moderately widespread

LITTLE-LEAFED LINDEN
(SMALL-LEAFED LIME)
Tilia cordata Mill.
Linden Family *Tiliaceae*

This pretty European tree is widely planted in Washington, but it is very difficult to distinguish from the hybrid European linden (*Tilia* x *europaea*), which is a cross between this species and the big-leafed linden (*Tilia platyphyllos*). President Franklin Delano Roosevelt planted two little-leafed lindens on the south lawn of the White House.

NATIVE HABITAT: Europe, the Caucasus, Siberia.
LEAVES: Simple, alternate, deciduous. Small, 1 - 3 in. (2.5 - 7.5 cm.) long, deeply heart-shaped. Apex abruptly pointed; margin sharply and finely toothed. Pale bluish green below, with orange tufts of hair in the vein axils.

FLOWERS AND FRUIT: Flowers in June; pale yellow, fragrant, in erect or spreading clusters attached to a leafy bract. Fruit small, round, *glabrous*, and nutlike; not ribbed or scarcely so; attached to the leafy bract.
OTHER FORMS: The 'Greenspire' linden sold by Princeton Nurseries is a cultivar of *Tilia cordata.*
SIMILAR SPECIES: The European linden (*Tilia* x *europaea*) has slightly larger leaves which tend to be more pubescent than those of the little-leafed linden. A very few small hairs scattered along the leaf margin of the European linden are often *visible with a hand lens*. Little-leafed linden leaves usually have no hairs along their margins.
LOCATIONS:
- ☐ The White House grounds
- ☐ National Park Service Headquarters, East Potomac Park
- ☐ U.S. Capitol grounds
- ☐ Streets and public buildings throughout the city

EUROPEAN LINDEN
(COMMON LIME)

Tilia x europaea L.
(*T. platyphyllos* x *T. cordata*)
Linden Family *Tiliaceae*

This hybrid of the big-leafed and little-leafed lindens is widely planted in Washington. It is very difficult to distinguish from the little-leafed linden, even for botanists.

LEAVES
Simple, alternate, deciduous. Very similar to the leaves of the little-leafed linden (*Tilia cordata*) above, but slightly larger, (2¼ - 4¼ in. (5.5 - 10.5 cm.) long), *sometimes* more pubescent below, and *sometimes* less deeply cordate at the base. A very few hairs are often visible along the margin *with a hand lens*.

FLOWERS AND FRUIT
Flower clusters slightly more pendulous than those of the little-leafed linden. Nutlike fruit *woolly pubescent* and faintly ribbed.

SIMILAR SPECIES
Little-leafed linden. There are two reasons why the distinguishing characteristics of the European linden are so hard to pin down: lindens, in general, are a difficult genus; and the European linden is the name for a large group of hybrids with widely varying characteristics.

LOCATIONS
☐ U.S. Capitol grounds
☐ Park Service Headquarters, East Potomac Park
　　(most trees in this planting are little-leafed lindens)
☐ Streets throughout the District

WEEPING SILVER LINDEN
(WEEPING SILVER LIME)

Tilia petiolaris DC.
Linden Family *Tiliaceae*

A beautiful weeping tree with leaves that look silvery below when blown by the wind. Quite rare in Washington.

NATIVE HABITAT: Origin unknown. Some botanists believe the tree to be a form of the silver linden (*Tilia tomentosa* Moench.), native to southeastern Europe and

western Asia. **LEAVES:** Simple, alternate, deciduous.
2½ - 5 in. (6.3 - 12.5 cm.) long, heart-shaped, sharply
toothed. Lower surface of leaf and petiole covered with
short, soft, white pubescence, giving the leaf its silvery
look. **FLOWERS:** Yellow, very fragrant, mid to late
June. Their nectar has a narcotic effect on bees.
SIMILAR SPECIES: The weeping habit combined with
the soft white undersides of the leaves distinguishes this
tree from other locally planted lindens.
LOCATIONS:
☐ The White House grounds
☐ The U.S. Capitol grounds

OTHER LINDENS OF THE WASHINGTON AREA:

Two other species of linden (*Tilia*) are cultivated in
Washington, though rarely.

The Caucasian linden or lime tree (*Tilia* x *euchlora*
K. Koch) is planted along a few streets in Washington.
Its leaves are a deep glossy green, 2 - 4 in. (5 - 10 cm.)
long, with large tufts of brownish hairs in the vein axils
below.

Even rarer is a linden believed to be one of the
parents of the hybrid Caucasian linden. A single
specimen of *Tilia dasystyla* Stev. is growing at the Tidal
Basin. This tree has leaves that are 3 - 5½ in. (7.5 - 14
cm.) long, with tufts of whitish-yellow hairs in the vein
axils below.

ROSE-OF-SHARON
OR SHRUBBY ALTHAEA

Hibiscus syriacus L.
Mallow Family *Malvaceae*

The rose-of-sharon is very conspicuous in Washington during its long blooming time, from mid-summer
until mid-autumn. Although usually a shrub, it is
sometimes trained as a small tree.

NATIVE HABITAT
China, India.

FLOWERS
May be pink, red, white, purple, blue or a combination
of colors. Vaguely rose-like.

LEAVES
Simple, alternate, deciduous. Usually three-lobed, with
coarse, rounded or pointed teeth; 1¾ - 4 in. (4.5 - 10
cm.) long.

SIMILAR SPECIES
Viburnums have opposite leaves.

LOCATIONS
☐ Very common throughout city
☐ U.S. Capitol grounds
☐ National Arboretum

CHINESE PARASOL TREE
OR PHOENIX-TREE
Firmiana simplex (L.) W.F. Wight
Sterculia Family *Sterculiaceae*

Very rare.

NATIVE HABITAT
China, Japan.

LEAVES
Simple, alternate, deciduous. Palmately 3 - 5 lobed. Size
varies. Most leaves 6 - 10 in. (15 - 25.5 cm.) long, but
some are much larger. Petiole as long or almost as long
as blade.

BARK
Very smooth, gray-green.

HABIT
Trunk very straight. Branches form a compact, rounded
crown. Overall appearance vaguely suggests a parasol.

LOCATIONS
☐ National Arboretum (near the duck pond)

COMMON BOX

Buxus sempervirens L.
Box Family *Buxaceae*

Dozens of varieties of the common box are planted
in Washington. Although most are shrubs, the box can
become a small tree. Several attractive tree-like
specimens are growing on the Capitol grounds.

NATIVE HABITAT
Europe and northern Africa.

tar Magnolia   *Magnolia stellata*   Japan

aucer Magnolia   *Magnolia x soulangeana*   Asian Hybrid

Southern Magnolia   *Magnolia grandiflora*   Southéastern United States

Flowering Dogwood   *Cornus florida*   Eastern United States

Kousa Dogwood   *Cornus kousa*   Asia

Cornelian Cherry   *Cornus mas*   Europe & Asia

Yoshino Cherry   *Prunus x yedoensis*   Japanese Hybrid

Weeping Cherry   (Single-Blossom)   *Prunus subhirtella pendula*   Japan

Kwanzan Cherry   *Prunus* (Sato-zakura group) 'Sekiyama'   Asia

Honey Locust   *Gleditsia triacanthos*   Eastern North America

Japanese Pagoda Tree   *Sophora japonica*   China, Korea

Mimosa or Silk-Tree   *Albizia julibrissin*   Asia, Asia Minor

Black Locust *Robinia pseudoacacia* Eastern United States

Redbud *Cercis canadensis* Eastern North America

Common Horse-Chestnut *Aesculus hippocastanum*
Southeastern Europe

Crape-Myrtle   *Lagerstroemia indica*   Asia

Paulownia   *Paulownia tomentosa*   China

Golden-Rain-Tree   *Koelreuteria paniculata*   Asia

Catalpa *Catalpa speciosa* Central United States

Fringe-Tree *Chionanthus virginicus* Eastern United States

Linden *Tilia x europaea* European hybrid

Bradford Pear   *Pyrus calleryana* 'Bradford'   Asian Cultivar

Flowering Crabapple   *Malus floribunda*   Asia

Hawthorn   *Crataegus*

LEAVES
Simple, opposite, evergreen. Tiny, ½ - 1¼ in. (1.3 - 3.2 cm.) long, elliptic or ovate, dark glossy green.

LOCATIONS
- ☐ U.S. Capitol grounds
- ☐ White House grounds (form known as "American box" planted by President Harry S. Truman)
- ☐ Dumbarton Oaks
- ☐ Common throughout the city

THE CHERRIES AND PEACHES AND PLUMS
Prunus L.
Rose Family *Rosaceae*

The crème de la crème of Washington's flowering trees are, unfortunately, among the most botanically illusive. Centuries of hybridization (mostly in Japan) have rendered many specimens of the genus virtually inscrutable, even to botanists specializing in the field. Thanks to one man, Roland Jefferson of the National Arboretum, the history and taxonomy of Washington's famous Japanese flowering cherry trees are being untangled and preserved. See Part One, for the ongoing story of these living symbols of international friendship.

CHARACTERISTICS OF THE GENUS

LEAVES: Simple, alternate, deciduous, usually toothed. **FLOWERS:** Petals-five. Blossom color white, pink or red (rarely green). **FRUIT:** Usually one-seeded drupe. **DISTRIBUTION:** About 200 species, mostly in the temperate zone. Descriptions of the most commonly planted cherries, plums and peaches follow. See also color close-up section.

FALL-BLOOMING CHERRY
Prunus subhirtella Miq. 'Autumnalis'
Rose Family *Rosaceae*

The fall-blooming cherry belongs to the same species as the weeping cherry. In late autumn and early winter, this unique tree puts forth pale pink, gently nodding blossoms. Then again, in spring, the tree becomes covered with blossoms before the leaves appear, continuing to bloom for a time after they've unfolded.

LOCATIONS:
- ☐ U.S. Capitol grounds
- ☐ Dumbarton Oaks

YOSHINO CHERRY
OR SOMEI-YOSHINO

Prunus x yedoensis Matsum.
(Hybrid of unknown origin)
Rose Family *Rosaceae*

This is the lovely Japanese flowering cherry tree of Tidal Basin fame. Some of the original trees given to the United States by Japan in 1912 are still alive today.

FLOWERS
Late March or early April, before the leaves. Pale pink at first; later turning white or nearly white, then often blushing pink near the base before falling. In clusters of two to five. (See color close-up.)

LEAVES
Simple, alternate, deciduous. Elliptic-obovate, coarsely toothed, about 6 in. (15 cm.) long. Pubescent along the veins below.

FRUIT
Early summer; bright red and yellow, then black. Obovoid-ellipsoid, less than ½ in. (1 cm.) long.

OTHER FORMS
In the 1920s the slightly pinker 'Akebono' was selected and propagated in a California nursery. This American form of the Japanese tree is widely planted in Washington today. Many of the old Yoshino cherries have been replaced by specimens of Akebono.

YOSHINO LOCATIONS
□ Tidal Basin
□ U.S. Capitol grounds
□ Library of Congress grounds
□ Fort McNair

AKEBONO LOCATIONS
□ Tidal Basin
□ Washington Monument
□ East Potomac Park
□ U.S. Capitol grounds
□ Dumbarton Oaks

WEEPING CHERRY

Prunus subhirtella pendula Maxim.
Prunus subhirtella pendula 'Flora Plena'
Rose Family *Rosaceae*

The delicate weeping cherry is one of Washington's most spectacular flowering trees. In early spring its pendulous branchlets put forth clouds of pink or white blossoms.

NATIVE HABITAT: Japan. **FLOWERS.** Late March or early April, before the leaves. Pink (or rarely white), *either double or single.* The single blossoms are star-like; the double blossoms bell-shaped. (See color close-up.)
LEAVES: Simple, alternate, deciduous. Oblong-elliptic; 2½ - 5 in. (6.3 - 12.5 cm.) long. Sharply, sometimes doubly, toothed; pubescent along the veins below.
FRUIT: Less than ½ in. (about 8 mm.) long; black.
HABIT: Gracefully weeping tree with delicate, very pendulous branchlets.
LOCATIONS:
SINGLE-BLOSSOMED PINK FORM
□ U.S. Capitol grounds
□ Dumbarton Oaks
□ Brookings Institution
□ East Potomac Park
□ Smithsonian Air and Space Museum
DOUBLE-BLOSSOMED PINK FORM
□ Smithsonian Air and Space Museum
□ National Arboretum
SINGLE-BLOSSOMED WHITE FORM
□ East Potomac Park

BLACK CHERRY
OR RUM CHERRY

Prunus serotina Ehrh.
Rose Family *Rosaceae*

The black cherry, native to most of the eastern United States, blooms in Washington in May. Its small white blossoms are borne in thin, 4 - 5 in. (10 - 12.5 cm.) long clusters.

LEAVES: Simple, alternate, deciduous, elliptic to oblong-lanceolate, 2 - 6 in. (5 - 15 cm.) long, with small, incurved teeth. **FRUIT:** Nearly black, ¼ - ½ in. (6 - 12 mm.) across; edible, but slightly bitter. **SIMILAR SPECIES:** The usually shrubby common choke cherry (*Prunus virginiana* L.), another native cherry, has red fruit and leaves with spreading, rather than incurved, teeth.

LOCATIONS:
□ National Arboretum
□ Montrose Park
□ Parks and woodlands throughout the city

KWANZAN CHERRY
Prunus (Sato-zakura group) 'Sekiyama'
(*Prunus serrulata* Lindl. 'Kwanzan')
Rose Family *Rosaceae*

A deep pink, double-blossomed Japanese cherry which blossoms approximately two weeks later than the Yoshino and Akebono. Kwanzan cherries are planted extensively in East Potomac Park.

NATIVE HABITAT: Origin unknown. Possibly a Chinese tree introduced into Japan early on as a single-flowered form. **FLOWERS:** Mid to late April. Large, medium to deep pink, in dense clusters of three to five. (See color close-up.) **LEAVES:** Simple, alternate, deciduous. Coppery or purplish at first, becoming green. Ovate to ovate-lanceolate (rarely obovate), doubly toothed. 3 - 7½ in. (7.5 - 17.8 cm.) long. **HABIT:** Very distinctive upright habit; branches form an inverse pyramid. **SIMILAR SPECIES:** Several other double-blossomed cherries were part of the original 1912 gift from Japan to the United States. The Kwanzan is the only one that is still around in any numbers. One of the trees sent to the U.S. by Japan, which is very rare to-day, was the Gyoiko, with unique, pale green blossoms shaped much like the Kwanzan's. The Gyoiko was planted on the White House grounds, but the specimens have since died. A large Gyoiko tree is thriving at the Glenn Dale Plant Introduction Station.

LOCATIONS:
☐ East Potomac Park
☐ U.S. Capitol grounds
☐ Library of Congress grounds
☐ Pan American Union
☐ Saint Elizabeth's Hospital

CAROLINA LAURELCHERRY
Prunus caroliniana (Mill.) Ait.
Rose Family *Rosaceae*

The Carolina laurelcherry, which grows from North Carolina to Texas, is just barely hardy here, if it is planted in a sheltered place. Its leaves are evergreen and its tiny white flowers are borne in long clusters in early spring.

LOCATIONS:
☐ White House grounds
☐ Saint Elizabeth's Hospital grounds
☐ Kenilworth Aquatic Gardens

PEACH
Prunus persica (L.) Batsch.
Rose Family *Rosaceae*

The peach has long been cultivated throughout Asia, Europe, and North America for its delicious fruit and lovely flowers. Several forms of the peach, with blossoms ranging from white to deep red, are planted in Washington. Some have large, double blossoms.

NATIVE HABITAT: Not known for certain, but believed to be China. **FLOWERS:** Red, pink, rose or white, in April.

LOCATIONS:
- U.S. Capitol grounds
- Pan American Union
- National Arboretum
- Quite widely planted in Washington

PURPLE-LEAVED PLUM
OR PISSARD PLUM
Prunus cerasifera Ehrh. 'Atropurpurea'
Rose Family *Rosaceae*

The purple-leaved plum is one of Washington's loveliest ornamentals. Its small, pale pink blossoms open in early spring and are soon offset by attractive, reddish-purple leaves. The species is native to the Balkan Peninsula and Asia.

LOCATIONS:
- B'nai B'rith Building (Rhode Island Avenue and 17th St., N.W.)
- Private yards throughout the city

DOUBLE CHERRY-PLUM
Prunus x *blireiana* André
(*P. cerasifera* 'Atropurpurea' x *P. mume.*)
Rose Family *Rosaceae*

The double cherry-plum is extremely rare in Washington. It has large, double, pink blossoms that open with the reddish-purple leaves in spring.

LOCATIONS:
- Dumbarton Oaks

OTHER MEMBERS OF THE GENUS
Mazzard Cherry *Prunus avium* L.
Sour Cherry *Prunus cerasus* L.
Prunus incisa Thunb.
Sargent Cherry *Prunus sargentii* Rehd.
Prunus subhirtella var. *ascendens* (Mak.) Wils.
Flowering Almond *Prunus triloba* Lindl.
Prunus serrulata 'Fugenzo'

THE FLOWERING CRABAPPLES

Malus Mill.
Rose Family *Rosaceae*

Washington's flowering crabapples are as important a part of the landscape as the Japanese flowering cherry trees. During April and early May a steady procession of crabapple blossoms adorns the city. For many years, until it was discontinued in the 1950s, a crabapple festival was held in the nation's capital each spring, with nearly as much fanfare as the cherry blossom festival. A crabapple parade was held and a young lady was crowned crabapple queen. Today many of the old trees that were the focal point of those festivities still bloom each year along the banks of the Anacostia in southeast Washington.

The genus *Malus*, to which the flowering crabapples belong, is an extremely confusing one. So much hybridization has taken place among the crabapples that even botanists specializing in the genus have trouble distinguishing among these trees. Therefore, we've chosen one of the most commonly planted crabapples as an exemplary species. A list of some of Washington's other commonly cultivated crabapples follows.

CRABAPPLES WITH WHITE OR PALE PINK BLOSSOMS	LOCATIONS
Fuji Crab (*Malus sieboldii* (Reg.) Rehd.) 'Fuji' (This splendid new cultivar produces a profusion of double white blossoms.)	Glenn Dale Plant Introduction Station Glenn Dale, MD
Katherine Crab (*Malus* x 'Katherine')	White House Rose Garden Dumbarton Oaks
Arnold Crab (*Malus* x *arnoldiana* Sarg.) (*M. baccata* x *M. floribunda*)	Anacostia Park
Siberian Crab (*Malus baccata* (L.) Borkh.)	Dumbarton Oaks National Arboretum
Tea Crab (*Malus hupehensis* (Pampan.) Rehd.)	National Arboretum
Iowa or Prairie Crab (*Malus ioensis* (Wood) Britt.)	National Arboretum
Bechtel Crab (*Malus ioensis* 'Plena')	Dumbarton Oaks
Pear or Plum-leaved Crab (*M. prunifolia* (Willd.) Borkh.)	National Arboretum
Cherry Crab (*Malus* x *robusta* (Carr.) Rehd.) (*M. baccata* x *M. prunifolia*)	National Arboretum
Sargent Crab (*Malus sargentii* Rehd.)	Anacostia Park
Zumi Crab (*Malus* x *zumi* (Matsum.) Rehd.)	Anacostia Park
FLOWERS MEDIUM PINK, DARK PINK, REDDISH OR PURPLISH	LOCATIONS
Dorothea Crab (*Malus* x 'Dorothea')	Dumbarton Oaks
Hopa Crab (*Malus* x 'Hopa')	Library of Congress
Radiant Crab (*Malus* x 'Radiant')	Dumbarton Oaks

Carmine Crab (*Malus* x *atrosanguinea* (Spaeth) Schneid.)	Smithsonian National Museum of Natural History
Wild Sweet Crab (*Malus coronaria* (L.) Mill.)	National Arboretum
Purple Crab (*Malus* x *purpurea* (Barbier) Rehd.) (*M. atrosanguinea* x *M. pumila* var. *hiedzwetzkyana*)	Washington Circle National Arboretum
Scheidecker Crab (*Malus* x *Scheideckeri* (Spaeth.) Zab.) (*M. floribunda* x *M. prunifolia*)	Dumbarton Oaks
Toringo Crab (*Malus sieboldii* (Reg.) Rehd.)	National Arboretum
Chinese Flowering Crab (*Malus spectabilis* (Ait.) Borkh.)	Dumbarton Oaks

JAPANESE FLOWERING CRAB

Malus floribunda Sieb. ex Van Houtte
Rose Family *Rosaceae*

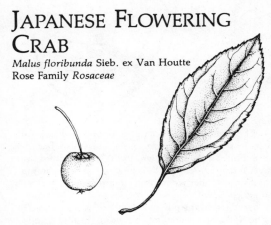

NATIVE HABITAT
Japan.

LEAVES
Simple, alternate, deciduous. 2 - 3 in. (5 - 7.5 cm.) long,
dark green, elliptic-ovate or oblong-ovate. Long pointed
apex, usually wedge-shaped base, sharply toothed
margin. Pubescent along the veins below or nearly
glabrous.

FLOWERS
Flower buds deep, rose pink; opening up paler pink to
nearly white. Blossoms 1 - 1¼ in. (2.5 - 3 cm.) across.
The deep pink buds against the paler pink blossoms and
dark green leaves present a striking picture. (See color
close-up.)

FRUIT
Yellowish or sometimes blushed red; small pome, ¼ - ½
in. (6 - 12 mm.) across.

HABIT
A small tree with widely spreading branches.

LOCATIONS
☐ Smithsonian National Museum of Natural History
☐ Washington Circle
☐ Tidal Basin
☐ Dumbarton Oaks
☐ National Arboretum
☐ Common throughout the city

The Pears

Pyrus
Rose Family *Rosaceae*

The pears have long been cultivated for their delicious fruit and showy spring blossoms. Pears are an important part of Washington's flowering spring.

Bradford Pear

Pyrus calleryana Dcne. 'Bradford'
Rose Family *Rosaceae*

The Bradford pear is an increasingly popular cultivar. Its snowy white, early spring flowers are borne on a beautiful egg-shaped crown. In the fall, Bradford pear leaves turn wine-red. With so much to recommend this tree it's no wonder we've heard it criticized....for being too perfect!

Dr. Creech, the plant explorer and former Director of the National Arboretum who wrote the foreword to *City of Trees*, was responsible for bringing the Bradford pear to the attention of the nursery trade in recent years.

NATIVE HABITAT: A cultivar of the Callery pear (*Pyrus calleryana*), which is native to China and Korea. **LEAVES:** Simple, alternate, deciduous. Egg-shaped or heart-shaped, with small, rounded teeth. Bright yellow-green when they unfold in the spring, becoming gray-green. Smooth, some pubescence when young, then becoming glabrous, 1½ -4 in. (4 - 10 cm.) long. **FLOWERS:** White, before or with the young leaves in early spring. Five-petaled blossoms have long stamens with purple or red anthers. (See color close-up). **FRUIT:** Small, round, slender-stalked fruit is less than ½ in. (about 1 cm.) in diameter. **HABIT:** Very distinctive egg-shaped crown with narrow, ascending branches. A small tree. **SIMILAR SPECIES:** The Bradford pear is best distinguished from other pears, cherries and apples by its clean, *egg-shaped crown*.
LOCATIONS:
☐ National Arboretum parking lot
☐ National Capital YMCA (Rhode Island Avenue)
☐ U.S. Botanic Gardens
☐ U.S.D.A., The Mall (planted by First Lady Lady Bird Johnson)
☐ Glenn Dale Plant Introduction Station (Glenn Dale, Md.)
☐ Common throughout the city

CALLERY PEAR

Pyrus calleryana Dcne.
Rose Family *Rosaceae*

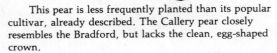

This pear is less frequently planted than its popular cultivar, already described. The Callery pear closely resembles the Bradford, but lacks the clean, egg-shaped crown.

LOCATIONS:
☐ National Arboretum

COMMON PEAR

Pyrus communis L.
Rose Family *Rosaceae*

Another flowering pear with beautiful, white spring blossoms. Specimens of this tree are planted in Lady Bird Johnson Park along the Potomac, where they are surrounded by a profusion of daffodils.

NATIVE HABITAT: Europe, Asia. **LEAVES:** Simple, alternate, deciduous. Egg-shaped, almost rounded or elliptic with wavy-toothed margin. 1 - 3 in. (2.5 - 7.5 cm.) long. **FLOWERS:** White, in early spring, about an inch across with five petals. **FRUIT:** Top-shaped or almost round, up to 4 in. (10 cm.) long. **HABIT:** A small to medium-sized tree with a rounded or pyramidal crown. **SIMILAR SPECIES:** *Pyrus ussuriensis* Maxim., mentioned here alone, is a rare species also planted in Lady Bird Johnson Park. This Asian native can be told from the common pear by the *sharp, bristly* teeth on its leaf margins. The Bradford and Callery pears (*Pyrus calleryana* and *Pyrus calleryana* 'Bradford') have very small fruit. Other pears are rarely planted in Washington.
LOCATIONS:
☐ Lady Bird Johnson Park
☐ Parks, public buildings and private homes

MEDLAR

Mespilus germanica L.
Rose Family *Rosaceae*

A single specimen of this rare tree or shrub stands on the grounds of the National Library of Medicine in Bethesda.

NATIVE HABITAT: Southeastern Europe, western Asia. **LEAVES:** Simple, alternate, deciduous. Margins with rounded teeth, sometimes nearly smooth. **FLOWERS:** White, with five petals, borne singly. **FRUIT:** A large, pome-like drupe that is open at the top. Edible only after it has decayed.

Chinese Photinia

Photinia serrulata Lindl.
Rose Family *Rosaceae*

A small tree or large shrub with shiny, evergreen leaves, attractive white blossoms, and bright red fruit.

NATIVE HABITAT
China.

LEAVES
Simple, alternate, evergreen. 3 - 7 in. (7.5 - 17.8 cm.) long, 1 - 1¾ in. (2.5 - 4.5 cm.) wide. Lustrous dark green above, paler below, leathery and glabrous. Reddish when young. Oblong, abruptly pointed, with a rounded or wedge-shaped base. Margin with small, rounded or pointed teeth.

FLOWERS
Tiny, white, in broad clusters 4 - 7 in. (10 - 17.8 cm.) across.

FRUIT
Small, red berry-like pomes in showy, stalked, flat-topped clusters that are up to 7 in. (17.8 cm.) across.

SIMILAR SPECIES
Hollies (*Ilex* species) bear fruit in smaller, shorter-stalked clusters.

LOCATIONS
☐ U.S. Capitol grounds (close to the House and Senate wings)

CHINESE QUINCE
Chaenomeles sinensis (Thouin) Koehne
Rose Family *Rosaceae*

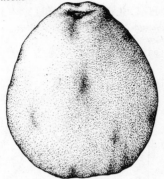

A beautiful little tree, with a fluted trunk, mottled bark, and large, fragrant fruit.

NATIVE HABITAT
China.

LEAVES
Simple, alternate, deciduous; elliptic-ovate or oblong-elliptic; 2 - 4 in. (5 - 10 cm.) long. Sharply and finely toothed.

FLOWERS
Pale pink, 1 - 1½ in. (2.5 - 3.8 cm.) across. After the leaves in spring.

FRUIT
Dark yellow, oblong, 4 - 6 in. (10 - 15 cm.) long.

SIMILAR SPECIES
Quince (*Cydonia oblonga* Mill.) (not included in this guide) is planted at the Arboretum. It has leaves that are downy below, with *smooth margins*.

LOCATIONS
☐ Dumbarton Oaks
☐ Pan American Union

COMMON OR DOWNY SERVICEBERRY

OR SHADBUSH, SHADBLOW OR JUNEBERRY

Amelanchier arborea (Michx. f.) Fern.
(*Amelanchier laevis* Wieg.)
Rose Family *Rosaceae*

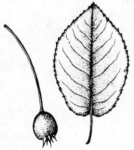

The common serviceberry or shadbush is one of the first trees to bloom in woodlands throughout the eastern United States and southeastern Canada. The tree was named serviceberry because it blooms soon after the ground has thawed, when burial services were traditionally held in the north for people who had died during the winter. Its blooming time also often coincides with the running of shad in the northeast; thus the names shadbush and shadblow. George Washington, who was fond of the serviceberry, planted it on the grounds of his Mount Vernon estate.

NATIVE HABITAT
New Brunswick to Florida; west to eastern Minnesota and eastern Texas.

LEAVES
Simple, alternate, deciduous. 1 - 3½ in. (2.5 - 9 cm.) long, obovate or ovate with small, sharply pointed teeth. Gradually or abruptly pointed apex and cordate or rounded base. Densely pubescent when young, especially on the lower surface, but may become glabrous.

FLOWERS
White, clustered, appearing when the small, young leaves are still folded. Each blossom has five thin petals.

FRUIT
June-August. Small, round, red, purple or blackish pome, ¼ - ⅓ in. (less than 1 cm.) in diameter. Rather dry and insipid tasting.

HABIT
Small tree or large shrub.

LOCATIONS
☐ Fern Valley, National Arboretum
☐ Mount Vernon
☐ Area woodlands

THE HAWTHORNS
Crataegus L.
Rose Family *Rosaceae*

English May
Crataegus oxyacantha

Hybrid Cockspur Thorn
Crataegus x lavallei

Because the hawthorns are extremely difficult even for botanists to identify, we simply describe the characteristics of the genus here, with a list of some of the species most commonly planted in Washington. The hawthorns are a large and complex genus, containing over 1,000 species. They are typically small trees or shrubs, which usually bear *sharp thorns*. The most interesting hawthorn in Washington is undoubtedly the rare Glastonbury thorn (*Crataegus monogyna* Jacq. 'Biflora'), which is planted in a circle near the Washington Cathedral. This rather scrappy looking old tree is reputed to have been raised from a cutting brought into the country from Glastonbury Abbey in England around the turn of the century. According to legend, the Glastonbury thorn blooms when royalty is present. But royalty or no, this particular tree has been known to bloom at nearly every time of the year.

CHARACTERISTICS OF THE HAWTHORNS
LEAVES: Simple, alternate, almost always deciduous. Lobed or unlobed; usually toothed. **FLOWERS:** White or pink with five petals (except in double-blossomed forms such as 'Paul's Scarlet') and five sepals. **FRUIT:** A small, often brightly colored pome, which resembles a tiny apple. Fruit on some species remains on the tree into the winter. **BARK AND TWIGS:** Bark scaly and/or shallowly furrowed. Twigs usually armed with sharp, stiff thorns. Winter buds small, round, brown, and scaly.

HAWTHORNS COMMONLY PLANTED LOCALLY
Cockspur Thorn C. *crus-galli* L.
English May or Hawthorn C. *oxyacantha* L.
Paul's Scarlet Hawthorn C. *oxyacantha* 'Paul's Scarlet'
Hybrid Cockspur Thorn C. *x lavallei* Herincq ex. Lav.
Downy Hawthorn C. *mollis* (Torr & Gr.) Scheele
Common Hawthorn C. *monogyna* Jacq.
Glastonbury Thorn C. *monogyna* 'Biflora'
Frosted Hawthorn C. *pruinosa* (Wendl.) K. Koch
Washington Thorn C. *phaenopyrum* (L.f.) Medic.
Dotted Hawthorn C. *punctata* Jacq.

LOCATIONS
☐ Parks, public buildings, and private homes

ROWAN TREE
OR EUROPEAN MOUNTAIN-ASH
Sorbus aucuparia L.
Rose Family *Rosaceae*

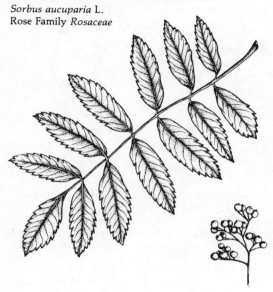

The Rowan tree or European mountain-ash is similar to the native American mountain-ash (*Sorbus americana* Marsh.), which grows in the northeastern states and in the mountains to northern Georgia. The Rowan tree is widely cultivated and has become naturalized in parts of the northern U.S. and Canada.

NATIVE HABITAT
Europe, Asia Minor, northern Africa.

LEAVES
Alternate, pinnately compound, deciduous. 6½ - 10 in. (16.5 - 25.0 cm.) long. Nine to fifteen sessile leaflets, each 1¼ - 3 in. (3 - 7.5 cm.) long. Margins evenly toothed, but smooth near the bases, which are slightly unequal; apices pointed. Pubescent below at first, but may become glabrous.

FLOWERS
White, after the leaves in spring, in upright clusters.

FRUIT
Upright clusters of yellow, then orange, then by mid-summer, brilliant red berry-like pomes, which are quickly devoured by birds.

SIMILAR SPECIES
The American mountain-ash (*Sorbus americana*) and the showy mountain-ash (*Sorbus decora* Schneid.), which are both native to northern states, are unlikely to be encountered in cultivation here.

LOCATIONS
☐ First Street, S.E. (near Capitol South Metro stop)

MIMOSA
OR SILK-TREE OR PERSIAN ACACIA

Albizia julibrissin Durrazz.
Pea Family *Leguminosae*

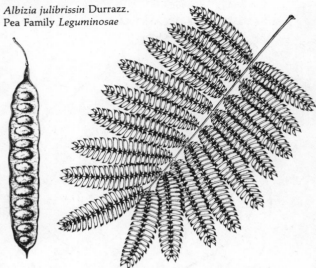

A small, delicate tree, conspicuous in summer with its wispy pink blossoms and feathery leaves.

NATIVE HABITAT
Central China to Iran. Escaped to the wild in the southeastern U.S.

LEAVES
Alternate, bipinnately compound, deciduous. 6 - 13 in. (15 - 33 cm.) long. Fern-like. Each tiny leaflet ¼ - ½ in. (about 1 - 1.5 cm.) long.

FLOWERS
Fragrant, in pink "powder puff" clusters; mid-June to late July. (See color close-up)

FRUIT
Many-seeded green pod, 3½ - 6 in. (9 - 15 cm.) long, about ¾ in. (2 cm.) wide; very thin. Seeds visible through pod, horizontally oval, 7 - 15 per pod.

BARK AND TWIGS
Bark smooth, light brown. Twigs slender, glabrous, with small winter buds and leaf scars.

GROWTH HABIT
A small tree with a broad crown, graceful branching pattern, and overall airy appearance.

SIMILAR SPECIES
The only other commonly grown trees in Washington with bipinnately compound leaves are the Kentucky coffee tree (*Gymnocladus dioicus*), honey locust (*Gleditsia triacanthos*), and devil's walking stick (*Aralia spinosa*). All have larger leaflets.

LOCATIONS
☐ A popular garden tree
☐ East Capitol Street and adjacent streets, Capitol Hill

Redbud

Cercis canadensis L.
Pea Family *Leguminosae*
STATE TREE OF OKLAHOMA

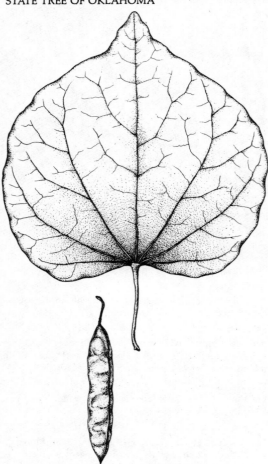

NATIVE HABITAT

Extreme southwestern New England to northern Florida;
west to Missouri, Texas, and northern Mexico.

LEAVES

The first leaves unfold at the tips of the branchlets when
the tree is in full bloom in the spring. Simple, alternate,
deciduous, heart-shaped; margin smooth. Mature leaf
2 - 5 in. (5 - 12.5 cm.) long, 3 - 5 in. (7.5 - 12.5 cm.)
wide. Five to seven palmately arranged veins arise from
the base. Petiole slender; small stipules soon fall.

FLOWERS
Deep purply-pink, rarely white, appearing in mid-April. Tiny pea-like blossoms cluster all along the branchlets, limbs, and even down the trunk of the tree. (See color close-up.)

FRUIT
2 - 3½ in. (5 - 9 cm.) light reddish-brown pod. Pointed at both ends, on thin stalk about ½ in. (1.2 cm.) long.

BARK AND TWIGS
Bark gray; may be smooth or scaly. Twig reddish-brown, heavily lenticelled, with small lateral buds and no terminal buds.

HABIT
Small tree with rounded crown or upright shrub with few ascending branches.

SIMILAR SPECIES
Very similar to Chinese redbud, described below. May also be confused with the catalpas (*Catalpa* sp.), but they have *whorled* or *opposite* leaves. See Katsura-tree (*Cercidiphyllum japonicum*) "Similar Species" section.

LOCATIONS
☐ Mount Vernon
☐ George Washington Memorial Parkway
☐ National Zoo
☐ National Arboretum
☐ Russell Senate Office Building, central courtyard
☐ Common citywide

Chinese Redbud
or Chinese Judas Tree
Cercis chinensis Bge.
Pea Family *Leguminosae*

Very similar to the native redbud with obscure differences in leaves and fruit. Chinese redbud blossoms tend to be deeper purply-pink and slightly larger than those of the native species. However, the best way to distinguish the two species is by habit: the Chinese redbud is usually *shrubby* in cultivation. While the native redbud is also shrub-like when young, it has fewer branches and is never as full as the Chinese species.

LOCATIONS
☐ U.S. Capitol grounds
☐ Quite common throughout the city

YELLOWWOOD
Cladrastis Kentukea (Dum.-Cours.) Rudd
(*Cladrastis lutea* (Michx.) K. Koch)
Pea Family *Leguminosae*

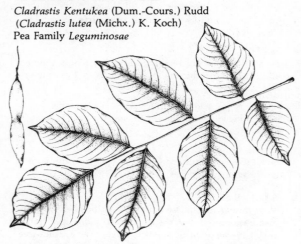

An attractive tree with smooth, gray bark, fragrant white flowers, and yellow autumn leaves.

NATIVE HABITAT
Kentucky, Tennessee, and western North Carolina; north to southern Indiana and southern Illinois; south to northern Georgia and Alabama. Also, southwestern Missouri, northwestern Arkansas, and northeastern Oklahoma.

LEAVES
Alternate, pinnately compound, deciduous. Leaflets five to eleven, each 2 - 4 in. (5 - 10 cm.) long; broadly ovate or, occasionally, obovate; more or less abruptly, and rather bluntly, pointed. Bases rounded, wedge-shaped or subcordate. Margins smooth. Leaflets glabrous above, sometimes silky below; each with a very short petiolule. Alternately arranged along rachis with a terminal leaflet. Full leaf size: 6 - 12 in. (about 15 - 30 cm.) long.

FLOWERS
Mid-May. Fragrant, white, in pendulous clusters. Each blossom ¾ - 1¼ in. (about 2 - 3 cm.) long.

FRUIT
Flat, pale green pod (turning brown), 2 - 4 in. (5 - 10 cm.) long, containing several seeds.

BARK AND TWIGS
Bark smooth, clear gray. (Wood underneath is yellow and roots yield a yellow dye.) Twigs slender, glabrous, with naked winter buds hidden by hollow petioles before leaves fall in autumn.

HABIT
Medium-sized tree with a lovely, rounded crown.

SIMILAR SPECIES
There is no other tree planted in our area with the combination of smooth, gray bark and alternate, odd-pinnately compound leaves. Naked buds distinguish it from the beeches (*Fagus* sps.) in winter. (Flowers and fruit are somewhat similar to black locust (*Robinia pseudoacacia*)).

LOCATIONS
☐ National Zoo
☐ Folger Park
☐ Lafayette Park
☐ Farragut Square
☐ Montrose Park

HONEY LOCUST
Gleditsia triacanthos L.
Pea Family *Leguminosae*

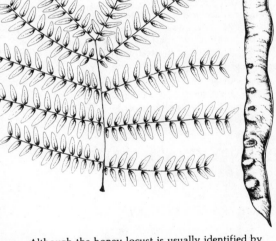

Although the honey locust is usually identified by its mean-looking thorns, nurseries are now propagating many *thornless* cultivars. Most trees planted for ornament in recent years are thornless.

NATIVE HABITAT
Western New York to South Dakota; south to Florida and Texas. Escaped from cultivation in many other parts of the eastern U.S. and southeastern Canada.

LEAVES
Alternate, pinnate or bipinnately compound, deciduous. Delicate and somewhat "feathery" looking. Individual leaflets ½ - 1 in. (1.2 - 2.5 cm.) long, elliptic-lanceolate, with blunt apices and rounded or wedge-shaped bases. Margins smooth or with very shallow, rounded teeth. Petiolules extremely short. Rachis grooved, pubescent.

FLOWERS
May. Narrow hanging clusters of small, closely arranged, greenish-yellow blossoms. (See color close-up.)

FRUIT
Very long, twisted, rust-brown pod, 8 - 18 in. (20 - 45.5 cm.). Contains many flattened oval seeds with sweet pulp between them.

BARK AND TWIGS
Bark dark, fissured and scaly; with or without stout, often branched, thorns. Twigs with very small winter buds and false end buds.

HABIT
Wide-spreading, more or less flat-topped crown.

OTHER FORMS
Thornless Honey-Locust (*Gleditsia triacanthos* f. *inermis* (L.) Zab.). The thornless forms are now propagated for ornament, almost exclusively. Many new thornless cultivars of this tree have been developed recently, including: 'Sunburst,' 'Skyline,' 'Majestic,' 'Imperial,' and 'Shademaster.'

SIMILAR SPECIES
In the absence of distinctive flowers or mature fruit, leaflet *size*, *shape*, and *margin* are the characteristics that set the honey locust apart from other members of the pea family. (See leaf illustrations.)

LOCATIONS
☐ First Street, S.E. near Independence Avenue
☐ National Gallery of Art grounds
☐ C Street, N.E. near corner of Sixth Street
☐ Quite common throughout the city

KENTUCKY COFFEE-TREE
Gymnocladus dioicus (L.) K. Koch
Pea Family *Leguminosae*

STATE TREE OF KENTUCKY

Conspicuous from afar in winter with its large, "sickle"-shaped pods. During the Civil War, Kentucky coffee-tree seeds were roasted and used as a coffee substitute.

NATIVE HABITAT
Western New York and Pennsylvania west to Minnesota and Nebraska; south to Tennessee and Oklahoma.

LEAVES
Alternate, bipinnately compound, deciduous. Numerous leaflets; each smooth-margined, ovate, usually with sharply pointed apex. Bases most often rounded, but may be wedge-shaped. 1 - 2½ in. (2.5 - 6.3 cm.) long; glabrous or slightly pubescent below when young, on a short petiolule. Entire leaf 12 - 36 in. (about 30 - 90 cm.) long. Late to leaf out in spring.

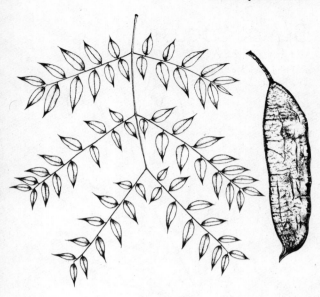

FLOWERS
Early to mid-May. Fragrant, pale greenish-white; males
and females on separate trees. Blossoms not typical of
pea family.

FRUIT
A thick, reddish-brown, somewhat sickle-shaped pod.
Formed by early fall (on female trees only), and remaining on the tree after the leaves have fallen. 3 - 9 in.
(7.5 - approx. 23 cm.) long. Contains several rounded
seeds with a sweet pulp between them.

BARK AND TWIGS
Bark gray or gray-brown, roughly fissured and scaly.
Twigs stout, somewhat whitened, with small, silky, par-
tially depressed winter buds and false end buds.

HABIT
A tall tree with an open crown.

SIMILAR SPECIES
The Kentucky coffee-tree is the only tree besides the
thorny devil's walkingstick *(Aralia spinosa)* in our area
with bipinnately compound leaves on which the leaflets
are more than an inch (2.5 cm.) long. Japanese pagoda
tree *(Sophora japonica)* and black locust *(Robinia
pseudoacacia)* are the most similar species.

LOCATIONS
☐ U.S. Capitol grounds and Canal Street parking lot,
   near Rayburn House Office Building
☐ St. Elizabeth's Hospital grounds
☐ Corregidor Street, N.W., near Massachusetts Avenue
☐ Washington Cathedral

BLACK LOCUST
OR FALSE ACACIA
Robinia pseudoacacia L.
Pea Family *Leguminosae*

The black locust has probably been more widely planted throughout the world than any other North American tree. Since it was first introduced in Europe in the seventeenth century, the black locust has been planted for timber and ornament in nearly every European country. The tree is the favorite North American ornamental in China, and is also widely grown in parts of Africa, Australia, New Zealand, and South America. The black locust is so well loved for its fragrant white blossoms and sturdy wood in other parts of the world that many foreign visitors to Washington may be more familiar with it than we are!

NATIVE HABITAT
Central Pennsylvania south to northern Georgia and Alabama; west to central Kentucky, Tennessee; parts of southern Indiana and Illinois. Also, southern Missouri, central and western Arkansas, and eastern Oklahoma. Naturalized in many other parts of the U.S. (including the D.C. area) and Europe.

LEAVES
Alternate, pinnately compound, deciduous. Seven to twenty one elliptic-ovate leaflets, including a terminal one. Each ¾ - 2¼ in. (2 - 5.7 cm.) long, with a smooth (or very slightly wavy) margin. Apex rounded or indented, often with a tiny spine barely visible. Base rounded, wedge-shaped, or almost straight across. Glabrous at maturity; may be finely pubescent below when young and along the short petiolule. Blue-green or gray-green. Entire leaf length: 6 - 11 in. (15 - 28 cm.)

FLOWERS
Fragrant, white, pendulous clusters of typically pea-like blossoms. Early to mid-May. Individual blossoms an inch (2.5 cm.) or less in length. (See color close-up.)

FRUIT
Flat, reddish-brown pod, tapered to a point at both ends. 2 - 4 in. (5 - 10 cm.) long, containing several flat brown seeds.

BARK AND TWIGS
Bark dark reddish-brown, deeply furrowed and scaly. Red-brown twigs usually have stipular spines about ½ in. (1.2 cm.) long. Winter buds small, pubescent. End bud false.

HABIT
Medium-sized tree with open, scraggly crown.

SIMILAR SPECIES
Honey locust (*Gleditsia triacanthos*) has smaller leaflets. Kentucky coffee-tree (*Gymnocladus dioicus*) has *bi*pinnately compound leaves. The Japanese pagoda tree (*Sophora japonica*) is the most similar, but its leaflets are *pointed at apices* and *whitened below*. Clammy locust (*Robinia viscosa*) discussed below.

LOCATIONS
☐ Frederick Douglass Home
☐ George Washington Memorial Parkway
☐ C&O Canal, between Georgetown and Great Falls, MD.
☐ Common throughout the city

CLAMMY LOCUST
Robinia viscosa Vent
Pea Family *Leguminosae*

Grows mostly in the mountains from Pennsylvania to Georgia and Alabama. Usually shrubby in our area, the clammy locust has pink blossoms and its branchlets have glands that exude a "clammy," sticky substance.

LOCATIONS:
☐ Along I-495 in Virginia
☐ Not common here

JAPANESE PAGODA TREE
OR CHINESE SCHOLAR TREE

Sophora japonica L.
Pea Family *Leguminosae*

During the Chou Dynasty (1122 - 240 B.C.) in
China, this tree was planted near the tombs of high
officials. Long cultivated on temple grounds in Japan,
the Japanese pagoda tree is gaining great popularity
in the west. Its profuse, fragrant blossoms provide
much-needed refreshment for those who spend July and
August in Washington!

NATIVE HABITAT
China, Korea. (Not native to Japan.)

LEAVES
Alternate, pinnately compound, deciduous. Seven to
seventeen ovate leaflets. Margins smooth, bases rounded
or wedge-shaped, *apices pointed.* Leaflets lustrous, dark
green above; *whitened* (glaucous) and very finely and
closely pubescent below. 1 - 2 in. (2.5 - 5 cm.) long on
short, pubescent petiolules. Entire leaf: 6 - 10 in. (about
15 - 25 cm.) long.

FLOWERS
Early to mid-July through much of August. (Some trees
bloom into September.) Fragrant, pale yellow-green or
creamy blossoms in spreading, loosely pyramidal
clusters. Individual blossoms typically pea-like, 1/3 - 2/3
in. (about 0.7 - 1.5 cm.) long. (See color close-up.)
Fallen blossoms carpet the ground.

FRUIT
Numerous clusters of sausage-like pods. Bright yellow-
green, divided into several round segments, each
containing a seed. Length varies according to the number
of segments. (Late summer through fall.)

BARK AND TWIGS
Bark gray-brown or brown, often with wavy ridges.
Young branchlets green, glabrous or nearly so. Winter
buds small, hidden by petioles before leaves fall.

HABIT
Usually with a full, rounded crown. Branches spreading.

SIMILAR SPECIES
Black locust (*Robinia pseudoacacia*) has leaflets that are
rounded or slightly indented at the apex and are *not
whitened* below. Kentucky coffee-tree (*Gymnocladus
dioicus*) has *bipinnately* compound leaves. No similar
species blooms in mid-summer, but from a distance the
ripening pods of the golden-rain-tree (*Koelreuteria
paniculata*) may be mistaken for Japanese pagoda tree
blossoms.

LOCATIONS
- ☐ U.S. Capitol grounds
- ☐ New Hampshire Avenue and 21st Street, N.W.
- ☐ Dupont Circle
- ☐ Embassy of the German Democratic Republic, Massa-
  chusetts Avenue
- ☐ Farragut Square
- ☐ Lincoln Park

Maackia
Maackia amurensis Rupr. & Maxim.
Pea Family *Leguminosae*

Rare tree, native to Manchuria. Somewhat similar
to yellowwood (*Cladrastis Kentukea*), but with leaflets
arranged *oppositely* along the rachis and white flowers
in upright clusters.

LOCATIONS:
- ☐ Glenn Dale Plant Introduction Station, Glenn Dale,
  MD.
- ☐ National Arboretum

Golden Chain Tree
or Common Laburnum
Laburnum anagyroides Med.
Pea Family *Leguminosae*

Small tree with alternate, clover-like leaves and hanging
clusters of bright yellow flowers in early May.

NATIVE HABITAT: Southern Europe. **LEAVES:** Alternate, deciduous, with trifoliate leaflets; smooth-
margined, usually elliptic, each 1¼ - 3¼ in. (about
3 - 8 cm.) long. Silky-pubescent below when young.
FLOWERS: Long, narrow, pendulous clusters of typically pea-like yellow blossoms. **FRUIT:** Twisted, brown
pod containing poisonous black seeds.
LOCATIONS:
- ☐ Private yards and gardens

Voss's Laburnum

Laburnum x *watererei* Dipp.
(L. anagyroides x. *L. alpinum)*
Pea Family *Leguminosae*

A hybrid, very similar to golden chain tree, but with fuller flower clusters and foliage. Produces fewer pods.

LOCATIONS
☐ Smithsonian Arts and Industries Building

Crape-Myrtle

Lagerstroemia indica L.
Loose-strife Family *Lythraceae*

From late July through September the crape-myrtles dominate the arboreal scene in Washington. Deep, dark pink is the most common color of the large clusters of frilly blossoms, but lavender, white, pale pink and cherry red forms are also planted in the city. Although the crape-myrtle is usually more of a shrub than a tree, it is often trained as a small tree and is simply too impressive to leave out of this book!

NATIVE HABITAT
China. Widely cultivated throughout the southern United States.

LEAVES
Opposite, sub-opposite or alternate, deciduous. Elliptic or obovate, 1¼ - 2¾ in. (3 - 7 cm.) long, on an extremely short petiole. Good autumn color: orange, yellow or red.

FLOWERS
Large, lilac-like clusters of crinkly (usually pink) blossoms, each about 1½ in. (3 - 4 cm.) across. (See color close-up.)

FRUIT
Small, round, woody capsule that resembles a flower
bud when closed; then opens like a blossom to release
seeds.

BARK
Very smooth, gray-brown and pink, with thin shreds
peeling away.

SIMILAR SPECIES
None. Blossoms and bark are unique.

LOCATIONS
☐ Very common throughout the city
☐ U.S. Capitol and Library of Congress grounds
☐ National Arboretum
☐ North Carolina Avenue and 7th Street, S.E.
☐ Folger Park
☐ 1st and C Streets, S.E.

EUROPEAN SMOKE-TREE
Cotinus coggygria Scop.
Cashew Family *Anacardiaceae*

A unique and desirable ornamental. In early summer
translucent, feathery fruiting panicles, which look like
puffs of smoke, appear on this tree. They last well into
summer, and are especially beautiful in the early morning
and evening light.

NATIVE HABITAT
Southern Europe to Central China and the Himalayas.

LEAVES
Simple, alternate, deciduous, 1¼ - 3½ in. (about 3 - 9
cm.) long. Ovate, elliptic or obovate. Rounded, broadly
pointed, or slightly indented apex and broadly wedge-
shaped or rounded base; becoming glabrous, but petiole
and midrib below may be pubescent when young.

FLOWERS AND FRUIT
The flowers and kidney-shaped fruit are small and
inconspicuous. The showy "smoky" erect or gently
drooping fruiting panicles are 6 - 9 in. (15 - 22.8 cm.)
long. The purplish or greenish smoky effect is created by
many small feathery hairs on the numerous sterile flower
stalks.

HABIT
Full, shrubby small tree.

OTHER FORMS
Form with purplish panicles and deep purple young
leaves (*C. coggygria purpureus* (Dupuy-Jamin) Rehd.)

LOCATIONS
□ National Arboretum (including purple form)
□ U.S. Capitol grounds
□ Fairly common in private yards and gardens

AMERICAN SMOKE-TREE

Cotinus obovatus Raf.
(*Cotinus americanus* Nutt.)
Cashew Family *Anacardiaceae*

The American smoke-tree is infrequently planted for ornament and is, therefore, extremely rare in the D.C. area.

NATIVE HABITAT: South-central states from central Tennessee and northwestern Alabama to Texas, eastern Oklahoma, northwestern Arkansas, and southwestern Missouri. The **LEAVES,** which turn brilliant orange and scarlet in the fall, are slightly longer than those of the European species, 2⅓ - 4¾ in. (6 - 12 cm.), and are covered with silky pubescence when young. The fruiting panicles are less spectacular than those of the European tree with rather inconspicuous brownish or purplish feathery hairs.

AILANTHUS OR TREE OF HEAVEN
Ailanthus altissima (Mill.) Swingle
Quassia Family *Simaroubaceae*

While the poetic Chinese name, "Tree of Heaven," refers to the short time it takes this tree to reach the sky, many residents of the District have far less ethereal feelings about the prolific, fast-growing ailanthus. Some Washingtonians consider it an attractive shade tree, but many others have been at war with ailanthus suckers and seedlings for years.

An ordinance, passed in the District of Columbia in 1875, declared ailanthus ownership a crime punishable by law.

'That ailanthus trees, the flowers of which produce offensive and noxious odors, in bloom, in the cities of Washington or Georgetown, or the more densely populated suburbs of said cities, are hereby declared nuisances injurious to health; and any person maintaining such nuisance, who shall fail, after due notice from this board, to abate the same, shall, upon conviction, be fined not less than five nor more than ten dollars for every such offense."

This ordinance is still on the books.

NATIVE HABITAT
China. Brought into the United States in the late eighteenth century and now naturalized over much of the east.

LEAVES
Large, alternate, odd-pinnately compound, deciduous. 7 - 27 in. (17.5 - 61 cm.) long. Thirteen to twenty-five leaflets, each 2 - 6 in. (5 - 15 cm.) long. Leaflets ovate-lanceolate, usually with one to four blunt or pointed teeth near the base. Glabrous or slightly pubescent below. Base straight across or unequal.

FLOWERS
Male and female flowers on the same tree or on separate trees. Mid-summer, in large, greenish clusters.

FRUIT
Large clusters of samaras remaining after the leaves have fallen. Each samara about 1½ inches (3.8 cm.) long, twisted, and with a single seed in the middle.

BARK AND TWIGS
Bark usually smooth, light brown or gray; sometimes with lighter vertical stripes or shallow ridges. Winter twigs distinctive: stout, yellowish or orange-brown, and soft to the touch. No terminal bud. Leaf scars large, heart-shaped; lateral buds, roundish, dark brown.

HABIT
Rapidly growing, produces many root-suckers and seedlings. Tropical-looking, with few branches and large, compound leaves.

SIMILAR SPECIES
Easily distinguished once learned. Somewhat similar to the Chinese Cedar (*Cedrela sinensis*), but far more commonly grown.

LOCATIONS
☐ Yards, parks, and grounds throughout D.C.
☐ Common in unused lots and fringes of parking lots and highways
☐ Rock Creek Park

AMUR CORK-TREE
Phellodendron amurense Rupr.
Rue Family *Rutaceae*

The beautiful Amur cork-tree is one of Washington's finest Asian ornamentals.

NATIVE HABITAT
China, Manchuria.

LEAVES
Opposite, compound, deciduous. 10 - 15 in. (25.3 - 38 cm.) long. Seven to thirteen ovate leaflets come to a long, somewhat curved point. Leaflets dark green; rachis and petiolules yellow-green. Glabrous below or with tufts of hair in the vein axils.

FRUIT
Small berry-like drupes in upright clusters; becoming black and sometimes remaining on the tree into the winter.

BARK
Thick, deeply fissured, with corky ridges; pale or medium gray.

CLOSELY RELATED SPECIES
The rare Japanese Phellodendron (*Phellodendron japonicum* Maxim.) is very difficult to distinguish from the more commonly grown Amur cork-tree. The Japanese species tends to be more pubescent. While a consensus has not yet been reached in Washington's botanical community, some botanists believe that the tree on the southeast side of the Library of Congress may be the rare Japanese species, while the tree standing just a few yards to the north is undoubtedly the more common Chinese tree.

LOCATIONS
☐ Library of Congress grounds   ☐ National Arboretum
☐ Tidal Basin

Trifoliate Orange

Poncirus trifoliata (L.) Raf.
Rue Family *Rutaceae*

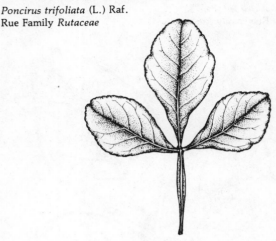

Small tree or shrub with thorny green branchlets.
Often used as a grafting stock for orange trees. Planted
in hedges in the southern states, where it has escaped
from cultivation in many places.

NATIVE HABITAT
China.

LEAVES
Alternate, compound, deciduous. Three clover-like
leaflets with slightly wavy margin, or a few shallow,
rounded teeth; petiole winged.

FLOWERS
White, 1¼ - 2 in. (about 3 - 5 cm.) across, before the
leaves in spring.

FRUIT
A small, yellow "orange" with bitter juice; up to 2 in.
(5 cm.) in diameter.

BRANCHLETS
Green, glabrous with thorns up to an inch or more in
length.

LOCATIONS
☐ U.S. Capitol grounds
☐ St. Elizabeth's Hospital
☐ Some gardens and grounds throughout the city

COMMON HOPTREE

Ptelea trifoliata L.
Rue Family *Rutaceae*

A small native tree or shrub.

NATIVE HABITAT
Scattered throughout eastern North America.

LEAVES
Alternate, compound, deciduous. Trifoliate, each leaflet
2 - 6 in. (5 - 15 cm.) long, the middle one usually
longest.

FRUIT
A roundish, flattened elm-like samara containing two
seeds.

SIMILAR SPECIES
The laburnums (*Laburnum* sp.) (including the golden
chain tree) and the trifoliate orange (*Poncirus trifoliata*)
also have alternate, trifoliate leaves, but their other
features differ.

LOCATIONS
☐ National Arboretum
☐ Some parks and private yards

CEDRELA OR CHINESE CEDAR

Cedrela sinensis Juss.
(*Toona sinensis* Roem.)
Mahogany Family *Meliaceae*

Rare in Washington.

NATIVE HABITAT
China.

LEAVES
Alternate, pinnately compound, deciduous. Similar to
tree of heaven (*Ailanthus altissima*), but with *no large
teeth* at leaflet bases. Ten to thirty leaflets (usually an
even number), each 3 - 6 in. (7.5 - 15.2 cm.) long. Long-
pointed, slightly unequal at base; margins nearly smooth
or with a few, small, distant teeth. Pubescent along the
veins below, or glabrous. Entire leaf very long, up to 24
in. (about 60 cm.)

FLOWERS
Fragrant clusters of small, white blossoms in early
summer.

FRUIT
Small, tulip-shaped woody capsule.

BARK
Dark, pinkish gray; becoming shaggy with age.

SIMILAR SPECIES
Tree of heaven is far more common and usually has an
odd number of leaflets with coarse teeth near their bases.

LOCATIONS
☐ U.S. Capitol grounds, near the Olmsted grotto
☐ Mount Hamilton, National Arboretum

THE MAPLES
Acer L.
Maple family *Aceraceae*

Famous for their autumn foliage, and attractive
throughout the year, maples abound in Washington. The
city's most popular maples hail from three continents:
From Asia, the Japanese maple (*Acer palmatum*); from
Europe, the Norway maple (*Acer platanoides*); and at
home right here, our native North American sugar
maple (*Acer saccharum*). The small, delicate Japanese
maple and its many cultivars are popular garden trees.
The larger, sturdier Norway and sugar maples are commonly planted as street trees. The Japanese maple's
autumn color is the most brilliant of the three in our
area, as the sugar maple rarely achieves the vivid reds it
is famous for further north.

Also popular as street trees are our native red (*Acer
rubrum*) and black maples (*Acer saccharum* var.
nigrum), the latter often considered a variety of the
sugar maple. Years ago, another native species, the silver
maple (*Acer saccharinum*) was Washington's most widely
planted street tree, but it proved to be impractical to
maintain and its popularity in cultivation has decreased.

CHARACTERISTICS OF THE GENUS

LEAVES
Opposite; simple and palmately veined, or pinnately
compound.

FLOWERS
Small, clustered, before or after the leaves.

FRUIT
Pairs of distinctive winged samaras which are sometimes
called "keys."

DISTRIBUTION
More than 100 species in North America, Europe, Asia
and northern Africa.

SIMILAR SPECIES
The sweetgum (*Liquidambar styraciflua* L.) has alternate
leaves and fruit that is a pendulous prickly ball. Some
hawthorns (*Crataequs* sps.) have small, maple-like leaves
but they are alternately arranged and hawthorn branches
are usually thorny. Viburnums (*Viburnum* sps.) are large
shrubs or, rarely, small trees.

Norway Maple

Acer platanoides L.

Maple Family *Aceraceae*

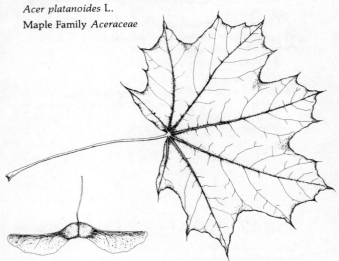

Widely planted throughout D.C. along streets, in parks, and around public buildings and private homes. The Norway maple retains its foliage until late autumn, when it turns orange and yellow.

NATIVE HABITAT
Europe, Caucasus.

LEAVES
Simple, opposite, deciduous. Five-lobed, with finely pointed teeth. Often slightly wider than long, 4 - 8 in. (10 - 20 cm.) across. Sinuses between lobes rather shallow. Thin-textured; bright green and glabrous above, slightly paler below with tufts of hair in the vein axils. *Petiole exudes a milky sap when broken.* (See "SIMILAR SPECIES.")

FLOWERS
Early spring, just before the leaves, then remaining after they've unfolded. Bright yellow-green, in erect, pubescent clusters.

FRUIT
Twin, winged samaras attached at a widely divergent angle. Each samara 1¼ - 2¼ in. (3 - 5.5 cm.) long, yellow-green, then turning brown.

BARK AND TWIGS
Bark light brown or gray; broken into thin, shallow, vertical ridges on mature trees. Winter buds large, ovoid, green or reddish.

HABIT
Well-formed tree with a full, rounded crown and dense foliage.

OTHER FORMS
Several forms with more or less purple leaves are
popular, including: 'Goldsworth Purple,' 'Crimson King,'
and 'Schwedleri.'

The columnar Norway maple (*Acer platanoides*
'Columnare') is showing great promise along streets
where a tree with a narrow crown is desirable, including:
□ I Street, N.W. and W Street, N.W.

SIMILAR SPECIES
The very similar sugar maple (*Acer saccharum*) has
leaves with petioles that do *not* exude a milky juice
when broken. Sugar maple bark on older trees is broken
into large scales or plates.

LOCATIONS
□ A popular street tree citywide
□ Private yards throughout the city
□ U.S. Capitol grounds
□ L'Enfant Plaza

SILVER MAPLE OR SOFT MAPLE

Acer saccharinum L.
(*Acer dasycarpum* Ehrh.)
Maple Family *Aceraceae*

Back in the 1870s and '80s Washington arborists
considered the fast-growing silver (or soft) maple to be
the ideal street tree. In 1883 more than 11,000 silver
maples were planted along the streets of the nation's
capital. Over the years, the silver maple lost its status
as Washington's favorite street tree because it proved to
be difficult to maintain. However, it remains common
throughout the District, both as a cultivated and naturally
occurring tree.

NATIVE HABITAT
Most of the eastern United States (excluding extreme south) and southeastern Canada; west to Minnesota, Nebraska, Kansas, and Oklahoma.

LEAVES
Simple, opposite, deciduous. 4 - 7 in. (10 - 17.5 cm.) long and wide. Bright green or yellowish-green above. Pale silvery white beneath. Five-lobed, very deeply cut, with the middle lobe itself sometimes three-lobed. Sharply, irregularly and sometimes doubly toothed. The leaf has a delicate, almost fern-like appearance. Petiole slender, often pink or red above, from 2½ - 5 in. (6.5 - 12.5 cm.) long. Autumn color usually pale yellow, occasionally reddish.

FLOWERS
Very early spring, before the leaves. May be yellow-green or reddish. Similar to red maple but with no petals.

FRUIT
Paired winged samaras, connected at a broad V-shaped angle or with one samara aborted. Green and glabrous, 1½ - 2½ in. (3.8 - 6.3 cm.) long. Maturing in spring, with the leaves. Soon falling.

BARK AND TWIGS
Bark smooth and gray on young trees. Very furrowed and flaking into large shaggy plates with age. Twigs slender, reddish, with dark red terminal winter buds; rank odor when broken.

HABIT
A fast-growing tree with a long, tall irregular crown.

SIMILAR SPECIES
The silver maple is distinctive in summer with its deeply lobed, sharply toothed leaves. See red maple (*Acer rubrum*) "Similar Species" section for similarities in early spring.

LOCATIONS
□ U.S. Capitol grounds
□ Streets, parks, and yards throughout the District
□ Rock Creek Park
□ C&O Canal, into Maryland

SUGAR MAPLE OR ROCK MAPLE

Acer saccharum Marsh.
Maple Family *Aceraceae*

STATE TREE OF NEW YORK, VERMONT, WEST
VIRGINIA, AND WISCONSIN

The sugar maple is the most important ingredient of
the world-renowned New England autumn. Its fall colors,
unrivaled even among maples, range from yellow to
deep crimson. Although our sugar maples here in
Washington rarely attain the glorious reds common
further north, they are beautiful nonetheless, often color-
ing a deep orange. This tree is also famous for being the
major source of the sap that is boiled down to make
maple syrup.

NATIVE HABITAT
Southeastern Canada; northeastern United States to
northern Georgia and Alabama; west to eastern
Missouri.

LEAVES
Simple, opposite, deciduous. 3 - 5 in. (7.5 - 12.5 cm.)
long, 3¼ - 6½ in. (8 - 16 cm.) wide. Dark green above,
paler and usually glabrous below. Three to five coarsely
and sparingly toothed lobes with fairly deep sinuses between them. Rounded base. Long, slender, glabrous
petiole.

FLOWERS
Yellowish, long-stemmed and drooping, with no petals.
Appearing as the leaves unfold in the spring.

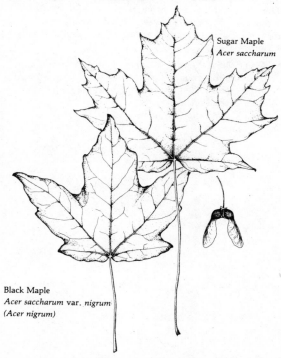

Sugar Maple
Acer saccharum

Black Maple
Acer saccharum var. *nigrum*
(*Acer nigrum*)

FRUIT
Wing-like, slightly divergent samaras, 1 - 1½ in. (2.5 - 4 cm.) long. Maturing in autumn.

BARK AND TWIGS
Bark gray, becoming deeply furrowed with age; often breaking into plates. Twigs reddish-brown and smooth. Winter buds pointed, reddish-brown, with four to eight pairs of scales.

HABIT
Branches widely spread into a full, rounded crown.

VARIETIES
See black maple (*Acer saccharum* var. *nigrum*).

SIMILAR SPECIES
The sugar maple is very similar in appearance to the Norway maple *(Acer platanoides)*. Although the Norway maple usually has wider, more shallowly sinused leaves, the best way to make a positive identification is to break off the tip of a petiole. If the liquid exuded is *milky* in color, the tree is a Norway maple. (The sugar maple exudes *clear* sap.) Sugar maple foliage turns earlier in autumn than that of the Norway maple. Also note the differences in fruits, flowers, and bark.

LOCATIONS
□ U.S. Capitol grounds
□ Walter Reed Army Medical Center grounds
□ Streets and parks citywide

BLACK MAPLE

Acer saccharum var. *nigrum* Brit.
(*Acer nigrum* Michx.)
Maple family *Aceraceae*

Although the black maple is considered to be a distinct species by some botanists, most prefer to classify this tree as a variety of the sugar maple. The black maple bears the same famous sap that goes into the making of maple syrup and, apart from the following characteristics, the two trees are very similar.

NATURAL HABITAT
Spotty distribution in northeastern states and southeastern Canada. More common from New York to West Virginia; west to South Dakota, Iowa, and Missouri.

LEAVES
Simple, opposite, deciduous. Similar to that of the sugar maple but usually with three not five, major lobes and fewer, more bluntly pointed, teeth. *Leaf margin gently drooping.* Leaf blade thicker than the sugar maple, lighter green beneath and slightly downy.

BARK AND TWIGS
Bark darker than the sugar maple, sometimes almost black; deeply furrowed. Twigs orange-brown.

LOCATIONS
□ Garfield Park
□ Streets, yards, and parks citywide

Red Maple

Acer rubrum L.
Maple Family *Aceraceae*

STATE TREE OF RHODE ISLAND

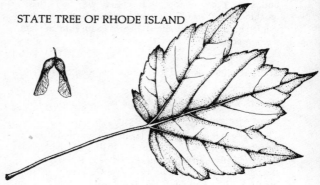

The first arboreal signs of spring in Washington are weeks ahead of the cherry blossoms. Early in March, along with the silver maple and the American elm, the red maple blooms at a time when it seems that winter will never end. With its abundant red blossoms and pale gray bark, the red maple is the most beautiful of Washington's first blooming trees.

NATIVE HABITAT
Newfoundland to Florida; west to Minnesota, Iowa, and Texas.

LEAVES
Simple, opposite, deciduous. 2 - 6 in. (5 - 15 cm.) long. Leaf width equal to or a little greater than length. Three or five broad lobes with shallow sinuses between them. Margin toothed. Dark green above, paler and glaucous beneath; usually pubescent on the veins. Petiole 2 - 4 in. (5 - 10 cm.) long, often red. Leaves turn red, yellow, and orange in autumn, sometimes with all three colors on a single leaf.

FLOWERS
Before the leaves in early spring. Usually red, sometimes yellow-green. Borne, with petals, in dense clusters. May be unisexual or perfect.

FRUIT
Twin winged samaras, usually ⅔ - 1 in. (1.5 - 2.5 cm.) long on long thin stalks. Pale pink to bright red wings connected at a V-shaped angle. Maturing in April or May.

BARK AND TWIGS
Bark smooth and pale gray on young trees. Darkening and breaking into large plates with age. Twigs reddish or orange with bright red winter buds. No unpleasant odor when twig is broken.

HABIT
A medium-sized tree with a rounded crown.

SIMILAR SPECIES
The red maple is easily distinguished from other maples
cultivated in the Washington area by its heavily toothed,
shallowly and broadly lobed leaves. A similar species,
the silver maple (*Acer saccharinum*), has very deeply
and narrowly sinused leaves and more coarsely flaking,
almost shaggy bark on mature trees. However, the two
trees are easily confused when they are both in bloom
before the leaves in early spring. Silver maple flowers
have no petals and are more often greenish-yellow than
red. Its twigs have a rank odor when crushed, while red
maple twigs do not.

LOCATIONS
□ City streets and parks throughout D.C.
□ U.S. Capitol grounds
□ White House grounds (planted by
   President Jimmy Carter)
□ Vietnam Veterans Memorial

FULLMOON MAPLE
OR DOWNY JAPANESE MAPLE
Acer japonicum Thunb.
Maple Family *Aceraceae*

The fullmoon maple is somewhat similar in appearance to the commonly planted Japanese maple (*Acer
palmatum*). This rare tree is now being carried by some
nurseries.

NATIVE HABITAT: Japan. **LEAVES:** Similar to
Japanese maple, but larger (3½–5½ in. (9–14 cm.) long
and wide) and less deeply lobed; very pubescent when
young and pubescent later, at least along the veins. Leaf
divided into seven to eleven lobes.
OTHER FORMS: The cultivar 'Aconitifolium' is gaining
popularity in this country. Its leaf is very similar to the
smaller Japanese fern leaf maple (*Acer palmatum* 'Dissectum') leaf, with deeply cut, delicate lobes. The 'Ancon-
itifolium' leaf is pubescent, at least along the veins
below, while the Japanese fern leaf maple is glabrous or
nearly so.
LOCATIONS:
□ U.S. Capitol grounds
□ Some private yards

JAPANESE MAPLE
Acer palmatum Thunb.
Maple Family *Aceraceae*

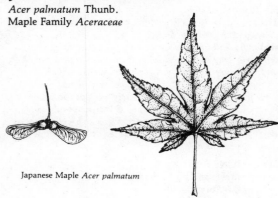

Japanese Maple *Acer palmatum*

In Japan the autumn colors of the Japanese maple
are as highly revered as the spring cherry blossoms.
Although the Japanese maples planted in Washington are
not nearly as well known as our famous Japanese cherry
trees, their fall colors are the most brilliant of all maples
in the city. Dozens of forms of this delicate tree are
popular here, with autumn colors ranging from bright
yellow to vivid scarlet.

NATIVE HABITAT
Japan, Korea.

LEAVES
Simple, opposite, deciduous. 1½ - 4 in. (3.8 - 10 cm.)
long and wide. Star-like, with five to seven pointed
lobes. Small, sharply pointed teeth; prominent palmate
venation. Base slightly cordate, straight across or broadly
wedge-shaped. Glabrous or with tufts of hair in the vein
axils below. Petiole slender, glabrous. Leaf bright green
in summer, or *in some forms, purplish, reddish, coppery, or yellow-green.* Autumn colors yellow, orange,
red, or scarlet.

FLOWERS
Purplish-red, in small erect or spreading clusters; with
the leaves in spring.

FRUIT
Small, delicate twin samaras attached at a wide angle
(sometimes nearly horizontally); each ½ - 1¼ in. (about
1 - 3 cm.) long.

BARK AND TWIGS
Bark smooth, light brown or gray, often marked with
pale, vertical stripes. Twigs slender, glabrous, with
small, ovoid (usually red) winter buds.

HABIT
Small, graceful tree with slender, sinuous branches forming a rounded or flat-topped crown.

OTHER FORMS
Many forms of the Japanese maple with varying leaf colors are planted in Washington. General color variations are described above in the "LEAVES" section. Two commonly planted cultivars are 'Atropurpureum,' with deep purple leaves, and 'Dissectum,' a weeping form with deeply cut, fern-like leaves. (See illustration of 'Dissectum' leaf.)

SIMILAR SPECIES
The small, star-like leaves are distinctive among maples. May be confused with the sweetgum (*Liquidambar styraciflua*) which has *larger, alternately arranged leaves* and fruit that is a pendulous, prickly ball.

LOCATIONS
- ☐ Dumbarton Oaks
- ☐ White House grounds (red-leafed weeping forms planted by Presidents Grover Cleveland and Jimmy Carter)
- ☐ Hillwood Estate
- ☐ Japanese ambassador's residence (not open to the public)
- ☐ Newark Street, N.W.
- ☐ Common around public buildings and private homes

'DISSECTUM' LOCATIONS
- ☐ Rock Creek Cemetery
- ☐ Hillwood Estate
- ☐ U.S. Capitol grounds
- ☐ Some public buildings and private homes

Fern-Leafed Japanese Maple
Acer palmatum 'Dissectum'

Box-Elder
OR ASH-LEAFED MAPLE
Acer negundo L.
Maple Family *Aceraceae*

The box-elder is the only commonly planted maple in the Washington area with compound, rather than simple, leaves.

NATIVE HABITAT
Much of the U.S.: New England to Florida; west to parts of California, with scattered occurrence throughout the west; southern Canada and parts of Mexico.

LEAVES
Opposite, deciduous, pinnately compound with three to five (rarely seven) leaflets. Each leaflet 1½ - 4 in. (3.8 - 10 cm.) long, ¾ - 1½ in. (2 - 3.8 cm.) wide. Ovate to lanceolate. Coarsely and irregularly toothed with the end leaflet sometimes three-lobed. Glabrous above, often slightly pubescent below. Petiole 2 - 3¼ in. (5 - 8 cm.) long, pale yellow or pinkish.

FLOWERS
Spring, with or before the leaves. Male and female flowers on separate trees. Small, with no petals, in hanging clusters.

FRUIT
Paired, winged, samaras in pendulous clusters. Each samara 1 - 1¾ in. (2.5 - 4.5 cm.) long; pair joined at acute angle. Wings slightly incurved; nutlet longer and narrower than on most maple samaras. Yellowish-green, becoming brown and persisting into winter.

BARK AND TWIGS
Twigs green, glabrous. Winter buds white, pubescent. Bark furrowed, pale gray, or light brown.

SIMILAR SPECIES
Ashes (*Fraxinus* sp.) and cork trees (*Phellodendron* sp.) also have opposite, pinnately compound leaves. See text and illustrations for distinguishing characteristics.

LOCATIONS
☐ Common throughout D.C., both in cultivation and in the wild

HEDGE MAPLE OR FIELD MAPLE

Acer campestre L.
Maple Family *Aceraceae*

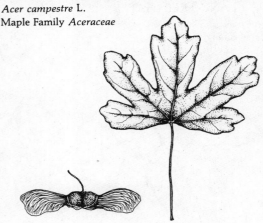

NATIVE HABITAT
Europe, W. Asia, N. Africa

LEAVES
Simple, opposite, deciduous. Usually five-lobed, the
middle three lobes with large, rounded teeth. 1¾ - 3 in.
(4.5 - 7.5 cm.) long. 2¼ - 4 in. (5.5 - 10 cm.) wide.
Lobe apices rounded. Glabrous, except for buff-colored
hairs along the veins below. Petiole slender, 1¼ - 3½ in.
(3 - 9 cm.) long.

AUTUMN COLOR
Yellow.

FLOWERS
Yellow-green, with the leaves in spring.

FRUIT
Paired samaras with pubescent nutlets and finely pubescent wings. Pair is attached at a wide angle and
resembles the silhouette of a bird in flight. Each samara
about 1 - 1¼ in. (2.5 - 3 cm.) long.

BARK AND TWIGS
Branchlets sometimes develop corky wings. Winter buds
reddish-brown with grayish pubescence at apices. Bark
of mature trees usually dark gray (sometimes brown)
with many thin vertical ridges and cracks.

HABIT
Short trunk, several long sinuous limbs, and broad
crown.

SIMILAR SPECIES
All other maples commonly cultivated or growing wild
in the Washington area have *pointed lobes*.

LOCATIONS
- ☐ U.S. Capitol and Library of Congress grounds
- ☐ Corner of 15th Street and Constitution Ave., N.W.
- ☐ Between 17th Street, N.W. and the Ellipse
- ☐ Soldiers' Home
- ☐ Some city parks

Sycamore Maple
or Plane-Tree Maple

Acer pseudoplatanus L.
Maple Family *Aceraceae*

A very attractive maple with large, pendulous clusters of flowers and fruit. Its leaves resemble the leaves of the London plane tree and American sycamore.

NATIVE HABITAT
Europe and western Asia.

LEAVES
Simple, opposite, deciduous. Usually five-lobed, 3 - 7 in. (7.5 - 17.7 cm.) long and often slightly wider than long. Margin with coarse, irregular, bluntly or sharply pointed teeth. Leaf thick, leathery, slightly wrinkly; deep dark green above, pale green or whitish beneath, with prominent veins. Glabrous or with some pubescence along the veins below. Petiole slender, reddish or yellow-green, 3 - 7½ in. (7.5 - 19 cm.) long.

FLOWERS
Greenish-yellow, in conspicuous hanging clusters. Late April and May, with the young leaves.

FRUIT
Twin samaras in long, hanging clusters. Samaras attached at varying angles, from acute to nearly horizontal; each 1 - 1¾ in. (2.5 — 4.5 cm.) long. Nutlet often pubescent. Late summer, fall.

BARK AND TWIGS
Bark gray or reddish-brown, flaking into scales. Twigs glabrous with green, ovoid winter buds.

HABIT
Large tree with spreading branches and a full, rounded crown.

SIMILAR SPECIES
The leaf shape and coarse, irregular teeth set the sycamore maple apart from other maples planted in Washington. (See illustration.) True sycamores and London plane trees (*Platanus* species) have alternate leaves and whitish, peeling bark.

LOCATIONS
- ☐ U.S. Capitol grounds
- ☐ Folger Park
- ☐ Smithsonian National Museum of Natural History
- ☐ Between 17th Street, N.W. and the Ellipse
- ☐ Some city parks, streets, public buildings, and private yards throughout Washington

AMUR MAPLE
Acer ginnala Maxim.
Maple Family *Aceracea*

A small, shrubby tree. Rare in the Washington area.

NATIVE HABITAT
China, Manchuria, Japan.

LEAVES
Simple, opposite, deciduous. Small, three-lobed, with the middle lobe the longest. Heavily toothed. 1½ - 3½ in. (3.8 - 9 cm.) long; 1 - 2½ in. (2.5 - 6.5 cm.) wide. Petiole thin, ¾ - 2 in. (2 - 5 cm.) long. Leaves turn red in autumn and fall early.

FLOWERS
Conspicuous, yellowish-white, fragrant, in late spring.

FRUIT
Twin-winged samaras in hanging clusters. Wings attached at an acute angle; each about an inch (2.5 cm.) long. Fruit persists into winter.

BARK AND TWIGS
Bark dark gray; twigs slender and glabrous; winter buds tiny, reddish-brown.

HABIT
Usually shrubby, with many upright limbs.

SIMILAR SPECIES
Trident maple (*Acer buergerianum*) leaves are smooth or barely toothed.

LOCATIONS
- ☐ National Arboretum
- ☐ National Zoo

CAPPADOCIAN MAPLE

Acer cappadocicum Gleditsch.
Maple Family *Aceraceae*

Rare in the Washington area. Tree growing on the Capitol grounds, mislabeled years ago, was once believed to be the largest mountain maple (*Acer spicatum* Lam.) in the United States!

NATIVE HABITAT
Caucasus Mountains, Himalayas, and China.

LEAVES
Simple, opposite, deciduous. Usually five-lobed; each lobe broad, tapering to a fine point at apex. Sinuses shallow, base broadly cordate, margin smooth. 3 - 6½ in. (7.5 - 16.5 cm.) wide, 2 - 4 in. (5 - 10 cm.) high. Glabrous but for tufts of hair in the vein axils beneath. Petiole slender, yellow or pinkish, 1½ - 3½ in. (3.8 - 9 cm.) long. Autumn color: yellow.

FLOWERS
Pale yellow, with the unfolding leaves.

FRUIT
Twin samaras, attached at a wide angle (nearly horizontal). Each samara ¾ - 2¾ in. (2 - 7 cm.) long.

BARK AND TWIGS
 Bark gray; winter bud small, ovoid.

HABIT
Trunk short; crown broad.

SIMILAR SPECIES
May be confused with Norway maple (*Acer platanoides*).

LOCATIONS
- ☐ Garfield Park, near intersection of 3rd St., S.E. and I-395
- ☐ Lafayette Park
- ☐ U.S. Capitol grounds (southwest section)

Trident Maple

Acer buergerianum Miq.
(A. *trinerve* Dipp.)
Maple family *Aceraceae*

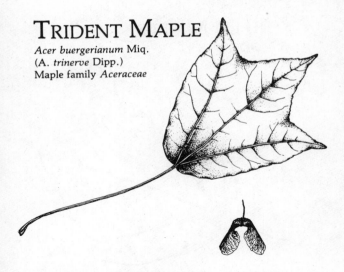

Rare in the Washington area.

NATIVE HABITAT
Eastern China, Japan.

LEAVES
Simple, opposite, deciduous. Three-lobed, with three
prominent veins radiating from the base. 1¾ - 3½ in.
(4.5 - 9 cm.) long. 1¼ - 2¾ in. (3 - 7 cm.) wide. Lobes
triangular; base broadly wedge-shaped, rounded or sub-
cordate. Margin smooth or barely toothed. Leaf somewhat leathery, dark green above, pale beneath. Petiole
very slender, 1¼ - 3¼ in. (3 - 8 cm.) long.

FLOWERS
Small, yellow, in early spring.

FRUIT
Small, twin samaras, about ¾ in. (2 cm.) long.

BARK AND TWIGS
Bark pinkish and flaking. Branchlets glabrous. Winter
buds reddish-brown, conic.

HABIT
A small tree with a full, rounded crown and gently
pendant branches.

SIMILAR SPECIES
Amur maple (*Acer ginnala*) leaves are sharply toothed.

LOCATIONS
☐ Walter Reed Army Medical Center, just inside the
16th Street gate, on a rise to the right
☐ National Arboretum bonsai collection (bonsai trees)

Striped Maple
or Moosewood Tree
or Goosefoot Maple

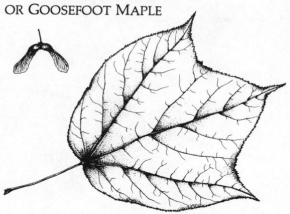

Acer pensylvanicum L.
Maple Family *Aceraceae*

A small, native maple, not commonly cultivated here. Distinguished by its thin green bark (sometimes becoming reddish with age) which is *vertically striped white*. LEAF is sharply toothed, shallowly three-lobed. SAMARAS in slender, pendulous clusters. Native to northeastern U.S. and southeastern Canada.

LOCATIONS
☐ Mount Vernon
☐ Fern Valley, National Arboretum

Golden-Rain-Tree
or Pride-of-India
or China-Tree
Koelreuteria paniculata Laxm.
Soapberry Family *Sapindaceae*

The golden-rain-tree is one of Washington's most beautiful exotic ornamentals. Its lovely fern-like leaves unfold early in spring and are followed by large clusters of yellow flowers in early summer, and pink lantern-shaped pods in autumn. During the Chou dynasty of ancient China the golden-rain-tree, one of five official memorial trees, was planted on the tombs of scholars.

NATIVE HABITAT
China, Korea, Japan.

LEAVES
Alternate, pinnately (or sometimes bipinnately) compound, deciduous. Seven to fifteen leaflets, each 1 - 3½ in. (2.5 - 9 cm.) long; ovate, with large teeth and often with one, two, or more small lobes. Glabrous above, glabrous or slightly pubescent below. Entire leaf 6 - 14 in. (15 - 35.5 cm.) long, feathery looking.

FLOWERS
June-July. Small bright yellow blossoms tinged with red in branched horizontal or erect clusters up to 13 in. (33 cm.) long. (See color close-up.)

FRUIT
Papery, lantern-like hanging pod, 1½ - 2 in. (3.8 - 5 cm.) long. Widest at the top, tapered to a point, and open at the bottom. Pale green when it first appears in summer, becoming coppery pink and remaining on the tree into the winter months. Contains three berry-like black seeds.

BARK AND TWIGS
Bark brown or purplish brown, roughly fissured and often marked with orange. Twigs light brown with darker brown, beaked, winter buds.

HABIT
Small to medium sized tree, with a rounded crown and sinuous, ascending limbs.

SIMILAR SPECIES
When the fruit pods first appear in the summer they may be confused with Japanese pagoda tree (*Sophora japonica*) blossoms from afar. Otherwise, not likely to be confused with any other species. The leaves, flowers, and fruit are unique among the trees planted in our area.

LOCATIONS
- ☐ National Zoo
- ☐ Forest Industries Building, 1619 Massachusetts Ave., N.W.
- ☐ U.S. Capitol and Library of Congress grounds
- ☐ Montrose Park
- ☐ Old D.C. Public Library, Mount Vernon Square
- ☐ E Street, S.E. between 4th and 6th Streets
- ☐ National Arboretum

THE HORSE-CHESTNUTS AND BUCKEYES

Aesculus L.
Horse-chestnut & Buckeye Family *Hippocastanaceae*

Horse-chestnuts and buckeyes are widely planted in Washington for their showy, upright clusters of blossoms and large, fan-shaped leaves. The most popular member of the genus is the common horse-chestnut (*Aesculus hippocastanum*) of southeastern Europe. In early May this tree puts forth large, pyramidal clusters of white blossoms. The sweet and Ohio buckeyes (*Aesculus octandra* and *Aesculus glabra*), which are native to the midwestern and southern U.S., are also popular ornamental trees in the District. Both have yellow blossoms that can be told apart by the length of their stamens (see species text). Ohio is known as "The Buckeye State" in honor of the Ohio buckeye. Other members of the genus in cultivation in our area are the red buckeye (*Aesculus pavia*) of the southeastern states and two hybrids, the red horse-chestnut (*Aesculus x carnea*) and the hybrid buckeye (*Aesculus x hybrida*).

Buckeyes are named for their shiny round seeds, each of which is marked with a single, pale, circular scar, or "buckeye." Although they look good enough to eat, most buckeye and horse-chestnut seeds are poisonous.

CHARACTERISTICS OF THE GENUS
LEAVES
Large, palmately compound, oppositely arranged. Five to nine toothed leaflets on a long petiole.

FLOWERS
May; in showy, upright clusters. White, yellow, pink, red, or a combination of colors.

FRUIT
Autumn. Smooth or spiny nut-like capsule which splits open to release one to three shiny seeds marked with characteristic "buckeye."

DISTRIBUTION
About twenty-five species in North America, Asia, and southeastern Europe.

KEY TO HORSE-CHESTNUTS AND BUCKEYES
COMMONLY CULTIVATED IN WASHINGTON, D.C.

1a) Flower clusters white. Leaflets stalkless. Autumn fruit capsule green or dark brown, prickly . . . .
. . . . Common Horse-Chestnut (*A. hippocastanum* L.)
1b) Flower clusters pink, red, yellow, or yellow and pink.
   2a) Flowers usually yellow.
      3a) Flowers pale yellow, *with stamens longer than petals*. Autumn fruit capsule tan, *prickly* . . Ohio Buckeye (*A. glabra* Willd.)
      3b) Flowers yellow or yellow and pink, *with stamens not longer than petals*. Autumn fruit capsule *smooth* . . . .
. . . . #2 Sweet Buckeye (*A. octandra* Marsh.)

2b) Flowers red, pink, or yellow and pink.
  4a) Blossoms dark red or dark pink, long, thin, with *tubular calyx* and *petals not spreading widely apart.* Leaflets pale to medium green, finely toothed. Autumn fruit capsule always smooth . . . . Red Buckeye (*A. pavia* L.)
  4b) Blossoms red, pink, or pink and yellow, with *petals spreading apart.*
    5a) Leaflets *deep, dark green* with *coarse, jagged teeth.* Autumn fruit capsule with a few small spines . . . . . .
    . . . . Red Horse-Chestnut (*A. x carnea* Hayne.)
    5b) Leaflets *pale to medium green* with *small, fine teeth.* Autumn fruit capsule always smooth . . . .
    . . . . Hybrid Buckeye (*A. x hydrida* DC.)

RED HORSE-CHESTNUT

Aesculus x carnea Hayne.
(*A. hippocastanum* x *A. pavia*)
Horse-Chestnut Family *Hippocastanaceae*

A cross between the common horse-chestnut of Europe and the red buckeye of the southeastern United States. The cultivar, 'Briotii,' is the most frequently planted form.

LEAVES: Opposite, deciduous, similar to common horse-chestnut (*Aesculus hippocastanum*), but darker, more coarsely toothed, and usually smaller. Five (sometimes seven) crinkly-textured leaflets on extremely short stalks. **FLOWERS:** Early May, in deep pink or red clusters. **FRUIT:** Smaller than common horse-chestnut, with fewer or no spines. **CULTIVAR:** *Aesculus x carnea* 'Briotii,' Flowers brighter red, leaves glossier green. **SIMILAR SPECIES:** Red buckeye (*Aesculus pavia*) has redder, but less spectacular blossoms with tubular calyxes, thinner leaflets on longer stalks, and fruit that is always smooth. (See, also, common horse-chestnut (*Aesculus hippocastanum*) and other buckeyes.)
LOCATIONS:
☐ Georgetown
☐ Saint Elizabeth's Hospital
☐ Fort McNair
☐ Private yards

HYBRID BUCKEYE

Aesculus x hybrida DC.
(*Aesculus octandra* x *Aesculus pavia*)
Horse-Chestnut Family *Hippocastanaceae*

A cross between the sweet buckeye (*Aesculus octandra*) and the red buckeye (*Aesculus pavia*).

LEAVES: Have five long-pointed leaflets that are pubescent along the veins below. Margins with small, pointed or rounded teeth. **FLOWERS:** *Reddish* and *yellow*, in upright clusters in late April, early May. **FRUIT:** Smooth, slightly etched, pale brown capsule; splitting to release shiny seed with characteristic "buckeye."
LOCATIONS:
☐ Mount Vernon. Tree planted by George Washington

COMMON HORSE-CHESTNUT

Aesculus hippocastanum L.
Horse-Chestnut Family *Hippocastanaceae*

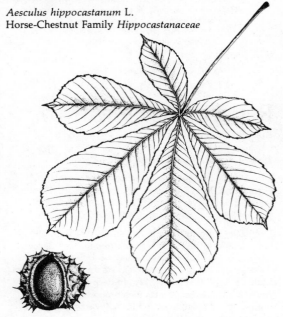

One of the most spectacular flowering trees in Washington.

NATIVE HABITAT
Greece, Albania.

LEAVES
Opposite, deciduous, large, palmately compound, with five to seven *stalkless* leaflets. Each leaflet 3 - 10 in. (7.5 - 25.5 cm.) long, very narrow at base, widening toward the apex, and ending in an abrupt point. Side leaflets smallest, middle ones largest. Margin irregularly toothed. Petiole up to 10 in. (25.5 cm.) long.

FLOWERS
In early May, in large, showy upright clusters. Overall color of cluster white, but individual blossoms are often tinged with red and yellow. (See color close-up.)

FRUIT
A dark brown, sharply and heavily spined capsule, splitting open to release one or two shiny, dark reddish-brown seeds. Each seed with whitish or pinkish circle (visible when free of capsule), approximately 1¼ to 2½ in. (3 - 5.5 cm.) long.

BARK AND TWIGS
Winter buds conspicuous: large, *sticky*, mahogany-colored. Branchlets usually glabrous. Bark often breaks into irregular scales that peel away slightly from trunk.

HABIT
May grow to be a large tree. Crown tall and rounded.

SIMILAR SPECIES
White flowers, stalkless leaflets, and (from late summer
through early spring) *sticky* buds distinguish the common
horse-chestnut from other horse-chestnuts and buckeyes
planted in the Washington area.

LOCATIONS
☐ U.S. Capitol grounds
☐ Stanton Park, Lafayette Park, and other
   parks throughout the city.
☐ Arlington Cemetery
☐ The Mall

SWEET BUCKEYE
OR YELLOW BUCKEYE

Aesculus octandra Marsh.
(*A. flava* Soland.)
Horse-Chestnut Family *Hippocastanaceae*

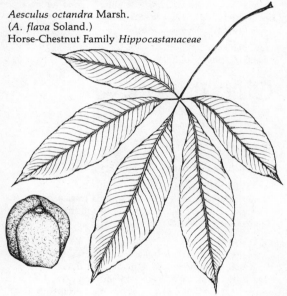

NATIVE HABITAT
Western Pennsylvania west to southern Illinois; south to
northern Georgia.

LEAVES
Opposite, deciduous, palmately compound, usually with
five leaflets. Each leaflet 4 - 10 in. (10 - 25.5 cm.) long;
widest in the middle, tapering smoothly and gradually to
apex and base. Yellow-green above, considerably paler
below. Finely toothed. May be glabrous, pubescent, or
partially pubescent below. Each leaflet *with a stalk*
which may be up to an inch (2.5 cm.) long. Petiole up to
8 in. (20 cm.) long. Autumn color: bright orange-yellow.

FLOWERS
Early May. Yellow, pink, or yellow and pink clusters.
Blossoms with the *stamens not longer than the petals.*

FRUIT
A smooth, tan, shallowly etched capsule, about the size and shape of a small plum. Splits open to release (usually two) shiny poisonous seeds, each with characteristic "buckeye."

BARK AND TWIGS
Bark gray and grayish pink, smooth underneath with shedding scales. Winter end buds large, but lighter-colored than common horse-chestnut (*Aesculus hippocastanum*), and *not sticky.*

HABIT
Crown broad and somewhat rounded.

SIMILAR SPECIES
Ohio buckeye (*Aesculus glabra*) has thick, furrowed bark, flowers with stamens extending beyond the petals, and a prickly fruit capsule. See other buckeyes and horse-chestnuts (*Aesculus* sp.).

LOCATIONS
☐ U.S. Capitol grounds

OHIO BUCKEYE
Aesculus glabra Willd.
Horse-Chestnut Family *Hippocastanaceae*

STATE TREE OF OHIO

The tree that named the "Buckeye State."

NATIVE HABITAT
Western Pennsylvania and W. Virginia to eastern Nebraska, Kansas, and Oklahoma; south through Tennessee to Alabama.

LEAVES
Opposite, deciduous, palmately compound, smallish for the genus, variable in size. Usually with five leaflets, each leaflet from 2 - 6 in. (5 - 15 cm.) long. Leaflet widest at the middle, or just above it, and tapering to a point at either end. Glabrous to pubescent below. *Leaflet stalks very short*, almost non-existent on some leaves. Finely toothed margin. Petiole thin, 2 - 6 in. (5 - 15 cm.) long.

FLOWERS
Bell-shaped, clustered, pale yellow or yellow-green in early May. *Stamens longer than petals.*

FRUIT
Capsule the color of coffee with cream. An inch or more in diameter, covered with small weak spines. Splits open to release one reddish-brown seed, marked with characteristic "buckeye."

BARK AND TWIGS
Bark thick, gray, furrowed and scaly. Twigs emit a foul odor when crushed. (The tree is sometimes known as "Fetid Buckeye.") Winter end buds reddish-brown, *not sticky*, with ridged scales.

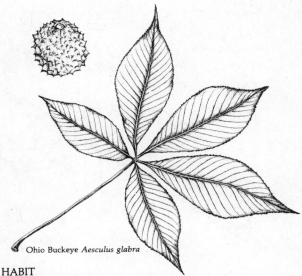

Ohio Buckeye *Aesculus glabra*

HABIT
A small tree with a broad, rounded crown.

SIMILAR SPECIES
See yellow buckeye (*Aesculus octandra*). Fruit similar to
common horse-chestnut (*Aesculuc hippocastanum*), but
smaller, lighter-colored, and with shorter, weaker spines.

LOCATIONS
- Hains Point
- Freer Gallery (west side)
- Walter Reed Army Medical Center
- Saint Elizabeth's Hospital

RED BUCKEYE

Aesculus pavia L.
Horse-Chestnut Family *Hippocastanaceae*

A small, infrequently cultivated tree.

NATIVE HABITAT: Virginia to Louisiana and Florida.
LEAVES: Similar to yellow buckeye (*Aesculus octandra*)
but with leaflets smaller and more irregularly toothed;
overall leaflet shape less symmetrical. Leaflet stalks vary
in size and may be ½ in. (1.2 cm.) or longer. **FLOWERS:**
Dark red, in May, in tall clusters. Each blossom has a
red, tubular calyx. **FRUIT:** Similar to yellow buckeye, but
smaller. Capsule contains one or two seeds. **SIMILAR
SPECIES:** See red horse-chestnut (*Aesculus x carnea*), other
buckeyes.
LOCATIONS:
- Private gardens

FLOWERING DOGWOOD
Cornus florida L.
Dogwood Family *Cornaceae*

STATE TREE OF MISSOURI AND VIRGINIA

STATE FLOWER OF NORTH CAROLINA

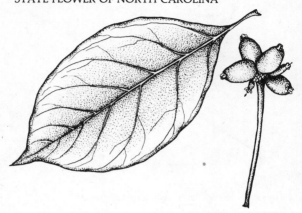

   Unsurpassed in beauty among our native flowering trees. In mid- to late April, the flowering dogwood puts forth its renowned white blossoms throughout Washington and our surrounding woodlands.

NATIVE HABITAT
Southern New England to Florida; west to Ontario, southern Michigan, eastern Kansas and eastern Texas.

LEAVES
Simple, opposite, deciduous, 2 - 6 in. (5 - 15 cm.) long. Elliptic or ovate, abruptly pointed with broadly wedge-shaped or rounded base. Veins, characteristic of dog-woods, curve along smooth or nearly smooth leaf margin. (See drawing.) Mostly glabrous above; paler below and usually glabrous, but may be somewhat pubescent, especially along the veins. Autumn color: bright crimson above, pale red below.

FLOWERS
Just before or with the leaves, mid-April to early May. Usually white, yellowish, or very pale green, but in some forms pink or red. (See "OTHER FORMS.") The four notched "petals" are actually large bracts which surround the tiny true flowers clustered in the center. (See color close-up.)

FRUIT
Small, scarlet, berry-like drupes in autumn, each ½ in. or less (about 1 cm.) in length; clustered.

BARK AND TWIGS
Bark is broken into many small, squarish plates. Twigs greenish or purple, with separate leaf and flower buds. Gray flower buds, located at the ends of twigs, are onion-shaped.

HABIT
A small tree with a flat, bushy crown.

SIMILAR SPECIES
The kousa dogwood (*Cornus kousa*) blooms *after* the
leaves are out. It has *pointed*, rather than notched,
petal-like bracts.

LOCATIONS
- □ U.S. Capitol grounds
- □ National Arboretum, Dogwood Collection and among
  the azaleas on Mount Hamilton
- □ Mount Vernon
- □ White House grounds
- □ Lady Bird Johnson Park and along the George
  Washington Memorial Parkway to Mount Vernon
- □ Franciscan Monastery
- □ Very common throughout the city in public places
  and private yards and gardens

OTHER FORMS
Dozens of cultivars and varieties of flowering dogwood
are propagated for ornament, many of which can be
seen at the National Arboretum's Dogwood Collection.
The following are some of the most noteworthy:

1. DOUBLE-FLOWERING DOGWOOD

Cornus florida 'Pluribracteata.' Blooms slightly later
than standard form and has *six or more* petal-like bracts.

LOCATIONS
- □ U.S. Capitol grounds
- □ National Arboretum, among the azaleas at
  Mount Hamilton

2. RED AND PINK FLOWERING DOGWOODS

Cornus florida f. *rubra* (West.) Schelle. Petal-like
bracts vary from very pale pink to red.

LOCATIONS
- □ U.S. Capitol grounds
- □ National Arboretum, Dogwood Collection

3. CHEROKEE CHIEF FLOWERING DOGWOOD

Cornus florida 'Cherokee Chief'. Popular cultivar
with red blossoms.

LOCATIONS
- □ National Arboretum, Dogwood Collection
- □ Private yards and gardens

Kousa Dogwood
or Japanese Dogwood

Cornus kousa Hance
Dogwood Family *Cornaceae*

A beautiful Asian tree or shrub. Similar to our
native flowering dogwood, but with *pointed* (rather than
notched) petal-like bracts, and a later and longer blooming time.

NATIVE HABITAT: Japan, Korea. (Form native to
China described under "OTHER FORMS.") **LEAVES:**
Simple, opposite, deciduous, 2 - 5 in. (5 - 12.6 cm.)
long. Elliptic-ovate, thinner and slightly less abruptly
pointed than flowering dogwood (*Cornus florida*), with
a smooth or barely wavy-toothed margin. Base broadly
wedge-shaped or (rarely) rounded. Characteristic
dogwood venation pattern. Glaucous below
with pale, minute flattened hairs along lower surface and longer, rusty-colored hairs in vein axils.
FLOWERS: After the leaves, from mid-or late May until
late June. Four pale green, white, or yellowish petal-like
bracts are gracefully pointed at apices. True flowers (or
flower buds) tiny in a prominent round, greenish head in
the center. (See color close-up.) **FRUIT:** Red, compound
drupe which looks like a raspberry or strawberry.
BARK: Brown, mottled. **HABIT:** Either shrub-like, with
spreading branches and a rounded crown, or with a
tallish, narrow crown. OTHER FORMS: CHINESE
KOUSA DOGWOOD. *Cornus kousa* var. *chinensis*
Osborn. Native to China, this form of kousa dogwood
has slightly larger petal-like bracts and leaves with very
little or no rusty pubescence in the vein axils below.
SIMILAR SPECIES: Flowering dogwood (*Cornus florida*)
blooms in April and early May and has *notched* (rather
than pointed) petal-like bracts.
LOCATIONS:
☐ U.S. Capitol northeast grounds (planted in honor of
   Lady Bird Johnson by Senate wives in 1968)
☐ Rock Creek Cemetery
☐ National Academy of Sciences
☐ Smithsonian National Museum of Natural History
☐ National Arboretum Dogwood Collection
☐ Beaver Valley, National Zoo

Table Dogwood

Cornus controversa Hemsl.
Dogwood Family *Cornaceae*

Native to Japan and China. Very similar to the
alternate-leaved dogwood, but with leaves usually
rounded at the base and slightly larger flower clusters that
are up to 4¾ in. (12 cm.) across.

CORNELIAN CHERRY

Cornus mas L.
Dogwood Family *Cornaceae*

This small tree or shrub is really a dogwood, but its fruit is cherry-like. It is one of the first trees to bloom in Washington in the early spring.

NATIVE HABITAT
Central and southern Europe and western Asia.

LEAVES
Simple, opposite, deciduous. Similar to flowering dogwood (*Cornus florida*) but smaller (1½ - 4 in. (4 - 10 cm.) long) and usually with tiny, pale, flattened hairs (visible with a hand lens) on both the upper and lower surfaces.

FLOWERS
March, or very early April, before the leaves. Round clusters of tiny yellow blossoms. (See color close-up.) Yellowish bracts are about as long as flower stalks. FRUIT is edible, red, up to ¾ in. (2 cm.) long; looks much like a cherry. BARK is brown and flaky.

HABIT
Usually a tall, full shrub in our area.

SIMILAR SPECIES
Rare Japanese Cornelian Cherry (*Cornus officinalis*) is described below.

LOCATIONS
☐ Library of Congress grounds
☐ Montrose Park
☐ Constitution Gardens
☐ Garfield Park
☐ Tidal Basin
☐ National Arboretum

JAPANESE CORNELIAN CHERRY

Cornus officinalis Sieb. & Zucc.
Dogwood Family *Cornaceae*

This rare tree or shrub, native to Japan and Korea, is very similar to the Cornelian cherry, described above. It differs in having leaves with conspicuous tufts of brownish hairs in the vein axils below, and flowers with stalks nearly twice as long as the bracts.

LOCATIONS:
☐ National Arboretum bonsai collection

Alternate-Leaved Dogwood

Cornus alternifolia L.f.
Dogwood Family *Cornaceae*

　　Most dogwoods have oppositely arranged leaves. However, this tree and the table dogwood (*Cornus controversa*) have leaves arranged *alternately*.

NATIVE HABITAT: New Brunswick west to Minnesota; south to Georgia and Alabama. **LEAVES:** Simple, alternate, deciduous, 2 - 5 in. (5 - 12.5 cm.) long. Ellipticovate, with wedge-shaped base. Flattened pubescence below (visible with a hand lens.) Typical dogwood curved venation pattern. **FLOWERS:** After the leaves, in late spring. Small, white, in flat-topped clusters, 1½ -2½ in. (4 - 6.3 cm.) across. **FRUIT:** Small, bluish-black berry-like drupe on a reddish stalk.
SIMILAR SPECIES:
See table dogwood.
LOCATIONS:
☐ National Arboretum; Fern Valley and the Dogwood Collection

Tupelo
or Black Gum or Sour Gum

Nyssa sylvatica Marsh.
Tupelo Family *Nyssaceae*

　　A handsome native tree. Leaves turn deep scarlet in early autumn.

NATIVE HABITAT
Southern Maine to southern Ontario and Michigan; south to Florida and Texas.

LEAVES
Simple, alternate, deciduous, 2 - 6 in. (5 - 15 cm.) long. Obovate. Apex bluntly pointed, base wedge-shaped or (rarely) rounded. Margin smooth or slightly wavy. Often pubescent along veins below. Petiole about ¾ in. (2 cm.) long. The most spectacular fall foliage of any native tree.

FLOWERS
Small, greenish white, with the leaves in spring. Males in many-flowered round heads; females, few per cluster

FRUIT
Egg-shaped, dark blue berry-like drupe, ⅓ - ⅔ in.
(about 1 - 1.5 cm.) long; on a slender stalk up to 1¾ in.
(4.5 cm.) long. Contains a stony, shallowly grooved, pit.

BARK AND TWIGS
Bark dark, furrowed, and often broken into squares.
Twigs slender, with diaphragmed pith. Winter buds:
scaly, pointed, ovoid, reddish-brown. Terminal bud
present.

HABIT
Crown rounded or cylindric and flat-topped. Branches
horizontal.

SIMILAR SPECIES
Common persimmon (*Diospyros virginiana*) has
somewhat similar leaves and bark. See persimmon,
"SIMILAR SPECIES," and compare leaf and fruit
illustrations.

LOCATIONS
☐ Kenilworth Aquatic Gardens
☐ White House lawn, just outside the Oval Office
☐ National Arboretum
☐ Rock Creek Park

DOVE TREE
OR HANDKERCHIEF TREE
Davidia involucrata Baill.
Tupelo Family *Nyssaceae*

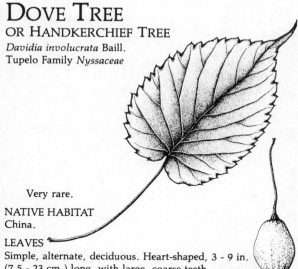

Very rare.

NATIVE HABITAT
China.

LEAVES
Simple, alternate, deciduous. Heart-shaped, 3 - 9 in.
(7.5 - 23 cm.) long, with large, coarse teeth.

FLOWERS
Large creamy white bracts are showy; true flowers
small, in a round cluster.

FRUIT
A hanging drupe, about 1½ in. (3.5 - 4 cm.) long.

SIMILAR SPECIES
Leaves of two other rare trees, the Japanese raisin tree
(*Hovenia dulcis*) and *Idesia polycarpa* are similar, but
the fruit of each is very distinctive.

LOCATIONS
☐ National Arboretum
☐ A few private yards

Devil's Walkingstick
OR HERCULES CLUB OR ANGELICA TREE
Aralia spinosa L.
Ginseng Family *Araliaceae*

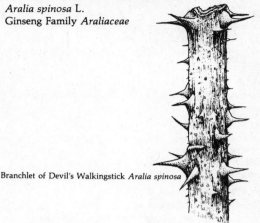

Branchlet of Devil's Walkingstick *Aralia spinosa*

A small, native tree, easily identified by its stout branchlets which are covered with thorns.

NATIVE HABITAT
Southern New York west to Illinois, Missouri, and eastern Texas; south to Florida.

LEAVES
Alternate, deciduous. Large, bipinnately compound, with prickly leaflets, stalks and petiole. Each toothed, ovate leaflet 2 - 3 in. (5 - 7.5 cm.) long; dark green above, glaucous below.

FLOWERS
Small, white, in huge clusters in mid or late summer.

FRUIT
Small, black berry-like drupe.

TWIGS
Very stout; covered with sharp thorns.

HABIT
Small tree or shrub.

SIMILAR SPECIES
Not likely to be confused with any other species. No other tree in our area is so thorny.

LOCATIONS
☐ National Arboretum
☐ Some private homes in D.C.

AMERICAN HOLLY

Ilex opaca Ait.
Holly Family *Aquifoliaceae*

STATE TREE OF DELAWARE

The lovely American holly perfectly complements the white marble monuments of Washington.

NATIVE HABITAT
Southern New England to Florida and Texas.

LEAVES
Alternate, simple, evergreen. 2 - 4 in. (5 - 10 cm.) long. Margin with spiny outcurved teeth. Leathery; rather dull green above, paler below.

FRUIT
Small, round, bright red berry-like drupe remaining on the tree through the winter.

SIMILAR SPECIES
The American holly is the most widely planted *tree*-sized holly in Washington. The shrubby osmanthus (*Osmanthus heterophyllus*) has similarly shaped leaves, but they are *oppositely* arranged.

OTHER FORMS
Ilex opaca f. *xanthocarpa* Rehd. has *yellow* fruit.

LOCATIONS
☐ Jefferson Memorial
☐ Lincoln Memorial
☐ U.S. Capitol grounds
☐ Smithsonian Castle
☐ Very common throughout Washington

OTHER HOLLIES OF THE WASHINGTON AREA:

The English holly (*ilex aquifolium* L.) and several Asian species, hybrids and cultivars are planted in Washington, but rarely become trees. The English holly has very shiny leaves [compared to the duller green of the American holly (*Ilex opaca*)]. The National Arboretum has a noteworthy holly collection.

WINGED EUONYMOUS
Euonymous alata (Thunb.) Sieb.
Staff-Tree Family *Celastraceae*

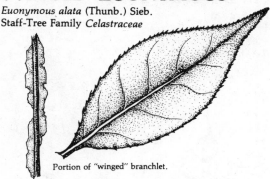

Portion of "winged" branchlet.

A large shrub, native to Asia, with unsurpassed autumn foliage. Easily identified with its *corky-winged branchlets*, small, opposite, simple leaves and bright scarlet fall color.

LOCATIONS
☐ U.S. Capitol grounds
☐ Washington Monument grounds
☐ Very common throughout the city

JAPANESE RAISIN-TREE
Hovenia dulcis Thunb.
Buckthorn Family *Rhamnaceae*

The rare Japanese raisin-tree has uniquely shaped, edible, raisin-like fruit. (See illustration.)

NATIVE HABITAT
China; cultivated in Japan and India.

LEAVES
Simple, alternate, deciduous. Broadly ovate to elliptic, 4 - 6 in. (10 - 15 cm.) long. Shallowly cordate or rounded at the base and often unequal. Apex pointed. Margin coarsely toothed.

FRUIT
Brown and raisiny textured; fleshy and juicy inside with a sweet, slightly fermented flavor. Ripens in autumn.

LOCATIONS
- ☐ Tidal Basin
- ☐ Kenilworth Aquatic Gardens
- ☐ National Arboretum (lower slopes of Mount Hamilton)

COMMON JUJUBE
Zizyphus jujuba Mill.
Buckthorn Family *Rhamnacea*

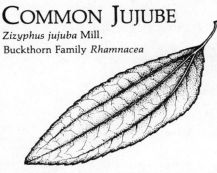

Every summer the jujube connoisseurs of Washington race to gather the fruit that falls on the Capitol grounds. Fresh, cooked or dried, the date-like jujube is a delicacy.

The jujube is cultivated throughout the Orient and the Mediterranean for its delicious fruit. While rare in Washington, several specimens grow on the grounds of the U.S. Capitol and Botanic Gardens.

NATIVE HABITAT
Southeastern Europe; Asia.

LEAVES
Simple, alternate, deciduous. ¾ - 3 in. (2 - 7.5 cm.) long, with shallow rounded or pointed teeth. Ovate to ovate-lanceolate with a pointed or blunt apex. Three main veins radiate from the base, which is usually slightly unequal. Spine-like stipules often present.

FLOWERS
Terminal clusters of small, greenish-white blossoms in spring.

FRUIT
Ovoid-oblong orange-red drupe, ½ - 1 in. (1 - 2.5 cm.) long.

LOCATIONS
- ☐ U.S. Capitol grounds
- ☐ Botanic Gardens (between Independence Avenue and Canal Street)

THE ASHES

Fraxinus L.
Olive Family *Oleaceae*

The white ash (*Fraxinus americana*) is quite commonly planted in Washington. The green or red ash (*Fraxinus pennsylvanica*) is common in the wild, but not in cultivation. The other species included here are rare.

CHARACTERISTICS OF THE GENUS

LEAVES
Opposite, odd-pinnately compound, deciduous.

FLOWERS
Unisexual or perfect. Small, in sometimes conspicuous clusters, with or before the leaves.

FRUIT
Usually single-seeded samara with a terminal wing.

DISTRIBUTION
About sixty-five species in the Northern Hemisphere; south to Mexico, Cuba, and Java.

WHITE ASH

Fraxinus americana L.
Olive Family *Oleaceae*

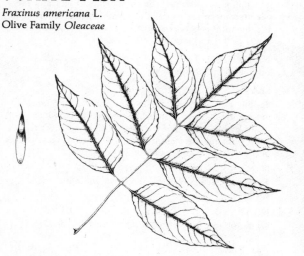

Magnificent specimens of this native tree are growing on the U.S. Capitol grounds.

NATIVE HABITAT
Southeastern Canada and eastern U.S. south to Florida; west to eastern Texas, eastern Nebraska, northern Michigan, and northern Wisconsin.

LEAVES
Opposite, compound, deciduous. 7 - 13 in. (17.8 - 33 cm.) long, composed of five to nine (usually seven) oblong—lanceolate to ovate leaflets. Leaflets 3 - 5 in. (7.5 - 12.5 cm.) long, with smooth or obscurely toothed margins. Usually glabrous. Petiolules ¼ - ½ in. (6-12 mm.) long.

FLOWERS AND FRUIT
Flowers in clusters in spring, before or with the leaves.
Fruit is a winged samara, 1 - 2 in. (2.5 - 5 cm.) long.

BARK AND TWIGS
Bark thick, dark gray, separating into vertical diamond-
shaped furrows and ridges. (Trees on Capitol grounds
have beautiful bark.) Twigs glabrous, lustrous grayish-
green with large "U"-shaped leaf scars and small, round,
dark brown winter buds.

HABIT
A medium-sized to tall tree with an open, pyramidal, or
rounded crown.

SIMILAR SPECIES
The similar green or red ash (*Fraxinus pennsylvanica*)
sometimes has glabrous leaves. It is not as widely cultivated as the white ash. Although the two species are
hard to tell apart, the green ash usually has *narrower
leaflets* and *narrower samaras*. Its bark is fissured and
ridged, but it is thin, brown, and scaly and does not
develop the handsome diamond furrows of the white
ash.

LOCATIONS
□ U.S. Capitol grounds
□ White House grounds
□ Saint Elizabeth's Hospital grounds
□ Parks, public buildings, and private homes through-
out the city

GREEN ASH
OR RED ASH
Fraxinus pennsylvanica Marsh.
Olive Family *Oleaceae*

Most botanists no longer recognize green and red
ashes as separate trees, although the more glabrous green
ash used to be considered a variety of the pubescent red
ash. Today the trees are lumped together under the
single name, *Fraxinus pennsylvanica.*

NATIVE HABITAT: Cape Breton Island, Nova Scotia
and New Brunswick south to northern Florida; west to
eastern Texas, northeastern Colorado, Montana, and
Saskatchewan. **LEAVES:** Opposite, compound,
deciduous. 10 - 12 in. (25.3 - 30.5 cm.) long, with five to
nine leaflets. Leaflets 4 - 6 in. (10 - 15 cm.) long, oblong-
lanceolate to elliptic. Margins smooth or toothed;
glabrous or pubescent below. Petiolules 1/8 - 1/4 in. (3 - 6
mm.) long, narrowly lanceolate. **BARK:** Brown, scaly
and fissured. (Not as thick as the white ash's (*Fraxinus
americana*). **SIMILAR SPECIES:** White ash usually has
slightly wider leaflets and samaras and thick, dark gray
bark separated into diamond-shaped furrows. The white
ash is more commonly cultivated.
LOCATIONS:
□ Kenilworth Aquatic Gardens
□ National Arboretum
□ Parks and private yards

EUROPEAN ASH
(COMMON ASH)

Fraxinus excelsior L.
Olive Family *Oleaceae*

The European ash is planted in some private yards in the District.

NATIVE HABITAT
Europe and Asia Minor.

LEAVES
Opposite, compound, deciduous. 7 - 14 in. (17.8 - 35.5 cm.) long, with 9 - 13 lanceolate or ovate-oblong leaflets. Margins with sharp, shallow teeth. White pubescence along veins below.

TWIGS
Winter buds *black*.

SIMILAR SPECIES
The black winter buds are the best distinguishing feature of the European ash. The white pubescence along the leaflet veins also separates it from other species.

LOCATIONS
☐ National Arboretum
☐ Private yards

CHINESE ASH

Fraxinus chinensis var. *rhynchophylla* (Hance) Hemsl.
Olive Family *Oleaceae*

This rare tree is planted in Lafayette Park.

NATIVE HABITAT: Northeastern Asia. **LEAVES:** Compound, opposite, deciduous. Leaflets usually five, ovate or obovate, with rounded to pointed teeth. usually pubescent below.

LOCATIONS:
☐ Lafayette Park (extremely rare in D.C.)

Blue Ash
Fraxinus quadrangulata Michx.
Olive Family *Oleaceae*

Several specimens of the rare blue ash are planted on the Potomac River side of the Tidal Basin. They can be distinguished from other ashes in the area by their stout, *four-sided* twigs.

NATIVE HABITAT: Midwest from southern Ontario and southern Wisconsin to Arkansas; northern Alabama and Georgia; and western West Virginia.

Osmanthus
Osmanthus heterophyllus (G. Don) P.S. Green
Olive Family *Oleaceae*

A large shrub or small tree with very fragrant autumn blossoms.

NATIVE HABITAT
Japan.

LEAVES
Simple, *opposite*, evergreen; closely resembling the hollies (*Ilex* sp.), which are arranged *alternately*. ¾ - 2½ in. (2 - 6.5 cm.) long, usually with a few sharp teeth, but sometimes smooth-margined. Lustrous, dark green above, pale below.

FLOWERS
October - November. Clusters of small, creamy white blossoms fill the air with their sweet perfume.

HABIT
Usually a many-branched, tall shrub.

SIMILAR SPECIES
The hollies (*Ilex* sp.) (For distinguishing characteristics, see under LEAVES).

LOCATIONS
☐ U.S. Capitol grounds
☐ Rayburn House Office Building
☐ Pan American Union
☐ Fairly common throughout the city

FRINGE-TREE
Chionanthus virginicus L.
Olive Family *Oleaceae*

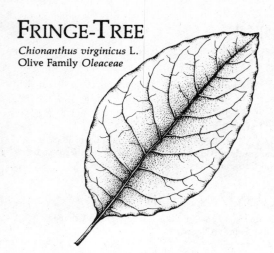

A small tree that puts forth cloud-like clusters of white blossoms in May.

NATIVE HABITAT
New Jersey west to southeastern Oklahoma and eastern Texas; south to Florida.

LEAVES
Simple, opposite, deciduous, 3½ - 8 in. (9 - 20 cm.) long. Ovate to oblong-elliptic. Smooth margin. Gradually or abruptly pointed apex. Round toward base, but finally narrowly wedge-shaped. Dark green and glabrous above; paler below and pubescent when young. Petiole ½ - 1 in. (1.2 - 2.5 cm.) long.

FLOWERS
Drooping, airy clusters of white blossoms in early or mid-May. Individual blossoms "fringe-like," with very slender, delicate petals. (See color close-up.) Male and female blossoms on separate trees.

FRUIT
Dark blue-black, oval drupe, ½ - ¾ in. (1.2 - 2 cm.) long. Contains a single stone.

BARK AND TWIGS
Bark reddish-brown, broken into thin scales. Twigs rather stout, often pubescent, with scaly winter buds and true end bud.

HABIT
Shrub or small tree.

SIMILAR SPECIES
Asian fringe-tree, discussed below.

LOCATIONS
- ☐ U.S. Capitol grounds
- ☐ Area between 17th Street, N.W. and the Ellipse
- ☐ Mount Vernon
- ☐ Gardens and grounds throughout city, but not very common

ASIAN FRINGE-TREE

Chionanthus retusus Lindl. & Paxt.
Olive Family *Oleaceae*

Very rare here. Native to China, Korea, and Japan.
Similar to our native fringe-tree, but with *shorter* and
relatively *wider leaves* that are often indented at the
apex, and blossoms with slightly *shorter, wider petals.*
The cloud-like clusters of blossoms are thicker and less
airy-looking than on our native tree, but are no less
beautiful.

LOCATIONS
☐ U.S. National Arboretum

THE LILACS

Syringa sp.
Olive Family *Oleaceae*

Common Lilac *Syringa vulgaris*

The lilacs are shrubs (rarely small trees) with opposite, heart-shaped or lance-shaped leaves, and upright or
drooping clusters of showy, often fragrant flowers.
Many forms of the lilac are grown in Washington, with
blossom color ranging from white to purple.

LOCATIONS
☐ The National Arboretum
☐ Private yards, public grounds and parks throughout
the city.

THE VIBURNUMS
Viburnum sp.
Honeysuckle Family *Caprifoliaceae*

The Viburnums are a large genus (approximately 150 species) of shrubs and small trees with opposite, simple leaves and usually showy flowers and fruit. The leaves may be lobed or unlobed, toothed or with smooth margins. Flowers are usually borne in large, flat-topped or rounded clusters and are most often a brilliant white. The berry-like fruit is red or black. The Washington area supports a large number of native and exotic viburnums.

We list a few of the most common species.

NANNYBERRY
Viburnum lentago L.

NATIVE HABITAT
Northeastern U.S., southeastern Canada.

LEAVES
Deciduous, 2 - 5 in. (5 - 12.5 cm.) long, rounded or wedge-shaped at the base, lanceolate, sharply pointed at the apex. Sharply toothed margins. Glandular below.

FLOWERS
Tiny white flowers in dense, rounded or flat-topped clusters.

FRUIT
Dark, blue-black in dense clusters.

HABIT
A small tree.

SMOOTH BLACKHAW
Viburnum prunifolium L.

NATIVE HABITAT
Eastern and midwestern U.S.

LEAVES
Similar to the preceding species, but more bluntly
pointed at the apex. Not glandular below.

SIEBOLD VIBURNUM
Viburnum sieboldii Miq.

NATIVE HABITAT (Japan)
A large shrub with leaves that are toothed toward the
tip and red fruit.

JAPANESE SNOWBALL
Viburnum plicatum Thunb.

This viburnum bears ball-shaped clusters of small,
white flowers.

DOUBLE-FILE VIBURNUM
Viburnum plicatum f. *tomentosum* (Thunb.) Rehd.

NATIVE HABITAT
Asia.

Small, white blossoms are surrounded by a circle of
larger ones.

VIBURNUM LOCATIONS
☐ National Arboretum
☐ Lyndon Baines Johnson Memorial Grove
☐ Parks, private yards and public building grounds
    throughout the city.

PAULOWNIA OR ROYAL PAULOWNIA OR EMPRESS TREE OR PRINCESS TREE

Paulownia tomentosa (Thunb.) Steud.
Figwort Family *Scrophulariaceae*

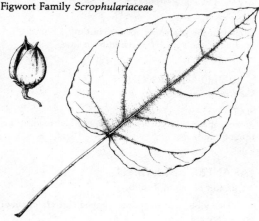

An Asian ornamental with tall clusters of fuzzy tan flower buds developing in autumn, and large lavender blossoms opening in May. Named after Anna Paulowna, a nineteenth century princess of the Netherlands.

NATIVE HABITAT
China, cultivated in Japan. Escaped from cultivation in the eastern states from southern New York to Georgia.

LEAVES
Simple, opposite, deciduous. Large, heart-shaped, downy all over. Margin smooth (young plants sometimes with two shallow lobes near the base). 4½ - 10 in. (11.5 - 25.3 cm.) long, or longer. Petiole 2½ - 8 in. (6.3 - 20.2 cm.) long, densely pubescent.

FLOWERS
Tall clusters of fragrant lavender blossoms in early May. Each erect cluster up to 12 in. (30.4 cm.) long; twenty or more blossoms per cluster. Blossoms bell-shaped, downy, yellow and white inside, with velvety tan sepals.

FRUIT
Upright clusters of woody, ovate nut-like capsules, each 1 - 1¾ in. (2.5 - 4.5 cm.) long, with a sharp beak at the apex; splitting in half to release winged seeds.

BARK AND TWIGS
Bark light brown or gray; may be slightly furrowed. Twigs stout, reddish-brown, with rounded leaf scars. (Pith chambered or hollow.) In winter, mature trees usually have clusters of both this year's fruit and next year's flower buds.

HABIT
Stout, spreading branches form a rounded crown.

SIMILAR SPECIES
The catalpas (*Catalpa* species) have white or yellow blossoms, long, thin pendulous fruit, usually *whorled* leaves, and twigs with solid piths.

LOCATIONS
- ☐ Parks citywide, including Garfield and Montrose
- ☐ National Zoo
- ☐ National Arboretum
- ☐ Walter Reed Army Medical Center
- ☐ C&O Canal, Georgetown
- ☐ Private yards throughout the city
- ☐ (Young trees in unused lots, along highways)

THE CATALPAS

Catalpa Scop.
Bignonia Family *Bignoniaceae*

The catalpas are among Washington's most beautiful flowering trees. The two native American species commonly grown here, the western or northern catalpa (*Catalpa speciosa*) and the southern or common catalpa (*Catalpa bignonioides*) produce many upright clusters of large, white blossoms. Because the catalpas are full-sized trees, and they bloom at a time when they have the scene pretty much to themselves, their effect, in flower, is dramatic. The western and southern catalpas are often confused with one another, but they are quite easily distinguished from the one Asian species commonly found in D.C., the yellow catalpa (*Catalpa ovata*). The Asian tree produces yellow flowers.

CHARACTERISTICS OF THE GENUS:

LEAVES
Simple, opposite or *whorled*, deciduous. Heart-shaped or with three to five shallow lobes.

FLOWERS
Late May and June. Showy upright clusters of white or yellow blossoms, usually marked with purple, orange and yellow.

FRUIT
Long, thin, bean-like capsule that splits open to release flat seeds with tufts of hair at either end.

DISTRIBUTION
About ten species in North America, the West Indies, and eastern Asia.

KEY TO THE CATALPAS COMMONLY CULTIVATED
IN WASHINGTON, D.C.

1a) Flowers Yellow: leaves often shallowly three-lobed, glabrous below at maturity or with pubescence only along the veins . . . .
. . . . Yellow catalpa (*Catalpa ovata* G. Don)
1b) Flowers White: leaves always heart-shaped, pubescent below.
    2a) Leaf with a foul odor when crushed; flowers early to mid-June, each 1¼ - 1¾ in. (3 - 4.5 cm.) across. Autumn and winter pods contain seeds with tufts of *hairs coming together at tips, nearly to a point* . . . . Southern catalpa (*Catalpa bignonioides* Walt.)
    2b) Leaf with no foul odor with crushed; flowers late May to early June, each 2 - 2½ in. (about 5 - 6 cm.) across. Autumn and winter pods contain seeds with *hairs not coming together at tips* . . . .
. . . . Western catalpa (*Catalpa speciosa* Warder)

Western Catalpa
or Northern Catalpa
(Catawba-Tree or Cigar Tree)
Catalpa speciosa Warder
Bignonia Family *Bignoniaceae*

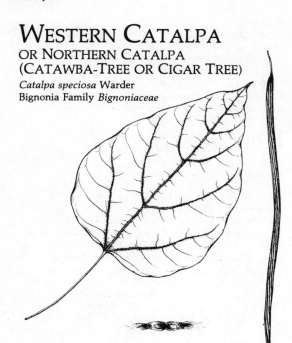

This tree and the southern or common catalpa
(*Catalpa bignonioides* Walt.) are very difficult to tell
apart. The western catalpa comes into bloom slightly
earlier than the southern catalpa.

NATIVE HABITAT
Southern Indiana and Illinois to northeastern Arkansas
and western Tennessee. Naturalized eastward.

LEAVES
Simple, opposite or whorled, deciduous. Heart-shaped,
6 - 12 in. (about 15 - 30 cm.) long. Apex abruptly or
gradually pointed; base heart-shaped, rounded, straight
across, or just barely wedge-shaped. (No foul odor when
crushed.) Pubescent below. Margin smooth. Petiole 3 - 7
in. (7.5 - 17.5 cm.) long.

FLOWERS
Late May-early June. Showy, white blossoms with small
yellow and purple spots in upright clusters. (See color
close-up.) Each blossom 2-2½ in. (about 5–6 cm.) across.

FRUIT
Bean-like capsule, 8 - 20 in. (20 - 50.5 cm.) long, remaining on the tree into winter. Contains many flat-winged
seeds with fringes of soft white hairs at either end.
(Hairs do *not* converge at tips. See illustration.)

BARK AND TWIGS
Bark brown or gray, fissured and scaly. Twigs glabrous,
stout, brown or gray, with round leaf scars and small
winter buds. End buds false. Pith solid.

HABIT
Medium-sized or tall tree with a pyramidal or rounded crown.

SIMILAR SPECIES
Very similar to the southern catalpa (*Catalpa bignonioides*), described below. The Asian yellow catalpa (*Catalpa ovata*) differs from the two native American species in having leaves that are often shallowly three-lobed. The paulownia (*Paulownia tomentosa*) has opposite leaves that are *never whorled*, lavender blossoms, a nut-like, woody fruit capsule, and twigs with chambered or hollow piths. Redbuds (*Cercis* sps.) have alternate leaves.

LOCATIONS
☐ Corner of E and First Streets, S.E.
☐ Quite widely planted throughout the city

SOUTHERN CATALPA
OR COMMON CATALPA

Southern or Common Catalpa *Catalpa bignonioides*

Catalpa bignonioides Walt.
Bignonia Family *Bignoniaceae*

This tree is very similar to the western catalpa (Catalpa speciosa). It differs from the preceding species in the following ways.

NATIVE HABITAT
Gulf coast states from Florida to Louisiana. (Naturalized as far north as southern New England, Ohio, and Michigan.) LEAF gives off a foul odor when crushed.

FLOWERS AND FRUIT
Slightly later than the western catalpa, in early or mid-June. Individual blossoms are not quite as wide, only about 1¼ - 1¾ in. (3 - 4.5 cm.) across, but they are more conspicuously marked with yellow, orange and purple. The bean-like fruit capsule is slightly shorter and thinner than that of the western catalpa, but the difference is nearly imperceptible. The best way to distinguish the two trees in the fall and winter is to split open a capsule and examine the seeds. The white fringe of hairs on either end of the southern catalpa's winged seeds *come together, nearly to a point*. (See illustrations for comparison.)

BARK
The southern catalpa's scaly bark is not as deeply furrowed as the western catalpa's.

SIMILAR SPECIES
See western catalpa "SIMILAR SPECIES" section.

LOCATIONS
☐ Washington Monument grounds
☐ Quite common throughout the city in parks and around public buildings and private homes

Yellow Catalpa
or Golden Catalpa
Catalpa ovata G. Don
Bignonia Family *Bignoniaceae*

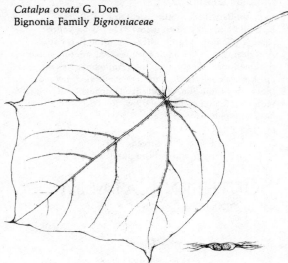

     This Asian tree, though lovely in bloom, is no match for our native American species in beauty.

NATIVE HABITAT
China. (Escaped from cultivation and naturalized from southern Ontario and Connecticut to Ohio and Maryland.)

LEAVES
Simple, opposite or whorled, deciduous. Similar to the leaves of the two native species, but often shallowly three-lobed and occasionally five-lobed. 4 - 10 in. (10 - 25.4 cm.) long and about as wide. Lobes sharply pointed; base heart-shaped, rounded, or straight across. Glabrous, or nearly so, below, except when young. Petiole 3 - 8 in. (7.5 - 20.3 cm.) long.

FLOWERS
Early June. Yellow, marked with purple and orange; in upright clusters. Except for color and size, very similar to the blossoms of the two native American species (see western catalpa color close-up). Individual blossoms up to ¾ in. (2 cm.) across.

FRUIT
Capsule looks like a string bean. Very thin, 8 - 13 in. (20 - 33 cm.) long, remaining on the tree into winter. Splits open to release small, flat seeds with fringes of soft, white hairs at either end. (Hairs do not converge at tips.)

BARK AND TWIGS
Twigs usually glabrous, similar to western catalpa, but thinner.

HABIT
Small tree with spreading branches.

SIMILAR SPECIES
Distinguished from the western (*Catalpa speciosa* Warder) and southern (*Catalpa bignonioides* Walt.) catalpas by its *yellow* flowers, usually *glabrous* and often *three-lobed* leaves, and *thinner* fruit capsules.

LOCATIONS
- ☐ U.S. Capitol, northwest grounds
- ☐ Washington Monument grounds
- ☐ Tidal Basin, south side
- ☐ Not as common in Washington as the two native American species

CHASTE-TREE
OR MONK'S PEPPER-TREE, OR HEMP-TREE, OR WILD LAVENDER
Vitex agnus-castus L.
Vervain Family *Verbenaceae*

This tall shrub or small tree is conspicuous in Washington from mid-summer until autumn with its upright clusters of blue or purple flowers. The common name, chaste-tree, stems from an ancient belief that the leaves and flowers of this plant could "cool the heat of lust."

NATIVE HABITAT
Southeastern Europe and western Asia; naturalized in the southeastern United States.

LEAVES
Opposite, deciduous, palmately compound, with a strong, spicy aroma. Five to seven lanceolate or narrowly elliptic leaflets are gray-green, 2 - 5 in. (5 - 12.6 cm.) long, with smooth or very sparsely toothed margins. Lower (and sometimes upper) surfaces of leaflets, petioles and branchlets are all covered with close, soft, grayish pubescence.

FLOWERS
Very attractive, narrowly pyramidal clusters of purple or
blue (rarely white) blossoms from *mid-summer* until
mid-autumn.

TWIGS
Four-sided.

SIMILAR SPECIES
Not likely to be confused with other species. The
combination of late-blooming flowers and opposite,
palmately compound leaves is distinctive.

LOCATIONS
□ U.S. Botanic Gardens, along Canal Street
□ U.S. Capitol grounds
□ D Street, S.E., near House Office Buildings
□ Private yards and public buildings citywide

BANANA
Musa x paradisiaca L.
Banana Family *Musaceae*

   While technically the banana is not a tree, we felt
that its presence in Washington could not go without
mention. When I moved to Washington from northern
New Hampshire I was very impressed by the fact that
there were real bananas growing in my neighborhood.
Visitors to my Capitol Hill apartment were given the full
tour: the Capitol, the Supreme Court, the Library of
Congress — and the bananas on Canal Street. These
little "trees", which are really herbaceous plants, are set
out each spring at the U.S. Botanic Gardens, the
Smithsonian National Museum of Natural History and
other locations in Washington. Before they are removed
in the fall, they produce small bunches of bananas. For
anyone who needs help identifying it, the banana plant
is illustrated .

ILLUSTRATED GLOSSARY
Text Follows on page 315

FIGURE 1
ALTERNATE LEAVES

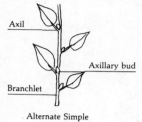

Alternate Simple

Alternate Compound

FIGURE 2
OPPOSITE LEAVES

Opposite simple

Opposite compound

Sub-opposite simple

Whorled simple

FIGURE 3
LEAVES

Simple

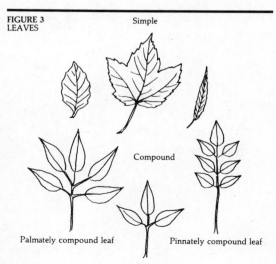

Compound

Palmately compound leaf

Pinnately compound leaf

Trifoliate leaf

FIGURE 4
PINNATELY COMPOUND LEAVES

Even-pinnately compound

Odd-pinnately compound

Bi-pinnately compound (see also Figure 6)

FIGURE 5
PARTS OF A LEAF

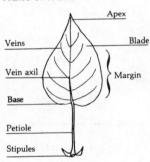

Apex

Veins   Blade

Vein axil   Margin

Base

Petiole

Stipules

Needle-like foliage

Scale-like foliage

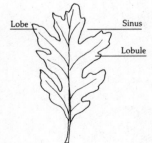

Lobe   Sinus

Lobule

Palmate venation

Pinnate venation

FIGURE 6
PARTS OF A COMPOUND LEAF

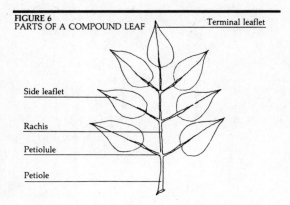

Terminal leaflet

Side leaflet

Rachis

Petiolule

Petiole

FIGURE 7
PARTS OF A FLOWER

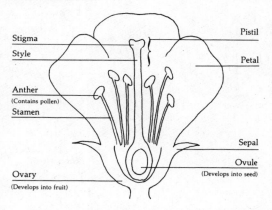

Stigma

Style

Anther
(Contains pollen)

Stamen

Ovary
(Develops into fruit)

Pistil

Petal

Sepal

Ovule
(Develops into seed)

FIGURE 8
LEAF SHAPES

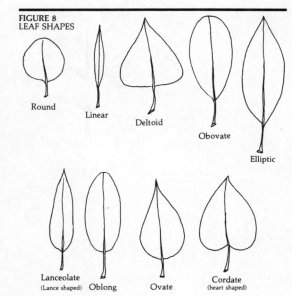

Round

Linear

Deltoid

Obovate

Elliptic

Lanceolate
(Lance shaped)

Oblong

Ovate

Cordate
(heart shaped)

FIGURE 8a
LEAF BASES

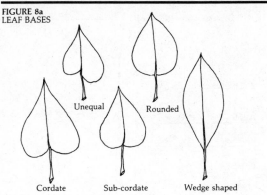

Unequal

Rounded

Cordate

Sub-cordate

Wedge shaped

FIGURE 9
LEAF MARGINS

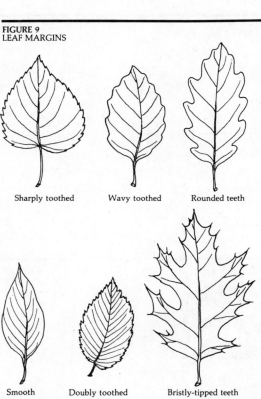

Sharply toothed

Wavy toothed

Rounded teeth

Smooth

Doubly toothed

Bristly-tipped teeth

FIGURE 10
WINTER TWIGS

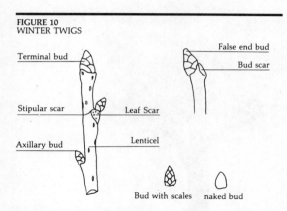

Terminal bud

False end bud

Bud scar

Stipular scar — Leaf Scar

Axillary bud — Lenticel

Bud with scales   naked bud

FIGURE 10a
TWIGS IN CROSS-SECTION

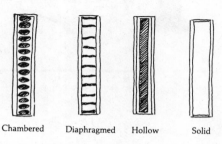

Chambered   Diaphragmed   Hollow   Solid

FIGURE 11
GROWTH HABITS OF TREES

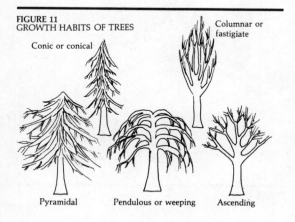

Conic or conical

Columnar or fastigiate

Pyramidal   Pendulous or weeping   Ascending

FIGURE 12
WOODY PLANTS

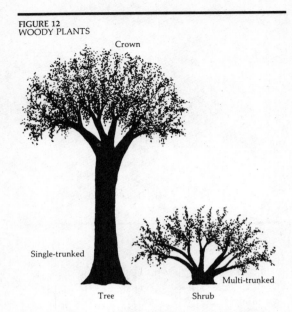

Crown

Single-trunked

Multi-trunked

Tree   Shrub

FIGURE 13

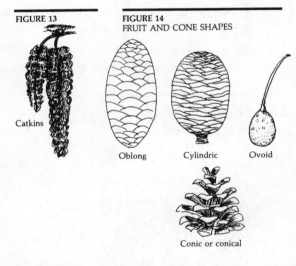

Catkins

FIGURE 14
FRUIT AND CONE SHAPES

Oblong   Cylindric   Ovoid

Conic or conical

FIGURE 15

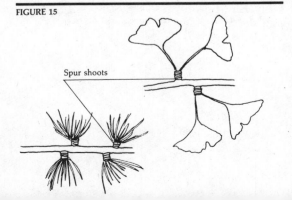

Spur shoots

Achene. A dry, one-seeded fruit that does not split open.

Aggregate. A compound fruit, developing from many parts of the same flower. (See also *multiple fruit*).

Alternate. Describes a common leaf arrangement in which the leaves are *not opposite* each other on the branchlet. (See Figure 1).

Angiosperm. Belonging to the class of plants that produce seeds *within ovaries*. (See *Gymnosperm*). Most trees of the Angiosperm class are broad-leaved.

Anther. The pollen-producing part of the stamen. (Figure 7).

Apex (plural: apices). The *tip* of a leaf blade, lobe, bud, fruit, etc. (the part farthest from the base). (See Figure 5.)

Appressed. Lying flat or close against the surface.

Arbor. Used in *City of Trees* to mean a grove of trees.

Arboreal. Pertaining to trees.

Arboretum. A place where trees are exhibited and studied. Most frequently used in *City of Trees* in reference to the United States National Arboretum in northeast Washington. May also be used informally to refer to a noteworthy collection of trees.

Aril. A seed covering. Used in *City of Trees* to describe the red berry-like covering of the yew seed.

Ascending. Pointing upward. Refers to a fairly common branching pattern (See Figure 11.)

Axil. The upper angle formed where two veins or the petiole and branchlet meet. (See Figures 1 & 5.)

Axillary bud. Bud located in the *axil* of the branchlet and petiole. (See Figures 1 & 10).

Base. The part of a leaf blade, cone or fruit that is closest to the stem or branch and farthest from the apex. (See Figures 5 & 8a.)

Berry. Technically, a simple fruit with a fleshy or pulpy ovary. In *City of Trees*, we refer to fruit that *looks* like a berry, but is technically some other type as "berry-like".

Bipinnately compound. Refers to leaves that are twice pinnately compound. (See Figure 4).

Blade. The large, flat part of the leaf (excluding the petiole). (See Figure 5).

Bonsai. A dwarfed tree or shrub trained by pruning of the roots and limbs.

Botanical. Of or pertaining to plants, including trees.

Botanist. One who specializes in the study of plants, including trees.

Botany. The biological science of plants, including trees.

Bract. A leafy plant part sometimes located below a flower or flower cluster or lower down the stem or branchlet. In some cases (for instance, the dogwoods) the bracts are showier than the flowers themselves.

Branchlet. In *City of Trees* branchlet and twig are used interchangeably to refer to the leaf-bearing part of the branch. (See Figures 1 & 10).

Bristle-tipped. Describes a lobe, tooth or apex of a leaf that comes to a thin, sharp, thread-like point.

Broad-leaved tree. Flowering, fruiting tree of the Angiosperm class.

Bud. A small protuberance on a branchlet that contains the shoot, leaf, and/or flower in embryonic condition. Buds may be *naked* or covered with *scales*. (See Figures 1 & 10). See also *end bud, false end bud, axillary bud.*

Calyx. The outer part of a flower, consisting of leafy or, rarely, petal-like parts known as sepals. (See Figure 7).

Capsule. A dry fruit, which splits open to release two or more seeds.

Catkin. A long, thin cluster of tiny flowers. (See Figure 13).

Chambered pith. The center of a twig in cross-section may be chambered, diaphragmed, hollow or solid. (See Figure 10a.)

Clone. A plant propagated from a single parent by means of grafting, cutting, layering or budding. Many cultivars are clones.

Columnar. Describes trees with narrow, upright growth habits. (See Figure 11.)

Common name. The name or names by which a tree is known to lay people. (Red oak, sugar maple, etc.) Common names often differ from region to region and are difficult to translate into other languages. Therefore, botanists use Latin names. Latin is the universal language of the botanical community. In *City of Trees* the common name or names for the tree are presented in large type, followed by the Latin names in smaller italicized type.

Compound fruit. A fruit with more than one ovary.

Compound leaf. A leaf that is divided into three or more leaflets. (See Figures 3 & 4.)

Cone. The woody, scaly structure produced by most conifers, that bears the "naked" seeds.

Conic or Conical. Cone-shaped. Pointed at one end, evenly spreading outward. (See Figures 11 & 14.)

Conifer. Usually cone-producing trees of the Gymnosperm class. Seeds are "naked" (not enclosed in ovaries).

Cordate. Heart-shaped. May refer to the entire leaf blade or just the base. (See Figures 8 & 8a.)

Corky wings. Flat, woody, "wing-like" projections on the branches of some trees and shrubs.

Crown. The full, top part of a tree or shrub formed by the spreading branches. (See Figure 12.)

Cultivar. A plant variety derived by horticultural means and not occurring naturally. The cultivar name follows the species name of the plant and is presented in single quotes.

Cultivated. Describes plants, including trees, that are planted and nurtured by humans.

Cylindric. Shaped like a cylinder. (See Figure 14.)

Deciduous. Describes trees and shrubs that shed their leaves in autumn. (See evergreen).

Deltoid. Triangular. (See Figure 8.)

Diaphragmed. The center of a twig in cross-section may be diaphragmed, chambered, solid, or hollow. (See Figure 10a.)

Dimorphic. Of two types. Evergreen trees with dimorphic foliage have leaves that are scale-like and leaves that are needle-like on the same tree.

Dioecious. Male and female flowers are produced on separate trees of the same species.

Downy. Covered with fine, soft hairs.

Drupe. A fleshy fruit with a bony, single-seeded center. Peaches are drupes.

Elliptic. About twice as long as broad and widest in the middle. Describes a common leaf shape. (See Figure 8.)

End bud. (Also called terminal bud). Bud found at the precise end of the twig. (See Figure 10.) In some species, a "false end bud" develops. (See *false end bud*, below.)

Erect. Standing straight up; the opposite of pendulous.

Even-pinnately compound. A pinnately compound leaf with an even number of leaflets. (See Figure 4.)

Evergreen. Describes trees and shrubs that retain their leaves throughout the year. (See *deciduous*.)

Exotic. Not native to North America. Exotic trees in Washington come from Asia, Europe and Africa.

False end bud. Bud that forms at or near the end of the twig in the absence of a true end bud. The false end bud can be distinguished from the true end bud by the presence of an adjacent "bud scar". (See Figure 10.)

Family. The Gymnosperm and Angiosperm classes are divided into plant families, which are sub-divided into genera and individual species.

Fastigiate. A growth habit in which the branches of a tree or shrub stand erect and close together. (See Figure 11.)

Fissured. Vertically grooved; describes bark.

Flower. The reproductive part of a plant, which usually includes petals. (See Figure 7.)

Foliage. Leaves (including those that are needle-like or scale-like).

Follicle. A dry fruit that splits along only one seam to release seeds. (See also *legume*.)

Fruit. The ripened ovaries of a seed-bearing plant, containing the seeds. May be dry or fleshy.

Genus. *(Plural: genera.)* Plant families are sub-divided into genera and then individual species.

Glabrous. Hairless. Parts of trees are either *glabrous* or *pubescent*. Some leaves are pubescent in spring, then become glabrous at maturity.

Gland. Small structure that may secrete (sometimes sticky) liquid. Some leaves have small glands on their blades or petioles.

Glandular. Having small glands, sometimes visible only with a hand lens.

Glaucous. Chalky; covered with a white or bluish bloom.

Glossy. Shiny.

Gymnosperm. Belonging to the class of plants more commonly known as conifers. Gymnosperm seeds are "naked" (not protected by ovaries). They are usually borne beneath woody cone scales. Gymnosperm foliage is typically needle-like or scale-like. (See Angiosperm.)

Habit or growth habit. The overall shape or silhouette of a tree. (See Figure 11.)

Hardy. Able to survive in a particular climate. A plant is not "hardy" in Washington if it cannot survive the cold of winter or the heat of summer.

Herbaceous. Describes plants that *do not have woody stems.* (Includes grasses, wildflowers, garden flowers, herbs, etc.)

Herbarium. A plant library containing dried plants labeled and organized for scientific study.

Horticulture. The science of cultivated plants, particularly those used for ornament.

Horticulturist. One trained in the science of horticulture.

Hybrid. A cross between unlike parents. Most of the hybrids described in *City of Trees* are the result of crosses between two species of the same genera.

Lanceolate. Lance-shaped. A common leaf shape. (See Figure 8.)

Lateral bud. Synonymous with axillary bud. (See Figure 10.)

Latin name. The scientific name of a plant family, genus, or species. The Latin name is given in italics after the common name.

Leaf. The food-producing part of the plant. On broad-leaved trees may be simple or compound. On conifers, typically needle-like or scale-like. (See Figure 5.)

Leaf base. The portion of a leaf closest to the petiole (See Figures 5 & 8a.)

Leaf blade. The broad, flat portion of a leaf, excluding the petiole. (See Figure 5.)

Leaf margin. The *edge* of a leaf. May be smooth or toothed. (See Figures 5 & 9.)

Leaf scar. The "scar" on the branchlet which remains when the leaf falls off the tree. In winter, the shape of a leaf scar can be used to help identify the tree. (See Figure 10.)

Leaflet. A leaf-like portion of a compound leaf (See Figures 3 & 6.)

Legume. A pod, which splits along two sides to release seeds. Members of the pea family are leguminous.

Lenticel. Variously shaped markings on the bark or branchlets of trees or shrubs. Lenticels serve as pores, allowing gases to pass in and out of the tree's interior.

Lobe. A portion of a leaf blade which may be rounded or pointed and is separated from other lobes by deep or shallow sinuses. (See Figure 5.)

Lobule. A small lobe, which is often part of a larger lobe. (See Figure 5.)

Margin. The edge of a leaf. May be smooth or toothed. (See Figures 5 & 9).

Monotypic. The sole member of its group, such as the only species of a genus and family.

Multiple fruit. A compound fruit, which develops from many different flowers. (See aggregate fruit.)

Naked bud. A bud with no scales. (See Figure 10.)

Native. Growing in the wild; indigenous.

Native Habitat. The region where a plant occurs naturally.

Naturalized. Escaped from cultivation and established as an independent population in the wild. Some Asian species, for instance, have become naturalized in the eastern United States.

Needle-like. Describes the needle-shaped foliage of many conifers (such as pines and spruces).

Nut. A hard, one-seeded fruit—such as an acorn—that does not split open.

Nut-like. Resembling a nut, but not fitting the technical description.

Oblong. About three times as long as wide, with nearly parallel sides. (See Figures 8 & 14.)

Obovate. Inversely ovate. (See Figure 8.)

Odd-pinnately compound. A pinnately compound leaf with an odd number of leaflets. (See Figure 4.)

Opposite. Describes leaves arranged opposite each other on the branchlet. Also includes whorled and sub-opposite leaf arrangements. (See Figure 2).

Ovary. The part of the pistil which develops into the fruit and contains the seeds. (See Figure 7.)

Ovate. Egg-shaped. A common leaf shape. (See Figure 8.)

Ovoid. Egg-shaped (usually refers to fruit or cone). (See Figure 14.)

Ovule. A plant's "egg", contained in the ovary, which—after fertilization—develops into the seed. (See Figure 7.)

Palmate. (See *palmate venation* and *palmately compound*).

Palmate venation. Leaf veins arranged in a pattern shaped like an open hand. (See Figure 5.)

Palmately compound. Leaflets arranged in a pattern shaped like an open hand. (See Figure 3 and *pinnately compound*).

Peltate. In *City of Trees* describes cone scales that are attached at the *center* rather than the base of the cone.

Pendulous. Hanging. Describes hanging branches, fruit, etc. (See Figure 11.)

Perfect Flower. A flower that possesses both male and female parts.

Petals. Flower parts that surround the center of the blossom. Petals are usually colored, and are often fragrant. Their primary function is to attract insects in order to facilitate fertilization. (See Figure 7.)

Petiole. The leafstalk. (See also *petiolule*, *rachis*, and Figures 5 & 6.)

Petiolule. The stalk of a leaflet that attaches to the petiole or rachis. (See Figure 6.)

Pinnate. (See *pinnate venation* and *pinnately compound*.)

Pinnate venation. Leaf veins arranged in a feather-like pattern. (See Figure 5.)

Pinnately compound. Leaflets arranged in a feather-like pattern. (See Figures 3 & 4.)

Pistil. The female part of the flower, including the ovary, the stigma and the style. (See Figure 7.)

Pith. The inner core of a twig. In order to examine the pith, cut the twig in half *lengthwise* with a sharp knife. The pith may be hollow, solid, chambered or diaphragmed. (See Figure 10a.)

Pod. A dry fruit that splits open to release seeds. (See *legume*.)

Pollen. Male seed (usually a fine powder) produced within the anther of a flower. (See Figure 7.)

Pome. A fleshy fruit, like the apple or pear, that contains several seeds. (See also *drupe*.)

Pubescent. Covered with hair. Parts of trees are either *glabrous* (without hair) or pubescent. Some species bear leaves that are pubescent in the spring, becoming glabrous in the summer or fall. Pubescence may be very obvious—as when the entire lower surface of a leaf blade is covered with hair—or it may only be visible with a hand lens. Frequently, hairs are borne only in the axils of leaf veins.

Pyramidal. Shaped like a pyramid. Describes a common growth habit of trees. (See Figure 11.)

Rachis. A term used in *City of Trees* to describe the portion of the petiole on a compound leaf that bears the leaflets. (See *petiole, petiolule* and Figure 6.)

Radiate. To spread outward from a common point.

Resinous. Containing or covered with resin, a usually sticky liquid exuded by some trees.

Samara. A dry, flattened fruit that doesn't split open. Maples and elms bear samaras.

Scales. Most often used in *City of Trees* to describe the woody "leaves" of cones. Also, describes broken sections of outer bark.

Scaly. Most often used to descibe bark that is broken into many small, flaky sections.

Seed. The fertilized, mature ovule. (See Figure 7.)

Seedling. A tree, shrub or herbaceous plant grown from seed (as opposed to grafting or other horticultural means).

Sepal. A portion of the calyx or outer part of the flower. Most flowers have a circle of *petals* (which are usually brightly colored) surrounded by a smaller, inconspicuous circle of sepals. Sepals are usually leafy and green, but in some cases the sepals are petal-like. (See Figure 7.)

Sessile. Having no petiole or stalk.

Shoot. Used in *City of Trees* to describe the newest growth at the end of a branchlet.

Shrub. A multi-trunked woody plant that usually stands no higher than 20 feet (about 5½ meters). (Figure 12.)

Silky. Covered with fine, soft hairs.

Simple fruit. Fruit that contains a single ovary.

Simple leaf. A leaf that is not divided into leaflets. (See Figures 1 & 2).

Sinus. The recess between the lobes of a leaf. (See Figure 5.)

Smooth margin. A leaf margin with no teeth. (See Figure 9.)

Species. An individual member of a genus. (May be divided into varieties or cultivars.)

Spine. A sharply pointed woody projection. Used synonymously with thorn in *City of Trees.*

Spur shoot. A short branchlet bearing clusters of leaves. (See Figure 15.)

Stamen. The male part of the flower, which includes the pollen-bearing anther. (See Figure 7.)

Stigma. The part of the style that receives pollen from the anther. (See Figure 7.)

Stipular scar. The scar left on a twig where a stipule has fallen off. (See Figure 10.)

Stipule. A leaf-like appendage at the base of the petiole. Not present on all species. (See Figure 5.)

Style. The long portion of the pistil between the stigma and the ovary.

Subcordate. Shallowly heart-shaped. Describes the leaf base (See Figure 8a.)

Sub-opposite. Describes a leaf arrangement in which the leaves are *nearly* opposite on the branchlet. (See Figure 2.)

Sucker. A sprout arising from the roots of the tree. Some species are more apt to produce suckers than others.

Terminal bud. The bud found at the end of the twig. (Also called *end bud*.) (See Figure 10.)

Terminal leaflet. The leaflet located at the apex of a pinnately compound leaf. When the terminal leaflet is present, the leaf is "odd-pinnately compound".(Figures 4 & 6.)

Toothed. Describes a leaf margin with "teeth". (See Figure 9.)

Tree. A usually single-trunked woody plant that stands more than 20 feet (about 5½ meters) high. (See Figure 12.)

Trifoliate. Describes a compound leaf with three leaflets. (See Figure 3.)

Trunk. The main stem of a tree which connects the roots with the crown.

Twig. Used synonymously with branchlet to refer to the leaf-bearing part of the branch. Often used to describe the branchlet in winter. (See Figures 1 & 10.)

Unequal base. Describes the leaf base in which the two sides of the base do not attach to the petiole at opposite places. (See Figure 8a.)

Unisexual. Of one sex only. Some trees bear separate male and female flowers rather than "perfect flowers". (See also *perfect flowers*.)

Variety. A naturally occurring variance which is not considered a separate species and yet has characteristics that differ from those typical of the species.

Veins. The slender vascular bundles which transport sap through the leaf. (See Figure 5.)

Venation. Arrangement of the veins in a leaf. (See Figure 5.)

Wavy-toothed margin. A leaf margin with undulating "teeth". (See Figure 9.)

Wedge-shaped. Shaped like the narrow end of a piece of pie. Describes the leaf base. (See Figure 8a.)

Weeping. Describes the crown of a tree in which the branches are pendulous. (See Figure 11.)

Whorled. A leaf arrangement in which three or more leaves are attached to the branchlet opposite one another. (See Figure 2.)

Wing. A thin, woody appendage on the branches of some woody plants.

Winter buds. Buds that develop during the summer or fall and stay on the tree throughout the winter until they unfurl the following spring.

Woody plant. A tree or shrub.

Woolly. Covered with short, soft hairs.

BLOOMING DATES

FLOWERING TREES IN BLOOM IN MARCH

Carolina Laurelcherry   *Prunus caroliniana*
Cornelian Cherry   *Cornus mas*
Japanese Flowering Cherry Trees:
  Some commonly planted Japanese Flowering
    Cherries:
  Akebono *   *Prunus* x *yedoensis* 'Akebono'
  Fall-Blooming Cherry   *Prunus subhirtella*
    'Autumnalis'
  Weeping Cherry* (including pink, white and
    double-blossomed forms)   *Prunus
    subhirtella pendula*
  Yoshino or Somei-Yoshino*   *Prunus* x
    yedoensis
Magnolia, Kobus   *Magnolia kobus*
Magnolia, Saucer   *Magnolia* x *soulangeana*
Magnolia, Star   *Magnolia stellata*
Magnolia, Yulan   *Magnolia denudata*
    (*Magnolia heptapeta*)
Peach   *Prunus persica*
Pear
  Some commonly planted Pears:
  Bradford   *Pyrus calleryana* 'Bradford'
  Callery   *Pyrus calleryana*
  Common   *Pyrus communis*
Plum, Purple-Leaved or Pissard   *Prunus
  cerasifera* 'Atropurpurea'
Serviceberry, Shadblow or Shadbush
    Amelanchier arborea

FLOWERING TREES IN BLOOM IN APRIL

Bradford Pear *Pyrus calleryana* 'Bradford'
Buckeye, Hybrid   *Aesculus* x *hybrida*
Buckeye, Ohio   *Aesculus glabra*
Buckeye, Red   *Aesculus pavia*
Buckeye, Sweet or Yellow   *Aesculus octandra*
Carolina Silverbell *Halesia carolina*
Cornelian Cherry   *Cornus mas*
Crabapples   *Malus* sp.
Dogwood, Flowering   *Cornus florida*
European Mountain-Ash (Rowan Tree)
    Sorbus aucuparia
Golden Chain Tree   *Laburnum anagyroides*
Hawthorns   *Crataegus* sp.

*Trees planted in West and East Potomac
Parks (Tidal Basin and Hains Point).

Horse-Chestnut,   Common *Aesculus hippocastanum*

Horse-Chestnut,   Red *Aesculus* x *carnea*

Japanese Flowering Cherry Trees:

   Akebono   *Prunus* x *yedoensis* 'Akebono'*

   Gyoiko (RARE)   *Prunus serrulata* 'Gyoiko'

   Fall-Blooming Cherry   *Prunus subhirtella* 'Autumnalis' (Also Blooms in November-December)

   Kwanzan   *Prunus serrulata* 'Kwanzan'*

   Weeping Cherry   *Prunus subhirtella pendula* *

   Yoshino or Somei-Yoshino   *Prunus* x *yedoensis*.*

Laburnum, Common   (See Golden Chain Tree)

Laburnum, Voss's   *Laburnum* x *waterei*

Magnolia, Kobus   *Magnolia kobus*

Magnolia, Lily   *Magnolia liliflora* (*Magnolia quinquepeta*)

Magnolia, Saucer   *Magnolia* x *soulangeana*

Magnolia, Star   *Magnolia stellata*

Magnolia, Umbrella   *Magnolia tripetala*

Magnolia, Yulan   *Magnolia denudata* (*Magnolia heptapeta*)

Paulownia or Princess Tree   *Paulownia tomentosa*

Peach   *Prunus persica*

Pear   *Pyrus* sp.

Plum, Purple-Leaved or Pissard   *Prunus cerasifera* 'Atropurpurea'

Redbud   *Cercis canadensis*

Redbud, Chinese   *Cercis chinensis*

Shadbush, Shadblow or Serviceberry   *Amelanchier arborea*

Spice-Bush   *Lindera benzoin*

Tamarisks   *Tamarix* sp.

Trifoliate Orange   *Poncirus trifoliata*

Viburnum species   *Viburnum* sp.

FLOWERING TREES IN BLOOM IN MAY

Black Locust (False Acacia)   *Robinia pseudoacacia*

Buckeye, Hybrid   *Aesculus* x *hybrida*

Buckeye, Ohio   *Aesculus glabra*

Buckeye, Red   *Aesculus pavia*

Buckeye, Sweet (Yellow)   *Aesculus octandra*

Carolina Silverbell   *Halesia carolina*

Catalpa, Western (Northern)   *Catalpa speciosa*

Catalpa, Yellow (Golden)   *Catalpa ovata*

Cherry, Black   *Prunus serotina*

Chinese Chestnut   *Castanea mollissima*

Chokecherry   *Prunus virginiana*

*Trees planted in West and East Potomac Parks (Tidal Basin and Hains Point).

Crabapples, Flowering   *Malus* sp.
  Some commonly planted Flowering Crabapples:
  Carmine   *M.* x *atrosanguinea*
  Dorothea   *M.* x 'Dorothea'
  Hopa   *M.* x 'Hopa'
  Japanese Flowering   *M. floribunda*
  Katherine   *M.* x 'Katherine'
  Purple   *M.* x *purpurea*
  Siberian   *M. baccata*
  Southern   *M. angustifolia (Pyrus angustifolia)*

Dogwood, Flowering   *Cornus florida*
  (including Double-Flowering Dogwood *C. florida* 'Pluribracteata' and Pink and Red Flowering Dogwoods *C. florida* f. *rubra*)

Dogwood, Kousa (Japanese)   *Cornus kousa*

European Mountain-Ash (Rowan Tree)
  Sorbus aucuparia

European Smoke-Tree   *Cotinus coggygria*

Fragrant Snowbell (Bigleaf Storax)
  Styrax obassia

Fringe-Tree   *Chionanthus virginicus*

Fringe-Tree, Asian   *Chionanthus retusus*

Golden Chain Tree (Common Laburnum)
  Laburnum anagyroides

Hawthorn   *Crataegus* sp.
  Some commonly planted Hawthorns:
  Cockspur Thorn   *C. crus-galli*
  English May   *C. oxyacantha*
  Paul's Scarlet   *C. oxyacantha* 'Paul's Scarlet'
  Washington Thorn   *C. phaenopyrum*

Honey Locust   *Gleditsia triacanthos*

Horse-Chestnut, Common   *Aesculus hippocastanum*

Horse-Chestnut, Red   *Aesculus* x *carnea*

Japanese Snowbell   *Styrax japonica*

Kentucky Coffee-Tree   *Gymnocladus dioicus*

Lime (see Lindens)

Linden, European   *Tilia* x *europaea*

Linden, Large-Leafed   *Tilia platyphyllos*

Linden, Silver   *Tilia tomentosa*

Linden, Small-Leafed   *Tilia cordata*

Magnolia, Bigleaf   *Magnolia macrophylla*

Magnolia, Cucumber (Cucumber-Tree)
  Magnolia acuminata

Magnolia, Southern (Bull-Bay or Evergreen)
  Magnolia grandiflora

Magnolia, Sweetbay   *Magnolia virginiana*

Magnolia, Umbrella   *Magnolia tripetala*

Paulownia (Royal Paulownia, Princess Tree)
  Paulownia tomentosa

Redbud   *Cercis canadensis*

Redbud, Chinese   *Cercis chinensis*

Spice-Bush   *Lindera benzoin*

Trifoliate Orange   *Poncirus trifoliata*

Tulip Poplar (Yellow Poplar, Tulip-Tree)
  Liriodendron tulipifera

Voss's Laburnum   *Laburnum* x *waterei*

Yellowwood   *Cladrastis kentukea*
  (*Cladrastis lutea*)

FLOWERING TREES IN BLOOM IN JUNE

Catalpa, Common   *Catalpa bignonioides*
Catalpa, Western (Northern)   *Catalpa speciosa*
Catalpa, Yellow (Golden)   *Catalpa ovata*
Chaste-Tree   *Vitex agnus-castus*
Chinese Chestnut   *Castanea mollissima*
European Mountain-Ash (Rowan Tree)
     Sorbus aucuparia
European Smoke-Tree   *Cotinus coggygria*
Golden Rain Tree   *Koelreuteria paniculata*
Japanese Raisin Tree   *Hovenia dulcis*
Kousa Dogwood (Japanese)   *Cornus kousa*
Lime (see Linden)
Linden, American   *Tilia americana*
Linden, European   *Tilia x europaea*
Linden, Large-Leafed   *Tilia platyphyllos*
Linden, Silver   *Tilia tomentosa*
Linden, Small-Leafed   *Tilia cordata*
Magnolia, Bigleaf   *Magnolia macrophylla*
Magnolia, Southern (Bull-Bay or Evergreen)
     Magnolia grandiflora
Magnolia, Sweetbay   *Magnolia virginiana*
Mimosa (Silk-Tree)   *Albizia julibrissin*

FLOWERING TREES IN BLOOM IN JULY

Catalpa, Common   *Catalpa bignonioides*
Chaste-Tree   *Vitex agnus-castus*
Chinese Chestnut   *Castanea mollissima*
Crape-Myrtle   *Lagerstroemia indica*
European Smoke-Tree   *Cotinus coggygria*
Golden Rain Tree   *Koelreuteria paniculata*
Japanese Pagoda Tree (Chinese Scholar Tree)
     Sophora japonica
Japanese Raisin Tree   *Hovenia dulcis*
Linden, American   *Tilia americana*
Magnolia, Southern (Bull-Bay or Evergreen)
     Magnolia grandiflora
Magnolia, Sweetbay   *Magnolia virginiana*
Mimosa (Silk-Tree)   *Albizia julibrissin*
Rose-of-Sharon   *Hibiscus syriacus*

FLOWERING TREES IN BLOOM IN AUGUST

Chaste-Tree   *Vitex agnus-castus*
Crape-Myrtle   *Lagerstroemia indica*
Franklin Tree   *Franklinia alatamaha*
Japanese Pagoda Tree (Chinese Scholar Tree)
   Sophora japonica
Magnolia, Southern (Bull-Bay or Evergreen)
   Magnolia grandiflora
Mimosa (Silk-Tree)   *Albizia julibrissin*
Rose-of-Sharon   *Hibiscus syriacus*

FLOWERING TREES IN BLOOM IN SEPTEMBER

Crape-Myrtle   *Lagerstroemia indica*
Franklin Tree   *Franklinia alatamaha*
Japanese Pagoda Tree (Chinese Scholar Tree)
   Sophora japonica
Rose-of-Sharon   *Hibiscus syriacus*

TREES BEARING CONSPICUOUS FALL FRUITS IN WASHINGTON, D.C.:

Black Locust   *Robinia pseudoacacia*
Buckeyes and Horse-Chestnuts   *Aesculus* sp.
Catalpas   *Catalpa* sp.
Chinese Chestnut   *Castanea mollissima*
Crabapples   *Malus* sp.
Dogwoods   *Cornus* sp.
European Filbert   *Corylus avellana*
Fig-Tree   *Ficus carica*
Golden Rain Tree   *Koelreuteria paniculata*
Hackberries   *Celtis* sp.
Hawthorns   *Crataegus* sp.
Hickories   *Carya* sp.
Hollies   *Ilex* sp.
Honey Locust   *Gleditsia triacanthos*
Japanese Pagoda Tree   *Sophora japonica*
Kentucky Coffee-Tree   *Gymnocladus dioicus*
Magnolias   *Magnolia* sp.
Oaks   *Quercus* sp.
Osage-Orange   *Maclura pomifera*
Paulownia   *Paulownia tomentosa*
Persimmons   *Diospyros* sp.
Planes (Sycamore)   *Platanus* sp.
Sweetgum   *Liquidambar styraciflua*

FLOWERING TREES IN BLOOM IN OCTOBER

Franklin Tree   *Franklinia alatamaha*
Osmanthus   *Osmanthus heterophyllus*
Rose-of-Sharon   *Hibiscus syriacus*
Witch-Hazel, Common   *Hamamelis virginiana*

OCTOBER FALL COLOR IN WASHINGTON, D.C.

American Beech *Fagus grandifolia*
Ashes *Fraxinus* sp.
Buckeyes, Horse-Chestnuts *Aesculus* sp.
Dogwoods *Cornus* sp.
Elms *Ulmus* sp.
Hickories *Carya* sp.
Maples (particularly the Sugar Maple)
    Acer sp.
Oaks *Quercus* sp.
Sorrel Tree (Sourwood) *Oxydendrum
    arboreum*
Sweetgum *Liquidambar styraciflua*
Tupelo *Nyssa sylvatica*
Zelkovas *Zelkova* sp.

FLOWERING TREES IN BLOOM IN NOVEMBER

Fall-Blooming Cherry Tree *Prunus
    subhirtella* 'Autumnalis'
Osmanthus *Osmanthus heterophyllus*
Witch-Hazel, Common *Hamamelis virginiana*

NOVEMBER FALL COLOR IN WASHINGTON, D.C.

Bradford Pear *Pyrus calleryana* 'Bradford'
European Beech *Fagus sylvatica*
Ginkgo *Ginkgo biloba*
Maples (particularly Japanese, Red and
    Norway Maples) *Acer* sp.
Oaks *Quercus* sp.
Sweetgum *Liquidambar styraciflua*

FLOWERING TREES IN BLOOM IN DECEMBER

Fall-Blooming Cherry Tree *Prunus
    subhirtella* 'Autumnalis'
Witch-Hazel, Common *Hamamelis virginiana*

CONSPICUOUS WINTER FRUIT IN WASHINGTON, D.C.

Catalpas *Catalpa* sp.
Hawthorns *Crataegus* sp.
Hollies *Ilex* sp.
Kentucky Coffee-Tree *Gymnocladus dioicus*
Paulownia *Paulownia tomentosa*
Planes (Sycamore) *Platanus* sp.
Tulip Poplar *Liriodendron tulipifera*

SELECTED BIBLIOGRAPHY

Aikman, Lonnelle. *The Living White House* (revised edition). Washington, D.C.: White House Historical Association (with the cooperation of the National Geographic Society), (1966, 1967, 1970, 1973, 1975) 1978.

Andresen, John W. "The Greening of Urban America", *American Forests Magazine*, vol. 84, no. 11. Washington, D.C.: American Forestry Association, November 1978.

Ayensu, Edward S. and DeFilipps, Robert A. *Endangered and Threatened Plants of the United States.* Washington, D.C.: Smithsonian Institution and World Wildlife Fund, Inc., 1978.

Bean, W.J. *Trees and Shrubs Hardy in the British Isles.* London: J. Murray, 1970.

Cable, Mary. *The Avenue of the Presidents.* Boston: Houghton Mifflin Company, 1969.

Chadbund, Geoffrey. *Flowering Cherries.* London: Collins, 1972.

Clepper, Henry. "George Washington's Trees". *American Forests Magazine, vol. 82, no. 8. Washington, D.C.: The American Forestry Association, August, 1976.*

The Committee for a More Beautiful Capital. Beautification Summary. Washington, D.C.: 1965-1968.

Crockett, James Underwood and the Editors of Time-Life Books. *Flowering Shrubs.* Alexandria, Virginia: Time-Life Books, (1972) 1977.

Eberlein, Harold Donaldson and Hubbard, Cortlandt Van Dyke. *Historic Houses of Georgetown and Washington City.* Richmond: Dietz Press, Inc., 1958.

"Endangered and Threatened Plants". *Federal Register,* vol. 43, no. 238, December 11, 1978.

Fairchild, David Grandison. *Exploring for Plants.* New York: The MacMillan Company, 1931.

Federal Writers' Program of the Work Projects Administration. *Washington, D.C., a Guide to the Nation's Capital* (new revised edition, edited by Randall Bond Truett). New York: Hastings House Publishers, 1968.

Fernow, B.E. and Sudworth, George B. *Trees of Washington, D.C.* Washington, D.C.: printed by Bell Lithographing Company, 1891.

"5000 Brave Rain to See Crab Apple Blossom Parade". Washington *Post*, April 19, 1953.

"General Hains". Washington *Star*, April 13, 1946.

Gleason, Henry A. *The New Britton and Brown Illustrated Flora of the Northeastern United States and Adjacent Canada,* vols. 1, 2 &3. New York Botanical Garden (printed by Lancaster Press, Inc., Lancaster, Pa.), (1952) 1958.

Green, Constance McGlaughlin. *Washington: Village and Capital, 1800-1878.* Princeton, N.J.: Princeton University Press, 1962.

Gurney, Gene and Wise, Harold. *The Official Washington, D.C. Directory.* New York: Crown Publishers, Inc., 1977.

Hermann, Frederick J. *A Checklist of Plants in the Washington-Baltimore Area.* Washington, D.C.: Smithsonian Institution, 1946.

Hillier and Sons, *Hilliers' Manual of Trees and Shrubs.* Newport, Isle of Wight, England: Yelf Brothers Limited (1971, 1972, 1973) 1974.

Hitchcock, A.S. and Standley, Paul C. *Flora of the District of Columbia and Vicinity.* Washington, D.C.: Government Printing Office, 1919.

Jefferson, Roland M. and Kay Kazue Wain. *The Nomenclature of Cultivated Japanese Flowering Cherries* (Prunus): *The Sato-zakura Group.* National Arboretum contribution no. 5, United States Department of Agriculture, 1984.

Jefferson, Roland M. and Fusonie, Alan E. *The Japanese Flowering Cherry Trees of Washington, D.C.* Washington, D.C.: National Arboretum contribution no. 4, United States Department of Agriculture, 1977.

Jefferson, Roland M. *History, Progeny, and Locations of Crabapples of Documented Authentic Origin.* Washington, D.C.: National Arboretum contribution no. 2, United States Department of Agriculture, 1970.

Johnson, Hugh. *The International Book of Trees.* New York: Simon and Schuster, 1973.

Judge, Joseph. "New Grandeur for Flowering Washington". National Geographic, April 1967.

Kauffman, Erle. *Trees of Washington, The Man - The City.* Washington, D.C.: The Outdoor Press, 1932.

Kite, Elizabeth S. *L'Enfant and Washington.* New York: Arno Press and the New York *Times,* 1970.

Lanham, Clifford. *The Tree System of Washington.* Washington, D.C.: Judd & Detweiler, Inc., 1926.

Lewis, Pauline. "In Spring in the Capital, Fancies Turn to the Arboretum". New York *Times,* Sunday, May 14, 1978.

Lewis, Taylor, Jr. and Young, Joanne. *Washington's Mount Vernon.* New York: Holt, Rinehart and Winston, 1973.

Li, Hui-Lin. "The Discovery and Cultivation of Metasequoia". Morris Arboretum *Bulletin,* December 1957.

Li, Hui-Lin. *The Origin and Cultivation of Shade and Ornamental Trees.* Philadelphia: University of Pennsylvania Press, 1963.

"Lindens Stretch Seven Miles on Famous Avenue in Capital", Washington *Star,* August 12, 1923.

Little, Elbert L. *Sixty Trees from Foreign Lands.* Washington, D.C.: United States Department of Agriculture, 1961.

McAtee, Waldo Lee. *A Sketch of the Natural History of the District of Columbia.* Washington, D.C.: H.L. & J.B. McQueen, Inc., 1918.

Masson, Georgina. *Dumbarton Oaks, A Guide to the Gardens.* Washington, D.C.: Trustees for Harvard University, 1968.

Mattoon, Wilbur and Alburtis, Susan. *Trees of the District of Columbia* Including Some Foreign Trees.

Washington, D.C.: American Forestry Association, 1926.

Maury, William M. *Washington, D.C. Past and Present, The Guide to the Nation's Capital.* New York: CBS Publications, in cooperation with the United States Capitol Historical Society, 1975.

Mazzeo, Peter M. *Trees of Shenandoah National Park.* Luray, Virginia: The Shenandoah Natural History Association, Inc., (1967) 1979.

Mitchell, Alan. *A Field Guide to the Trees of Britain and Northern Europe.* Boston: Houghton Mifflin Company, 1974.

Mitchell, Henry. "Georgetown Gardens". The Washington *Post,* April 17, 1977.

Mount Vernon Ladies' Association of the Union, Mount Vernon, Virginia. *Mount Vernon, An Illustrated Handbook.* Washington, D.C.: printed by Judd & Detweiler, Inc., 1974.

National Register of Historic Places Inventory—Nomination Form for Federal Properties (East and West Potomac Parks). Washington, D.C.: United States Department of the Interior, November 30, 1973.

O'Hara, Mike. "Trees of Capitol Hill". *American Forests Magazine,* vol. 82, no. 8. Washington, D.C.: The American Forestry Association, August 1976. Huyck, Dorothy Boyle. "Washington—City of Trees", *American Forests Magazine,* vol. 80, no. 3. Washington, D.C.: The American Forestry Association, March 1974.

Ohwi, Jisaburo. *Flora of Japan.* Washington, D.C.: Smithsonian Institution edition, edited by Frederick G. Meyer and Egbert H. Walker, 1965.

Olszewski, George J. *History of the Mall, Washington, D.C.* Washington, D.C.: National Park Service, U.S. Department of the Interior, 1970.

Olszewski, George J. *The President's Park South.* Washington, D.C.: Office of History and Historic Architecture, U.S. Department of the Interior, 1970.

Pardo, Richard. "Our National Bonsai Collection". *American Forests Magazine,* vol. 83, no. 12. Washington, D.C.: American Forestry Association, December 1977.

Pariser, Ursula R. and Beatty, Noelle Blackmer. The Dumbarton Oaks Gardens, Their History, Design and Ornaments. Washington, D.C.: Trustees for Harvard University (distributed by Acropolis Books Ltd.), 1978.

Petrides, George A. *A Field Guide to Trees and Shrubs.* Boston: Houghton Mifflin Company, (1958) 1972.

Phillips, Roger. *A Photographic Guide to More than 500 Trees of North America and Europe.* New York: Random House, 1978.

Preston, Dickson J. "The Rediscovery of Betula Uber". *American Forests Magazine,* vol. 82, no. 8. Washington, D.C.: The American Forestry Association, August 1976.

Preston, Richard J. *North American Trees.* Iowa State University Press (third edition), 1976.

Princeton Nurseries Wholesale Price List. Princeton, N.J.: Fall, 1974.

Randall, Charles Edgar and Clepper, Henry. *Famous and Historic Trees*. Washington, D.C.: American Forestry Association, 1976.

Reeves, Craven. Landscape Restoration, Frederick Douglass Home (Plans and Supplementary Report and drawing no. 872/80, 001). Washington, D.C.: United States Department of the Interior, 1976.

Rehder, Alfred. *Manual of Cultivated Trees and Shrubs Hardy in North America*. New York: MacMillan Publishing Company, Inc., (1927) 1940.

Royal Horticultural Society, The. *Supplement to the Dictionary of Gardening*, edited by Patrick M. Synge, M.A., F.L.S. Oxford at the Clarendon Press, 1956.

Russell, Paul. *The Oriental Flowering Cherries*. Washington, D.C.: United States Department of Agriculture, 1934.

Sargent, Charles Sprague. *The Trees at Mount Vernon*, Report to the Council of the Mount Vernon Ladies' Association of the Union, 1926.

Shannon, J.H. "The Rambler". Washington *Star* columns appearing from 1915 to 1924.

Sheng, C.K. "Introduction of North American Trees into China". *Arnoldiana*, vol. 39, no. 4, July/August 1979.

Sites, Maud Kay. *The Japanese Cherry Trees*. Baltimore: Norman T.A. Munder, 1935.

"Southeast Cheers Crab Apple Blossom Festival and Parade". Washington *Star*, April 25, 1954.

Thomas, Lindsey Kay, Jr. *Geomorphology and Vegetation of Theodore Roosevelt Island*. Washington, D.C.: National Park Service, U.S. Department of the Interior, 1963.

U.S. Capitol Historical Society. *We the People: The Story of the United States Capitol*. Washington, D.C.: published in conjunction with the National Geographic Society, 1978.

Viertel, Arthur T. *Trees, Shrubs and Vines*. Syracuse, N.Y.: Syracuse University Press, 1970.

Washington, D.C. Ordinance to revise, consolidate and amend the ordinances of the board of health, to declare what shall be deemed nuisances injurious to health, and to provide for the removal thereof. (Nov. 19, 1875)

White House Conference on Natural Beauty. *Beauty for America: Proceedings of the White House Conference on Natural Beauty*. Washington, D.C.: May 24-25, 1965.

The White House Gardens and Grounds (booklet developed and distributed by the White House during the Reagan administration).

Williams, George Livingston. *The Gardens of Hillwood, A Guide Book with Map*. Washington, D.C.: printed by Corporate Press, 1965.

Wilson, Ernest Henry. *Plant Hunting*. Boston: The Stratford Company, 1927.

ENDNOTES

[1] Maury, William M. *Washington, D.C. Past and Present, The Guide to the Nation's Capital.* New York: CBS Publications, in cooperation with the United States Capitol Historical Society, 1975. p. 41.

[2] Kite, Elizabeth S. *L'Enfant and Washington.* New York: Arno Press and the New York *Times,* 1970. p. 23.

[3] Kauffman, Erle. *Trees of Washington, The Man—The City.* Washington, D.C.: The Outdoor Press, 1932. p. 56.

[4] Green, Constance McGlaughlin. *Washington: Village and Capital, 1800-1878.* Princeton, N.J.: Princeton University Press, 1962. pp. 105-106.

[5] Cable, Mary. *The Avenue of the Presidents.* Boston: Houghton Mifflin Company, 1969. p. 113.

[6] Henderson, Peter. "Street Trees of Washington". *Harper's Magazine,* 1889.

[7] Kauffman, Erle. *Trees of Washington, The Man—The City.* Washington, D.C.: The Outdoor Press, 1932. p. 57.

[8] Olszewski, George J. *History of the Mall, Washington, D.C.* Washington, D.C.: National Park Service, United States Department of the Interior, 1970. p. 51.

[9] Johnson, Lady Bird (Mrs. Lyndon Baines), Speech given at Yale University, 1967.

[10] "Washington the Nation's Capital". *National Geographic,* March 1915.

[11] "In the White House Looking Out". *U.S. News and World Report,* April 8, 1935.

[12] Von Eckardt, Wolf. "Verdant Vista is Memorial to J.F.K." Washington *Post,* May 31, 1964.

[13] National Archives and Records Service. *Washington, The Design of the Federal City.* Washington, D.C.: Acropolis Books Ltd., 1981. p. 14.

[14] *Ibid.*

[15] *Ibid.* p. 6

[16] Olmsted Brothers—Landscape Architects. "Report to the President of the United States on Improvements and Policy of Maintenance for the Executive Mansion Grounds", 1935. p. 62.

[17] *Ibid.*

[18] "Historic Trees on White House Lawn". *The Washington Post Magazine,* December 3, 1933.

[19] Aikman, Lonnelle. *The Living White House.* Washington, D.C.: White House Historical Association with the cooperation of the National Geographic Society, (1966, 1967, 1970, 1973, 1975) 1978. p. 124.

[20] *Ibid.*

[21] Washington *Star,* March 25, 1928.

[22] Von Eckardt, Wolf. "Verdant Vista is Memorial to J.F.K." The Washington *Post,* May 31, 1964.

[23] *Ibid.*

[24] Cheshire, Maxine (quoting Mrs. Johnson). "Only Her Name Could Grace Glowing Greensward". The Washington *Post,* April 23, 1965.

[25] *Ibid.*

26. Carter, Rosalynn (Mrs. Jimmy). "The White House Gardens and Grounds" (a brochure distributed during the Carter administration to visitors to the President's Park).

27. Smith, Margaret Bayard. *The First Forty Years of Washington Society*. New York: Scribners, 1906. p. 11.

28. "Historic Trees on White House South Lawn". *The Washington Post Magazine*, December 3, 1933.

29. "In the White House Looking Out". *U.S. News and World Report*. April 8, 1935.

30. "Historic Trees on White House Lawn".

31. Washington Newspaper story (source unknown) Washingtoniana Division, Martin Luther King Jr. Library.

32. "Historic Trees on White House Lawn".

33. Washington *Post*. August 25, 1933.

34. Warren, Virginia Burgess. "White House Trees". *American Forests*, March 1958.

35. *Ibid.*

36. La Hay, Wauhillau. "L.B.J. Plants for the Future". The Washington *Daily News*. October 17, 1964.

37. Olmsted, Frederick Law. Report contained in the Annual Report of the Architect of the United States Capitol. Washington D.C.: Government Printing Office, 1882. p. 13.

38. *Ibid.*

39. *Ibid.* p. 14.

40. *Ibid.*

41. *Ibid.* p. 15.

42. *Ibid.*

43. *Ibid.* p. 17.

44. *Ibid.* p. 16.

45. *Ibid.* p. 17.

46. *Ibid.* p. 15.

47. *Ibid.* p. 6.

48. *Congressional Record.* Speech by Senator Edward Kennedy, June 27, 1978.

49. Russell, Paul. *The Oriental Flowering Cherries*. Washington, D.C.: United States Department of Agriculture, Circular no. 313, 1934. p. 2.

50. *Ibid.* p. 1.

51. Keene, Donald (editor). *Anthology of Japanese Literature*, 1960. (Poem from "The Exile of Godaigo").

52. Ringle, Ken. "Where the City Gets Together." Washington *Post*, August 7, 1975.

53. Washington *Star*, January 19, 1913.

54. *Ibid.*

55. Letter dated June 27, 1927.

56. Eastern National Park & Monument Association. *The Lyndon Baines Johnson Memorial Grove on the Potomac.* Washington, D. C.: National Geographic Society, 1977. p. 3.

57. *Ibid.* p. 25.

58. *Ibid.* p. 3.

59. *Ibid.*

60. Washington, George. From his diary, March 26, 1786.

61. Lewis, Taylor, Jr. and Young, Joanne. *Washington's Mount Vernon*. New York: Holt, Rinehart and Winston, 1973.

62. Kauffman, Erle. *Trees of Washington, The Man—The City*. p. 5.

63. Mount Vernon Ladies Association of the Union. "The Mount Vernon Gardens", 1973. p. 9.

64. Lewis and Young. *Washington's Mount Vernon*.

65. *Ibid*.

66. Sargent, Charles Sprague. *The Trees at Mount Vernon*, 1926. p. 3.

67. Washington, George. From his diary, January 12, 1785.

68. *Ibid*. January 19, 1785.

69. Mount Vernon Ladies' Association. *Mount Vernon, An Illustrated Handbook*. Mount Vernon, Virginia: 1974. p. 28.

70. Sargent. *The Trees at Mount Vernon*. p. 6.

71. Washington, George. From his diary, August 18, 1785.

72. Federal Writers' Program. *Washington, D.C., a Guide to the Nation's Capital* (revised edition). New York: Hastings House, 1968.

73. Masson, Georgina. *Dumbarton Oaks, a Guide to the Gardens*. Washington, D.C.: Trustees for Harvard University, 1968. p. 6.

INDEX